武井宏之

Thinking of nothing. I love deer. When I'm around them, all my thoughts stop and my mind is at peace. Their awesome facial expressions seem to express that total lack of thought, that lack of consciousness. Whenever I watch them, I just end up sitting down and relaxing.

—*Hiroyuki Takei, 1999*
*(at Kofuku temple, Nara, Japan)*

Unconventional author/artist Hiroyuki Takei began his career by winning the coveted Hop Step Award (for new manga artists) and the Osamu Tezuka Award (named after the famous artist of the same name). After working as an assistant to famed artist Nobuhiro Watsuki, Takei debuted in **Weekly Shonen Jump** in 1997 with **Butsu Zone**, an action series based on Buddhist mythology. His multicultural adventure manga **Shaman King**, which debuted in 1998, became a hit and was adapted into an anime TV series. Takei lists Osamu Tezuka, American comics and robot anime among his many influences.

**SHAMAN KING VOL.6**
**The SHONEN JUMP Graphic Novel Edition**

This graphic novel contains material that was originally published in
English in **SHONEN JUMP** #23-27.

STORY AND ART BY
HIROYUKI TAKEI

English Adaptation/Lance Caselman
Translation/Lillian Olsen
Touch-up Art & Lettering/Kathryn Renta
Design/Sean Lee
Editor/Jason Thompson

Managing Editor/Elizabeth Kawasaki
Director of Production/Noboru Watanabe
Vice President of Publishing/Alvin Lu
Vice President & Editor in Chief/Yumi Hoashi
Sr. Director of Acquisitions/Rika Inouye
Vice President of Sales & Marketing/Liza Coppola
Publisher/Hyoe Narita

Printed in the U.S.A.

Published by VIZ, LLC
P.O. Box 77010
San Francisco, CA 94107

SHONEN JUMP Graphic Novel Edition
10 9 8 7 6 5 4 3 2 1
First printing, April 2005

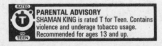

PARENTAL ADVISORY
SHAMAN KING is rated T for Teen. Contains
violence and underage tobacco usage.
Recommended for ages 13 and up.

THE WORLD'S
MOST POPULAR MANGA

SHONEN JUMP
GRAPHIC NOVEL

www.viz.com

www.shonenjump.com

SHONEN JUMP GRAPHIC NOVEL

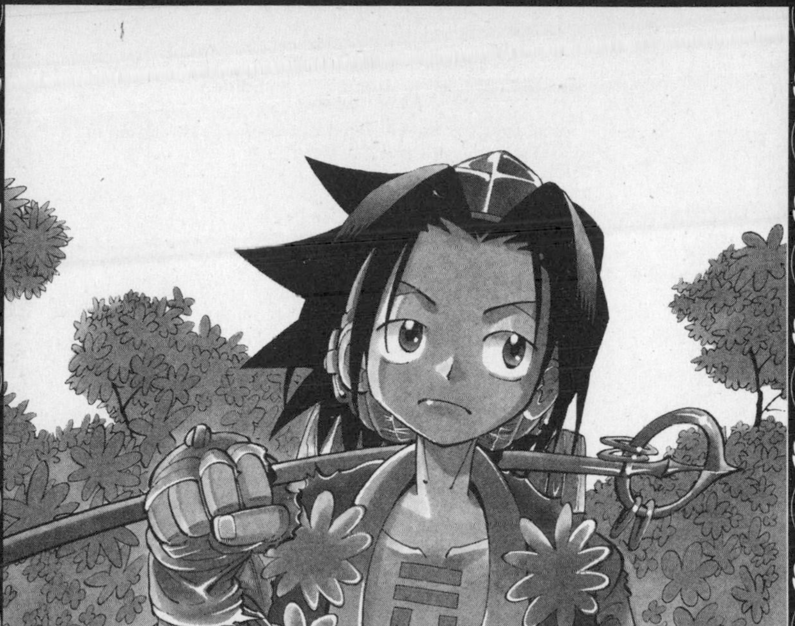
Shaman King

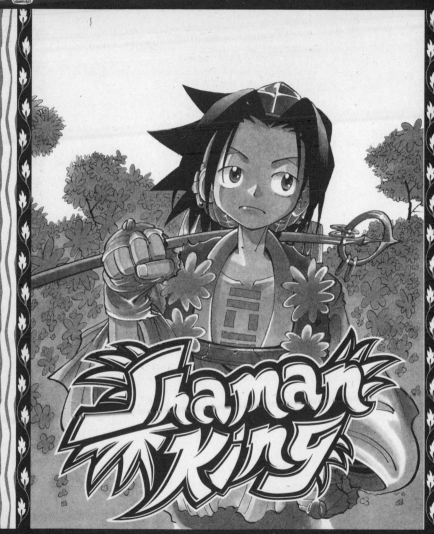

VOL. 6

# ROAD TRIP TO IZUMO

STORY AND ART BY

HIROYUKI TAKEI

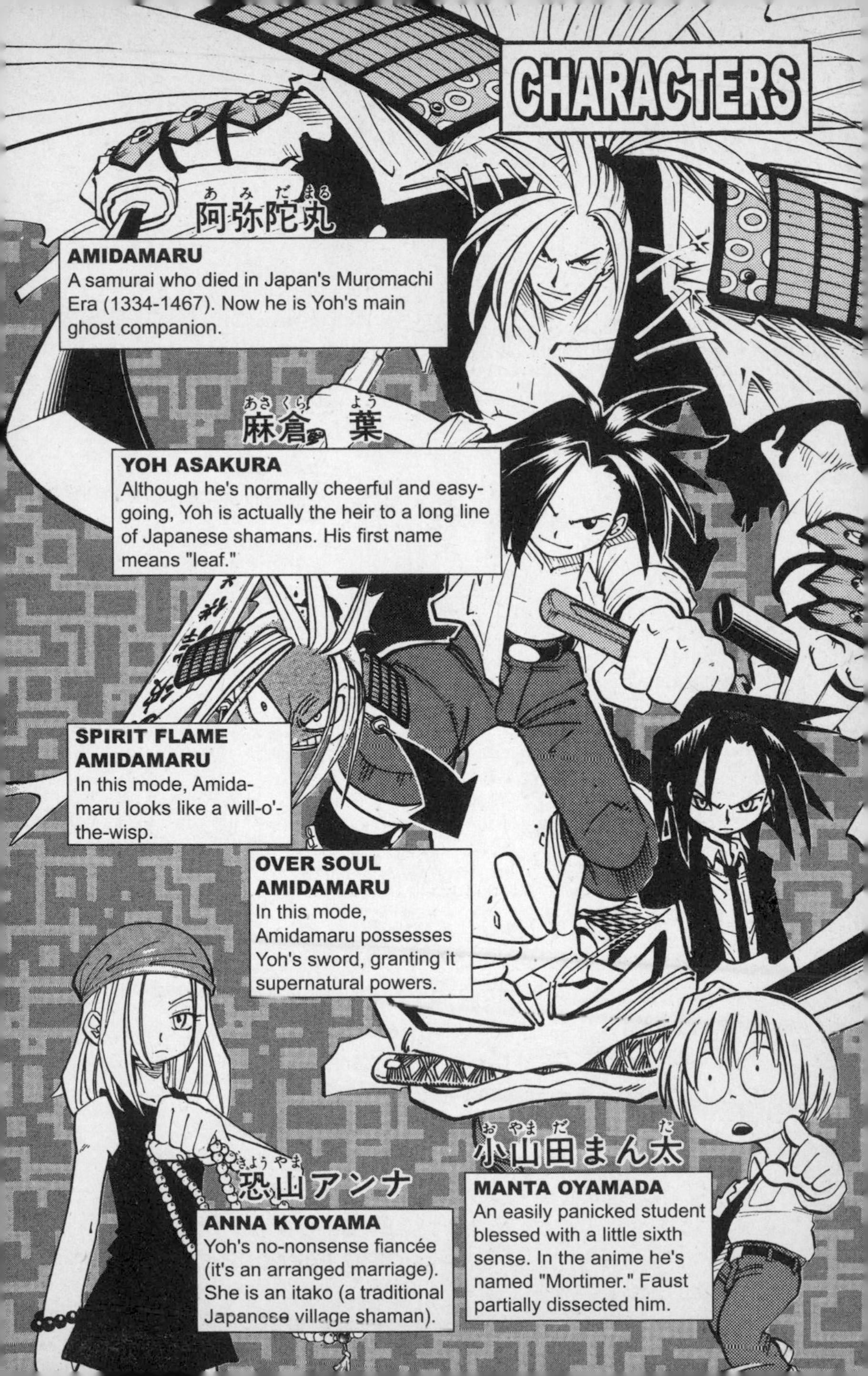

# CHARACTERS

阿弥陀丸

**AMIDAMARU**
A samurai who died in Japan's Muromachi Era (1334-1467). Now he is Yoh's main ghost companion.

麻倉葉

**YOH ASAKURA**
Although he's normally cheerful and easy-going, Yoh is actually the heir to a long line of Japanese shamans. His first name means "leaf."

**SPIRIT FLAME AMIDAMARU**
In this mode, Amidamaru looks like a will-o'-the-wisp.

**OVER SOUL AMIDAMARU**
In this mode, Amidamaru possesses Yoh's sword, granting it supernatural powers.

小山田まん太

**MANTA OYAMADA**
An easily panicked student blessed with a little sixth sense. In the anime he's named "Mortimer." Faust partially dissected him.

恐山アンナ

**ANNA KYOYAMA**
Yoh's no-nonsense fiancée (it's an arranged marriage). She is an itako (a traditional Japanese village shaman).

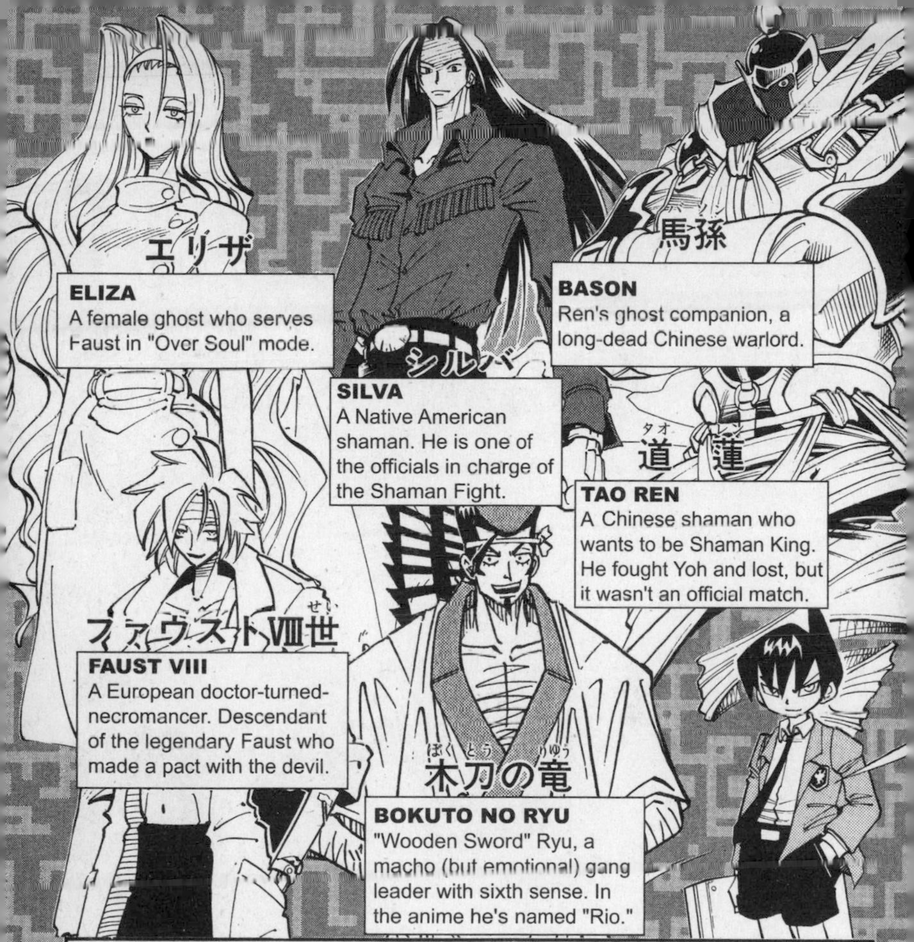
エリザ
ELIZA
A female ghost who serves Faust in "Over Soul" mode.
馬孫
BASON
Ren's ghost companion, a long-dead Chinese warlord.
シルバ
SILVA
A Native American shaman. He is one of the officials in charge of the Shaman Fight.
道 蓮
TAO REN
A Chinese shaman who wants to be Shaman King. He fought Yoh and lost, but it wasn't an official match.
ファウストVIII世
FAUST VIII
A European doctor-turned-necromancer. Descendant of the legendary Faust who made a pact with the devil.
木刀の竜
BOKUTO NO RYU
"Wooden Sword" Ryu, a macho (but emotional) gang leader with sixth sense. In the anime he's named "Rio."

## THE STORY SO FAR...

Yoh Asakura is a shaman--one of the gifted few who, thanks to training or natural talent, can summon spirits that most people can't even see. Once every 500 years, shamans from around the world gather to compete in the Shaman Fight, the grand tournament to see who can channel the "King of Spirits" and become the Shaman King. Already Yoh has fought against Native American, Chinese and Ainu shamans. But now he finds himself at the end of his rope against the European sorcerer Faust VIII...

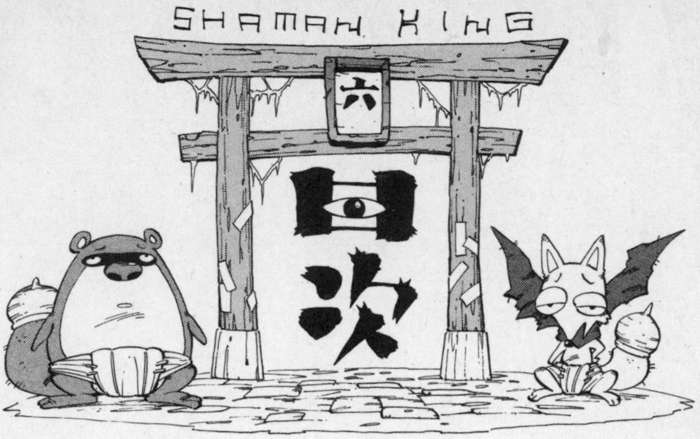
SHAMAN KING
六
目次

VOL. 6:
ROAD TRIP TO IZUMO

## CONTENTS

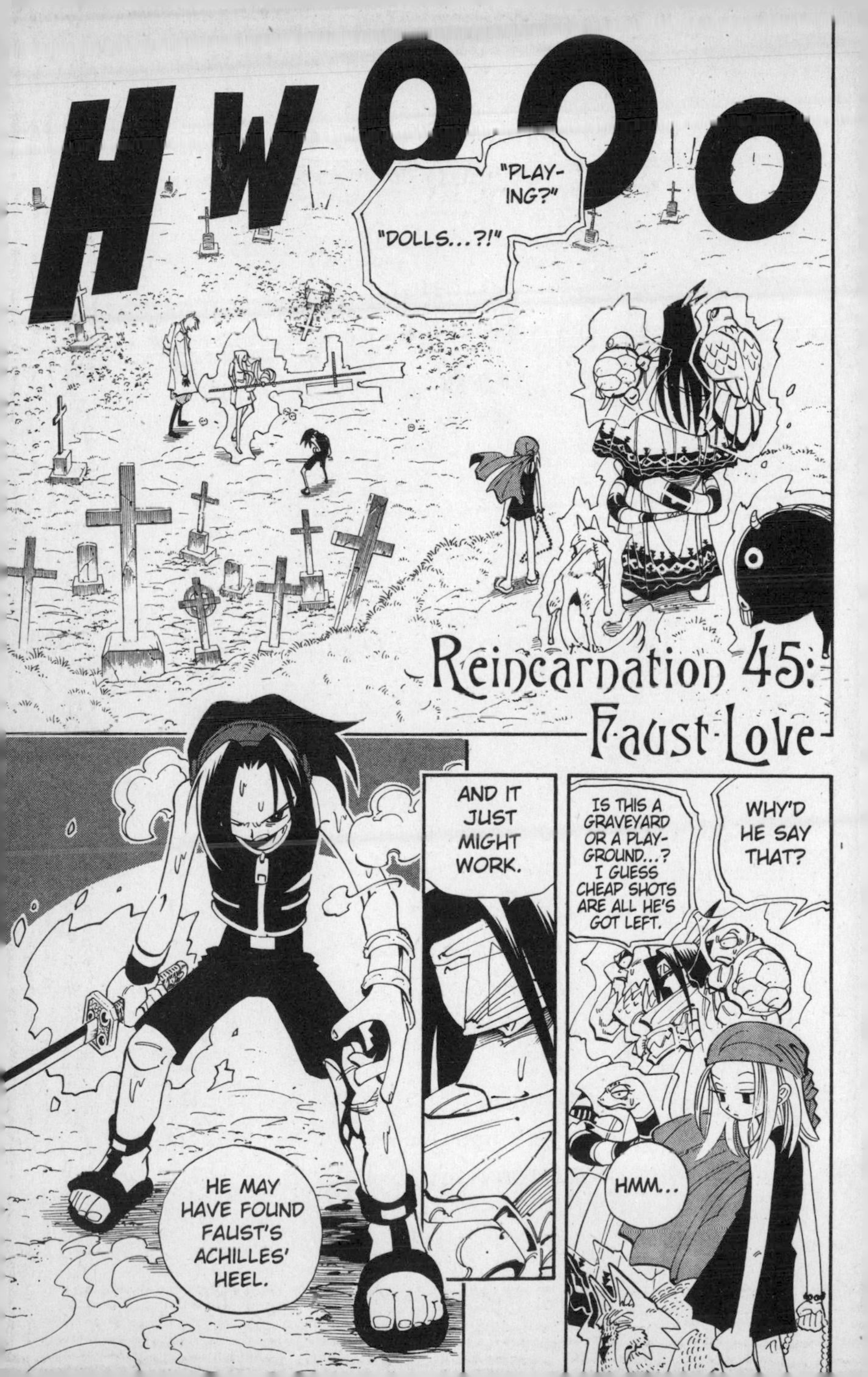
HWOOO
"PLAYING?"
"DOLLS...?!"
Reincarnation 45: Faust Love
WHY'D HE SAY THAT?
IS THIS A GRAVEYARD OR A PLAYGROUND...? I GUESS CHEAP SHOTS ARE ALL HE'S GOT LEFT.
HMM...
AND IT JUST MIGHT WORK.
HE MAY HAVE FOUND FAUST'S ACHILLES' HEEL.

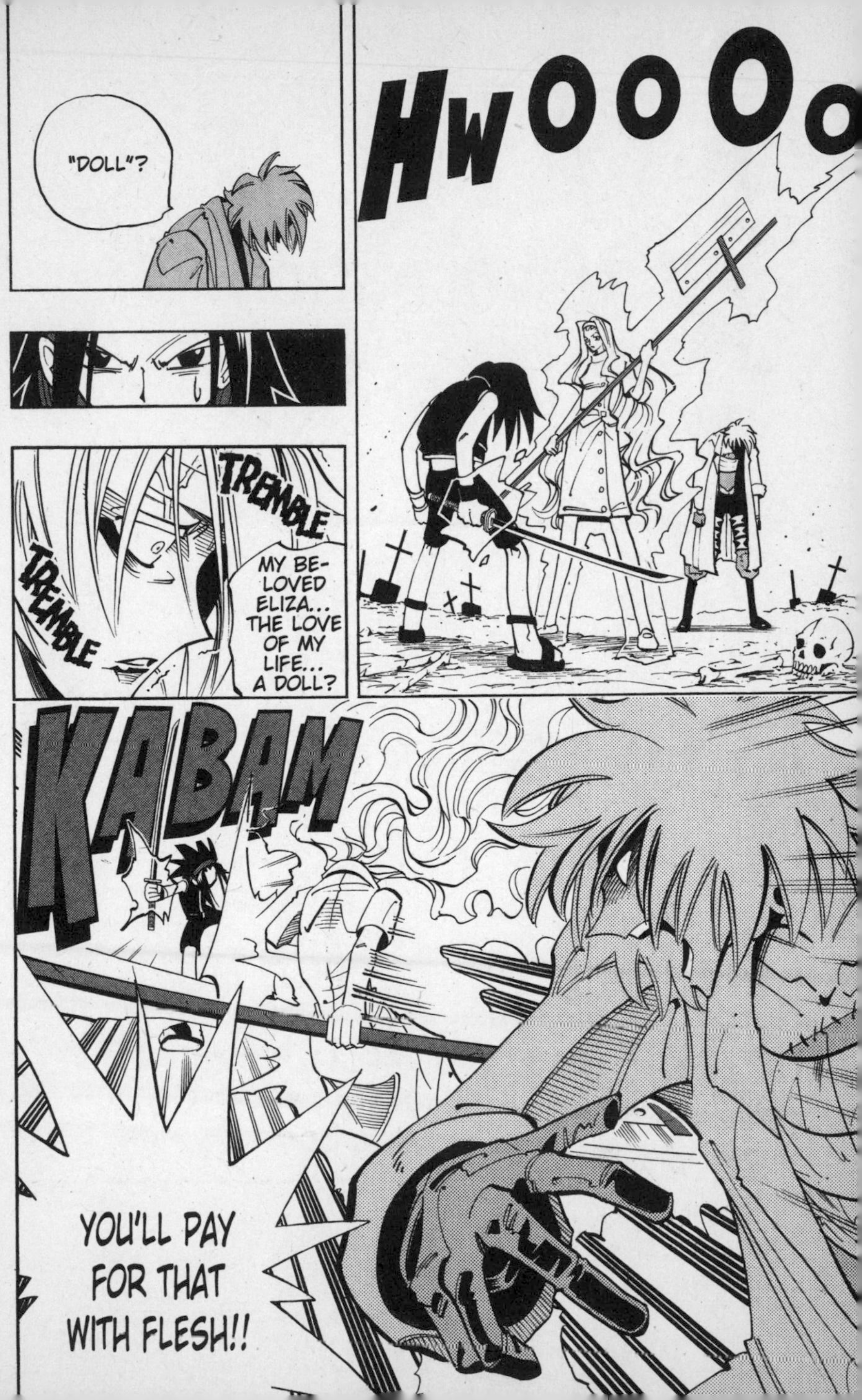
HWOOOOO
"DOLL"?
TREMBLE
MY BE-LOVED ELIZA... THE LOVE OF MY LIFE... A DOLL?
TREMBLE
KABAM
YOU'LL PAY FOR THAT WITH FLESH!!

# Reincarnation 45: Faust Love

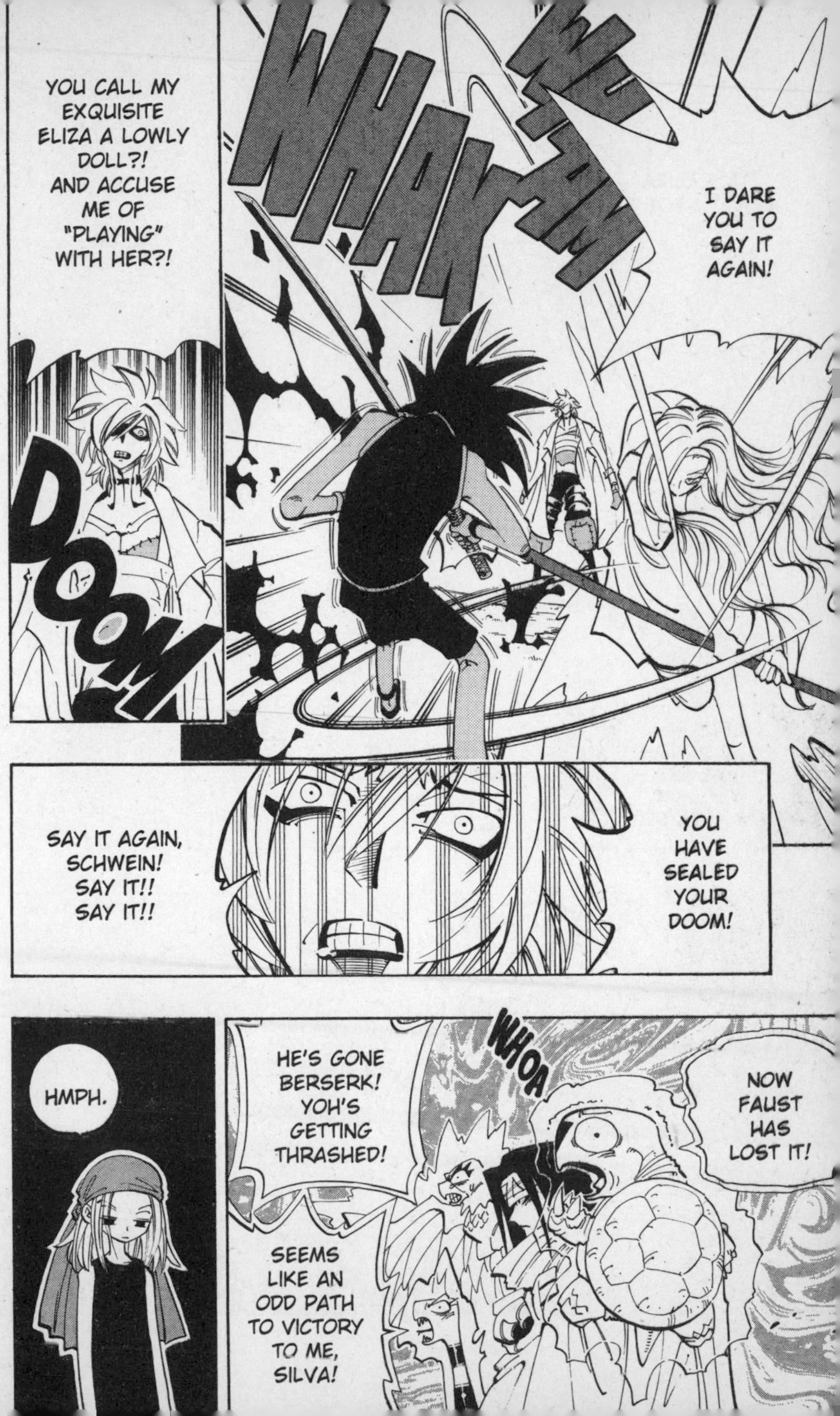
WHAK
I DARE YOU TO SAY IT AGAIN!
YOU CALL MY EXQUISITE ELIZA A LOWLY DOLL?! AND ACCUSE ME OF "PLAYING" WITH HER?!
DOOM
YOU HAVE SEALED YOUR DOOM!
SAY IT AGAIN, SCHWEIN! SAY IT!! SAY IT!!
NOW FAUST HAS LOST IT!
WHOA
HE'S GONE BERSERK! YOH'S GETTING THRASHED!
SEEMS LIKE AN ODD PATH TO VICTORY TO ME, SILVA!
HMPH.

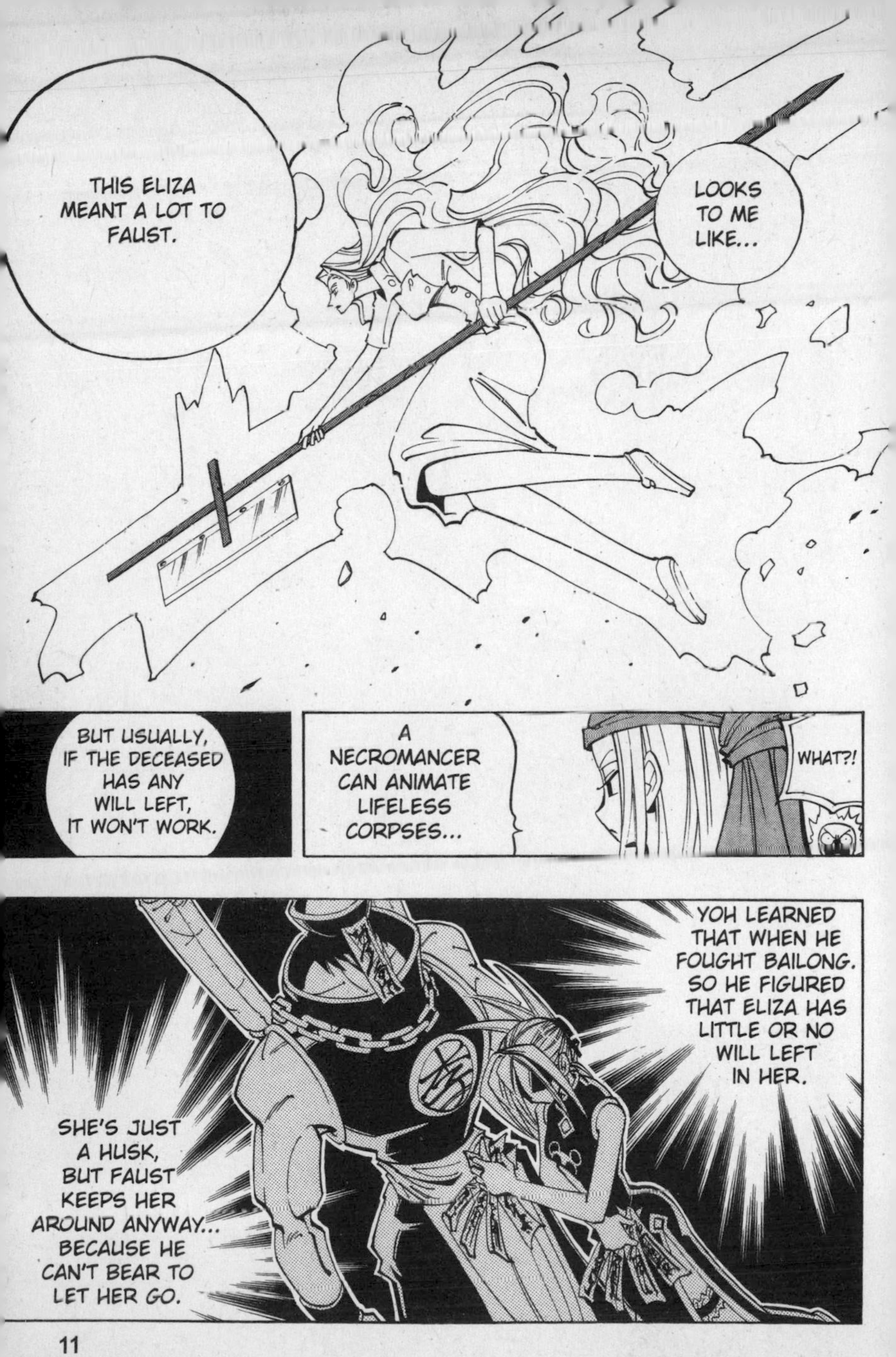
LOOKS TO ME LIKE...
THIS ELIZA MEANT A LOT TO FAUST.
WHAT?!
A NECROMANCER CAN ANIMATE LIFELESS CORPSES...
BUT USUALLY, IF THE DECEASED HAS ANY WILL LEFT, IT WON'T WORK.
YOH LEARNED THAT WHEN HE FOUGHT BAILONG. SO HE FIGURED THAT ELIZA HAS LITTLE OR NO WILL LEFT IN HER.
SHE'S JUST A HUSK, BUT FAUST KEEPS HER AROUND ANYWAY... BECAUSE HE CAN'T BEAR TO LET HER GO.

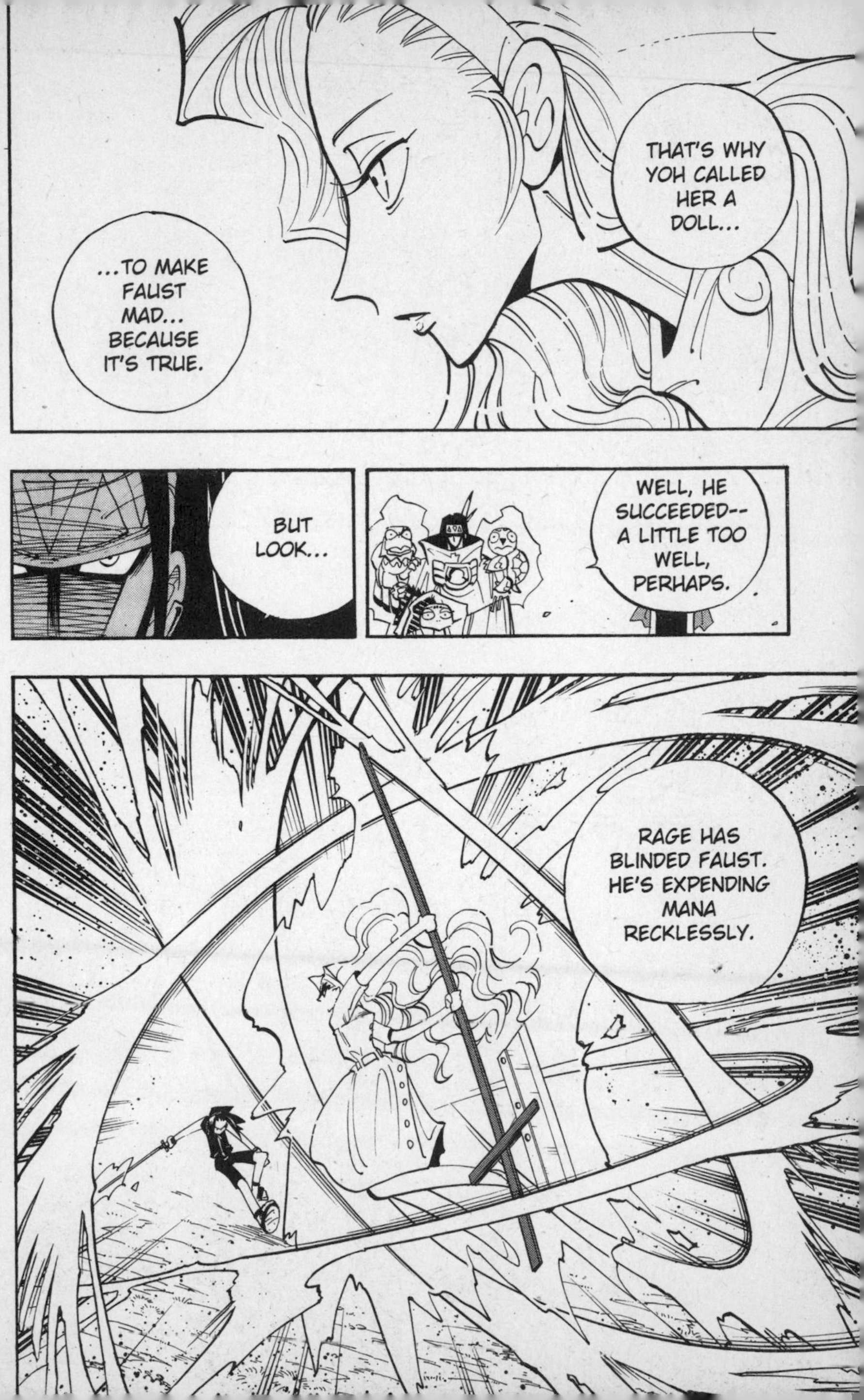
THAT'S WHY YOH CALLED HER A DOLL...
...TO MAKE FAUST MAD... BECAUSE IT'S TRUE.
WELL, HE SUCCEEDED-- A LITTLE TOO WELL, PERHAPS.
BUT LOOK...
RAGE HAS BLINDED FAUST. HE'S EXPENDING MANA RECKLESSLY.

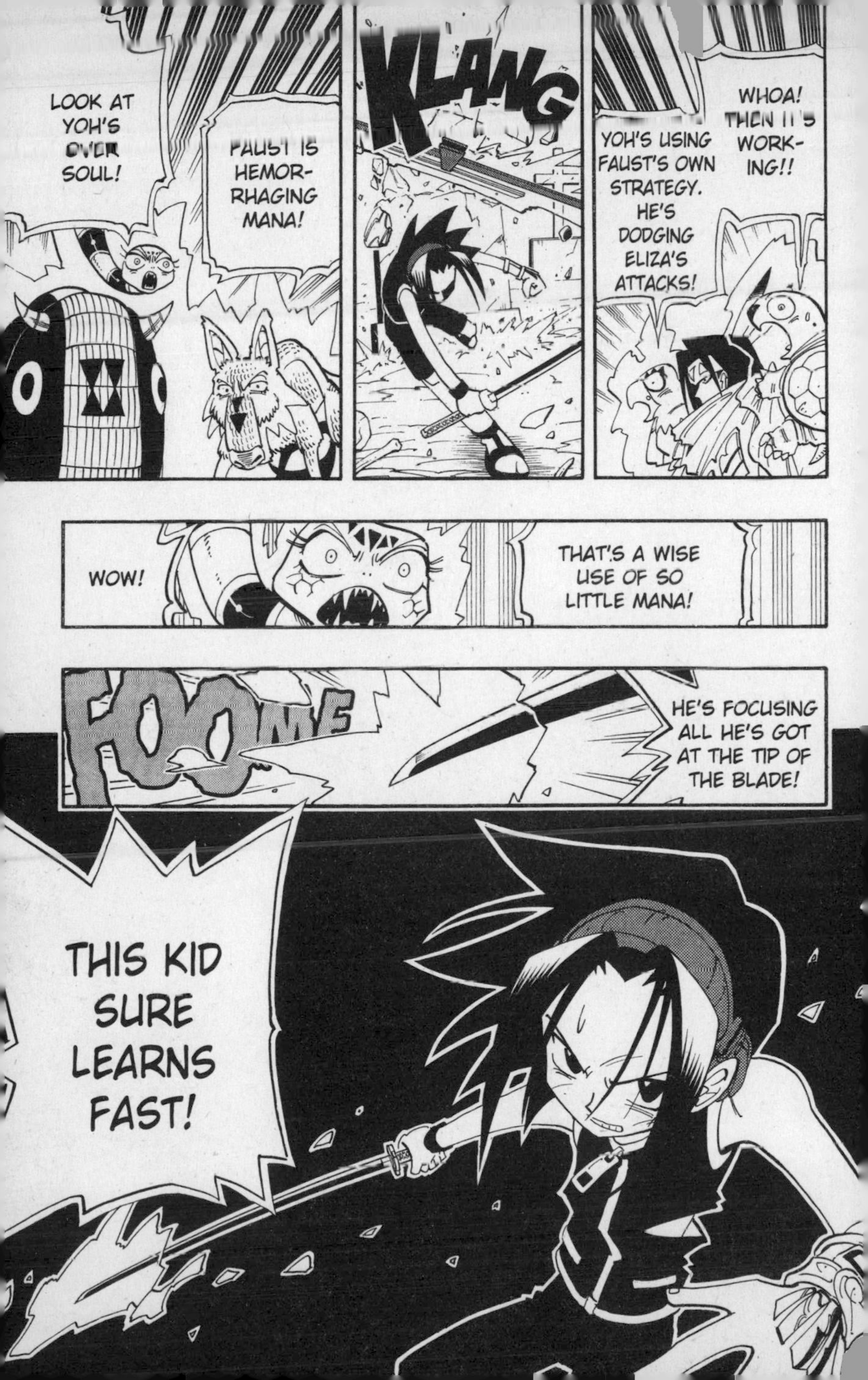
WHOA! THEN IT'S WORKING!!
YOH'S USING FAUST'S OWN STRATEGY. HE'S DODGING ELIZA'S ATTACKS!
KLANG
FAUST IS HEMORRHAGING MANA!
LOOK AT YOH'S OVER SOUL!
THAT'S A WISE USE OF SO LITTLE MANA!
WOW!
HE'S FOCUSING ALL HE'S GOT AT THE TIP OF THE BLADE!
FOOMF
THIS KID SURE LEARNS FAST!

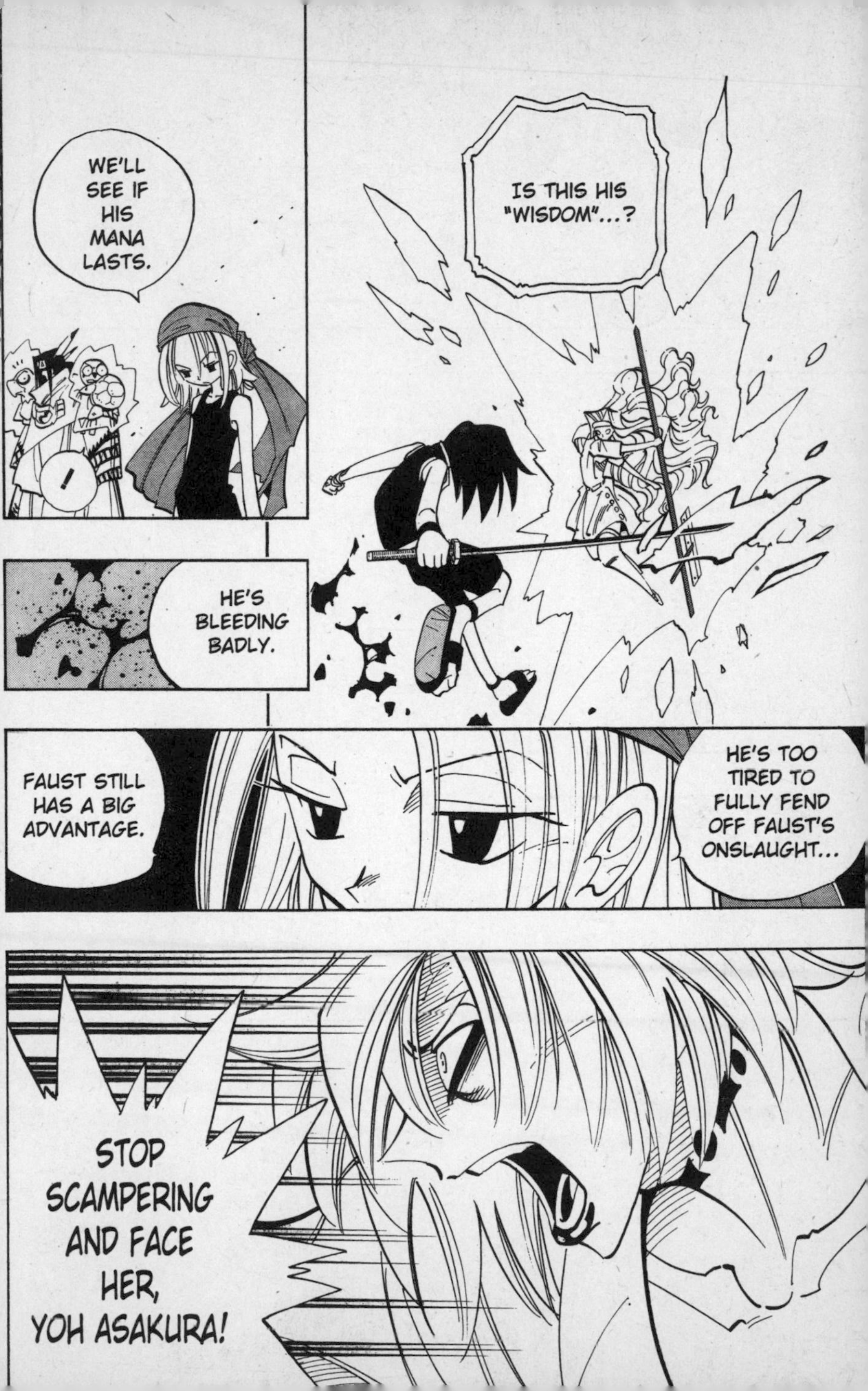
IS THIS HIS "WISDOM"...?
WE'LL SEE IF HIS MANA LASTS.
!
HE'S BLEEDING BADLY.
HE'S TOO TIRED TO FULLY FEND OFF FAUST'S ONSLAUGHT...
FAUST STILL HAS A BIG ADVANTAGE.
STOP SCAMPERING AND FACE HER, YOH ASAKURA!

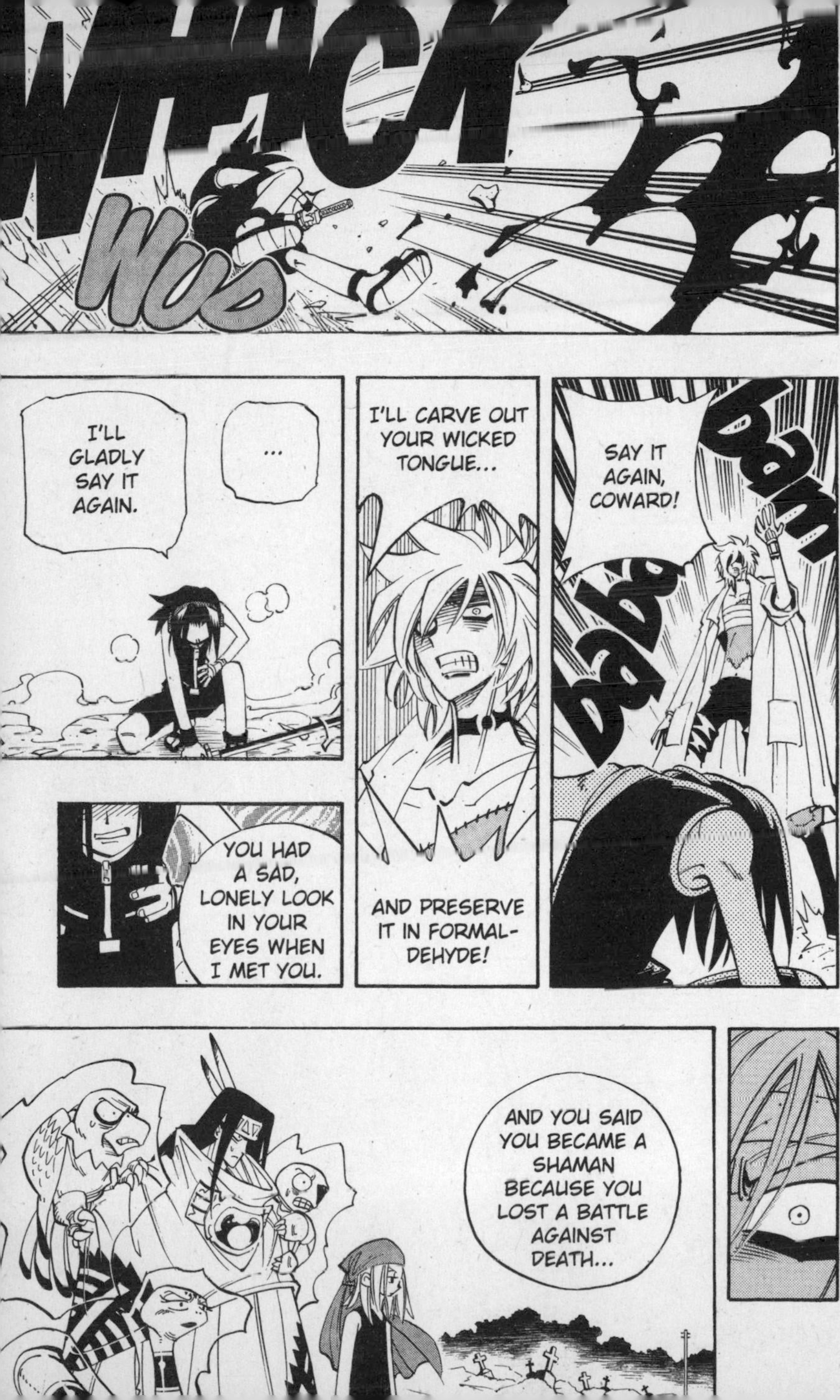
WHACK
WUD
SAY IT AGAIN, COWARD!
I'LL CARVE OUT YOUR WICKED TONGUE...
AND PRESERVE IT IN FORMAL-DEHYDE!
...
I'LL GLADLY SAY IT AGAIN.
YOU HAD A SAD, LONELY LOOK IN YOUR EYES WHEN I MET YOU.
AND YOU SAID YOU BECAME A SHAMAN BECAUSE YOU LOST A BATTLE AGAINST DEATH...

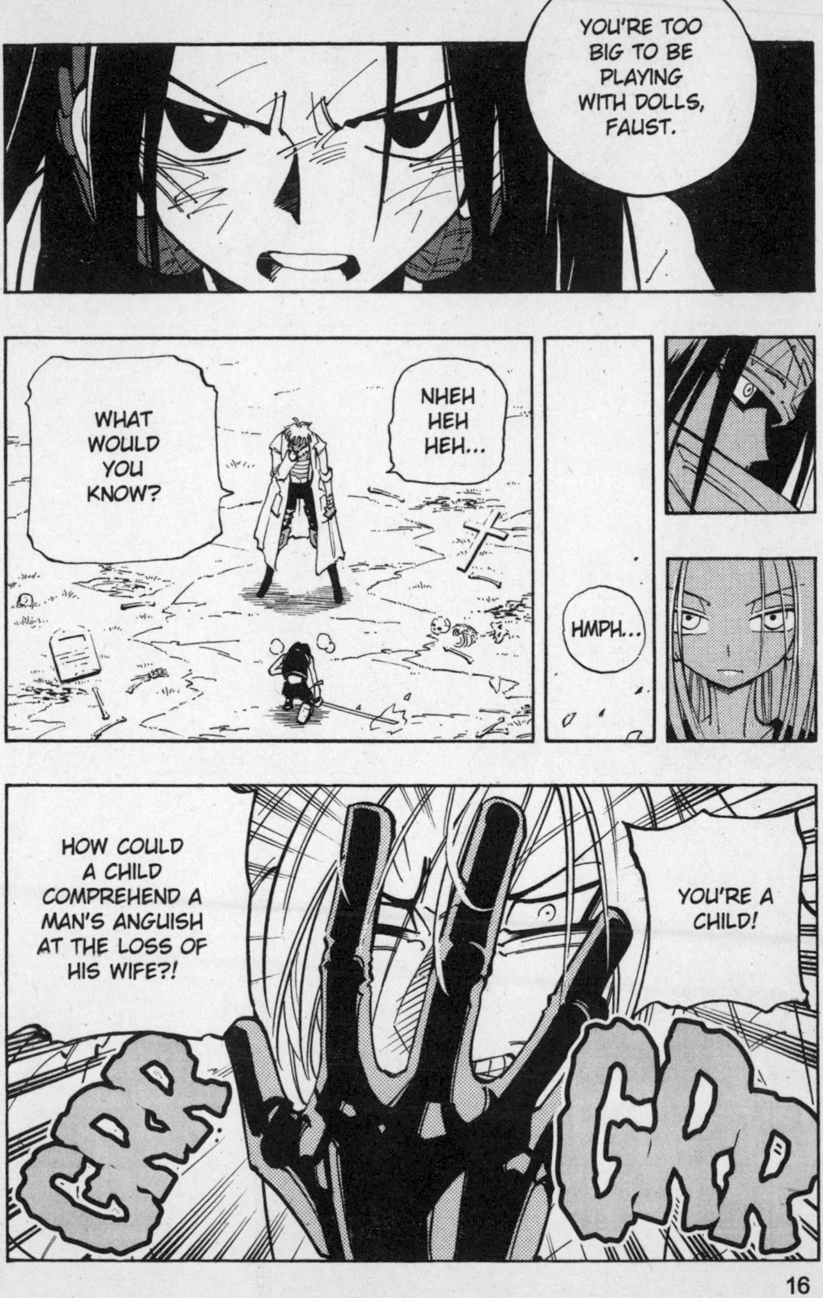
YOU'RE TOO BIG TO BE PLAYING WITH DOLLS, FAUST.
HMPH...
NHEH HEH HEH...
WHAT WOULD YOU KNOW?
YOU'RE A CHILD!
HOW COULD A CHILD COMPREHEND A MAN'S ANGUISH AT THE LOSS OF HIS WIFE?!
GRR
GRR

READ THIS WAY

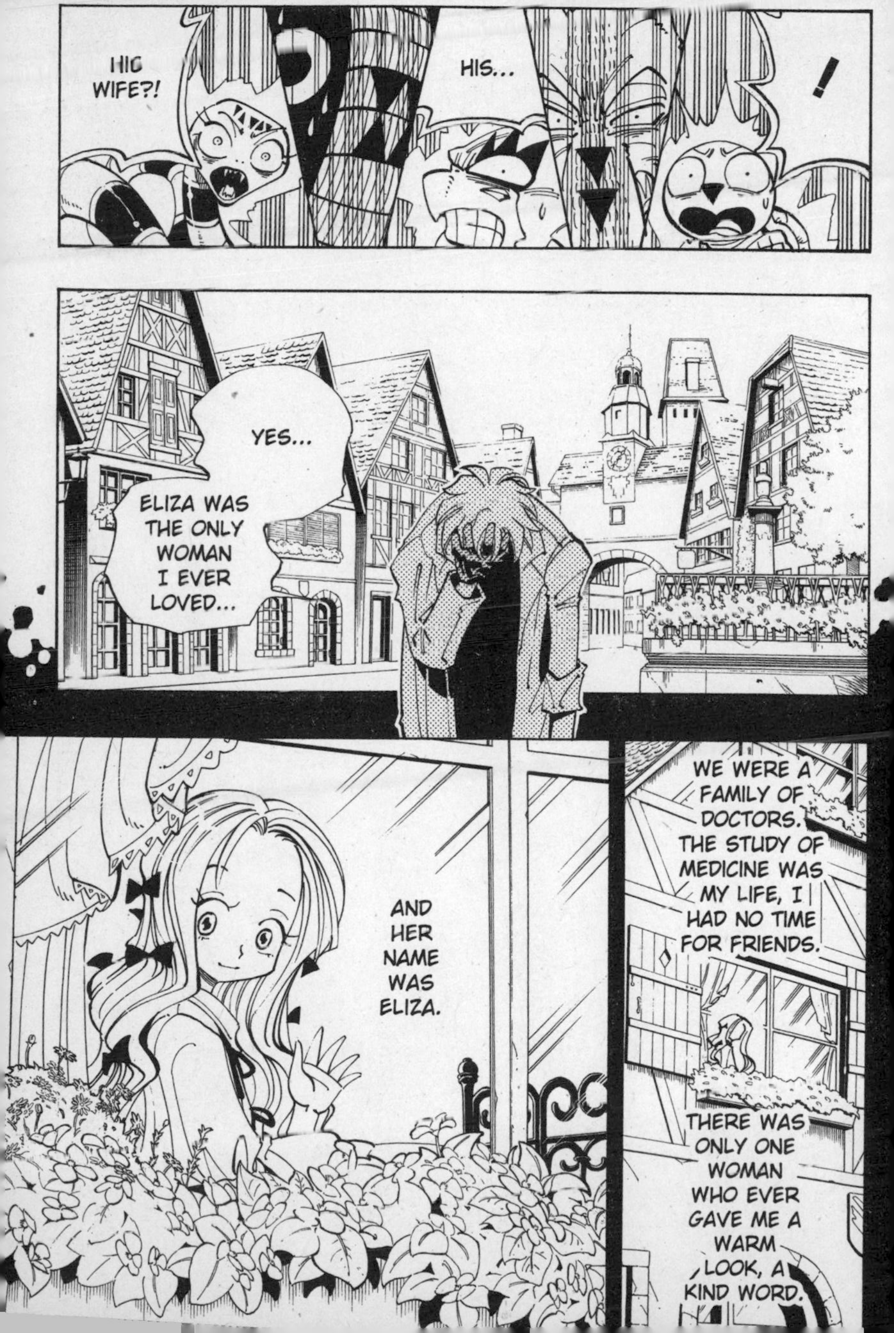
!
HIS...
HIS WIFE?!
YES...
ELIZA WAS THE ONLY WOMAN I EVER LOVED...
WE WERE A FAMILY OF DOCTORS. THE STUDY OF MEDICINE WAS MY LIFE, I HAD NO TIME FOR FRIENDS.
THERE WAS ONLY ONE WOMAN WHO EVER GAVE ME A WARM LOOK, A KIND WORD.
AND HER NAME WAS ELIZA.

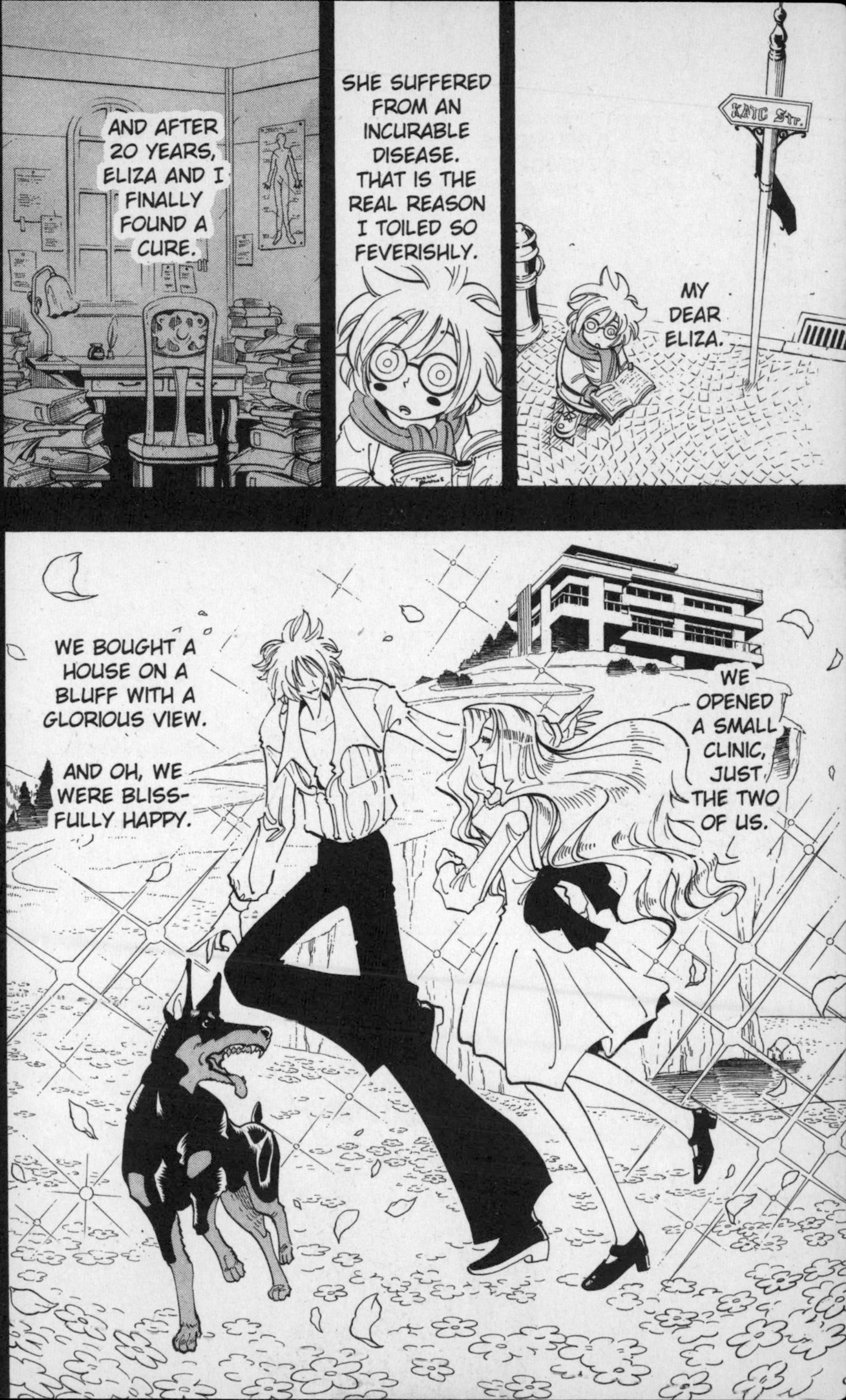
MY DEAR ELIZA.
SHE SUFFERED FROM AN INCURABLE DISEASE. THAT IS THE REAL REASON I TOILED SO FEVERISHLY.
AND AFTER 20 YEARS, ELIZA AND I FINALLY FOUND A CURE.
WE OPENED A SMALL CLINIC, JUST THE TWO OF US.
WE BOUGHT A HOUSE ON A BLUFF WITH A GLORIOUS VIEW.
AND OH, WE WERE BLISS-FULLY HAPPY.

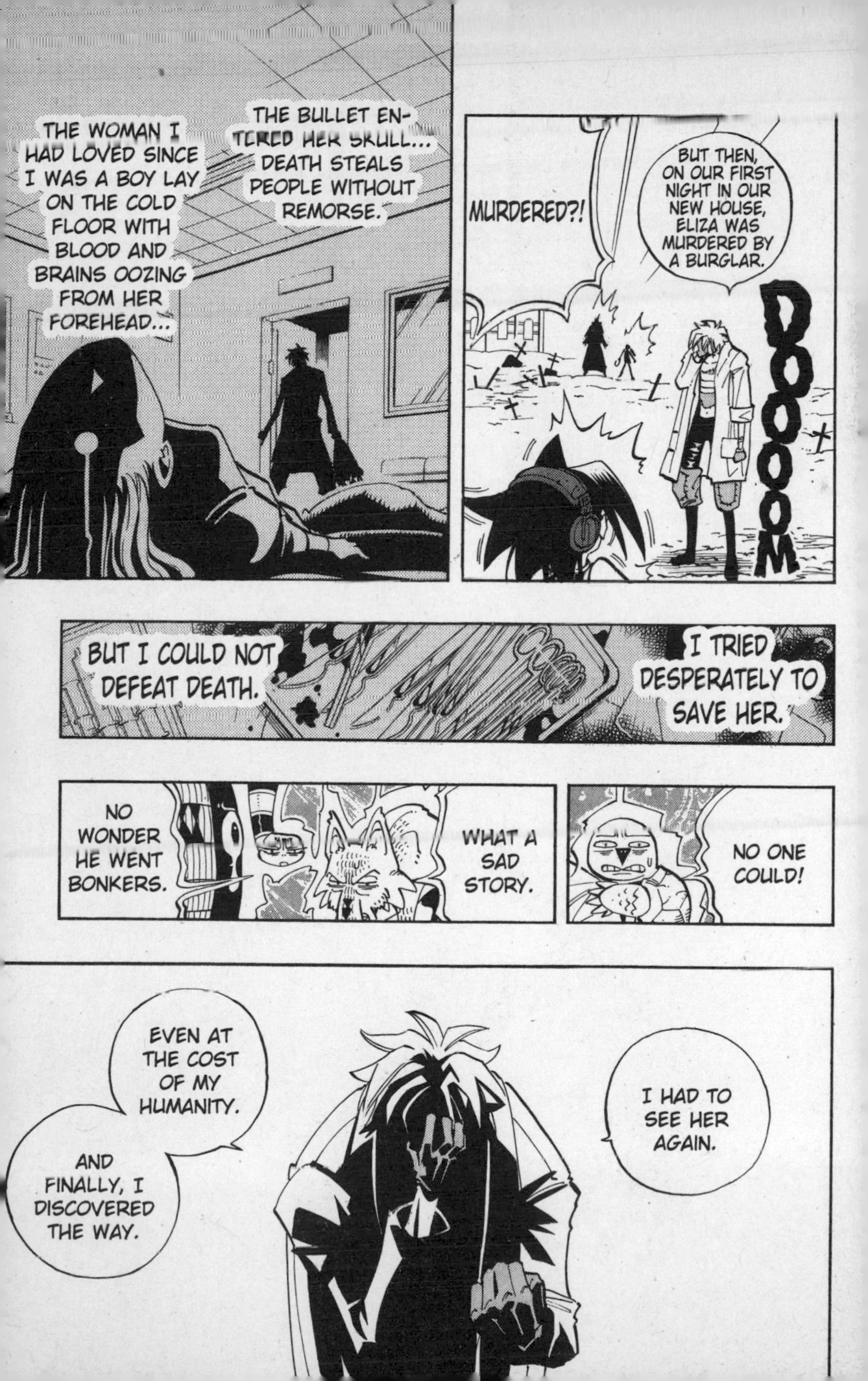
BUT THEN, ON OUR FIRST NIGHT IN OUR NEW HOUSE, ELIZA WAS MURDERED BY A BURGLAR.
MURDERED?!
DOOOOOM
THE BULLET ENTERED HER SKULL... DEATH STEALS PEOPLE WITHOUT REMORSE.
THE WOMAN I HAD LOVED SINCE I WAS A BOY LAY ON THE COLD FLOOR WITH BLOOD AND BRAINS OOZING FROM HER FOREHEAD...
I TRIED DESPERATELY TO SAVE HER.
BUT I COULD NOT DEFEAT DEATH.
NO ONE COULD!
WHAT A SAD STORY.
NO WONDER HE WENT BONKERS.
I HAD TO SEE HER AGAIN.
EVEN AT THE COST OF MY HUMANITY.
AND FINALLY, I DISCOVERED THE WAY.

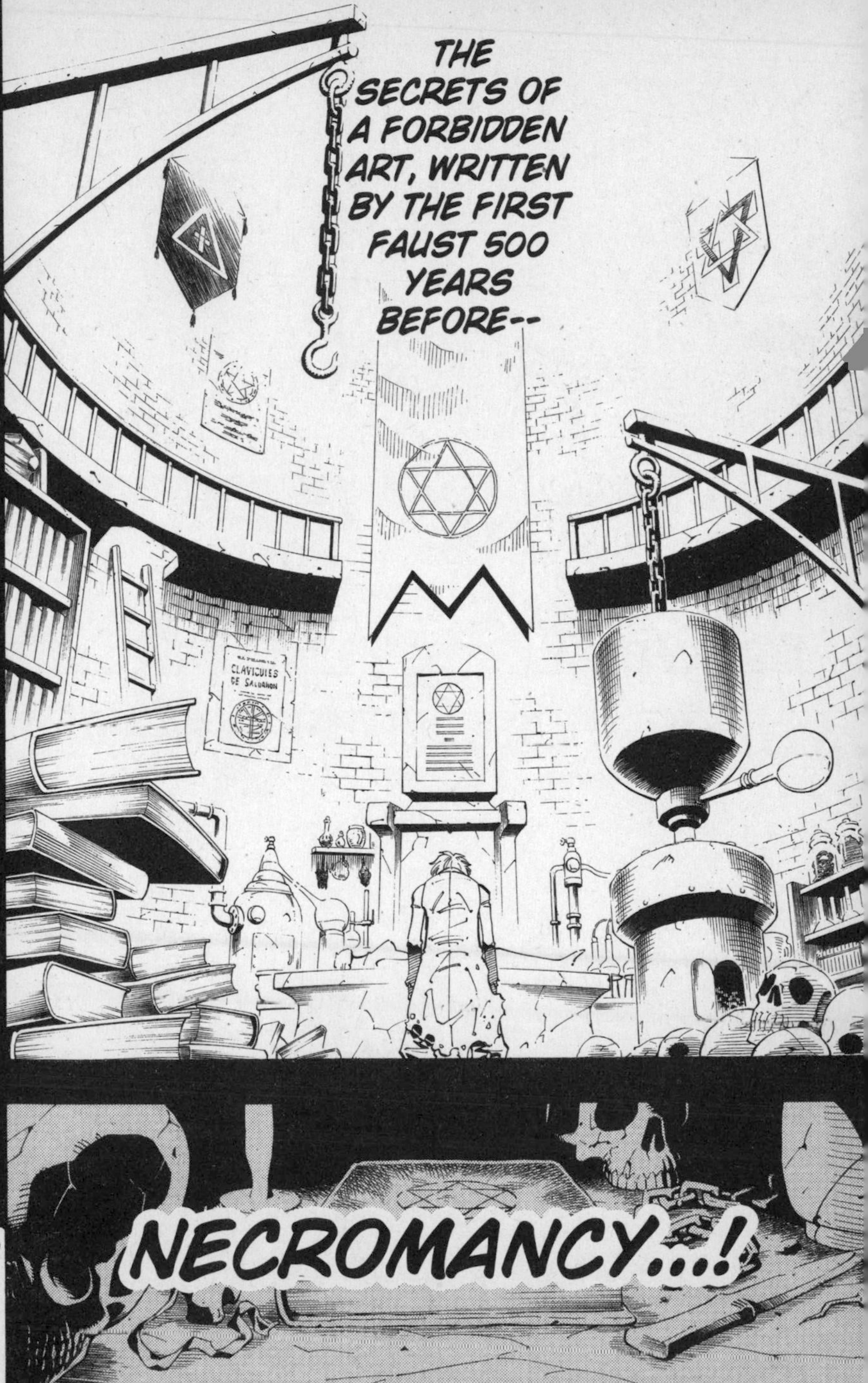
THE SECRETS OF A FORBIDDEN ART, WRITTEN BY THE FIRST FAUST 500 YEARS BEFORE--
NECROMANCY...!

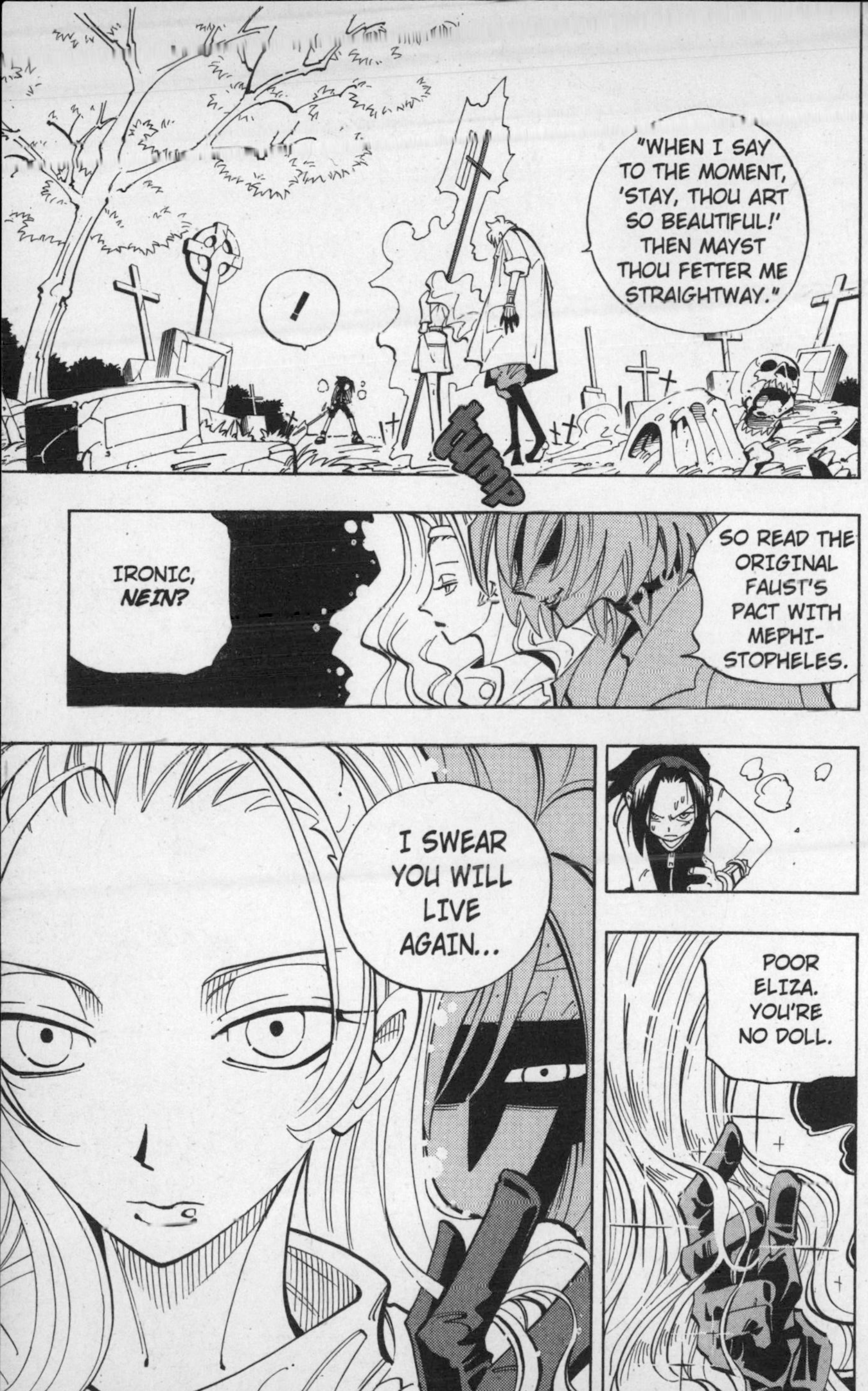
"WHEN I SAY TO THE MOMENT, 'STAY, THOU ART SO BEAUTIFUL!' THEN MAYST THOU FETTER ME STRAIGHTWAY."
!
TUMP
SO READ THE ORIGINAL FAUST'S PACT WITH MEPHI-STOPHELES.
IRONIC, *NEIN?*
POOR ELIZA. YOU'RE NO DOLL.
I SWEAR YOU WILL LIVE AGAIN...

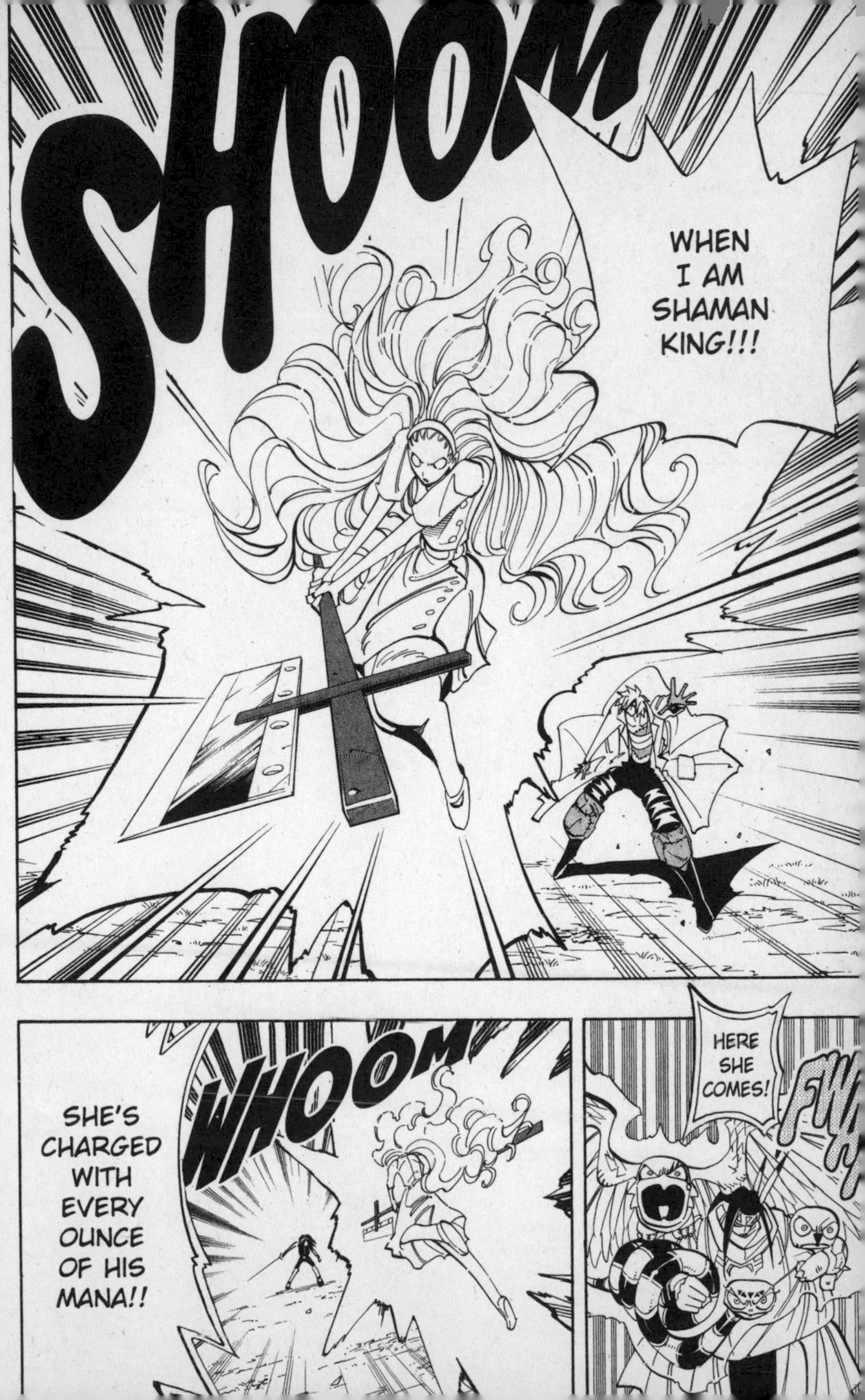
SHOOM
WHEN I AM SHAMAN KING!!!
HERE SHE COMES!
WHOOM
SHE'S CHARGED WITH EVERY OUNCE OF HIS MANA!!

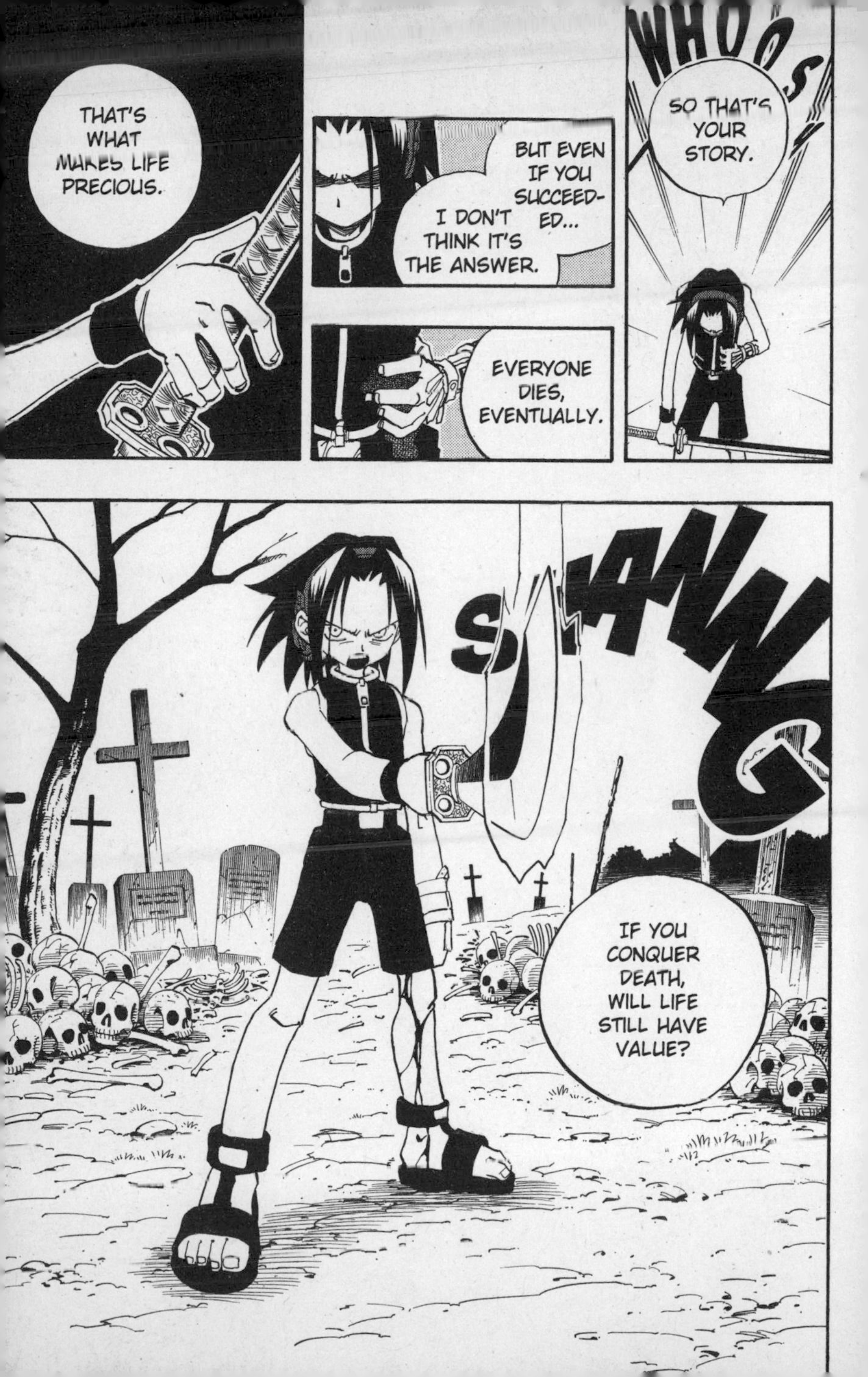
WHOOSH
SO THAT'S YOUR STORY.
BUT EVEN IF YOU SUCCEEDED...
I DON'T THINK IT'S THE ANSWER.
EVERYONE DIES, EVENTUALLY.
THAT'S WHAT MAKES LIFE PRECIOUS.
SHAWNG
IF YOU CONQUER DEATH, WILL LIFE STILL HAVE VALUE?

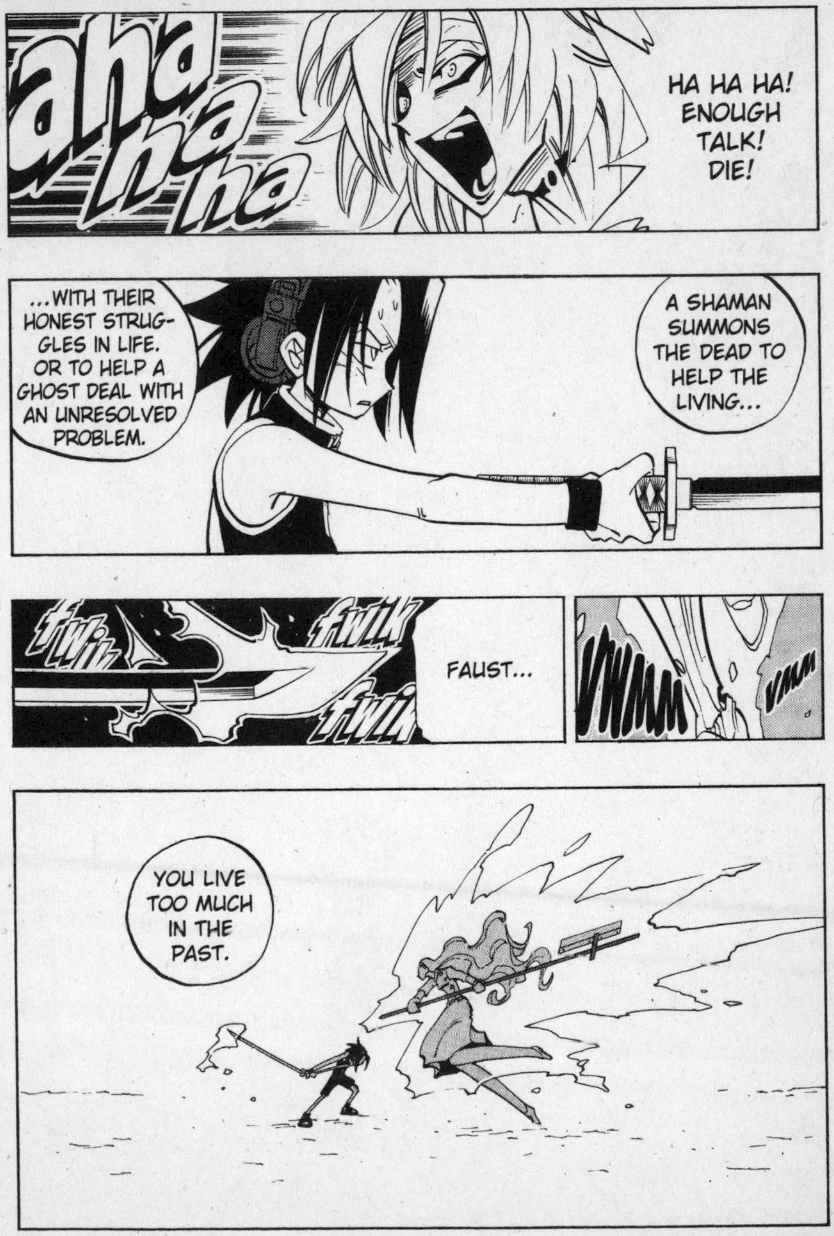

aha ha ha
HA HA HA! ENOUGH TALK! DIE!
A SHAMAN SUMMONS THE DEAD TO HELP THE LIVING...
...WITH THEIR HONEST STRUG- GLES IN LIFE. OR TO HELP A GHOST DEAL WITH AN UNRESOLVED PROBLEM.
VHMMM
VMMM
FAUST...
fwik
YOU LIVE TOO MUCH IN THE PAST.

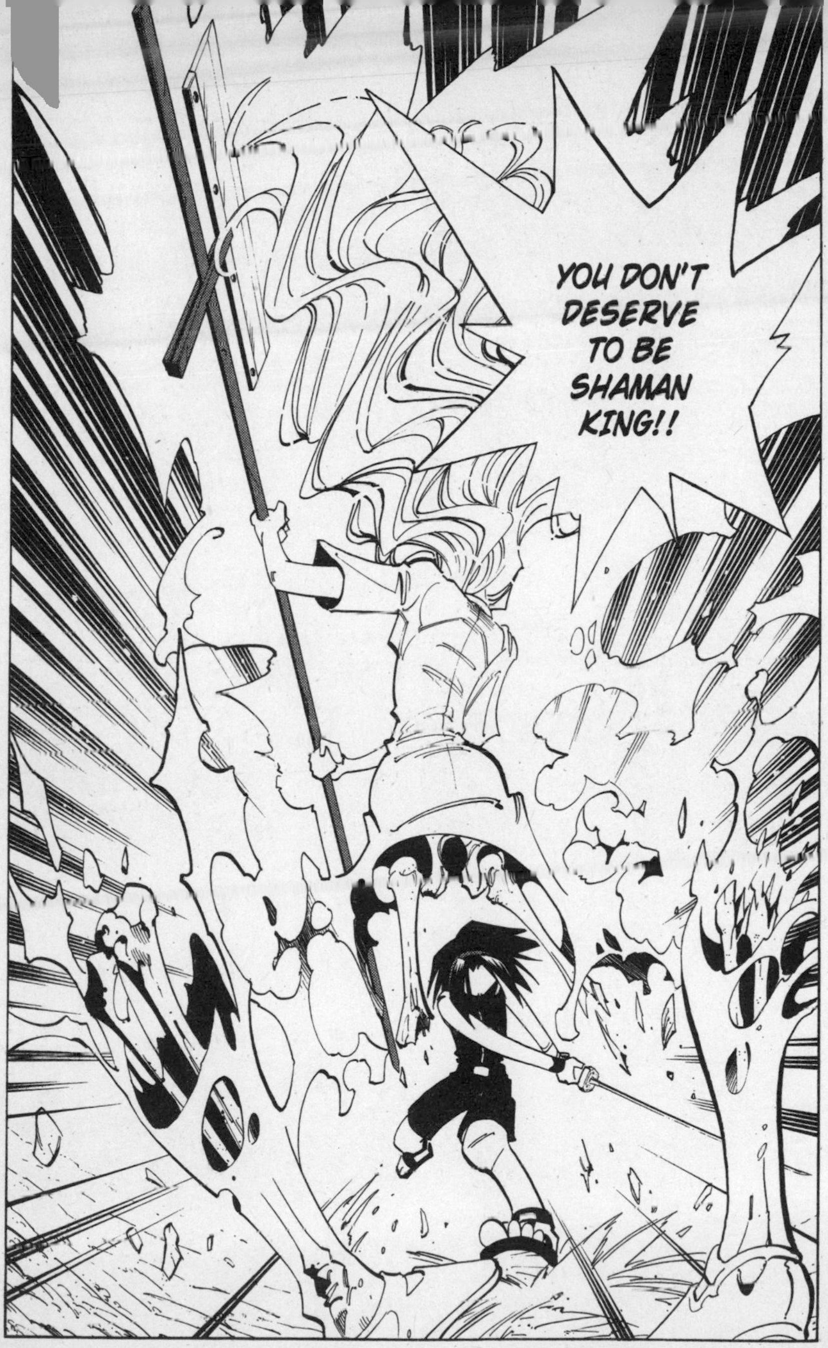
YOU DON'T DESERVE TO BE SHAMAN KING!!

## SHAMAN KING CHARACTER FILE No.24

# エリザ ファウスト

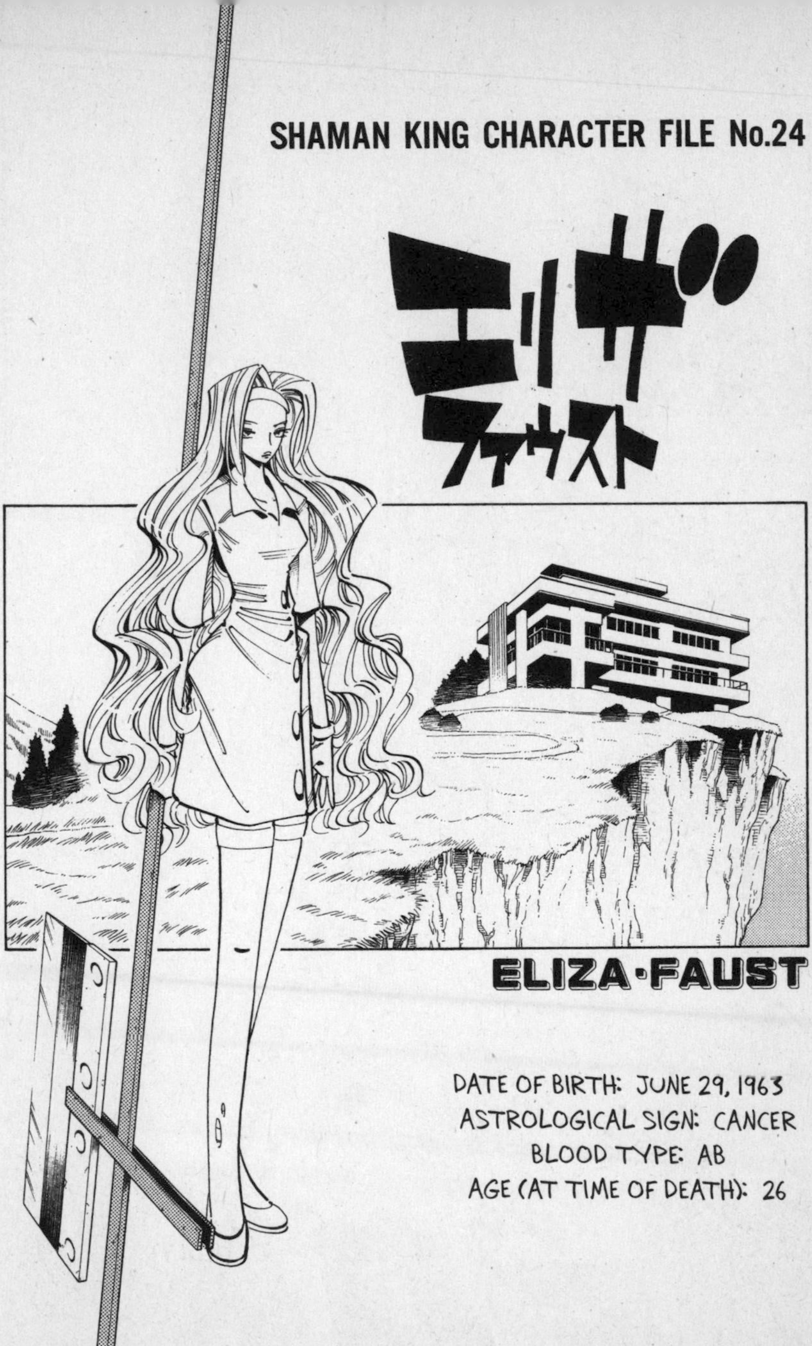

## ELIZA·FAUST

DATE OF BIRTH: JUNE 29, 1963
ASTROLOGICAL SIGN: CANCER
BLOOD TYPE: AB
AGE (AT TIME OF DEATH): 26

# Reincarnation 46: A Form of Courage

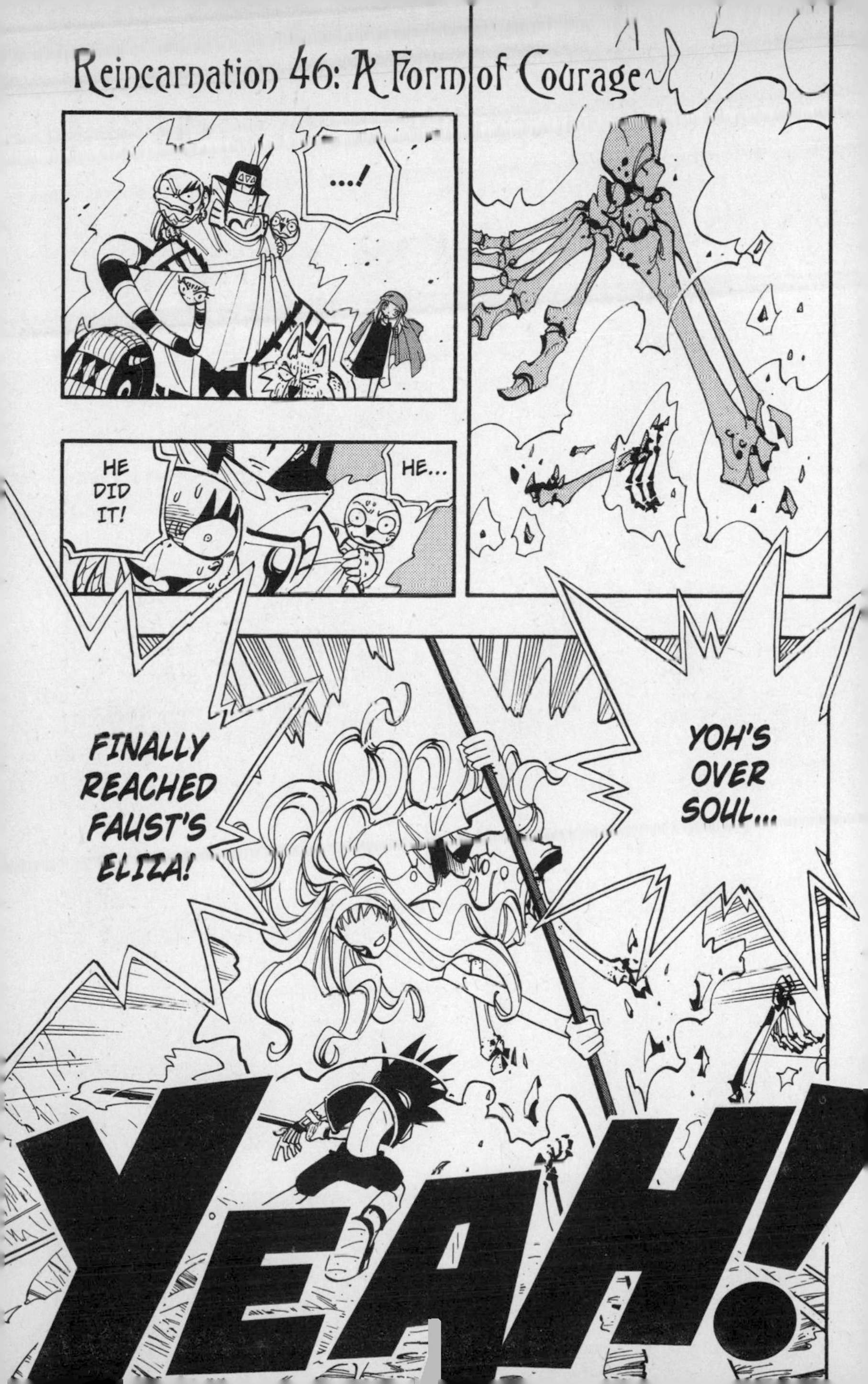
...!
HE...
HE DID IT!
YOH'S OVER SOUL...
FINALLY REACHED FAUST'S ELIZA!
YEAH!

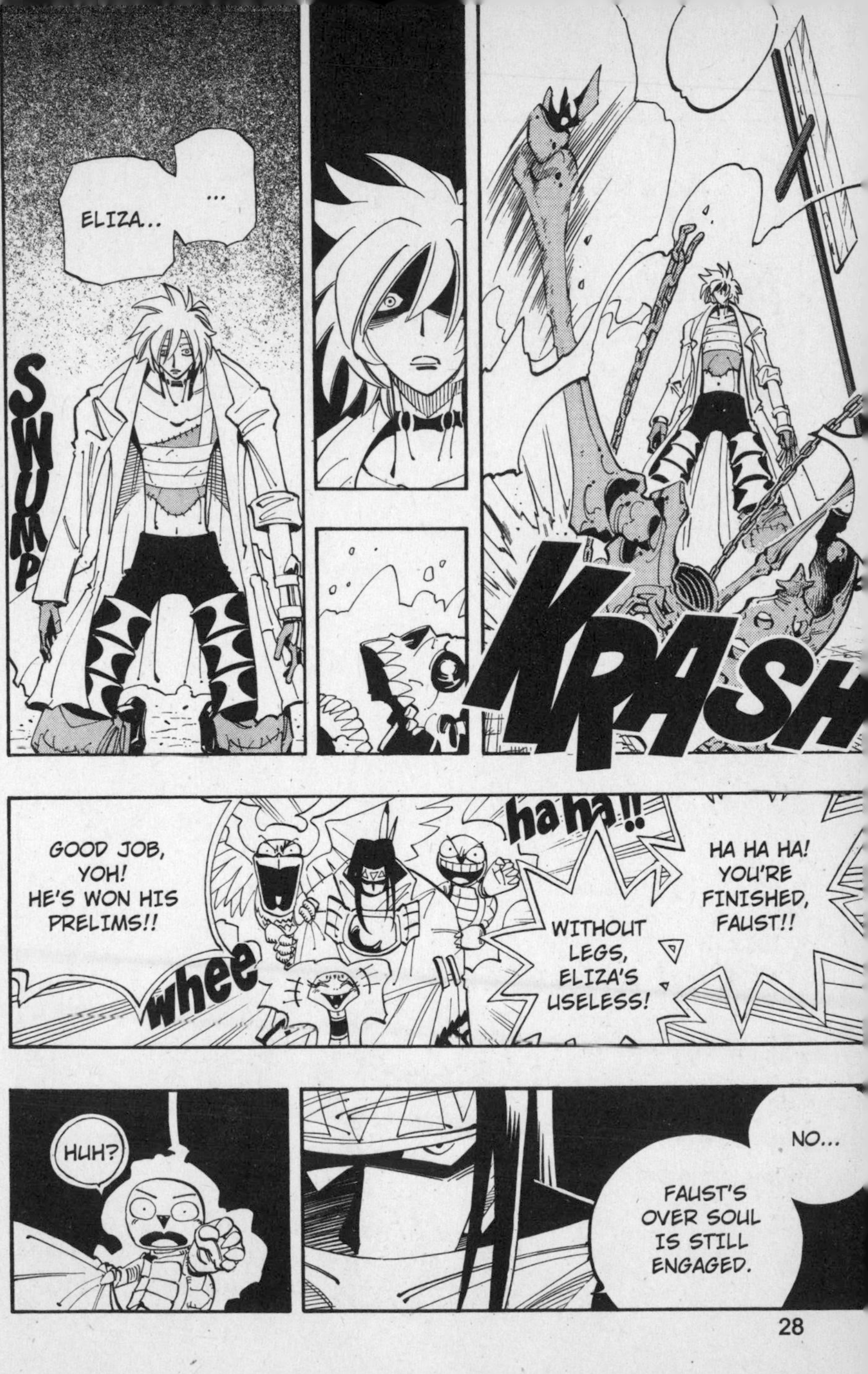
KRASH
...
ELIZA...
SWUMP
ha ha!!
HA HA HA! YOU'RE FINISHED, FAUST!!
WITHOUT LEGS, ELIZA'S USELESS!
GOOD JOB, YOH! HE'S WON HIS PRELIMS!!
whee
NO...
FAUST'S OVER SOUL IS STILL ENGAGED.
HUH?

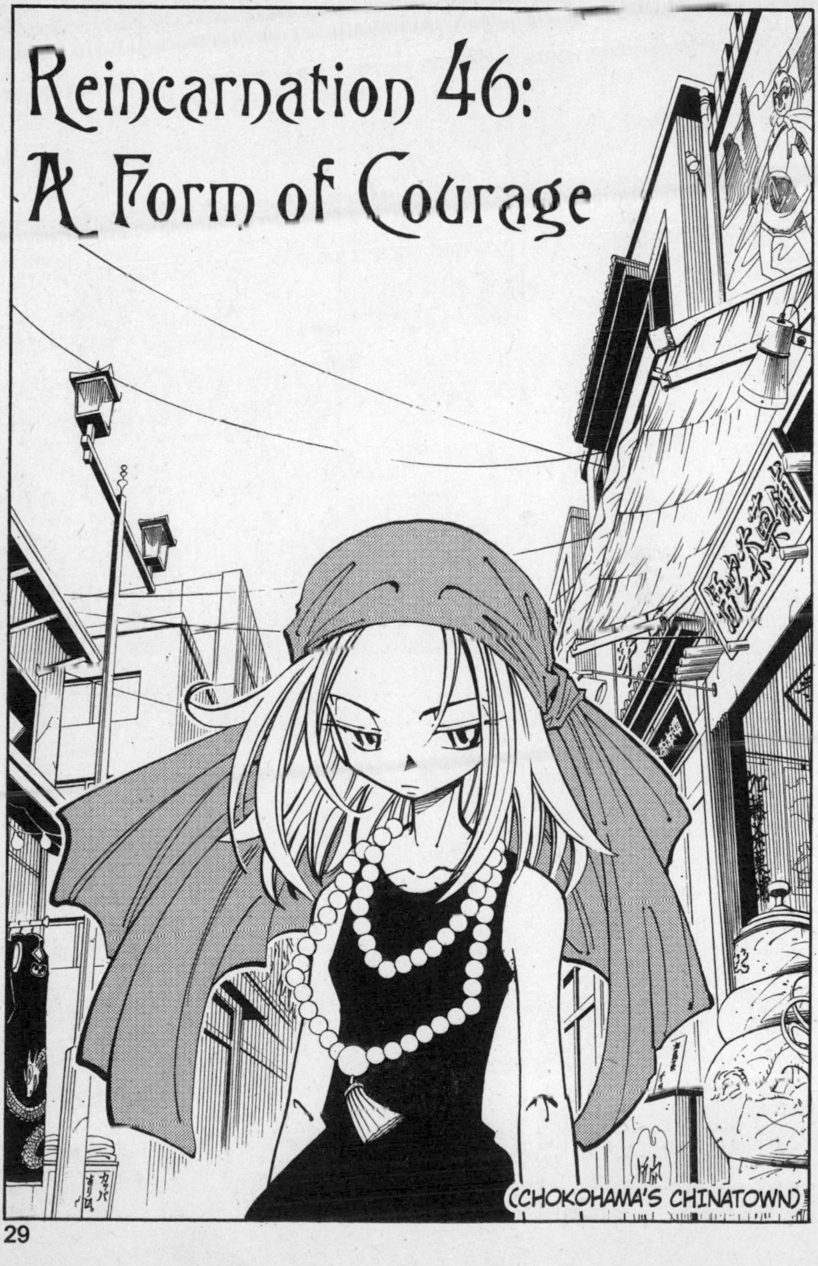
Reincarnation 46:
A Form of Courage
(CHOKOHAMA'S CHINATOWN)

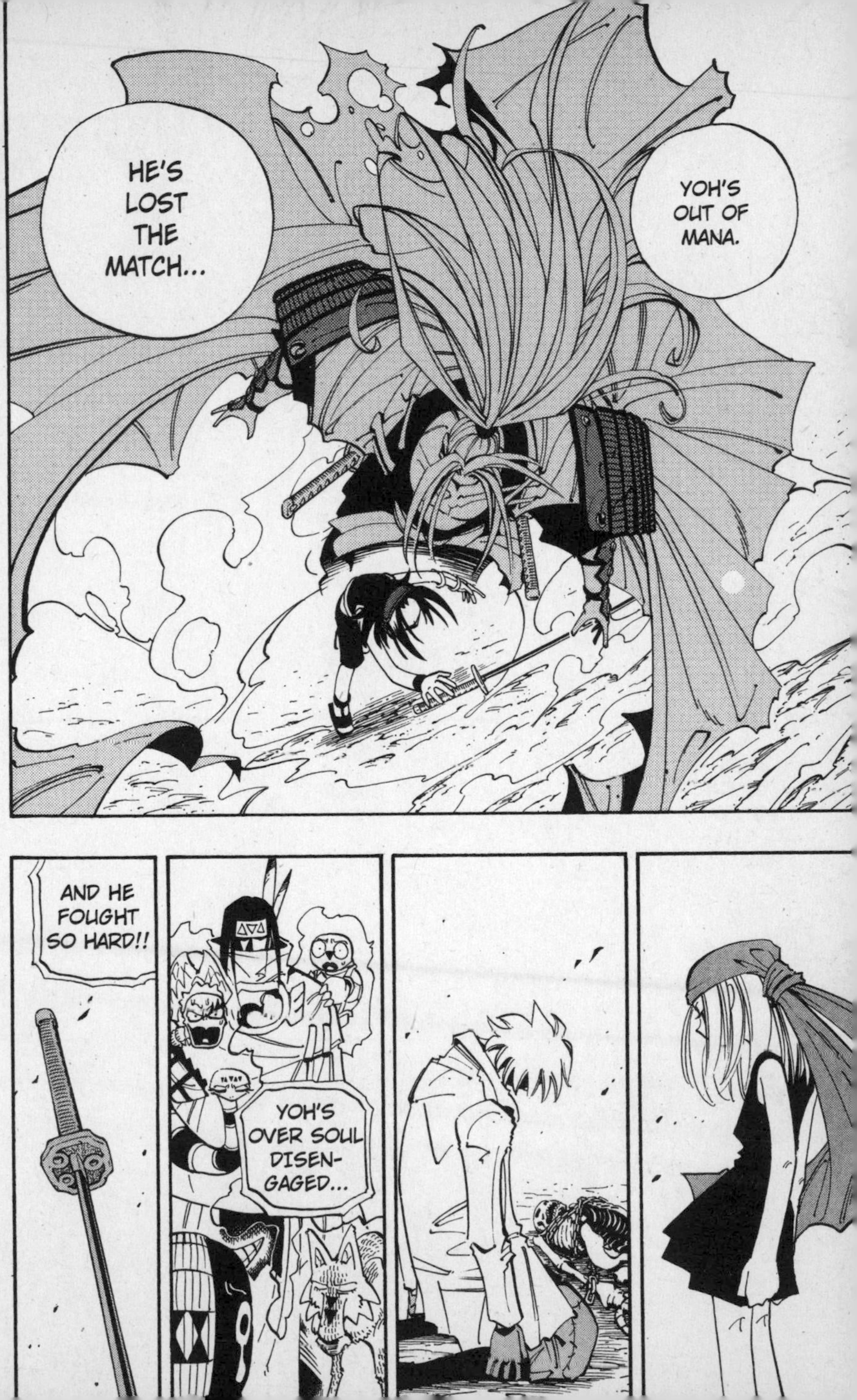
YOH'S OUT OF MANA.
HE'S LOST THE MATCH...
YOH'S OVER SOUL DISENGAGED...
AND HE FOUGHT SO HARD!!

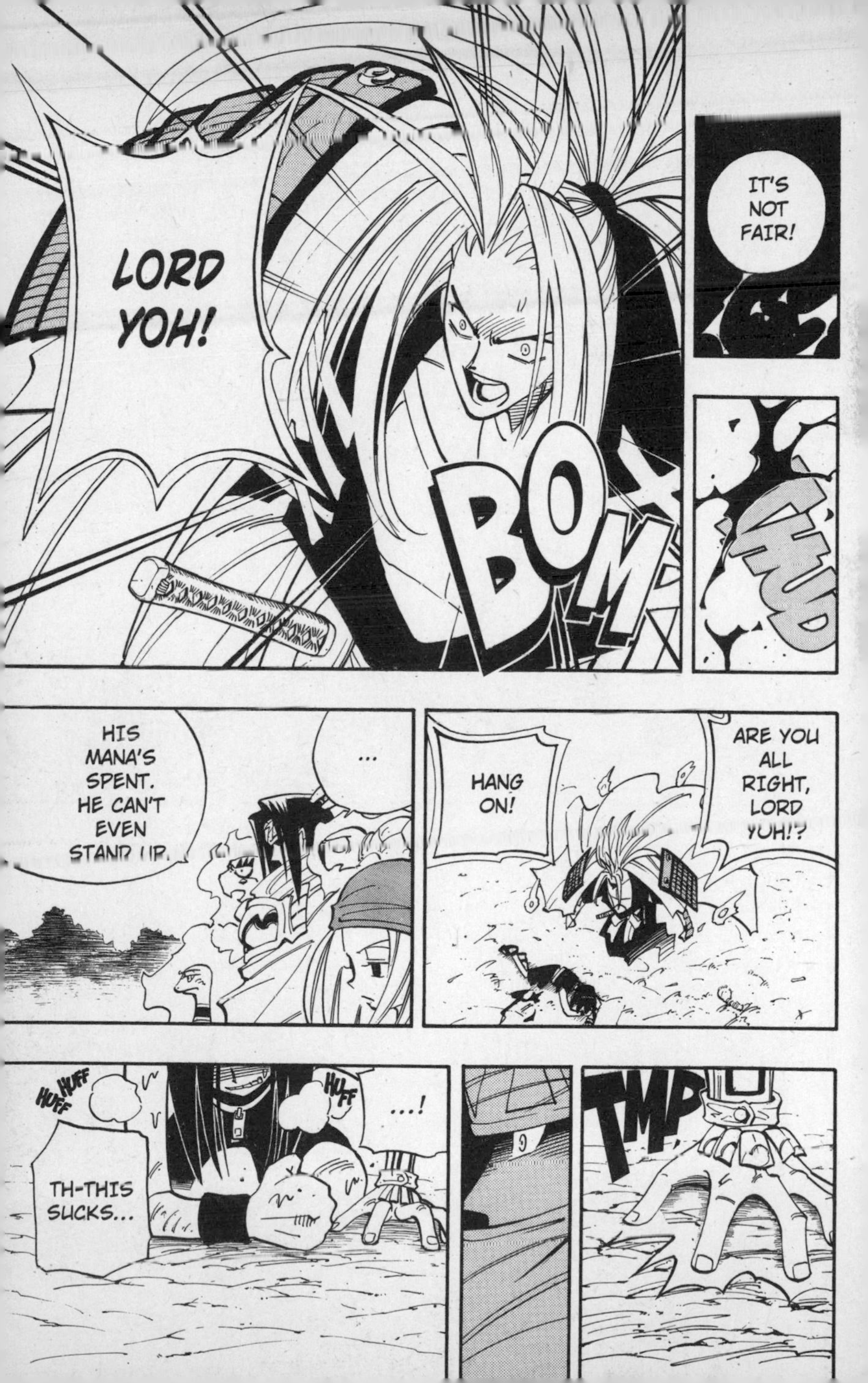
IT'S NOT FAIR!
THUD
LORD YOH!
BOOM
ARE YOU ALL RIGHT, LORD YUH!?
HANG ON!
...
HIS MANA'S SPENT. HE CAN'T EVEN STAND UP.
TMP
...!
HUFF
HUFF HUFF
TH-THIS SUCKS...

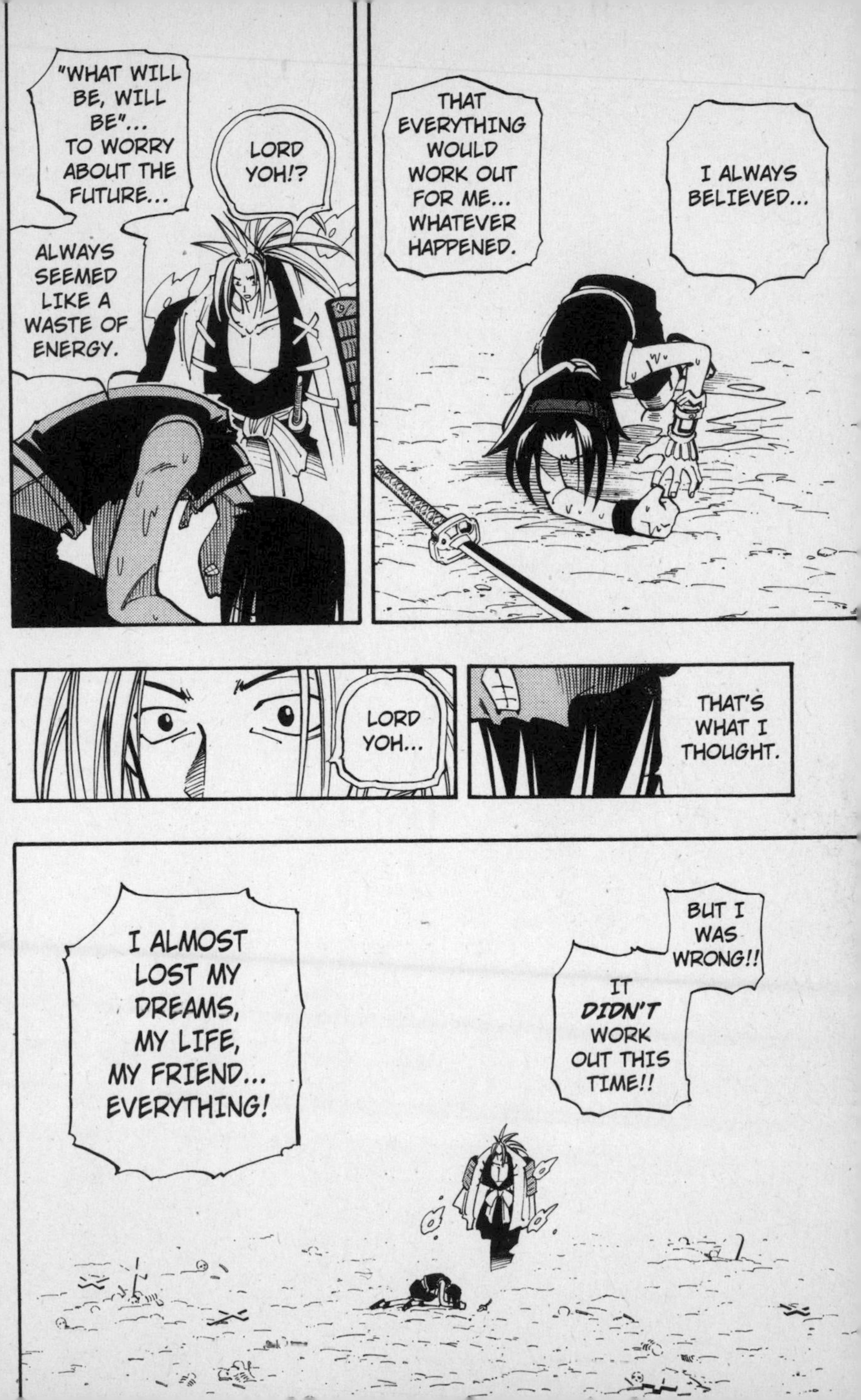
I ALWAYS BELIEVED...
THAT EVERYTHING WOULD WORK OUT FOR ME... WHATEVER HAPPENED.
"WHAT WILL BE, WILL BE"... TO WORRY ABOUT THE FUTURE...
ALWAYS SEEMED LIKE A WASTE OF ENERGY.
LORD YOH!?
THAT'S WHAT I THOUGHT.
LORD YOH...
BUT I WAS WRONG!!
IT *DIDN'T* WORK OUT THIS TIME!!
I ALMOST LOST MY DREAMS, MY LIFE, MY FRIEND... EVERYTHING!

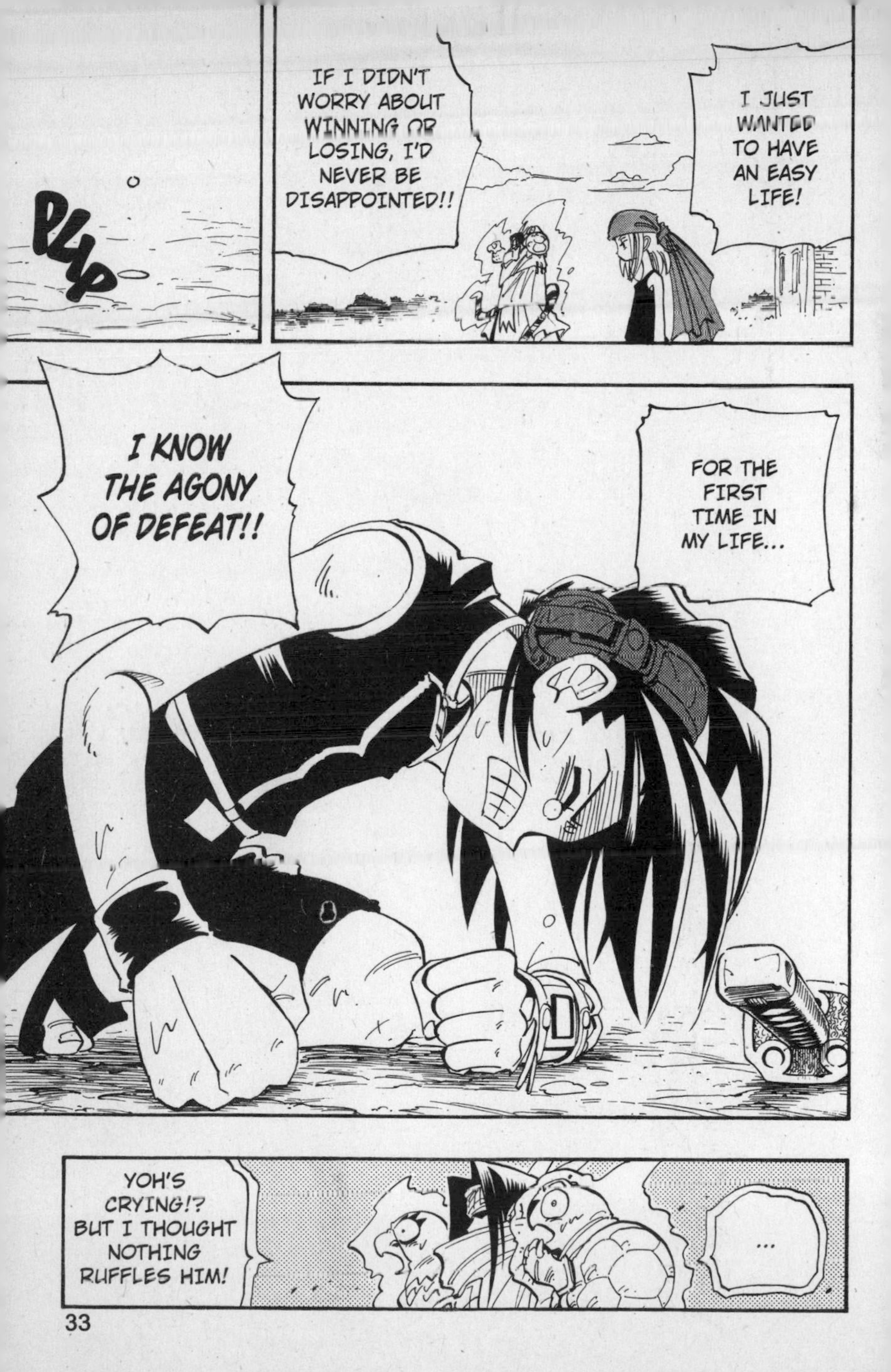
I JUST WANTED TO HAVE AN EASY LIFE!
IF I DIDN'T WORRY ABOUT WINNING OR LOSING, I'D NEVER BE DISAPPOINTED!!
PLIP
FOR THE FIRST TIME IN MY LIFE...
I KNOW THE AGONY OF DEFEAT!!
...
YOH'S CRYING!? BUT I THOUGHT NOTHING RUFFLES HIM!

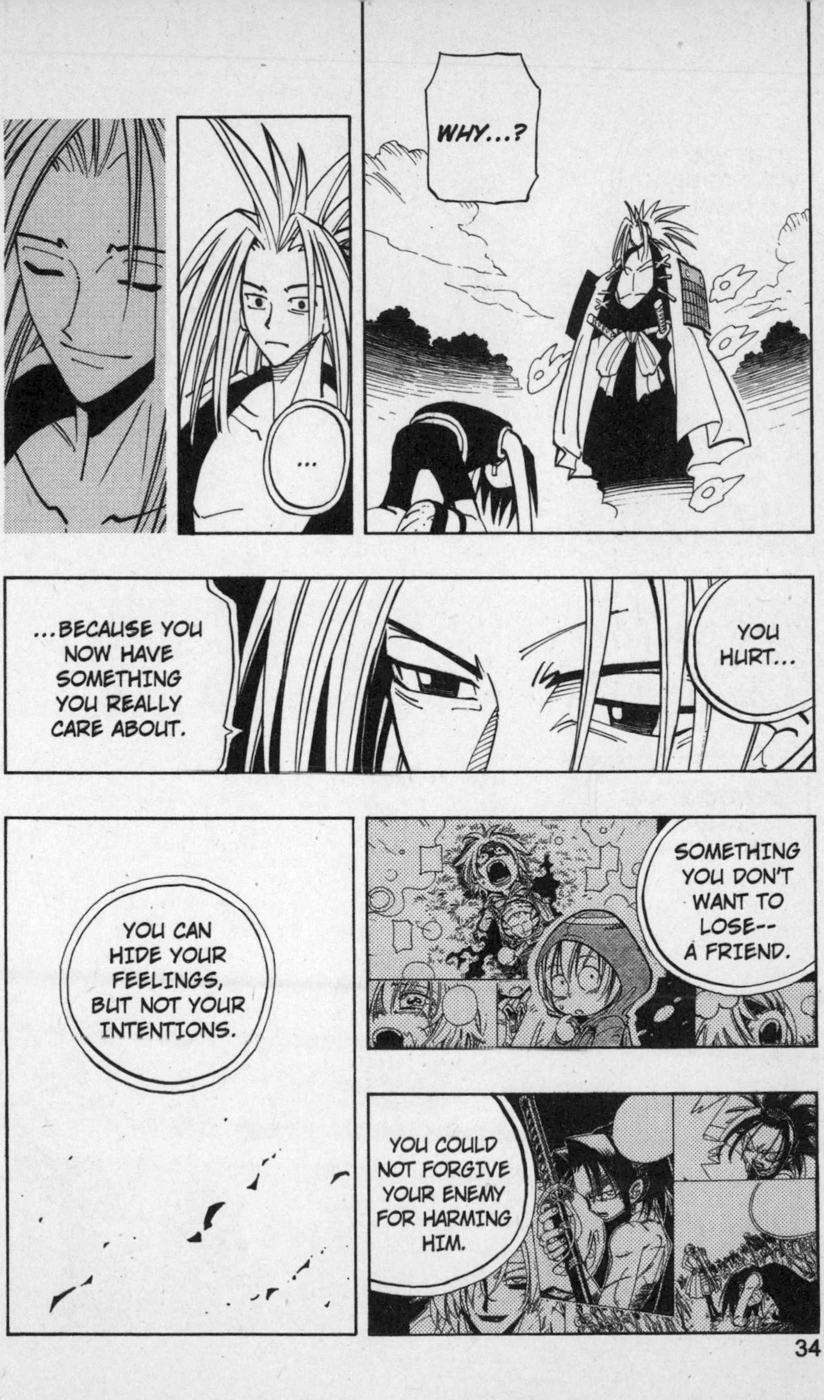
WHY...?
...
YOU HURT...
...BECAUSE YOU NOW HAVE SOMETHING YOU REALLY CARE ABOUT.
SOMETHING YOU DON'T WANT TO LOSE-- A FRIEND.
YOU COULD NOT FORGIVE YOUR ENEMY FOR HARMING HIM.
YOU CAN HIDE YOUR FEELINGS, BUT NOT YOUR INTENTIONS.

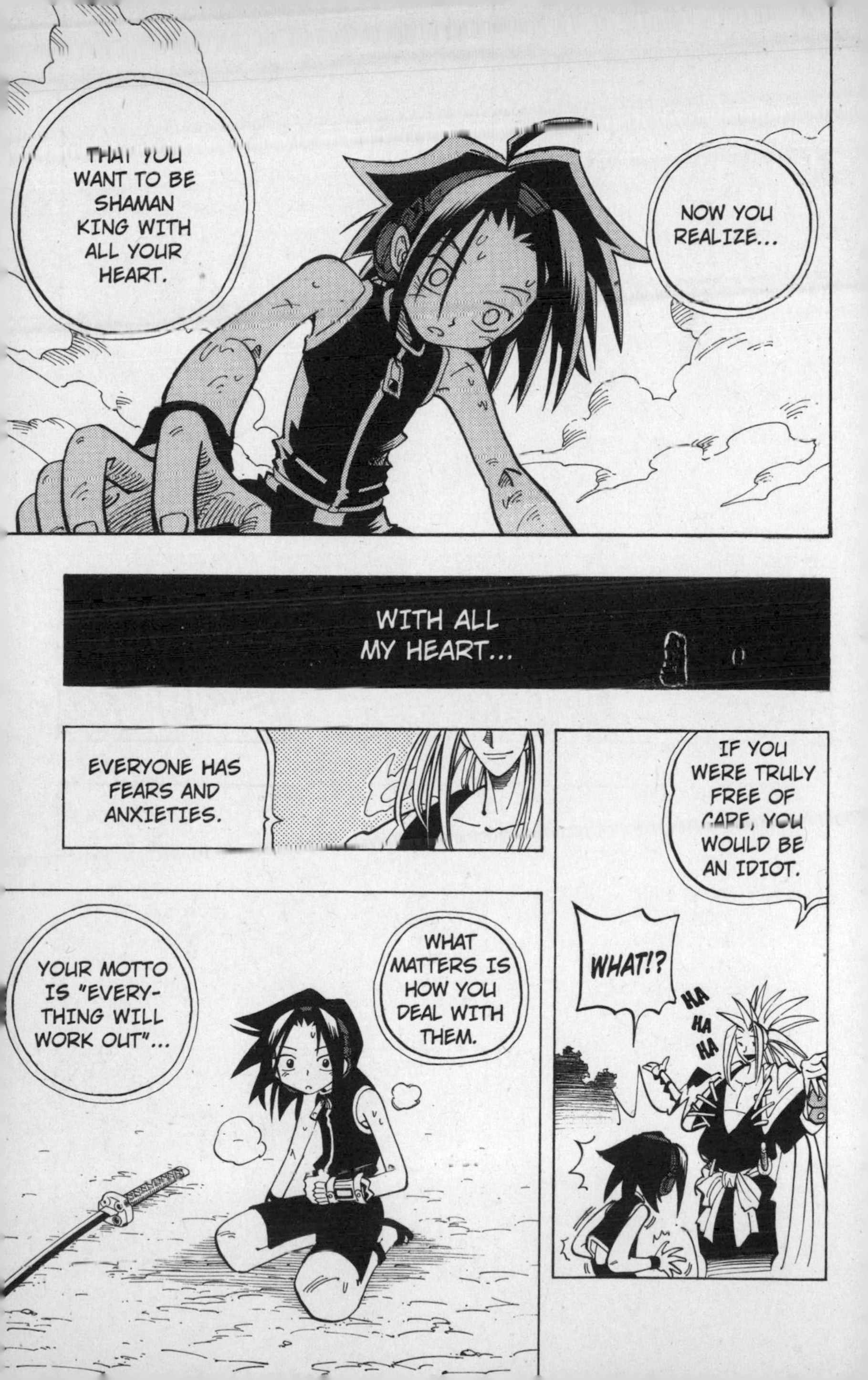
NOW YOU REALIZE...
THAT YOU WANT TO BE SHAMAN KING WITH ALL YOUR HEART.
WITH ALL MY HEART...
IF YOU WERE TRULY FREE OF CARE, YOU WOULD BE AN IDIOT.
WHAT!?
HA HA HA
EVERYONE HAS FEARS AND ANXIETIES.
WHAT MATTERS IS HOW YOU DEAL WITH THEM.
YOUR MOTTO IS "EVERY-THING WILL WORK OUT"...

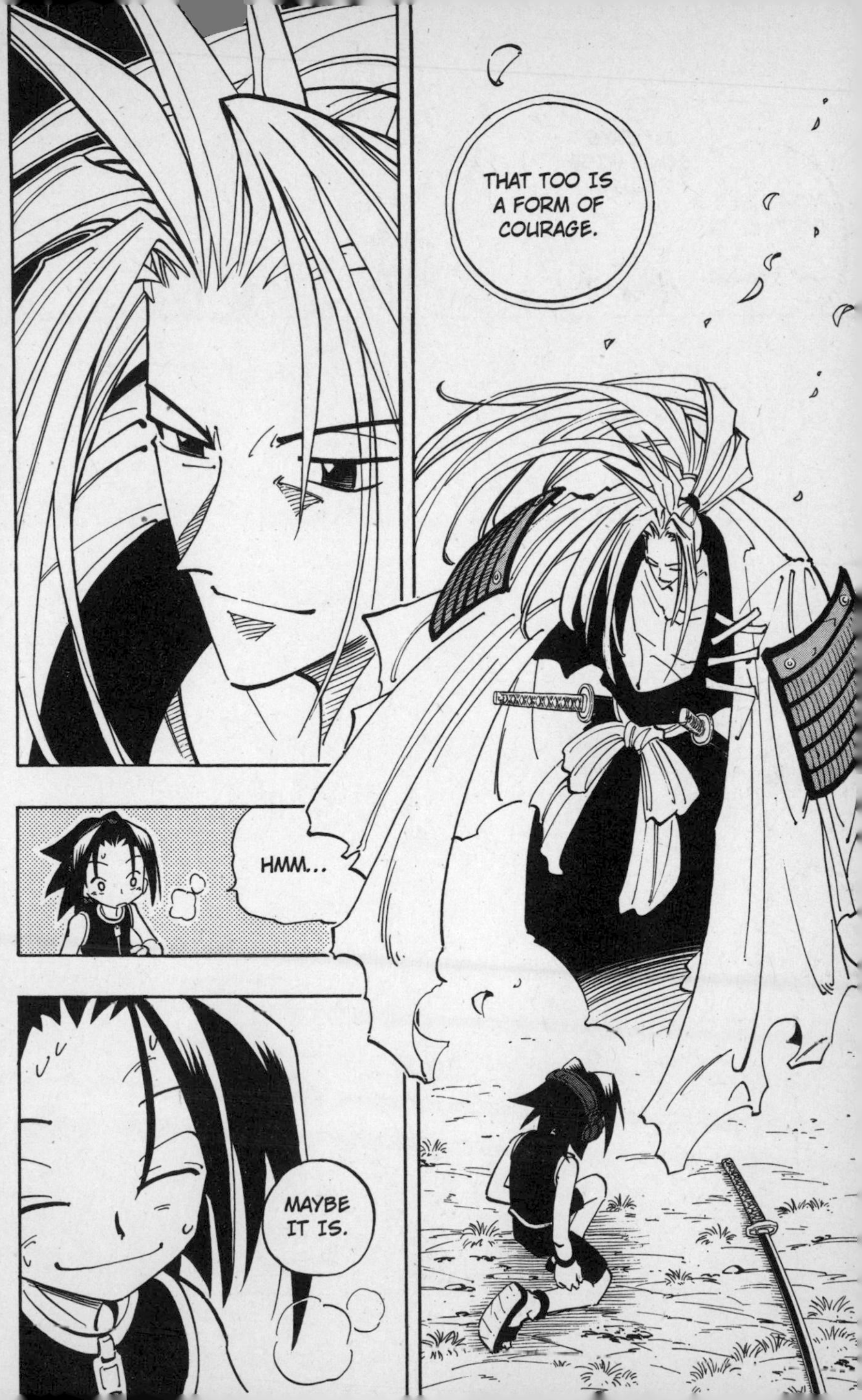
THAT TOO IS A FORM OF COURAGE.
HMM...
MAYBE IT IS.

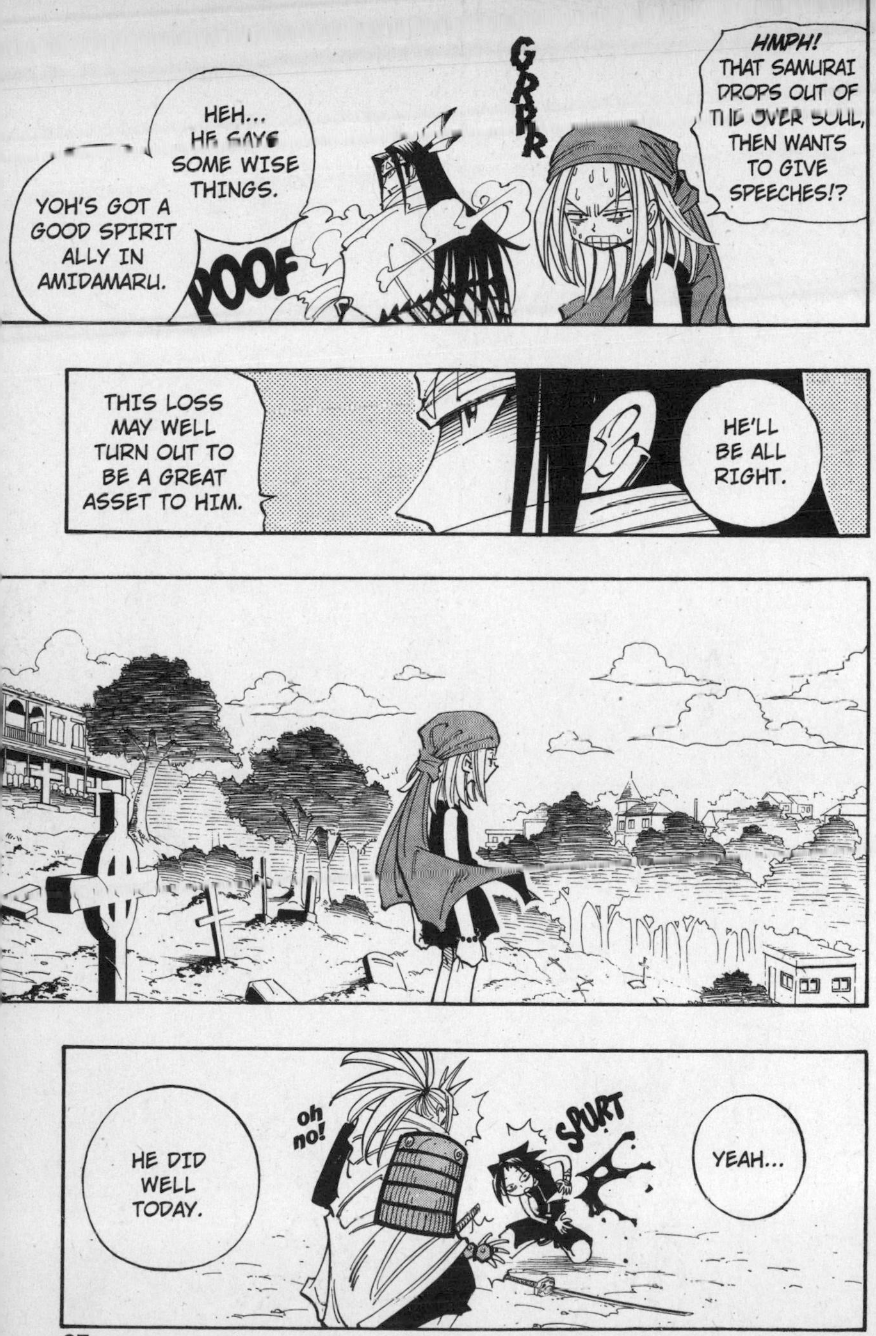
HMPH! THAT SAMURAI DROPS OUT OF THE OVER SOUL, THEN WANTS TO GIVE SPEECHES!?
GRRR
HEH... HE SAYS SOME WISE THINGS.
YOH'S GOT A GOOD SPIRIT ALLY IN AMIDAMARU.
POOF
HE'LL BE ALL RIGHT.
THIS LOSS MAY WELL TURN OUT TO BE A GREAT ASSET TO HIM.
YEAH...
SPURT
oh no!
HE DID WELL TODAY.

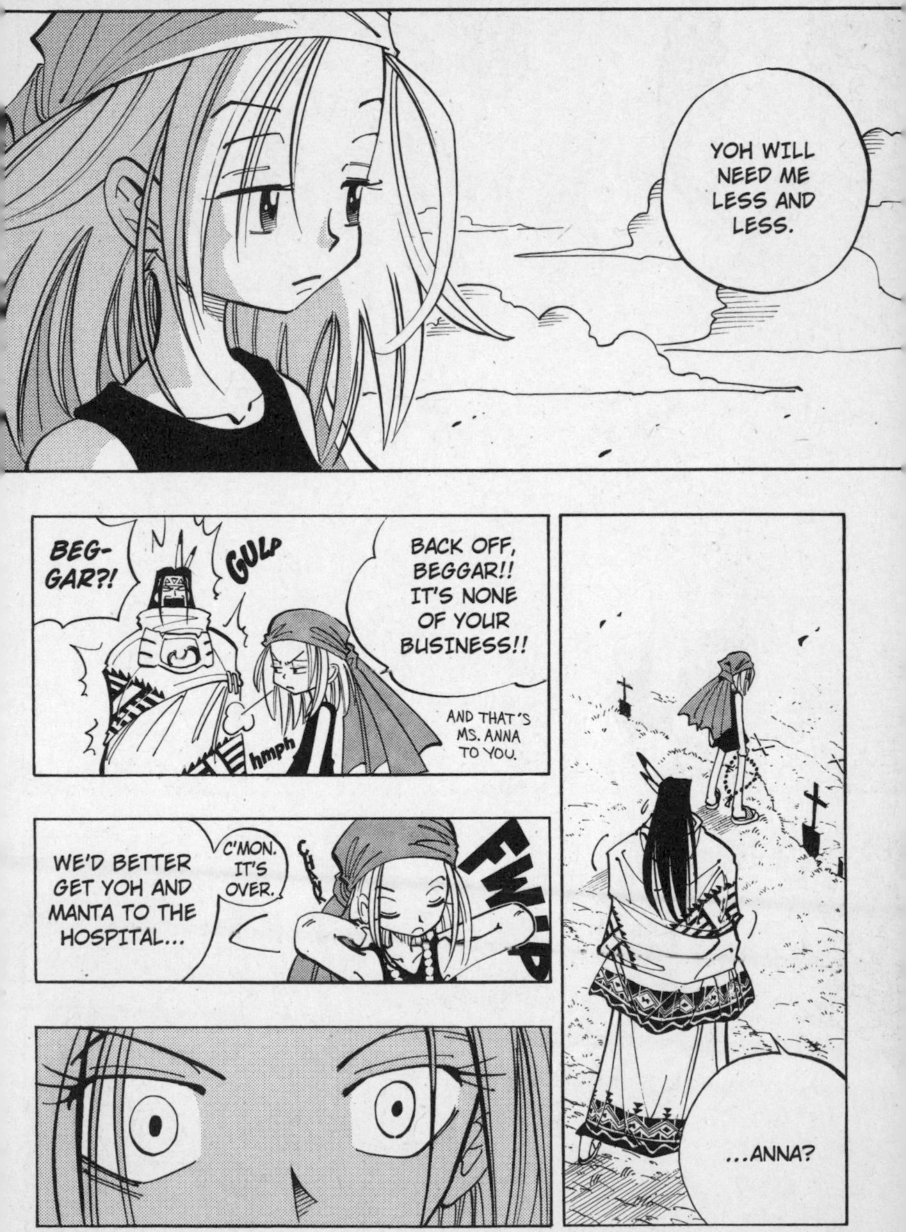
YOH WILL NEED ME LESS AND LESS.
...ANNA?
BACK OFF, BEGGAR!! IT'S NONE OF YOUR BUSINESS!!
GULP
BEG-GAR?!
AND THAT'S MS. ANNA TO YOU.
hmph
FWIP
C'MON. IT'S OVER.
WE'D BETTER GET YOH AND MANTA TO THE HOSPITAL...

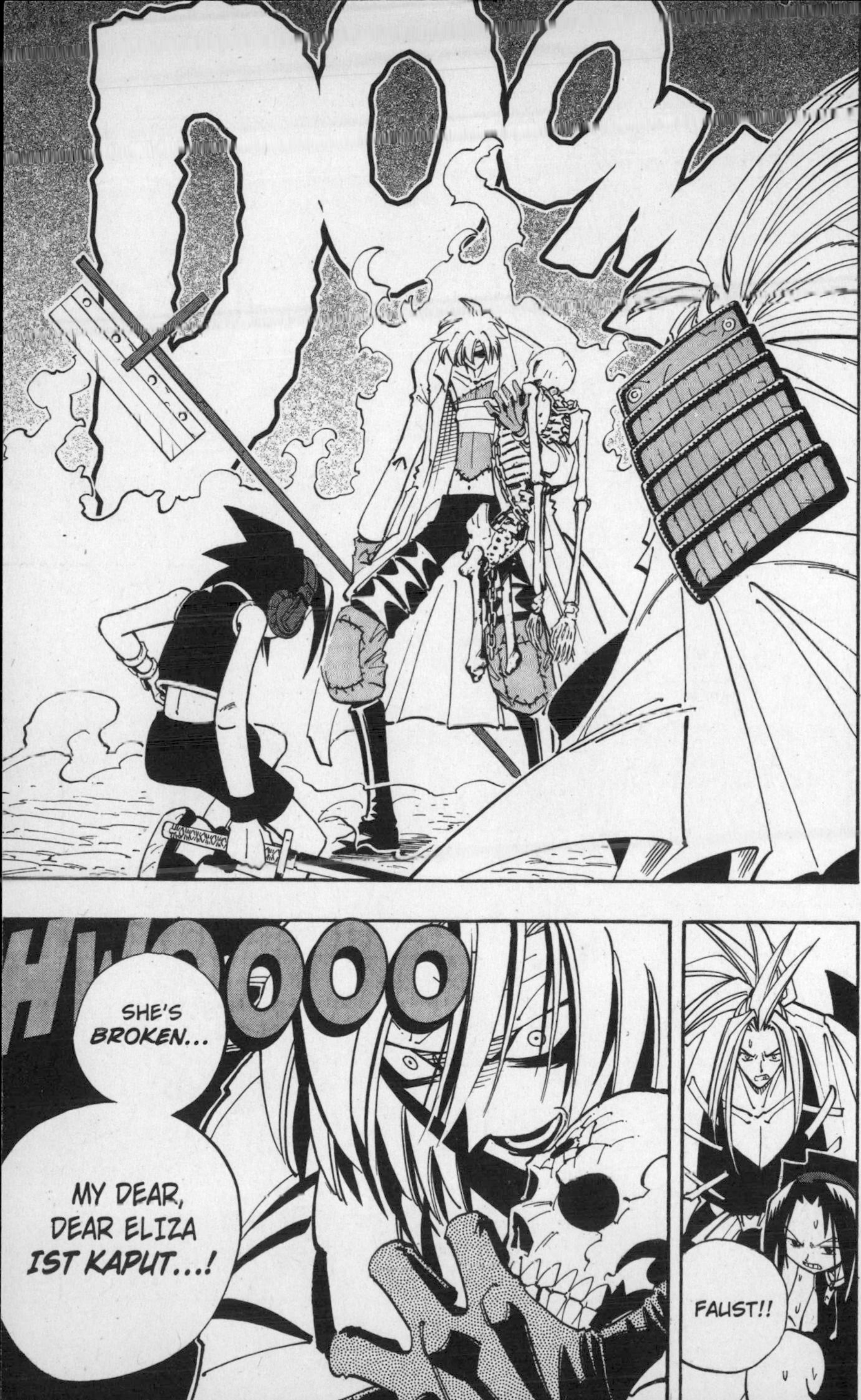
DOOM
FAUST!!
HWOOOO
SHE'S BROKEN...
MY DEAR, DEAR ELIZA IST KAPUT...!

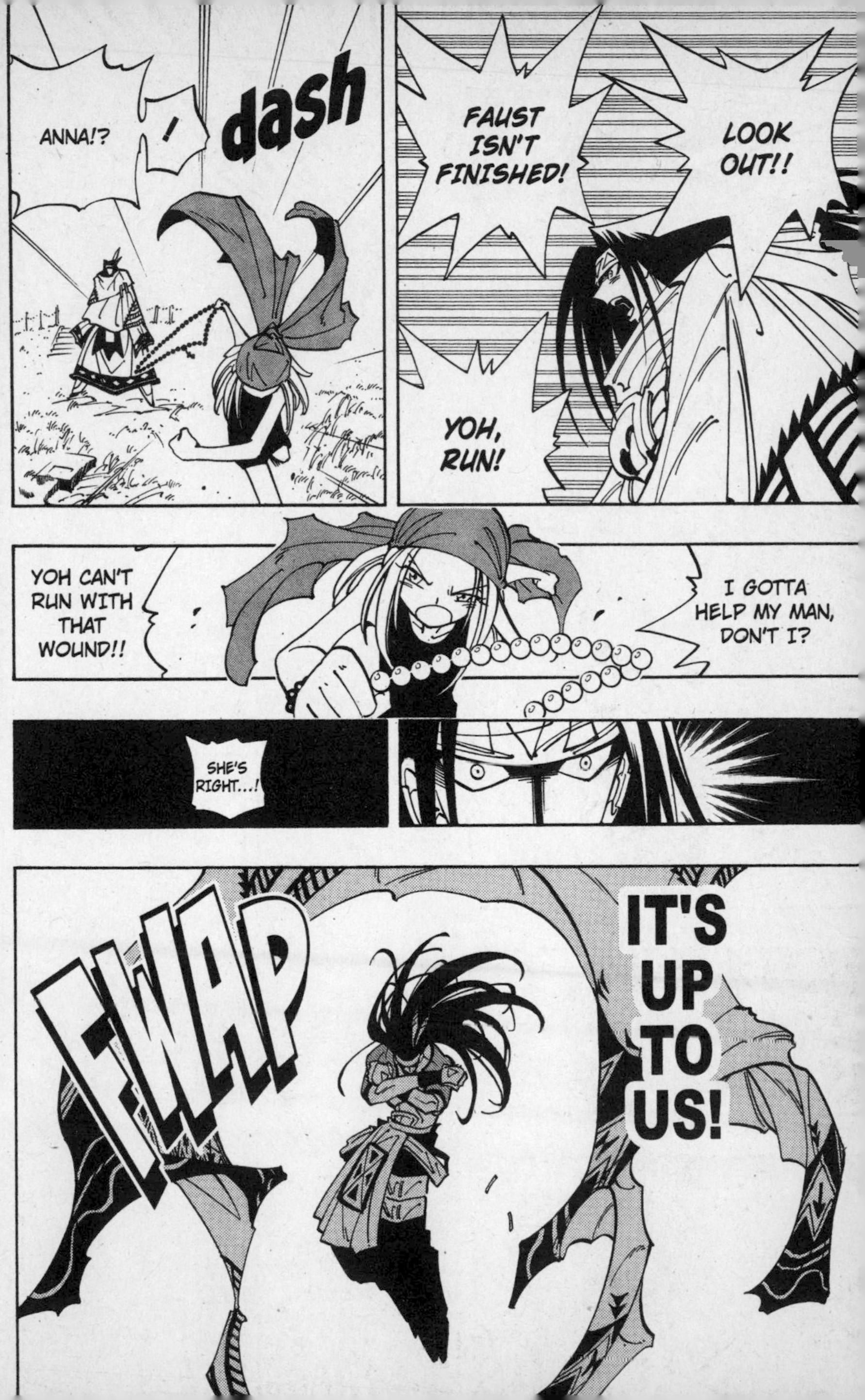
LOOK OUT!!
FAUST ISN'T FINISHED!
YOH, RUN!
dash
!
ANNA!?
I GOTTA HELP MY MAN, DON'T I?
YOH CAN'T RUN WITH THAT WOUND!!
SHE'S RIGHT...!
IT'S UP TO US!
FWAP

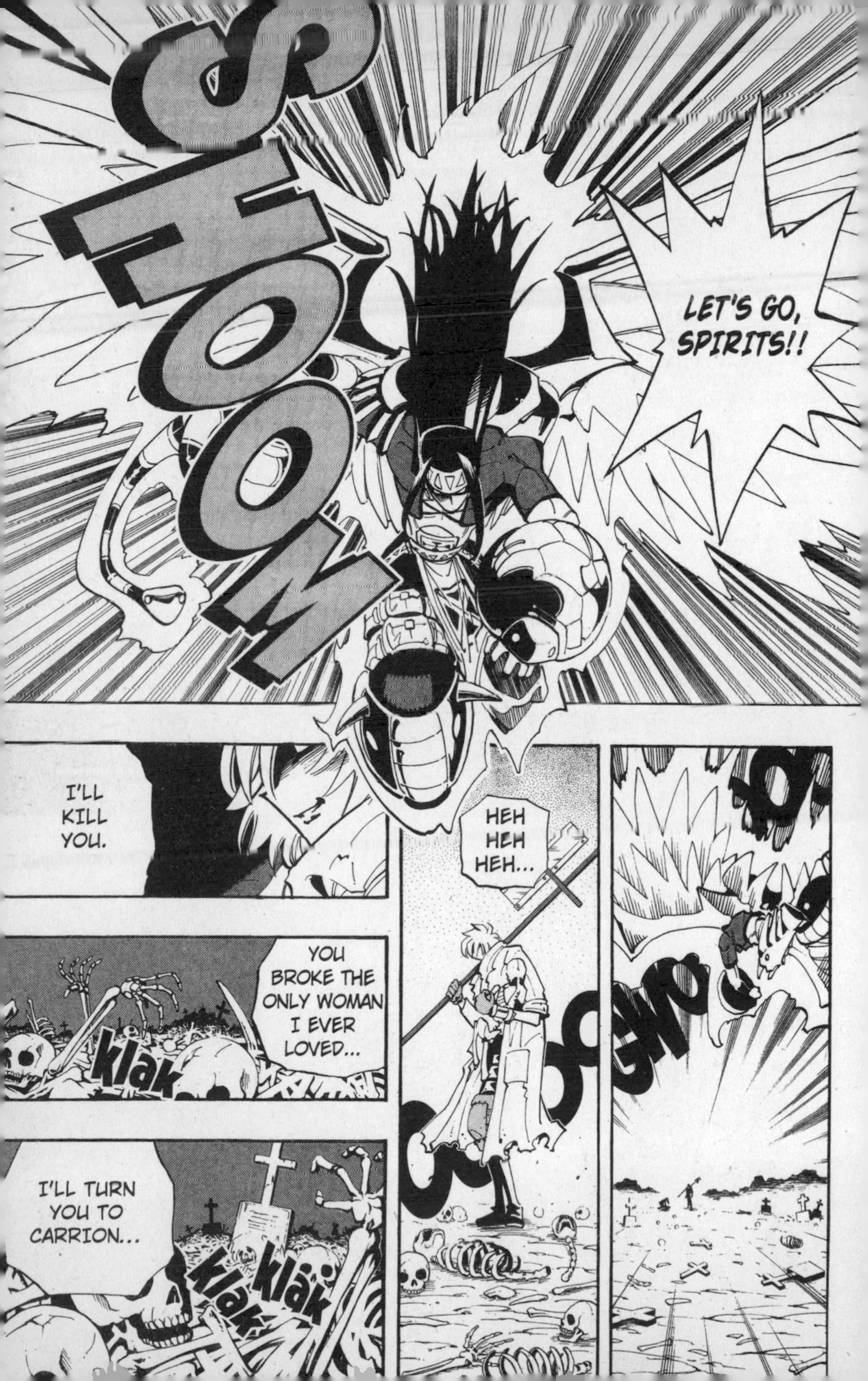
LET'S GO, SPIRITS!!
SHOOM
HEH HEH HEH...
I'LL KILL YOU.
YOU BROKE THE ONLY WOMAN I EVER LOVED...
klak
I'LL TURN YOU TO CARRION...
klak
klak
klak

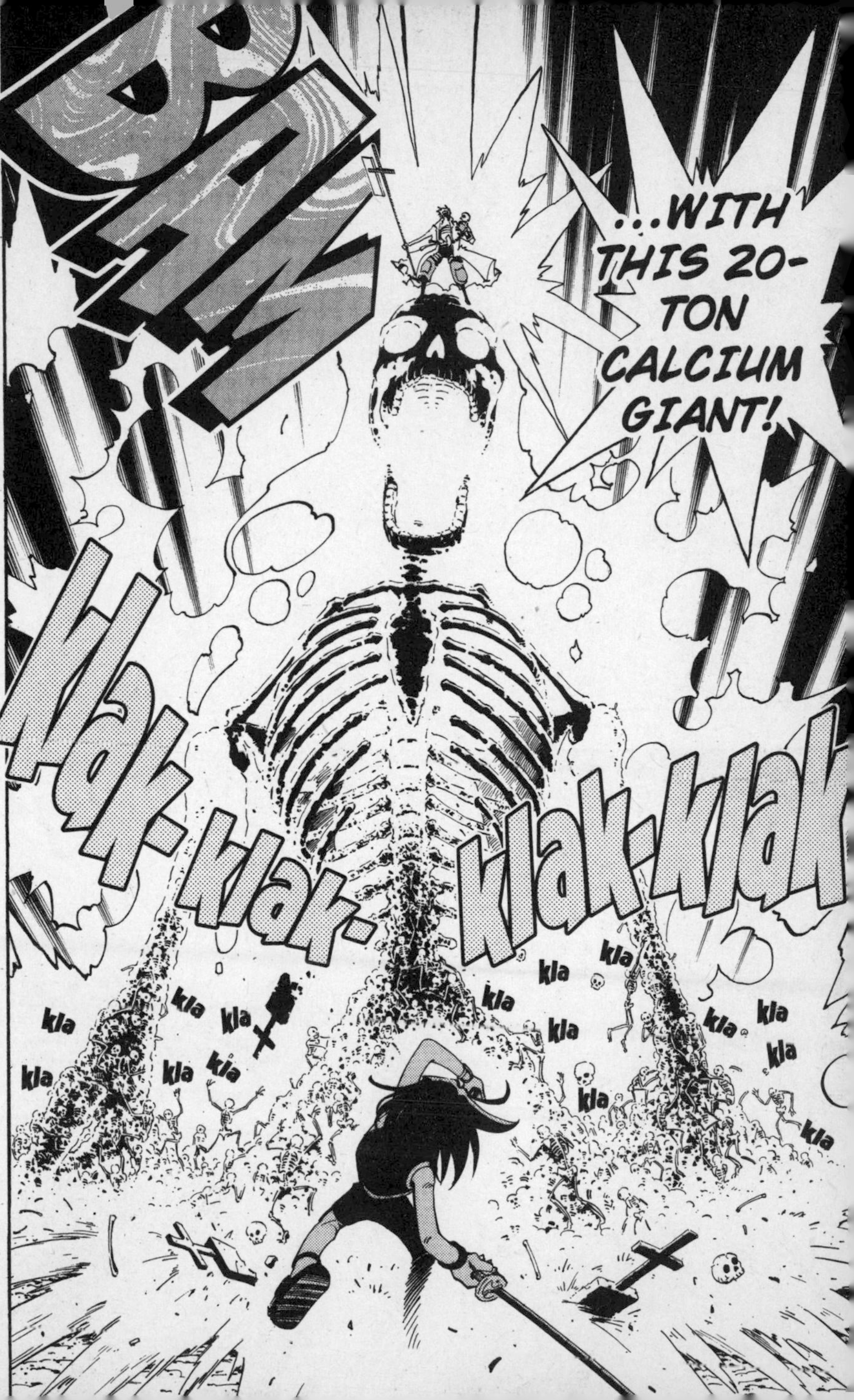
...WITH THIS 20-TON CALCIUM GIANT!
klak-klak-klak-klak-klak
kla kla kla kla kla kla kla kla kla kla kla kla kla kla kla

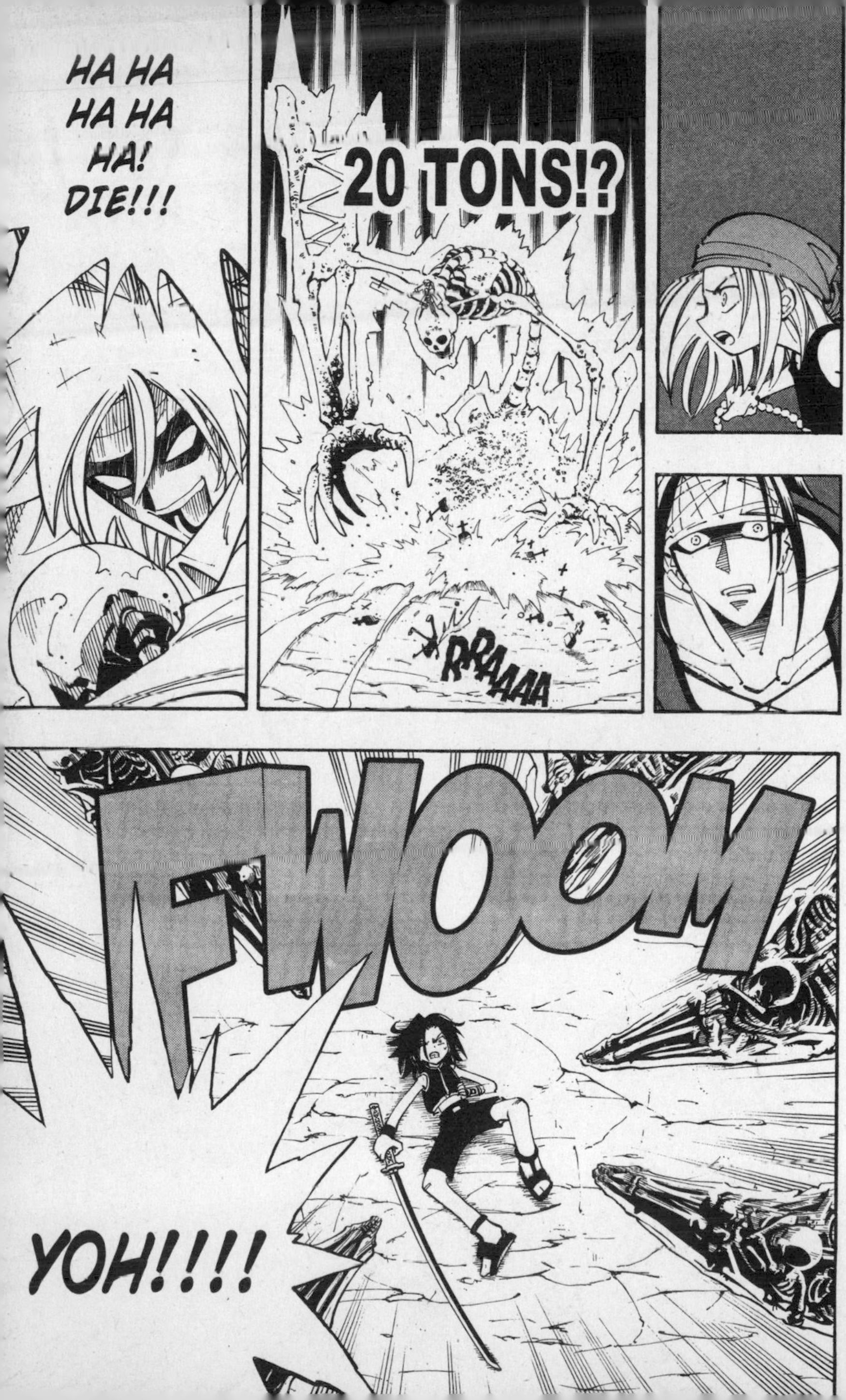
20 TONS!?
RRAAAAA
HA HA HA HA HA! DIE!!!
FWOOM
YOH!!!!

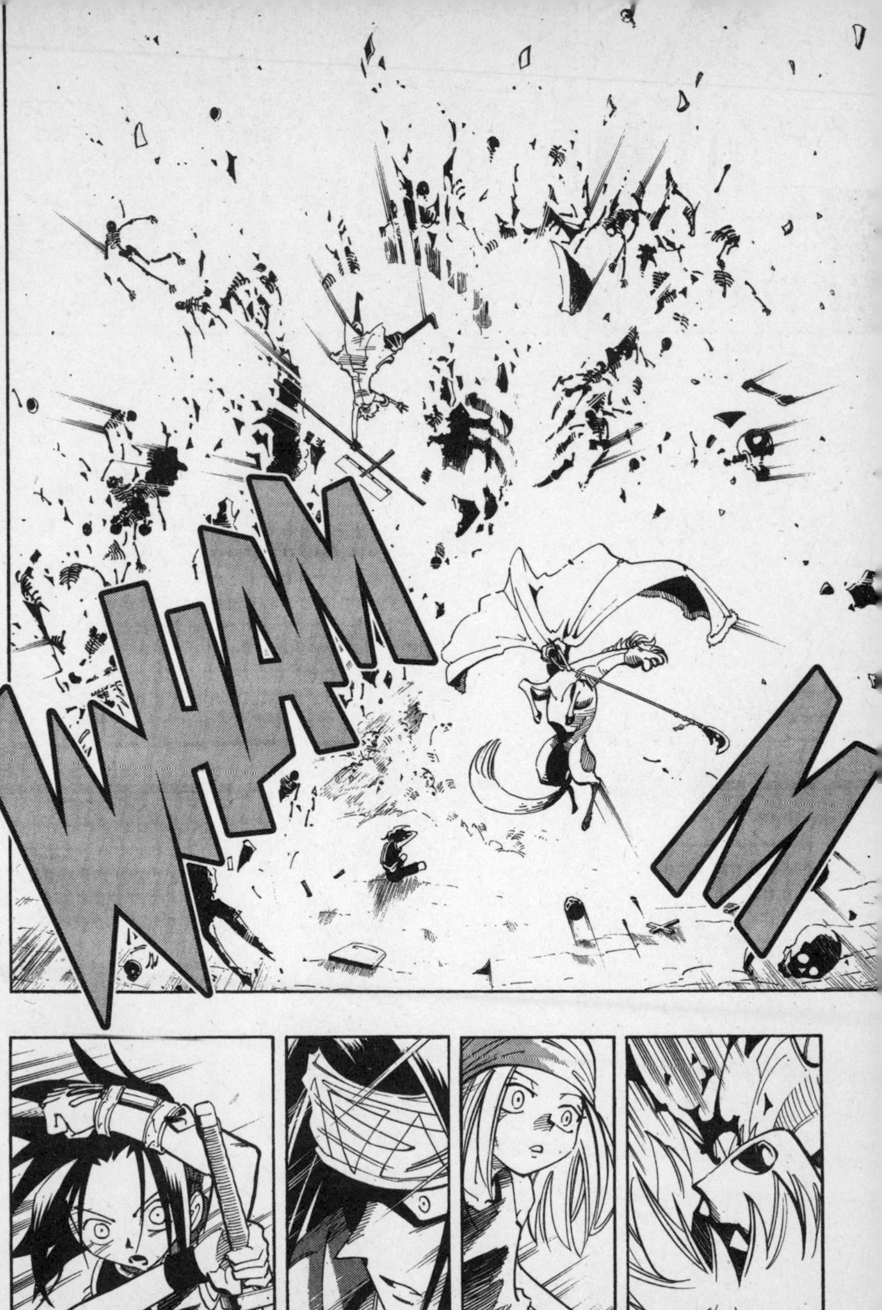
WHAMM

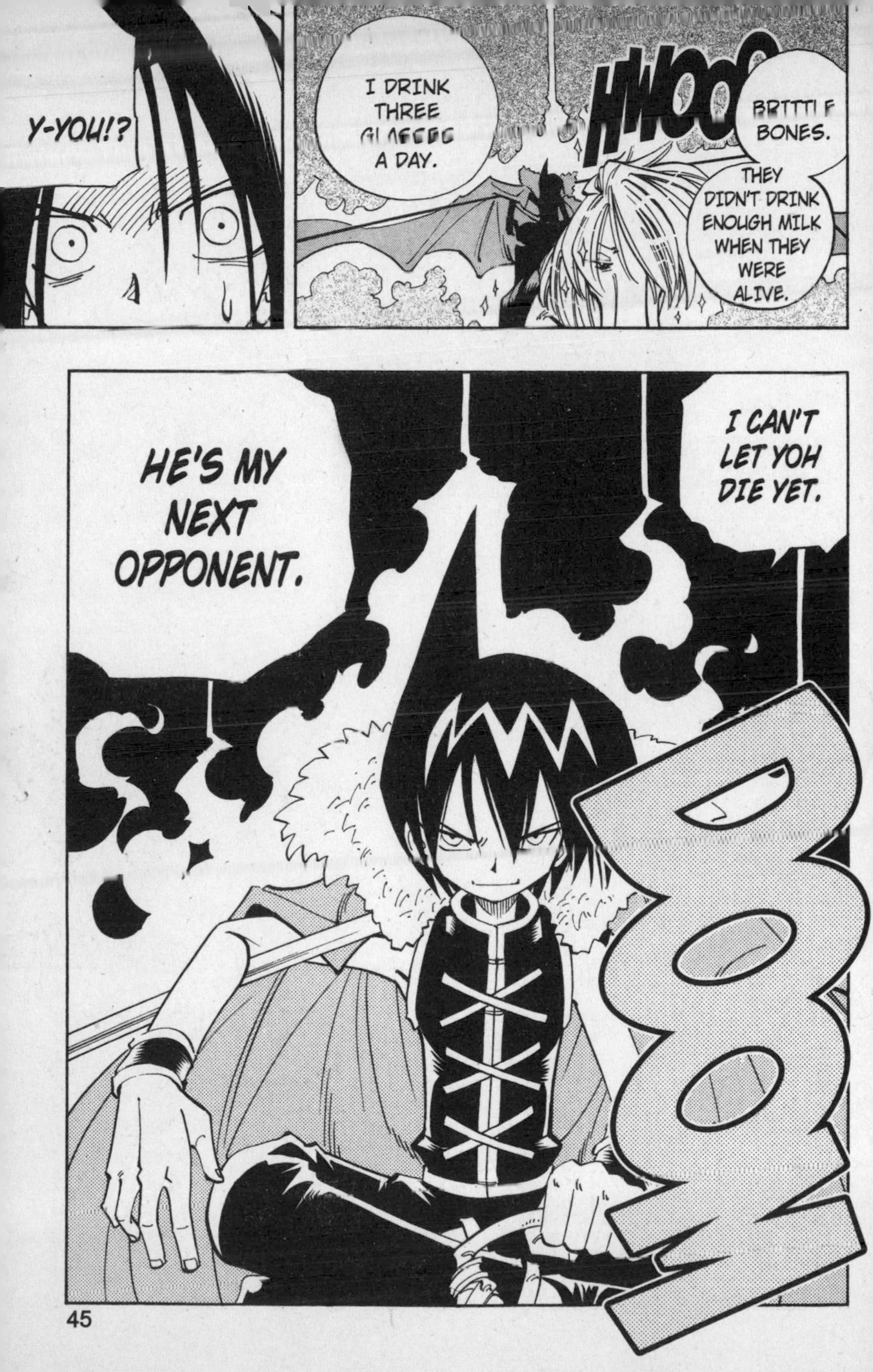
HWOO
BRITTLE BONES.
THEY DIDN'T DRINK ENOUGH MILK WHEN THEY WERE ALIVE.
I DRINK THREE GLASSES A DAY.
Y-YOU!?
I CAN'T LET YOH DIE YET.
HE'S MY NEXT OPPONENT.
BOOM

SHAMAN KING

6

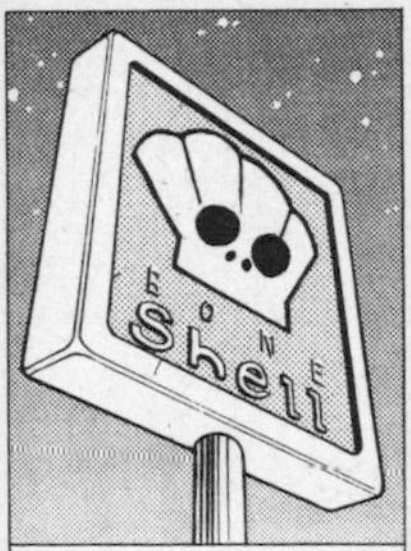
BONE
Shell

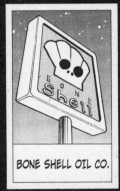

BONE SHELL OIL CO.

# Reincarnation 47: June Goodbyes

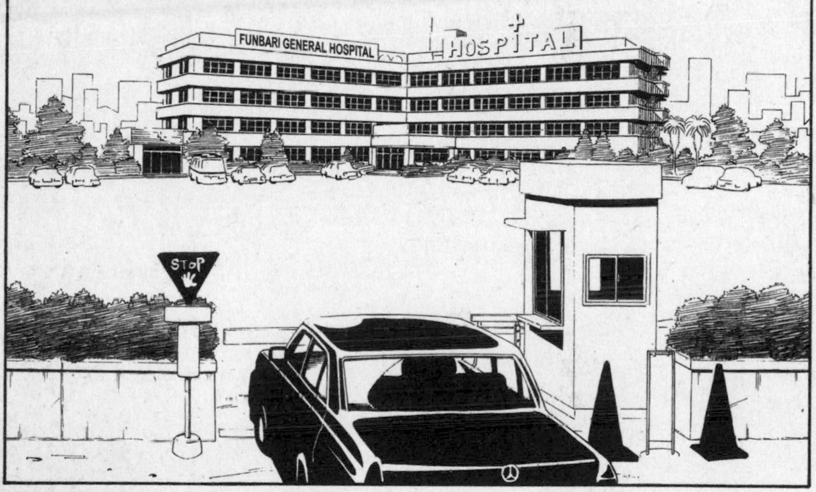
FUNBARI GENERAL HOSPITAL
HOSPITAL
STOP

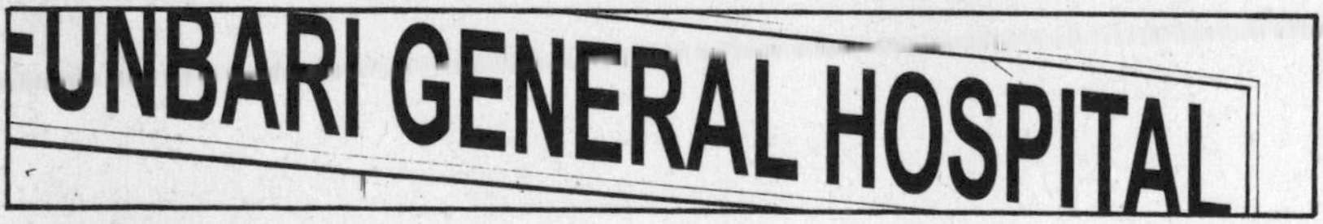
FUNBARI GENERAL HOSPITAL

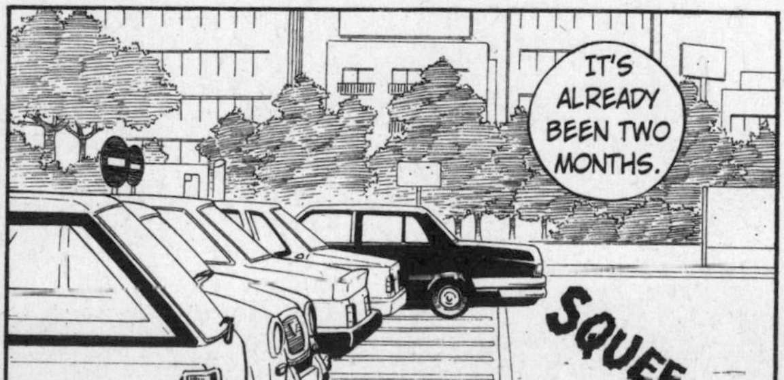
IT'S ALREADY BEEN TWO MONTHS.
SQUEE

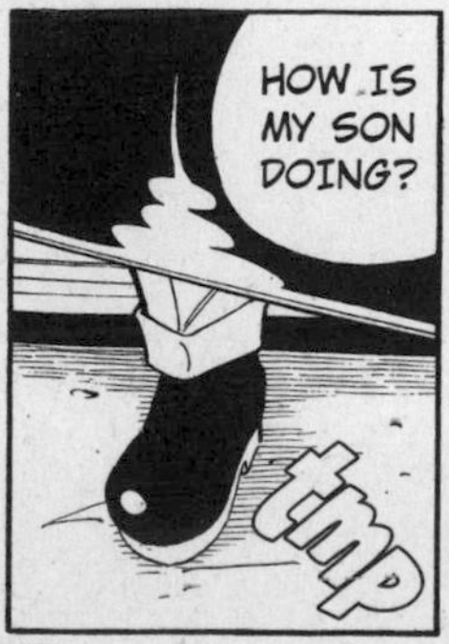
HOW IS MY SON DOING?
tmp

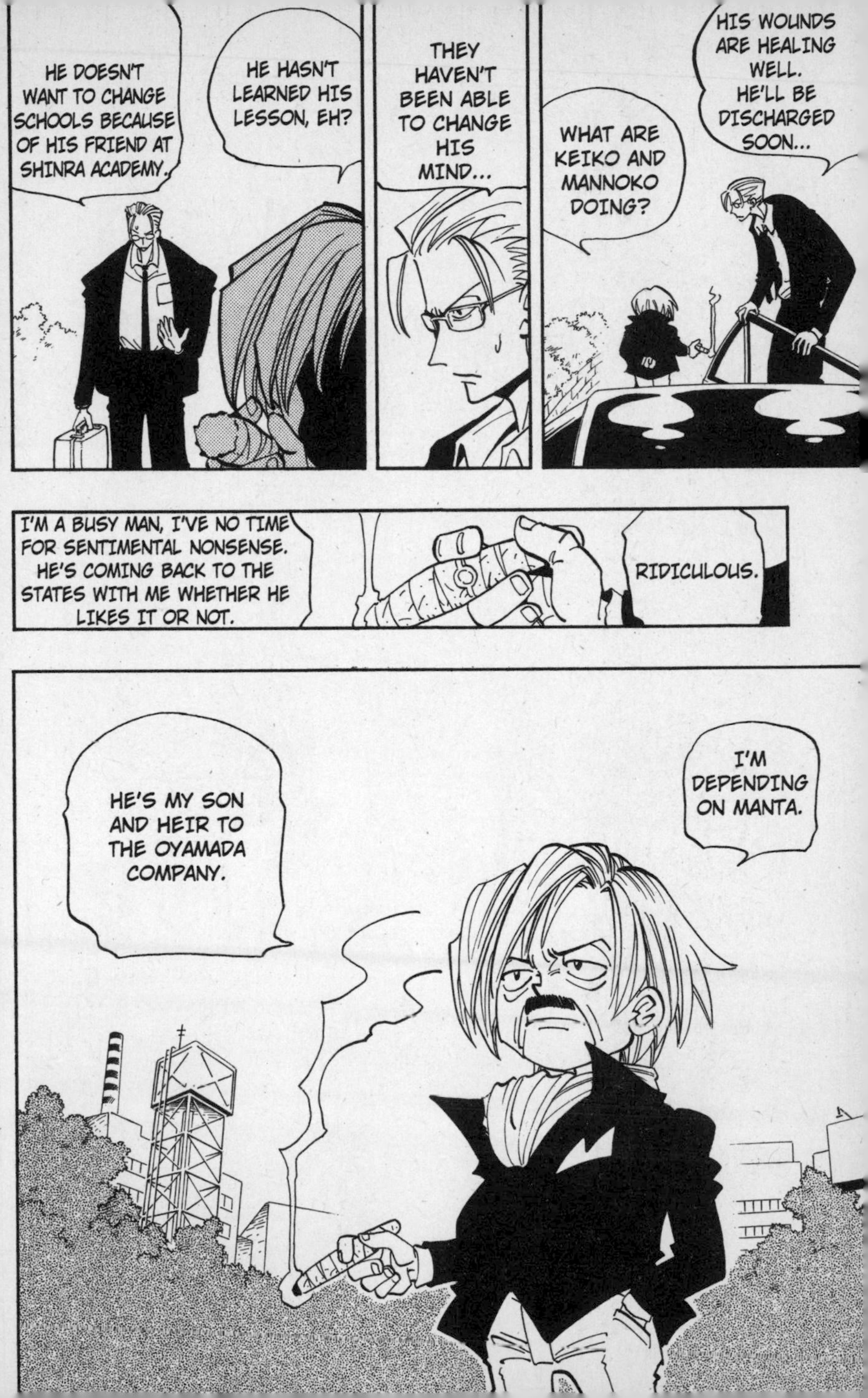
HIS WOUNDS ARE HEALING WELL. HE'LL BE DISCHARGED SOON...
WHAT ARE KEIKO AND MANNOKO DOING?
THEY HAVEN'T BEEN ABLE TO CHANGE HIS MIND...
HE HASN'T LEARNED HIS LESSON, EH?
HE DOESN'T WANT TO CHANGE SCHOOLS BECAUSE OF HIS FRIEND AT SHINRA ACADEMY.
RIDICULOUS.
I'M A BUSY MAN, I'VE NO TIME FOR SENTIMENTAL NONSENSE. HE'S COMING BACK TO THE STATES WITH ME WHETHER HE LIKES IT OR NOT.
I'M DEPENDING ON MANTA.
HE'S MY SON AND HEIR TO THE OYAMADA COMPANY.

# Reincarnation 47: June Goodbyes

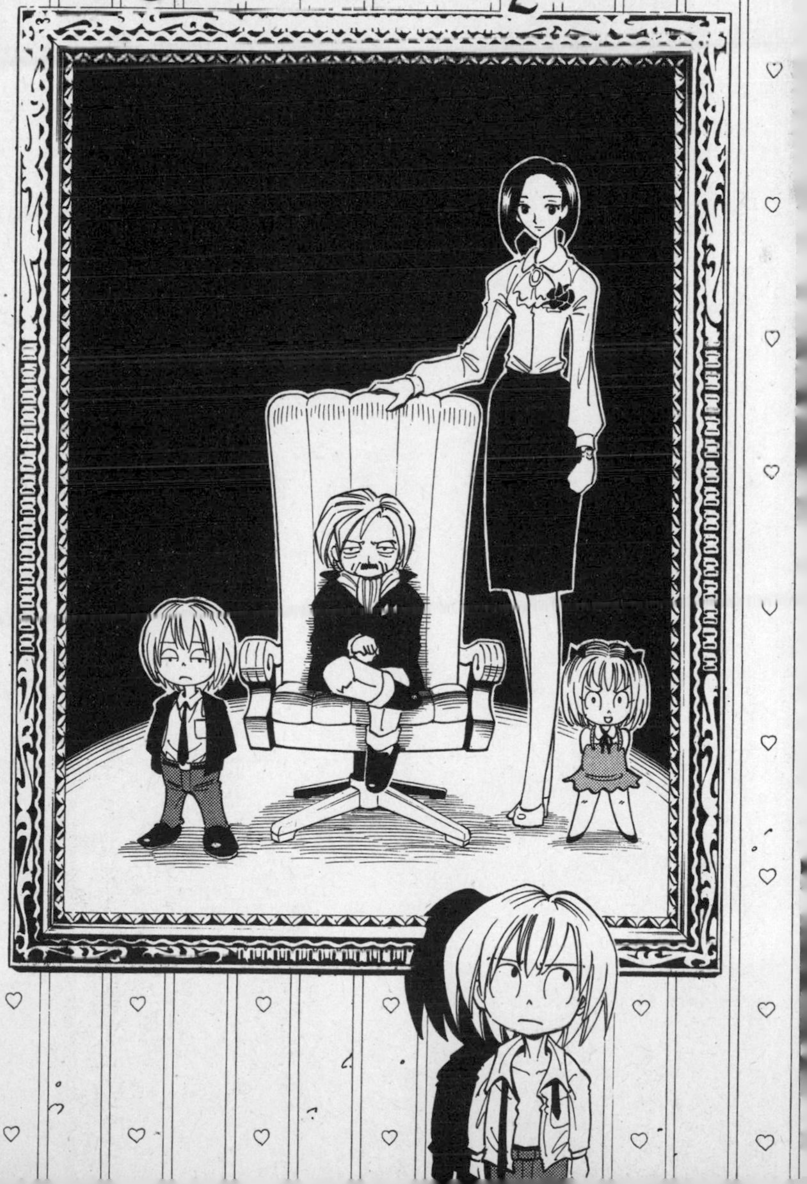

READ THIS WAY

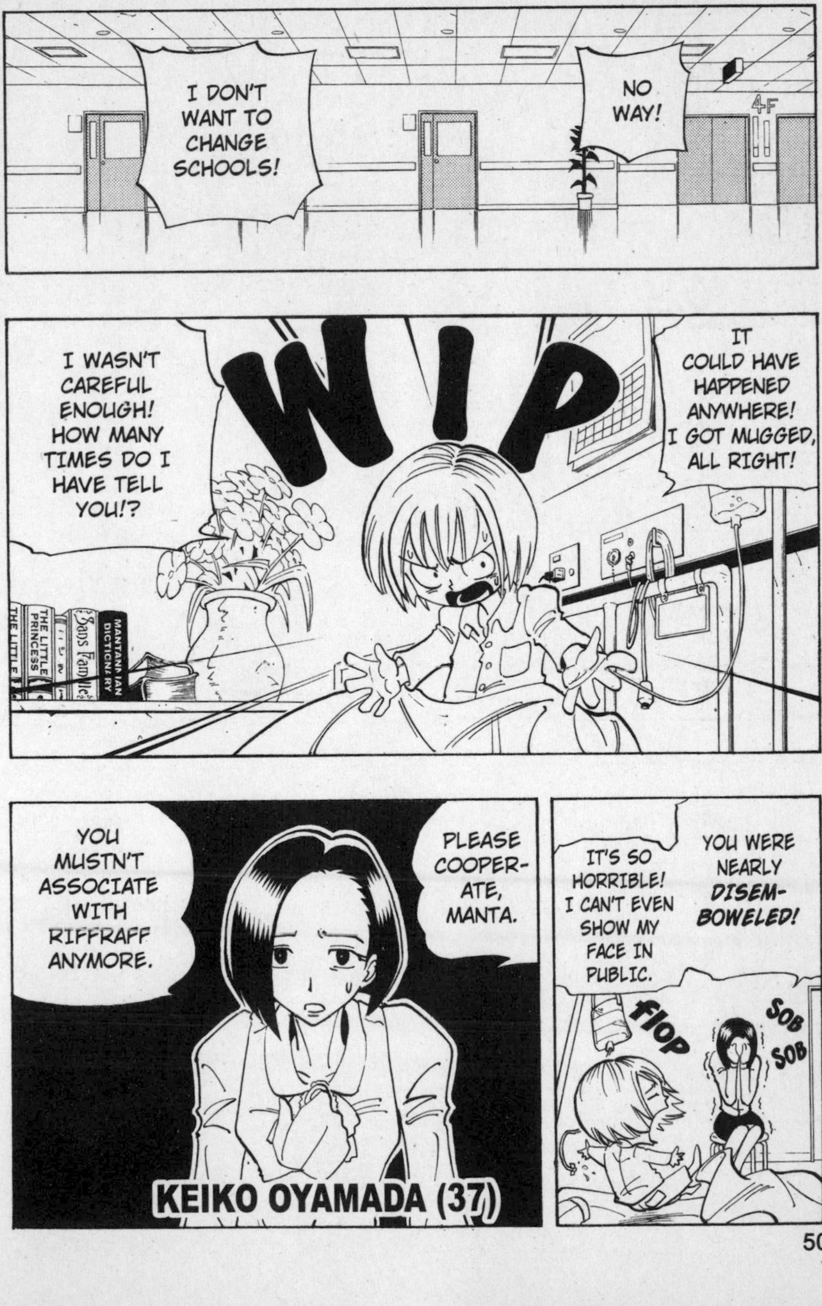

NO WAY!
I DON'T WANT TO CHANGE SCHOOLS!
IT COULD HAVE HAPPENED ANYWHERE! I GOT MUGGED, ALL RIGHT!
WIP
I WASN'T CAREFUL ENOUGH! HOW MANY TIMES DO I HAVE TELL YOU!?
MANTANN IAN DICTIONARY
Sans Famille
THE LITTLE PRINCESS
YOU WERE NEARLY DISEMBOWELED!
IT'S SO HORRIBLE! I CAN'T EVEN SHOW MY FACE IN PUBLIC.
SOB SOB
flop
PLEASE COOPERATE, MANTA.
YOU MUSTN'T ASSOCIATE WITH RIFFRAFF ANYMORE.
KEIKO OYAMADA (37)

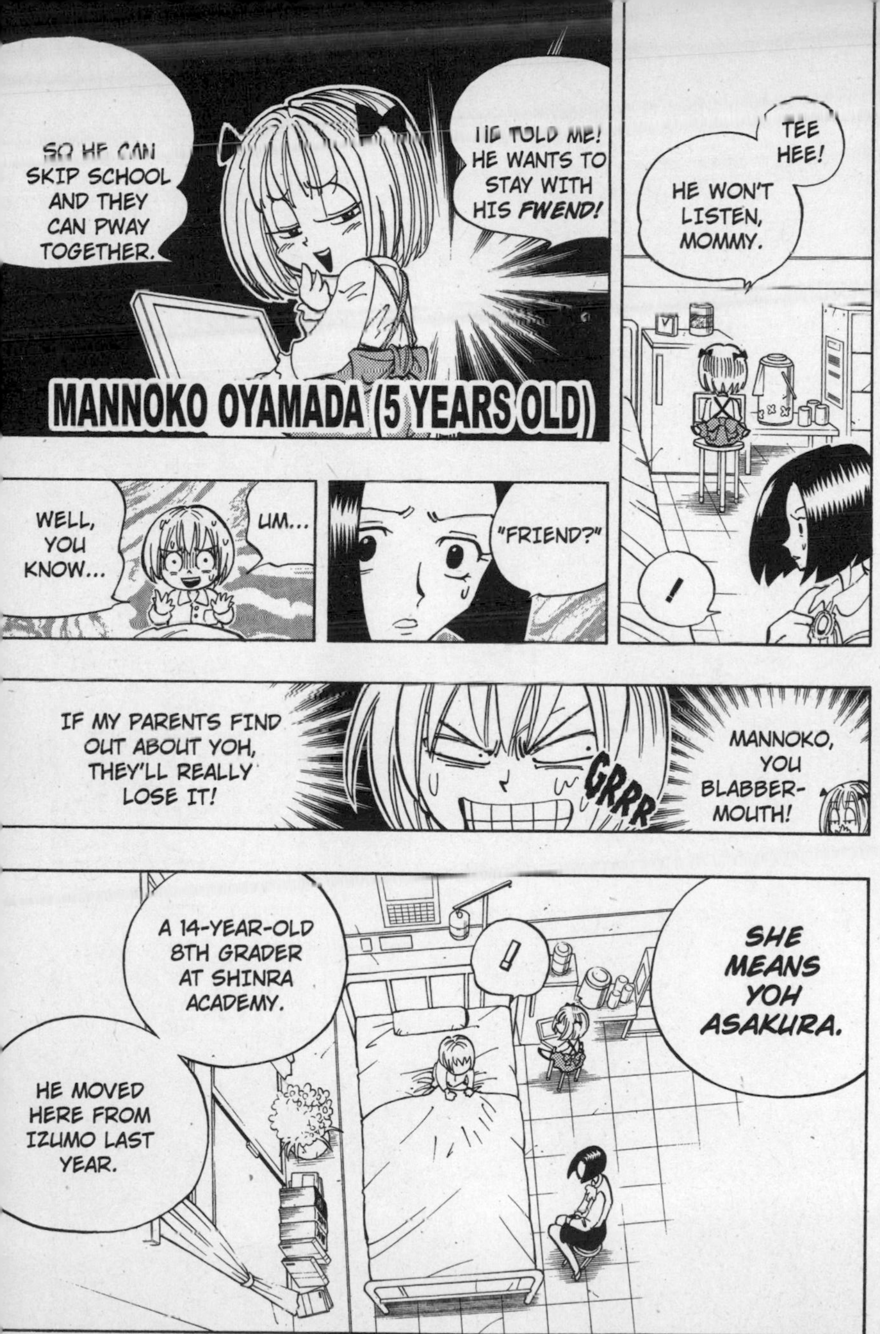
TEE HEE!
HE WON'T LISTEN, MOMMY.
!
HE TOLD ME! HE WANTS TO STAY WITH HIS *FWEND!*
SO HE CAN SKIP SCHOOL AND THEY CAN PWAY TOGETHER.
MANNOKO OYAMADA (5 YEARS OLD)
"FRIEND?"
UM...
WELL, YOU KNOW...
MANNOKO, YOU BLABBER-MOUTH!
GRRR
IF MY PARENTS FIND OUT ABOUT YOH, THEY'LL REALLY LOSE IT!
SHE MEANS YOH ASAKURA.
!
A 14-YEAR-OLD 8TH GRADER AT SHINRA ACADEMY.
HE MOVED HERE FROM IZUMO LAST YEAR.

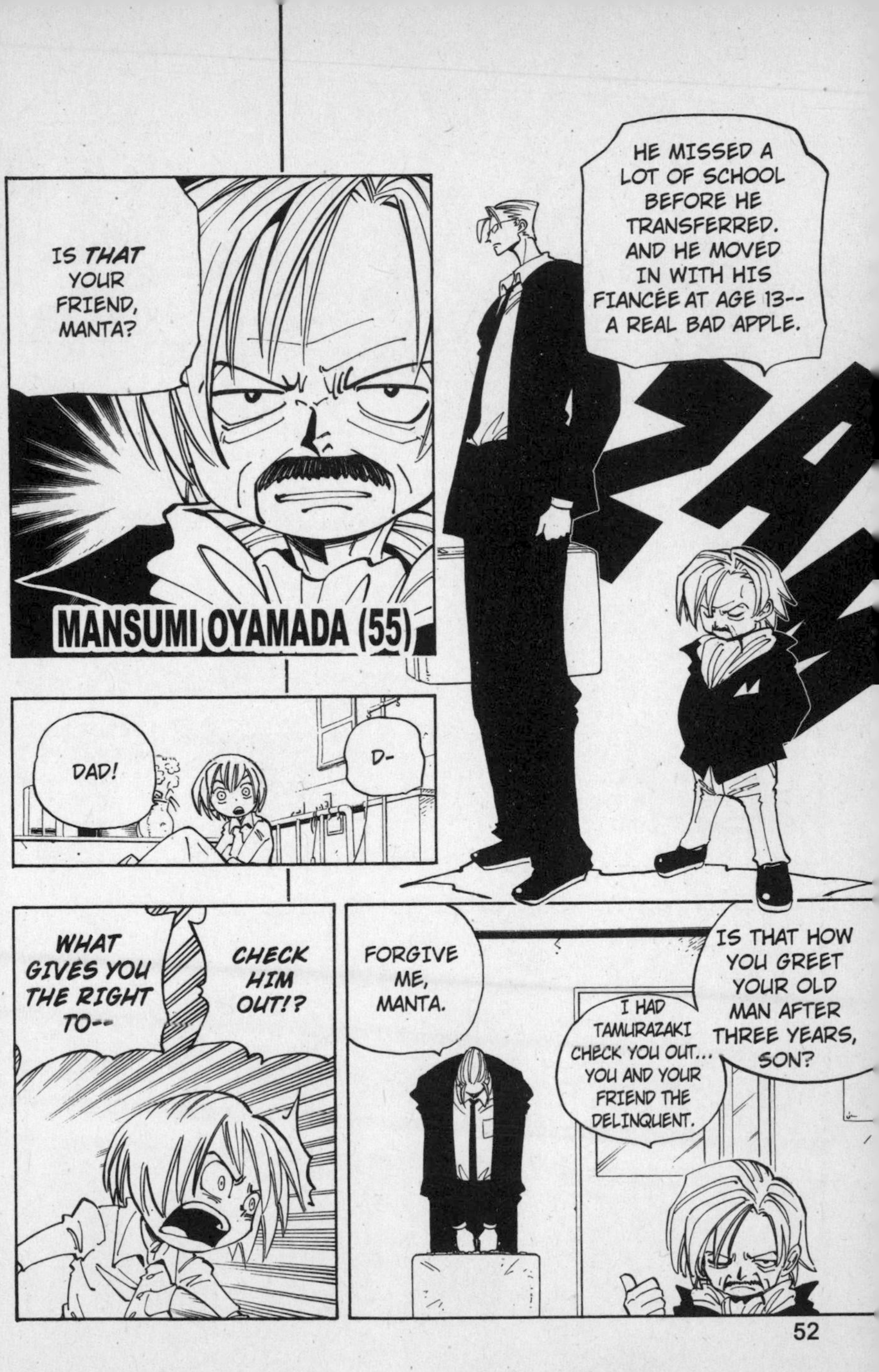
HE MISSED A LOT OF SCHOOL BEFORE HE TRANSFERRED. AND HE MOVED IN WITH HIS FIANCÉE AT AGE 13-- A REAL BAD APPLE.
IS *THAT* YOUR FRIEND, MANTA?
MANSUMI OYAMADA (55)
D-
DAD!
IS THAT HOW YOU GREET YOUR OLD MAN AFTER THREE YEARS, SON?
I HAD TAMURAZAKI CHECK YOU OUT... YOU AND YOUR FRIEND THE DELINQUENT.
FORGIVE ME, MANTA.
CHECK HIM OUT!?
WHAT GIVES YOU THE RIGHT TO--

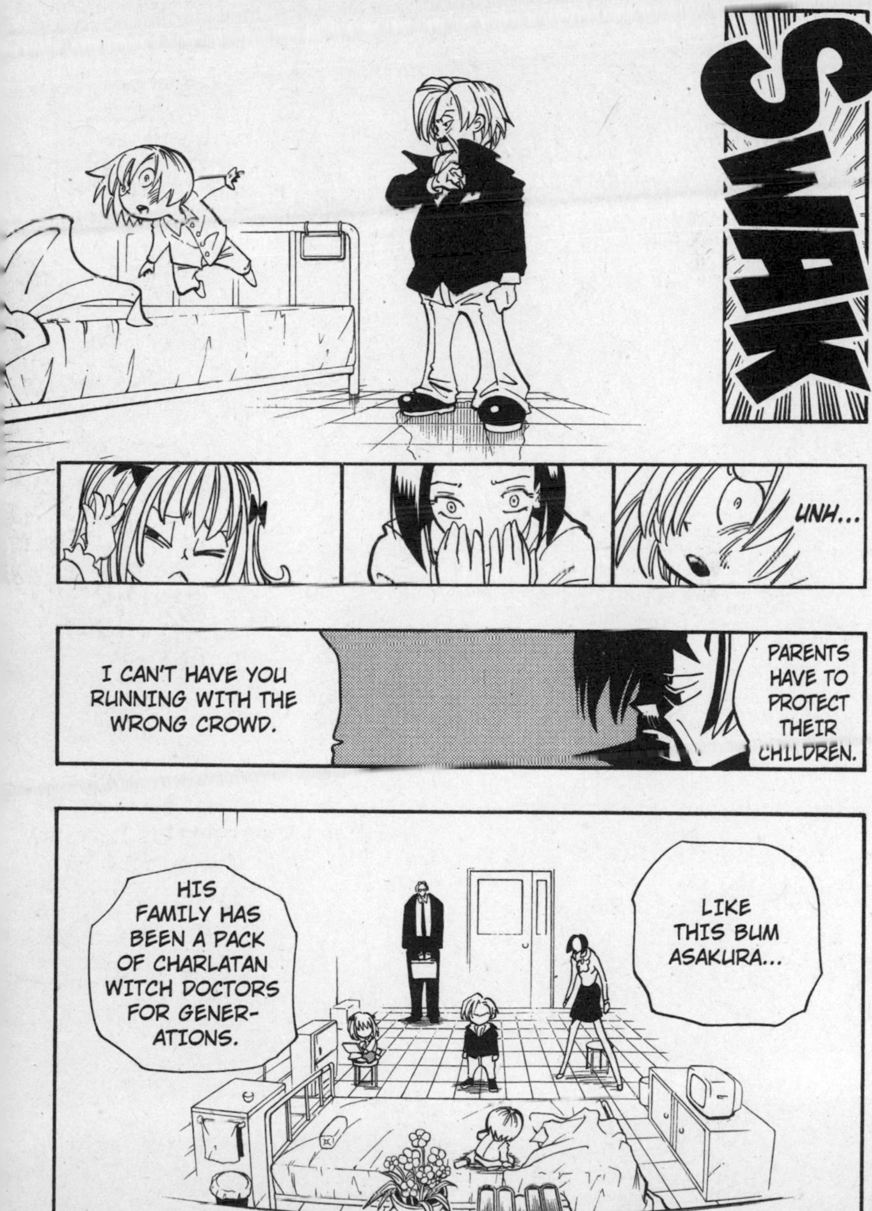
SMAK
UNH...
PARENTS HAVE TO PROTECT THEIR CHILDREN.
I CAN'T HAVE YOU RUNNING WITH THE WRONG CROWD.
LIKE THIS BUM ASAKURA...
HIS FAMILY HAS BEEN A PACK OF CHARLATAN WITCH DOCTORS FOR GENERATIONS.

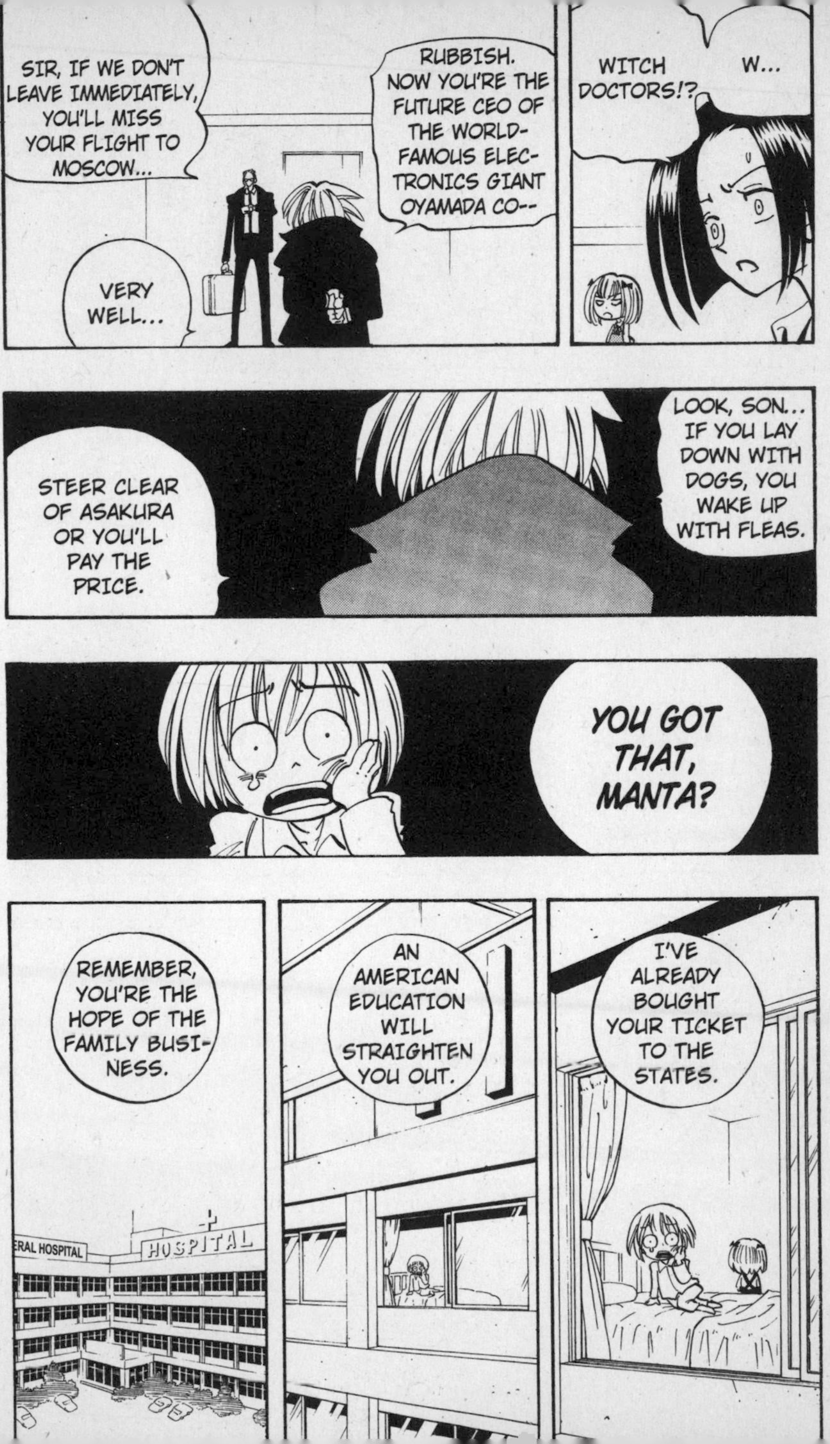
W... WITCH DOCTORS!?
RUBBISH. NOW YOU'RE THE FUTURE CEO OF THE WORLD-FAMOUS ELEC-TRONICS GIANT OYAMADA CO--
SIR, IF WE DON'T LEAVE IMMEDIATELY, YOU'LL MISS YOUR FLIGHT TO MOSCOW...
VERY WELL...
LOOK, SON... IF YOU LAY DOWN WITH DOGS, YOU WAKE UP WITH FLEAS.
STEER CLEAR OF ASAKURA OR YOU'LL PAY THE PRICE.
YOU GOT THAT, MANTA?
I'VE ALREADY BOUGHT YOUR TICKET TO THE STATES.
AN AMERICAN EDUCATION WILL STRAIGHTEN YOU OUT.
REMEMBER, YOU'RE THE HOPE OF THE FAMILY BUSI-NESS.
HOSPITAL
ERAL HOSPITAL

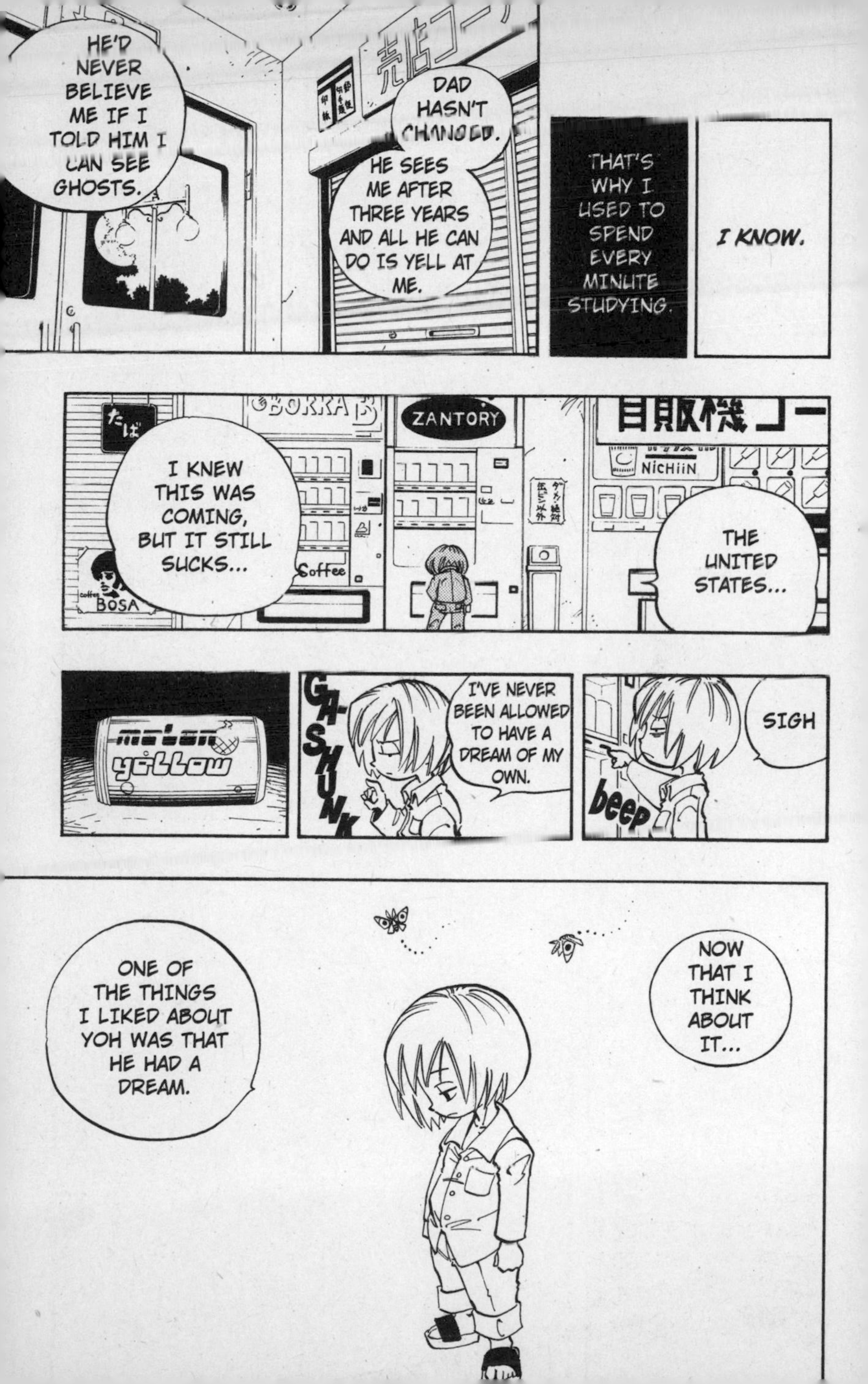
I KNOW.
THAT'S WHY I USED TO SPEND EVERY MINUTE STUDYING.
DAD HASN'T CHANGED.
HE SEES ME AFTER THREE YEARS AND ALL HE CAN DO IS YELL AT ME.
HE'D NEVER BELIEVE ME IF I TOLD HIM I CAN SEE GHOSTS.
THE UNITED STATES...
ZANTORY
I KNEW THIS WAS COMING, BUT IT STILL SUCKS...
SIGH
beep
I'VE NEVER BEEN ALLOWED TO HAVE A DREAM OF MY OWN.
GA-SHUNK
melon yellow
NOW THAT I THINK ABOUT IT...
ONE OF THE THINGS I LIKED ABOUT YOH WAS THAT HE HAD A DREAM.

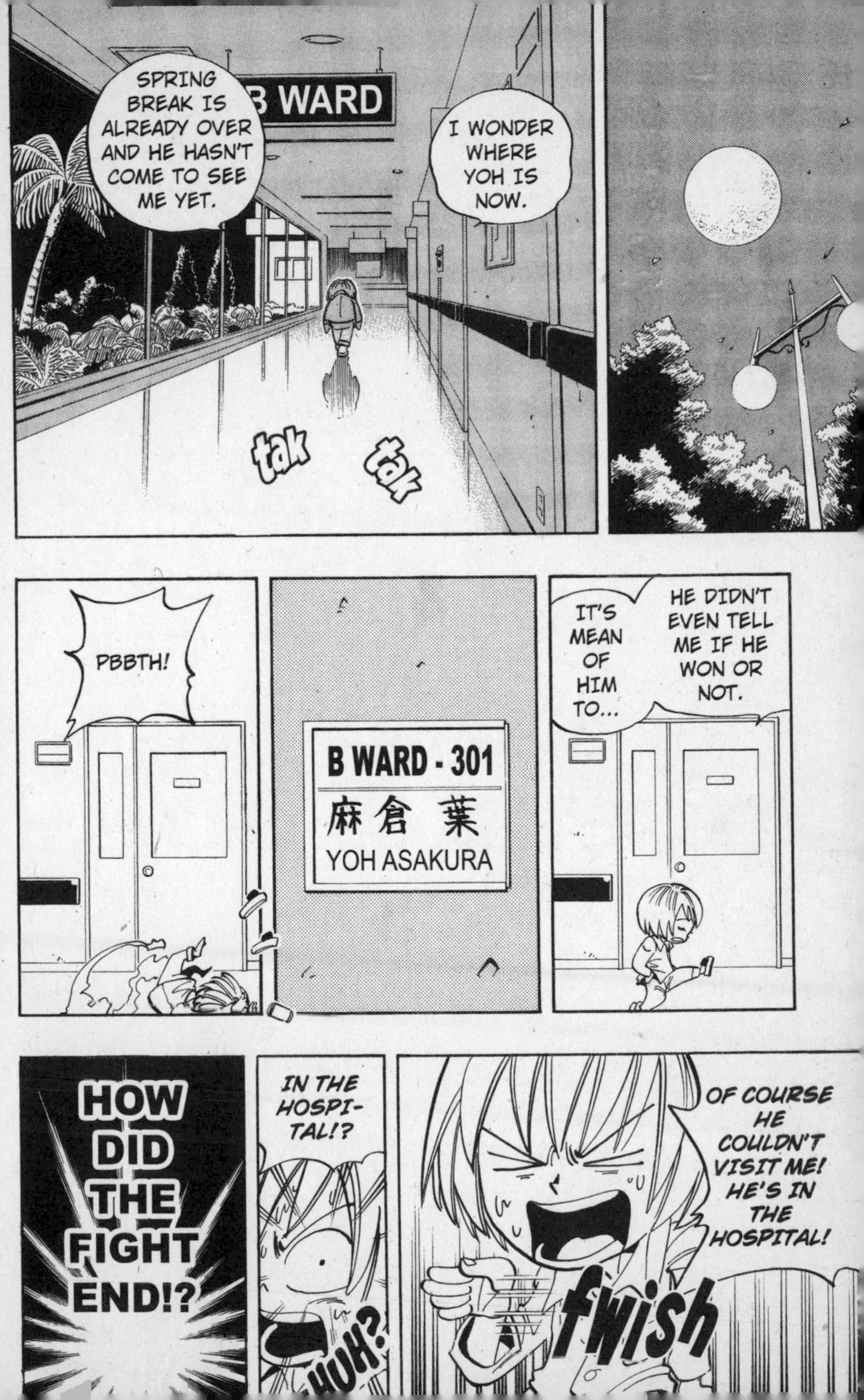
I WONDER WHERE YOH IS NOW.
B WARD
SPRING BREAK IS ALREADY OVER AND HE HASN'T COME TO SEE ME YET.
tak
tak
HE DIDN'T EVEN TELL ME IF HE WON OR NOT.
IT'S MEAN OF HIM TO...
B WARD - 301
麻倉 葉
YOH ASAKURA
PBBTH!
OF COURSE HE COULDN'T VISIT ME! HE'S IN THE HOSPITAL!
fwish
IN THE HOSPI-TAL!?
HUH?
HOW DID THE FIGHT END!?

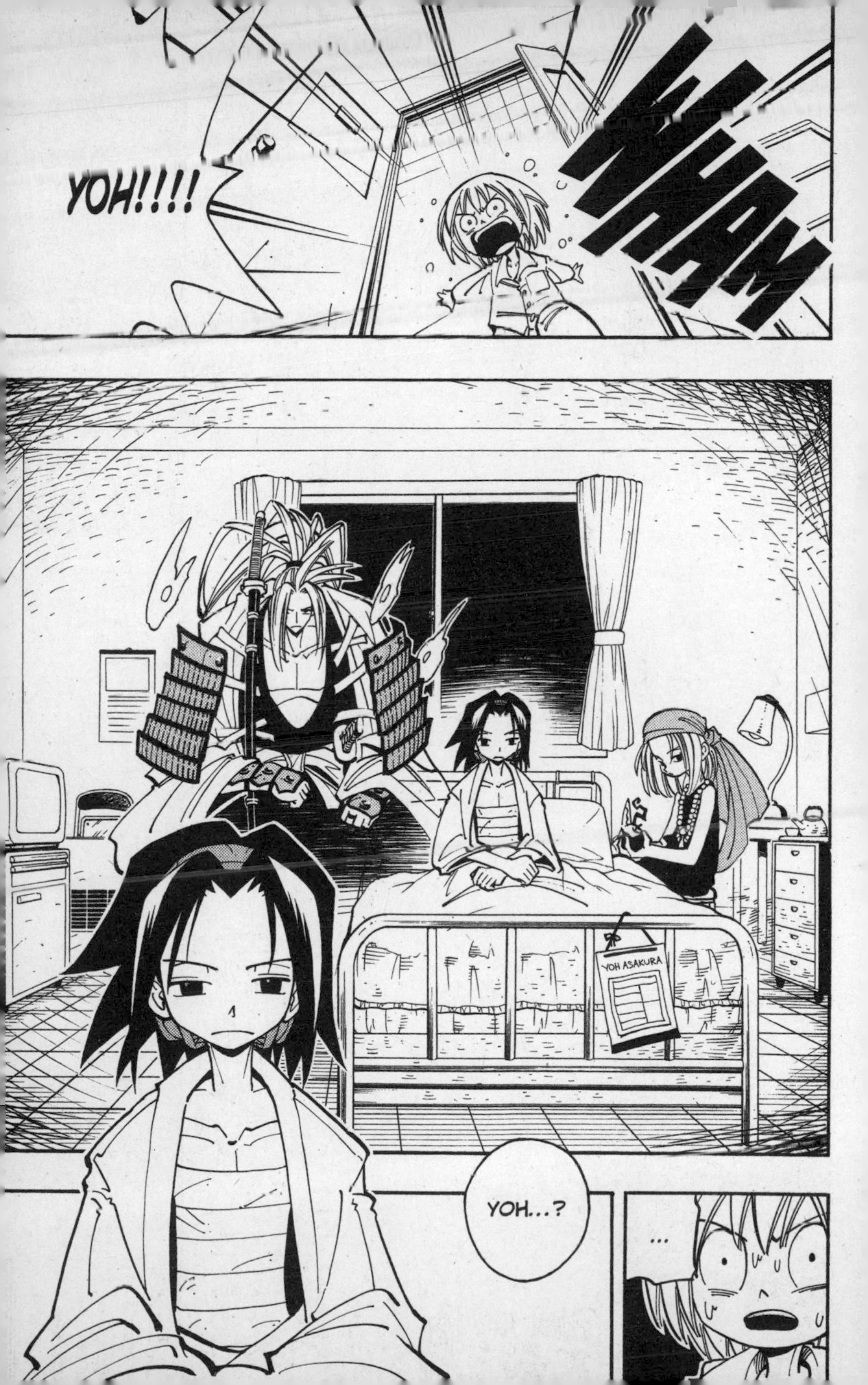
WHAM
YOH!!!!
YOH ASAKURA
YOH...?
...

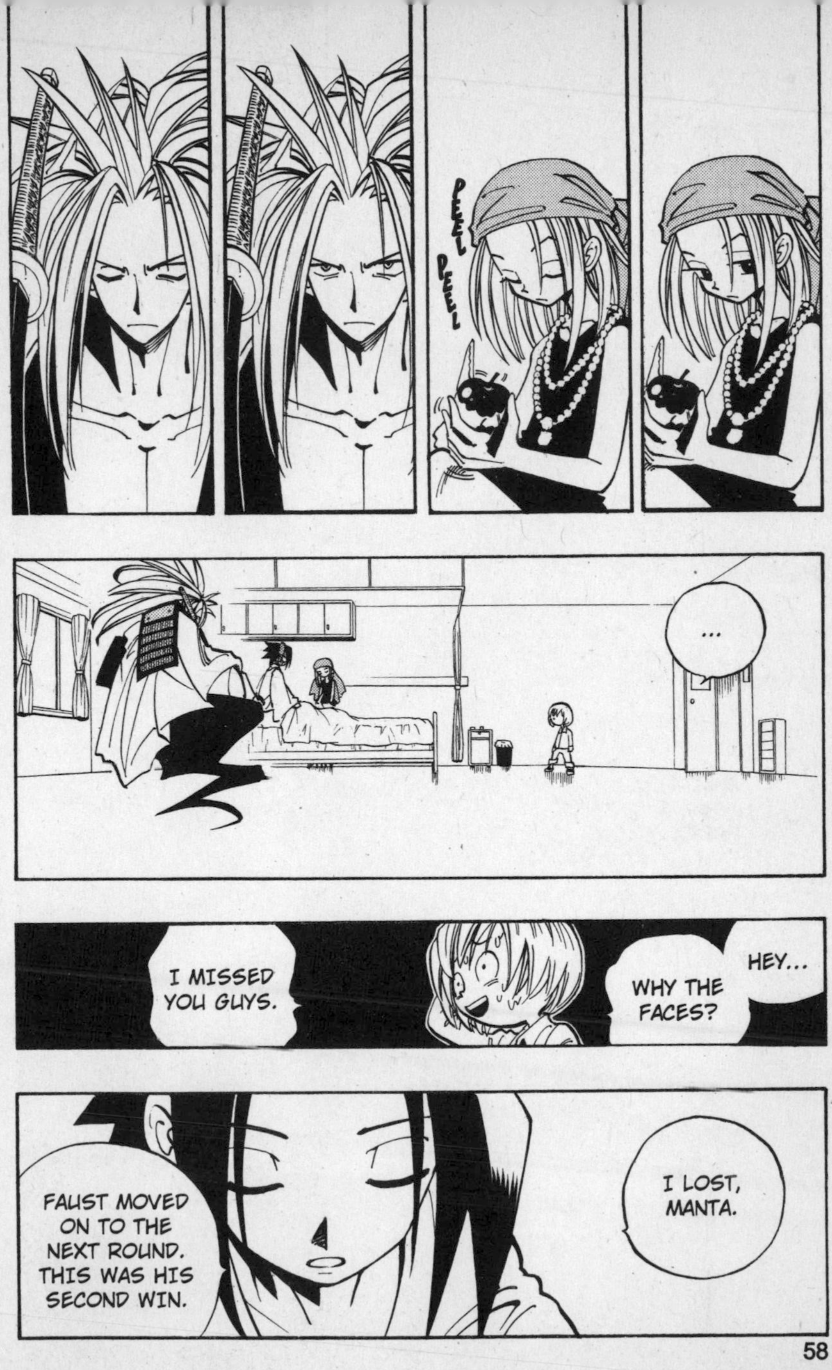
PEEL PEEL
...
HEY...
WHY THE FACES?
I MISSED YOU GUYS.
I LOST, MANTA.
FAUST MOVED ON TO THE NEXT ROUND. THIS WAS HIS SECOND WIN.

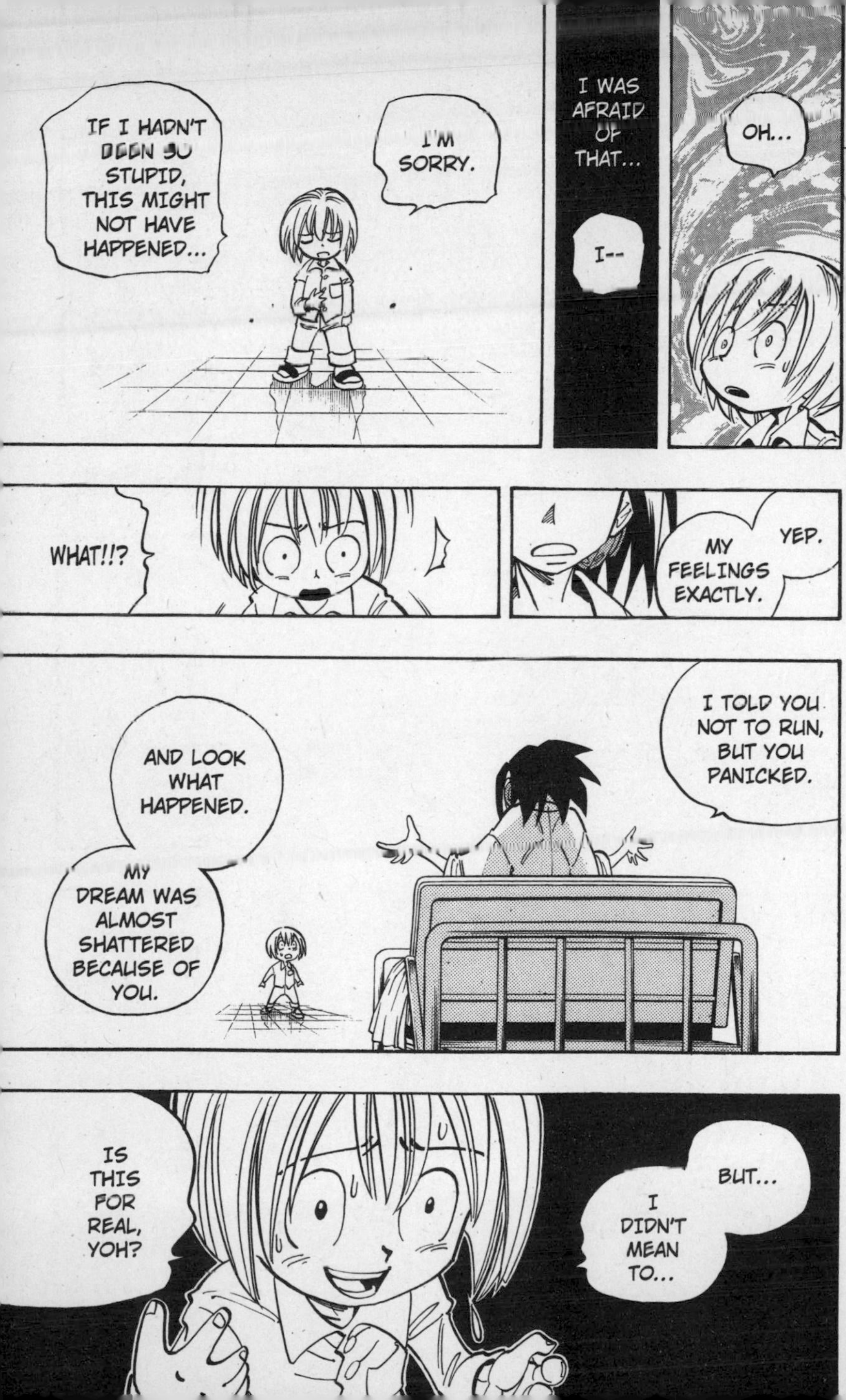
OH...
I WAS AFRAID OF THAT...
I--
I'M SORRY.
IF I HADN'T BEEN SO STUPID, THIS MIGHT NOT HAVE HAPPENED...
YEP.
MY FEELINGS EXACTLY.
WHAT!!?
I TOLD YOU NOT TO RUN, BUT YOU PANICKED.
AND LOOK WHAT HAPPENED.
MY DREAM WAS ALMOST SHATTERED BECAUSE OF YOU.
BUT...
I DIDN'T MEAN TO...
IS THIS FOR REAL, YOH?

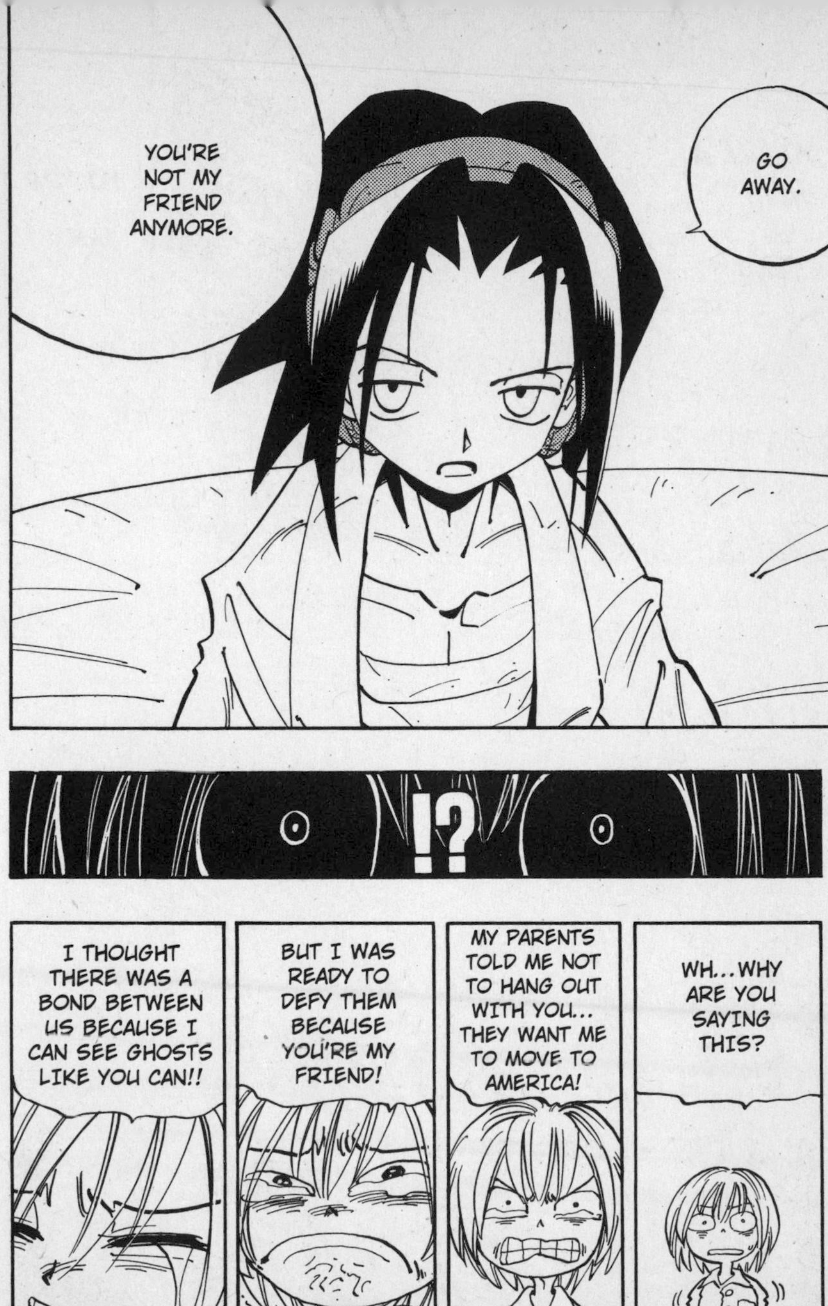
GO AWAY.
YOU'RE NOT MY FRIEND ANYMORE.
!?
WH...WHY ARE YOU SAYING THIS?
MY PARENTS TOLD ME NOT TO HANG OUT WITH YOU... THEY WANT ME TO MOVE TO AMERICA!
BUT I WAS READY TO DEFY THEM BECAUSE YOU'RE MY FRIEND!
I THOUGHT THERE WAS A BOND BETWEEN US BECAUSE I CAN SEE GHOSTS LIKE YOU CAN!!

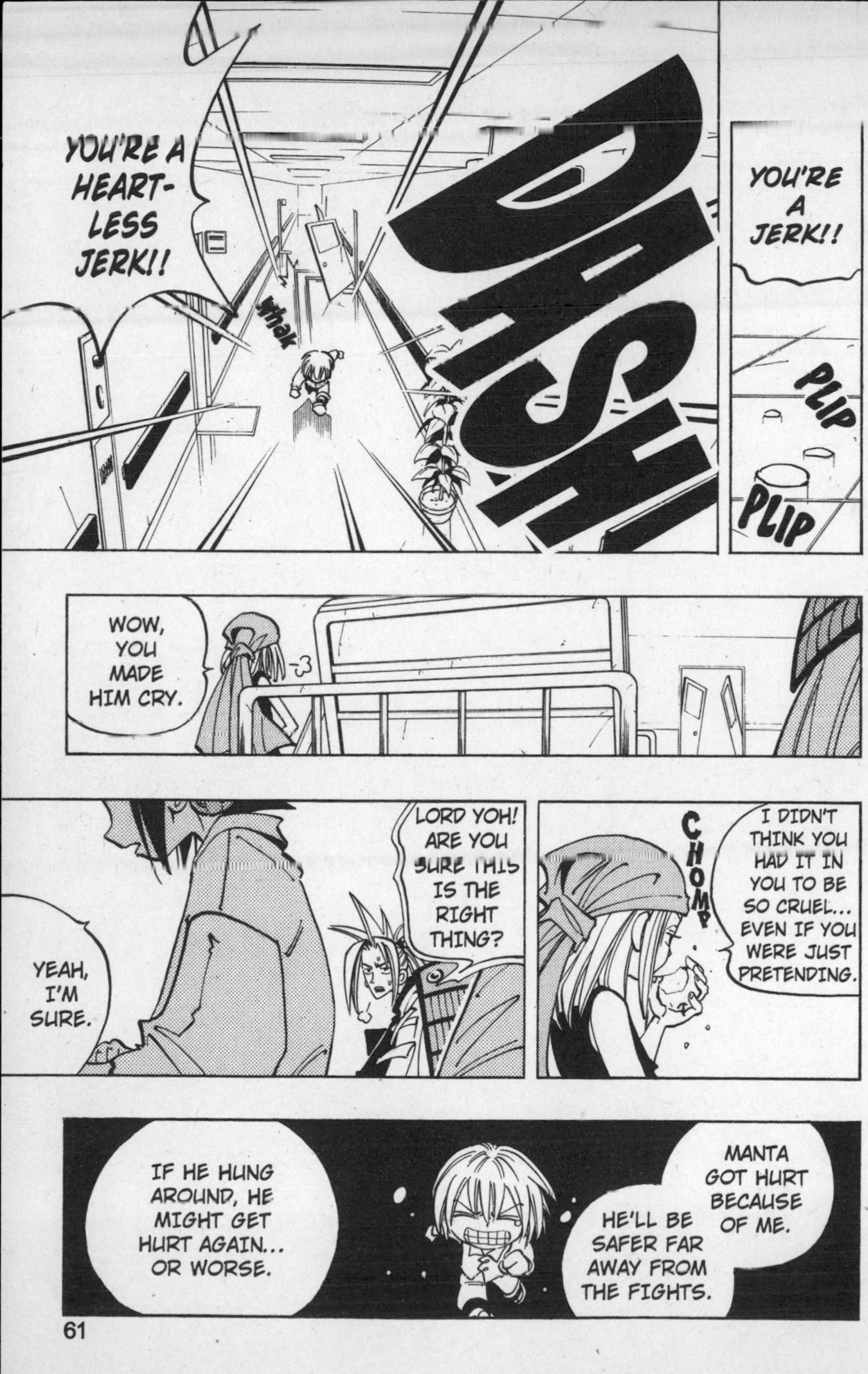
YOU'RE A JERK!!
PLIP
PLIP
DASH
YOU'RE A HEART-LESS JERK!!
whak
WOW, YOU MADE HIM CRY.
I DIDN'T THINK YOU HAD IT IN YOU TO BE SO CRUEL... EVEN IF YOU WERE JUST PRETENDING.
CHOMP
LORD YOH! ARE YOU SURE THIS IS THE RIGHT THING?
YEAH, I'M SURE.
MANTA GOT HURT BECAUSE OF ME.
HE'LL BE SAFER FAR AWAY FROM THE FIGHTS.
IF HE HUNG AROUND, HE MIGHT GET HURT AGAIN... OR WORSE.

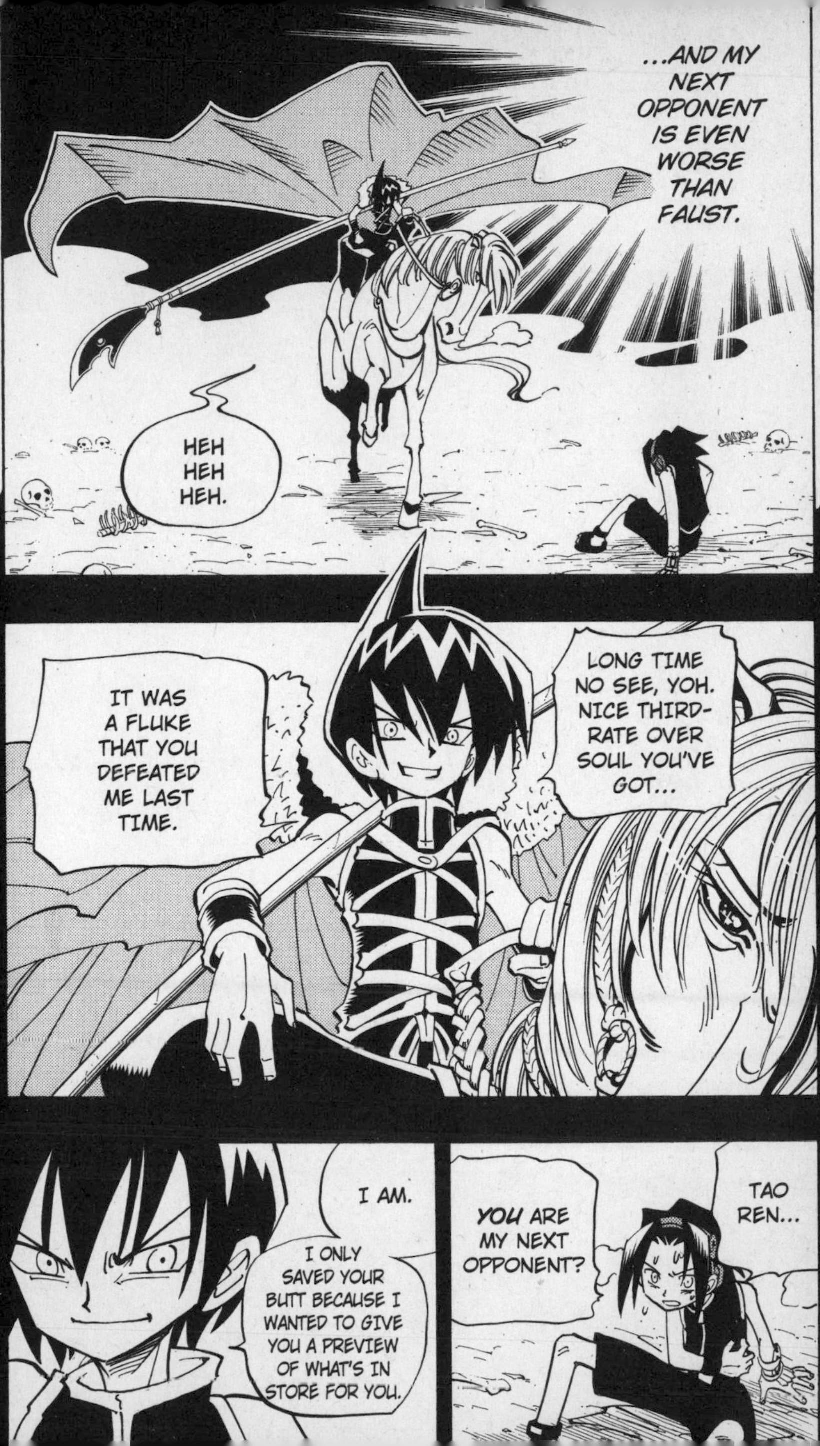
...AND MY NEXT OPPONENT IS EVEN WORSE THAN FAUST.
HEH HEH HEH.
LONG TIME NO SEE, YOH. NICE THIRD-RATE OVER SOUL YOU'VE GOT...
IT WAS A FLUKE THAT YOU DEFEATED ME LAST TIME.
TAO REN...
*YOU* ARE MY NEXT OPPONENT?
I AM.
I ONLY SAVED YOUR BUTT BECAUSE I WANTED TO GIVE YOU A PREVIEW OF WHAT'S IN STORE FOR YOU.

READ THIS WAY

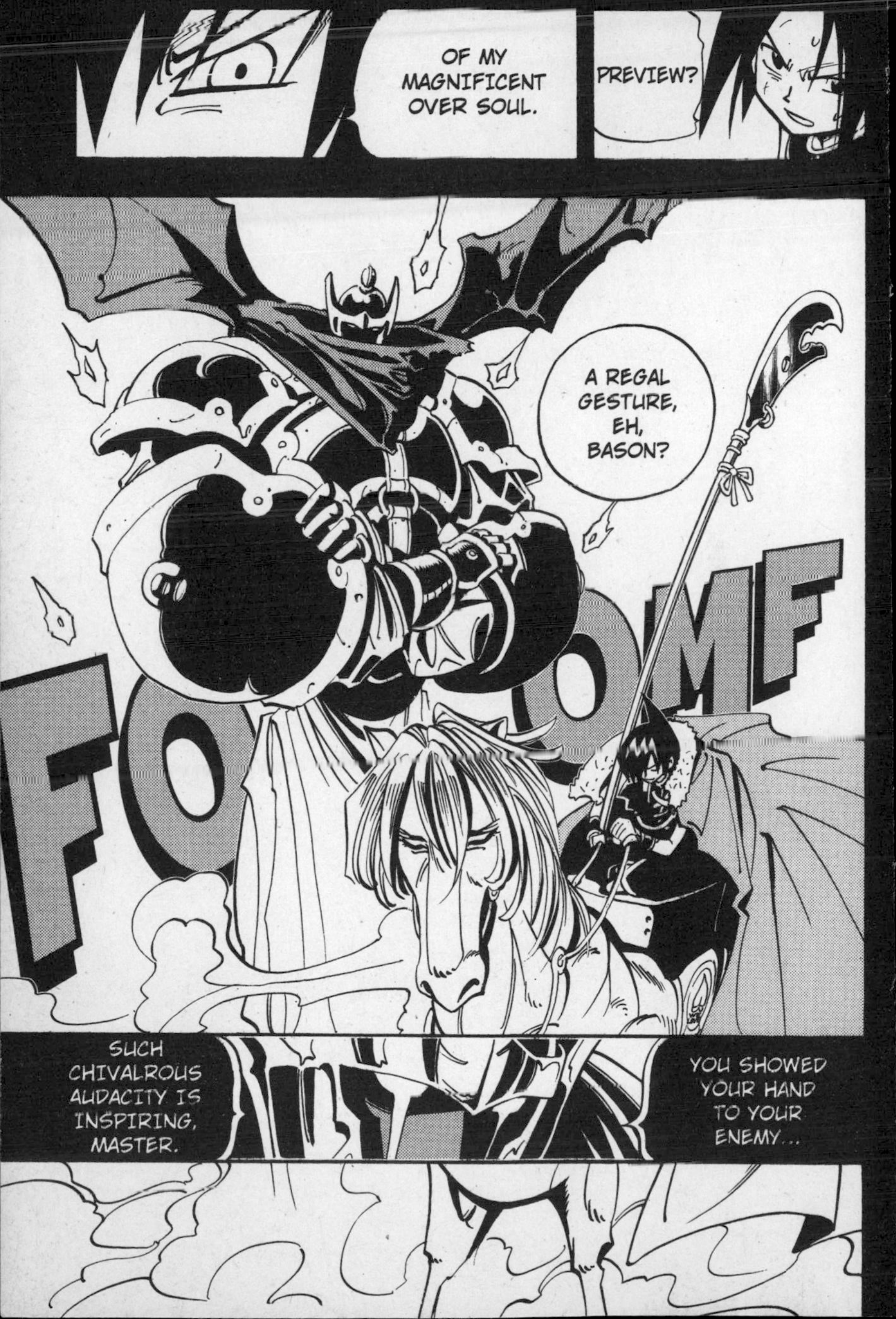
PREVIEW?
OF MY MAGNIFICENT OVER SOUL.
A REGAL GESTURE, EH, BASON?
FOOMF
YOU SHOWED YOUR HAND TO YOUR ENEMY...
SUCH CHIVALROUS AUDACITY IS INSPIRING, MASTER.

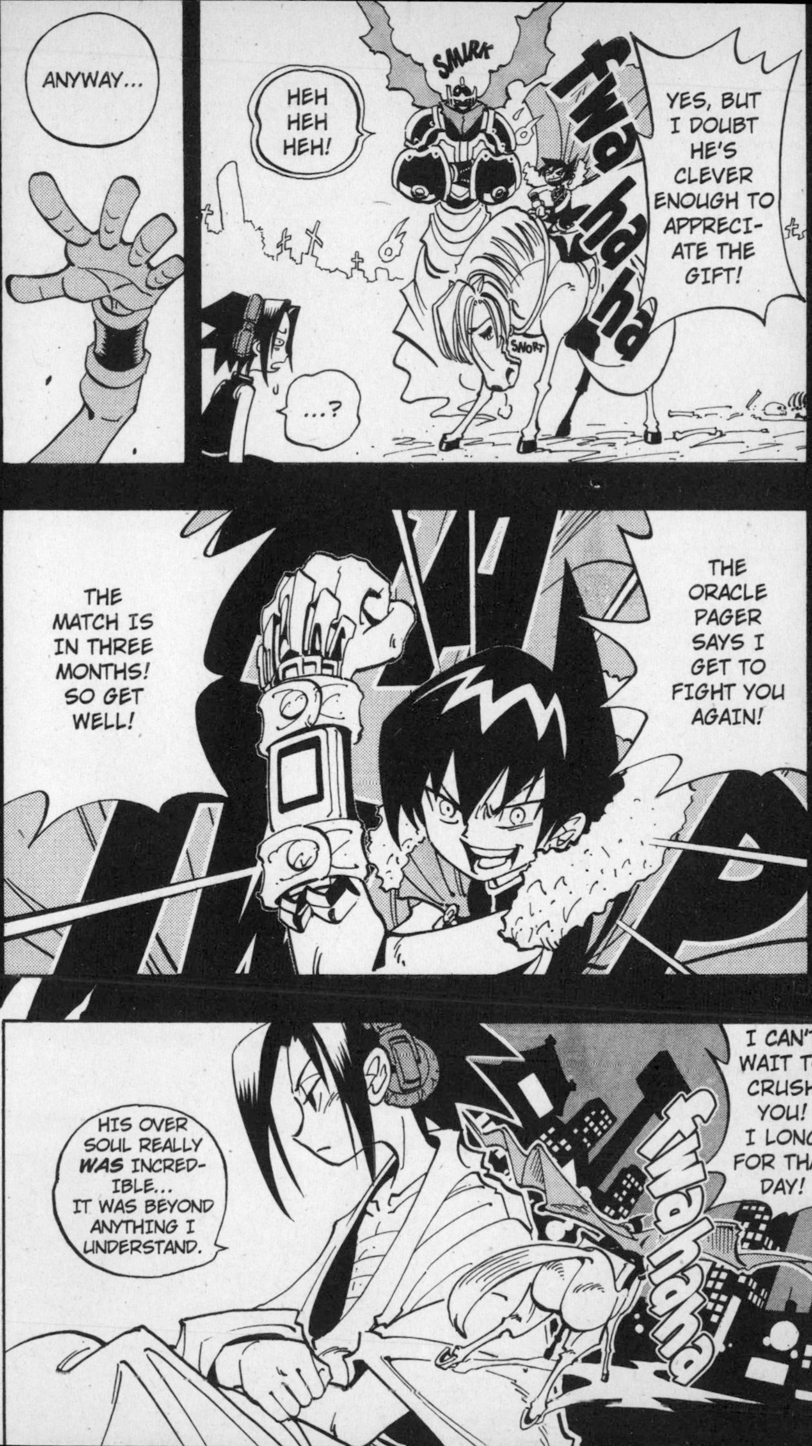
YES, BUT I DOUBT HE'S CLEVER ENOUGH TO APPRECI-ATE THE GIFT!
fwa ha ha ha
SMIRK
HEH HEH HEH!
SNORT
...?
ANYWAY...
THE ORACLE PAGER SAYS I GET TO FIGHT YOU AGAIN!
THE MATCH IS IN THREE MONTHS! SO GET WELL!
I CAN'T WAIT TO CRUSH YOU! I LONG FOR THAT DAY!
fwahaha
HIS OVER SOUL REALLY *WAS* INCRED-IBLE... IT WAS BEYOND ANYTHING I UNDERSTAND.

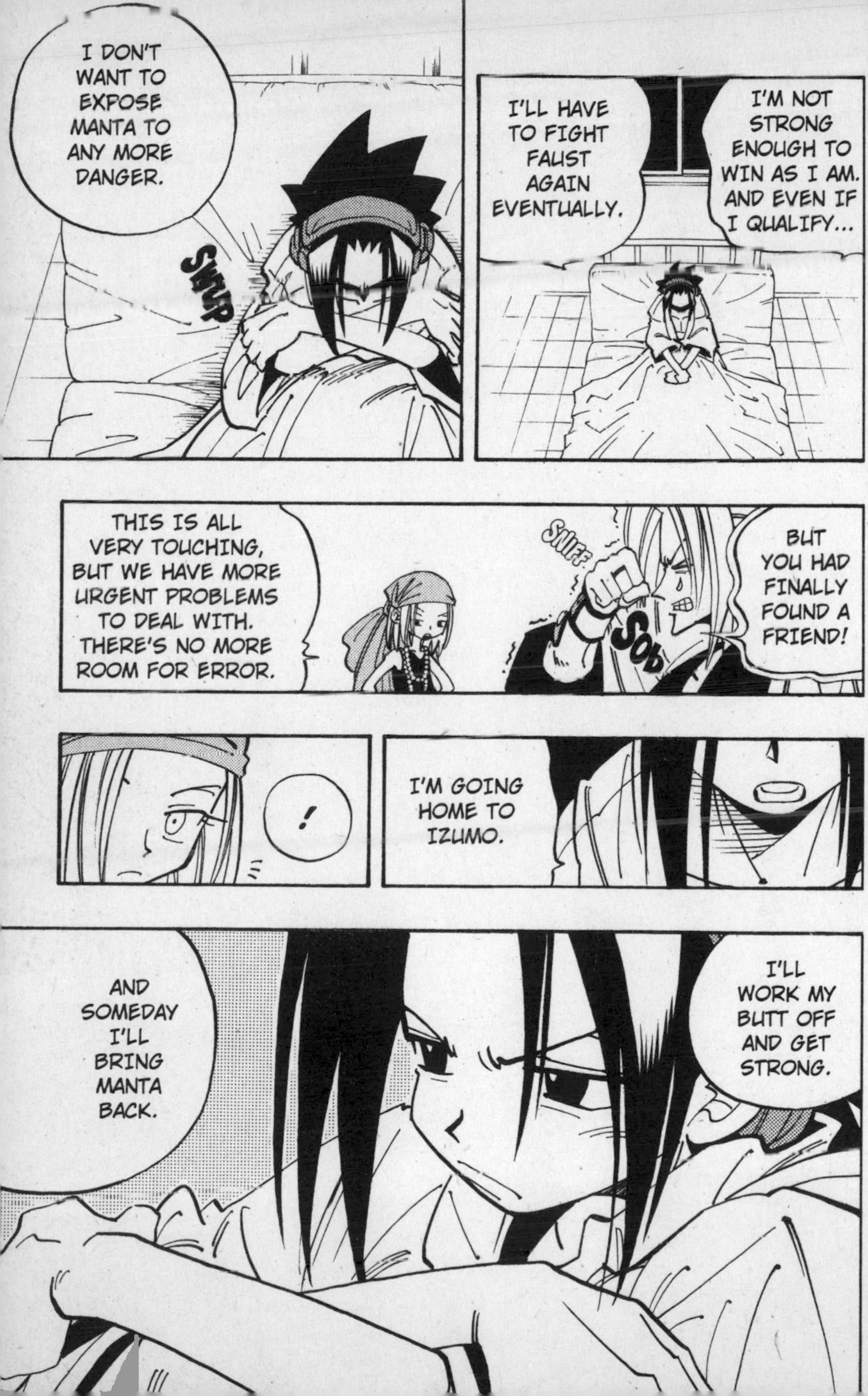
I'M NOT STRONG ENOUGH TO WIN AS I AM. AND EVEN IF I QUALIFY...
I'LL HAVE TO FIGHT FAUST AGAIN EVENTUALLY.
I DON'T WANT TO EXPOSE MANTA TO ANY MORE DANGER.
SWUP
BUT YOU HAD FINALLY FOUND A FRIEND!
SNIFF
SOB
THIS IS ALL VERY TOUCHING, BUT WE HAVE MORE URGENT PROBLEMS TO DEAL WITH. THERE'S NO MORE ROOM FOR ERROR.
I'M GOING HOME TO IZUMO.
!
I'LL WORK MY BUTT OFF AND GET STRONG.
AND SOMEDAY I'LL BRING MANTA BACK.

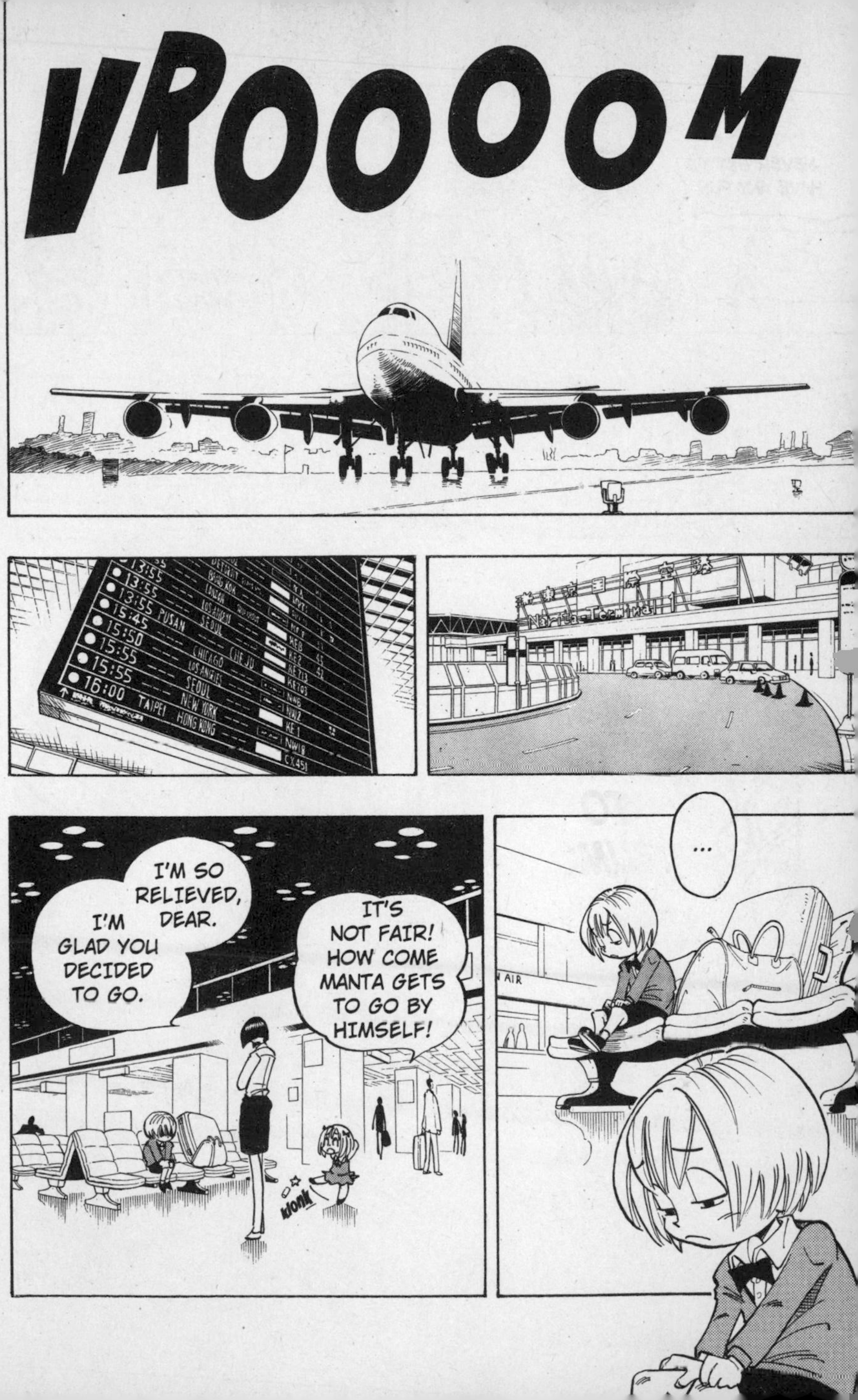
VROOOOM
...
I'M SO RELIEVED, DEAR. I'M GLAD YOU DECIDED TO GO.
IT'S NOT FAIR! HOW COME MANTA GETS TO GO BY HIMSELF!
klonk

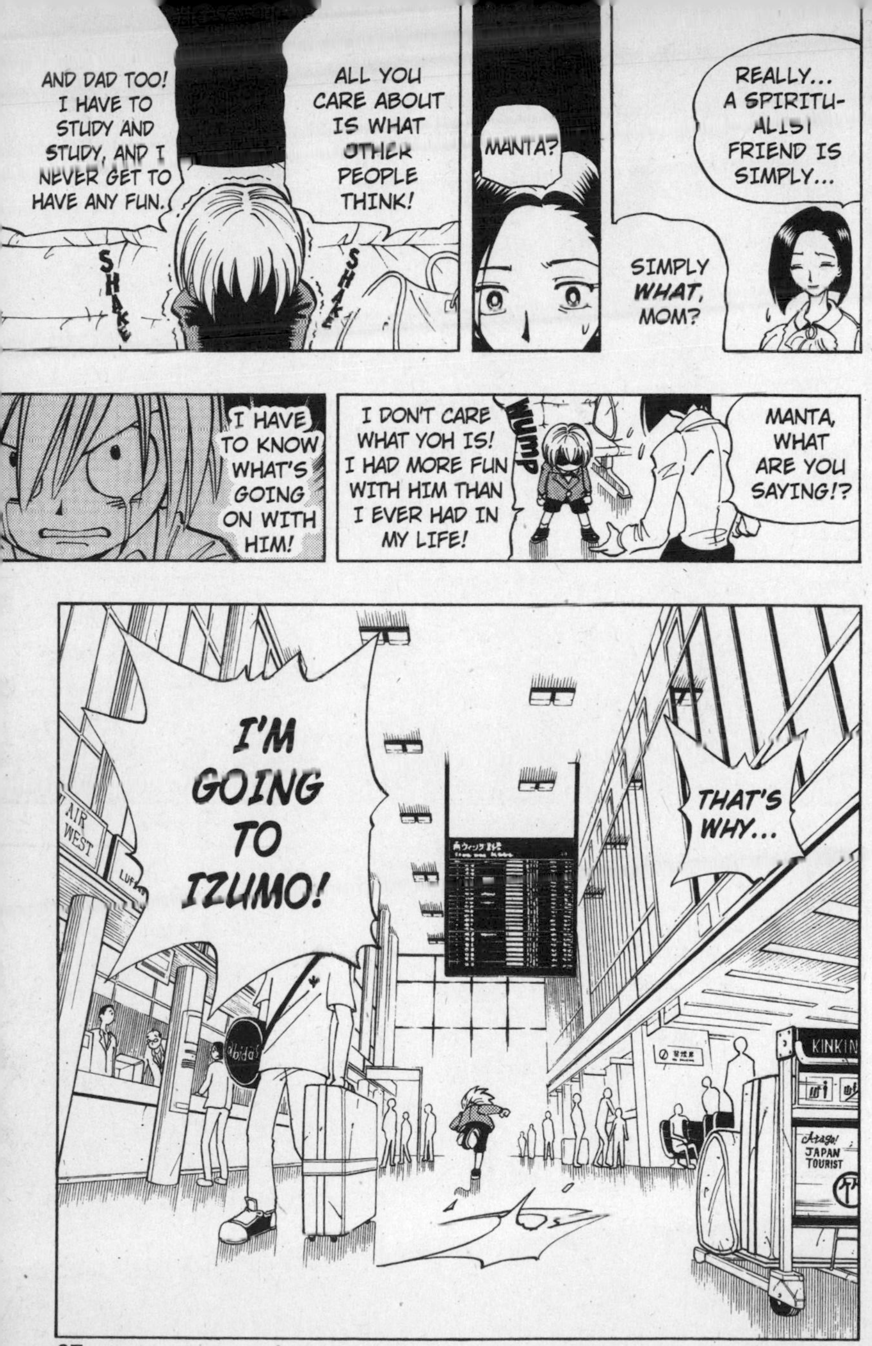
REALLY... A SPIRITU-ALIST FRIEND IS SIMPLY...
SIMPLY WHAT, MOM?
MANTA?
ALL YOU CARE ABOUT IS WHAT OTHER PEOPLE THINK!
AND DAD TOO! I HAVE TO STUDY AND STUDY, AND I NEVER GET TO HAVE ANY FUN.
SHAKE
SHAKE
MANTA, WHAT ARE YOU SAYING!?
HUMP
I DON'T CARE WHAT YOH IS! I HAD MORE FUN WITH HIM THAN I EVER HAD IN MY LIFE!
I HAVE TO KNOW WHAT'S GOING ON WITH HIM!
THAT'S WHY...
I'M GOING TO IZUMO!
AIR WEST
KINKIN
JAPAN TOURIST

SHAMAN KING CHARACTER FILE No.25

# フランケンシュタイニー

## FRANKENSTEINY

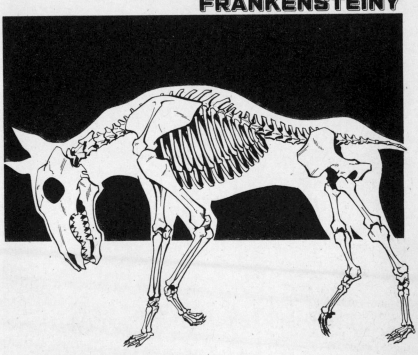

BLOOD TYPE: D2

AGE (AT TIME OF DEATH): 4

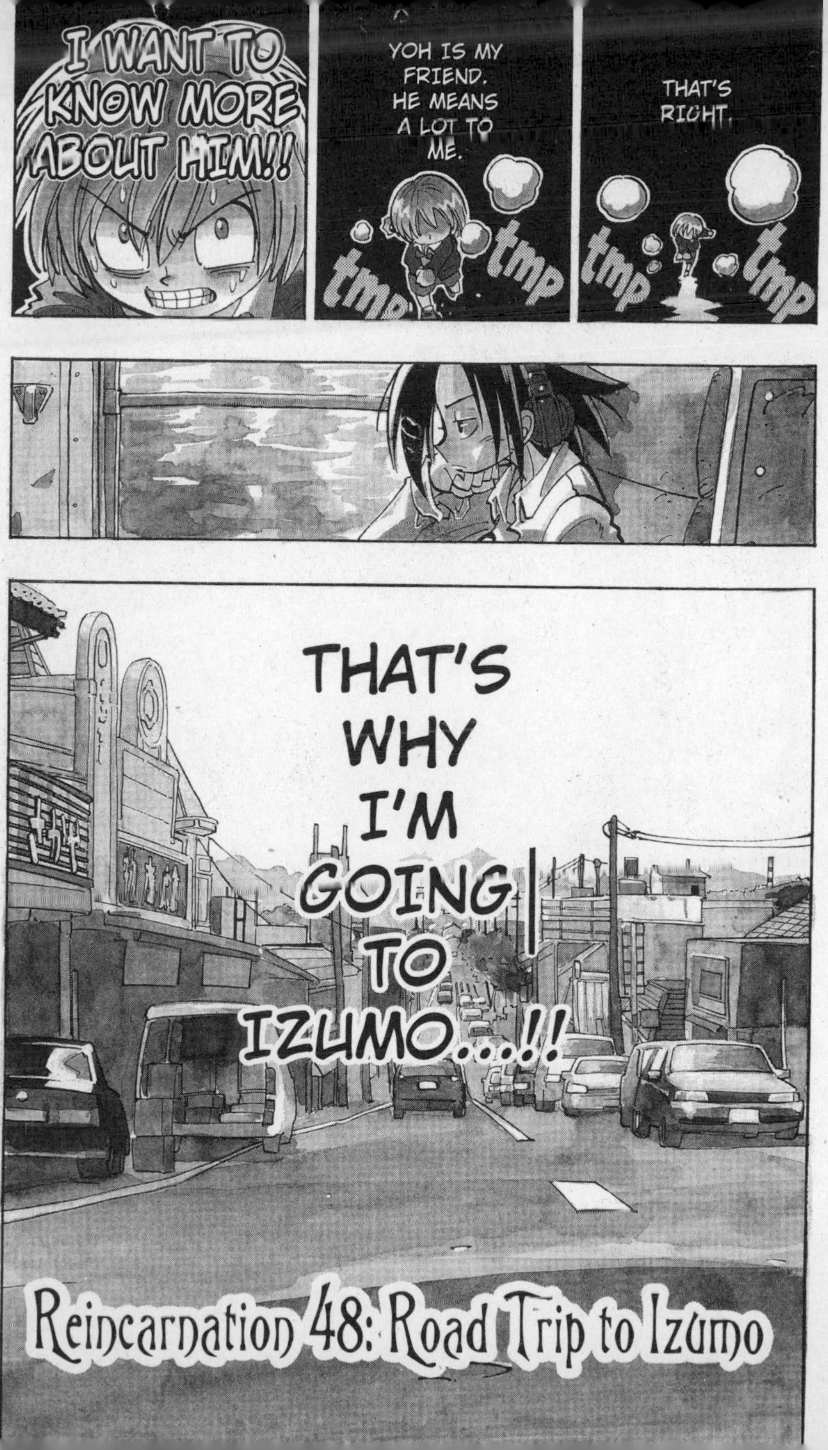
THAT'S RIGHT.
tmp tmp
YOH IS MY FRIEND. HE MEANS A LOT TO ME.
tmp tmp
I WANT TO KNOW MORE ABOUT HIM!!
THAT'S WHY I'M GOING TO IZUMO...!!
Reincarnation 48: Road Trip to Izumo

# Reincarnation 48: Road Trip to Izumo

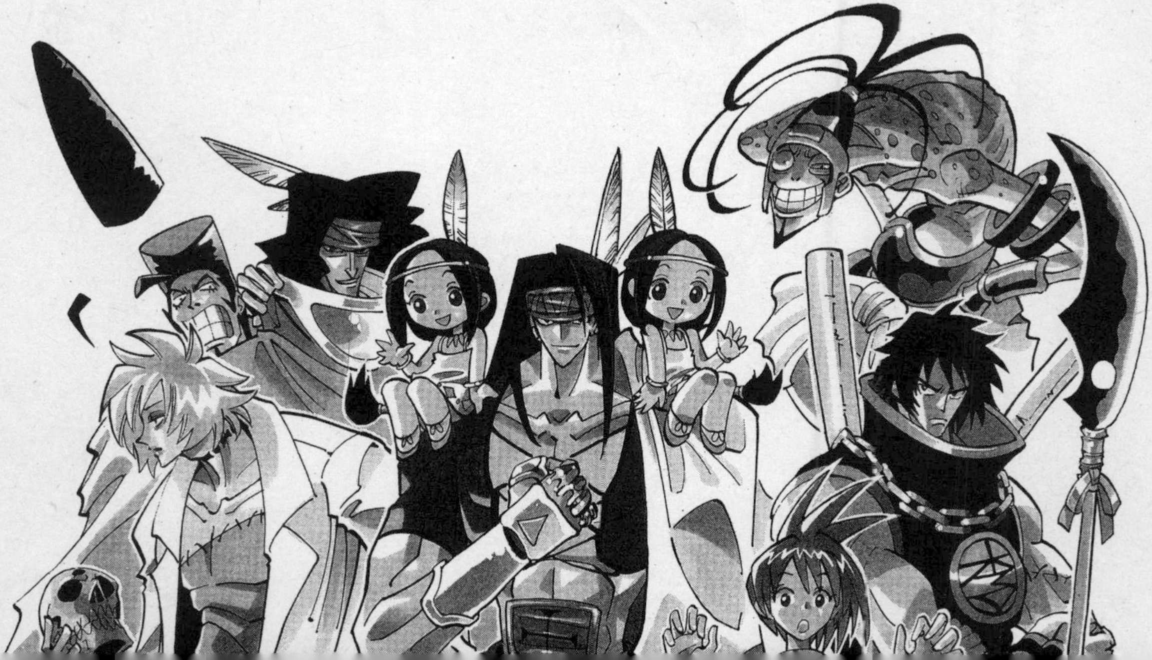

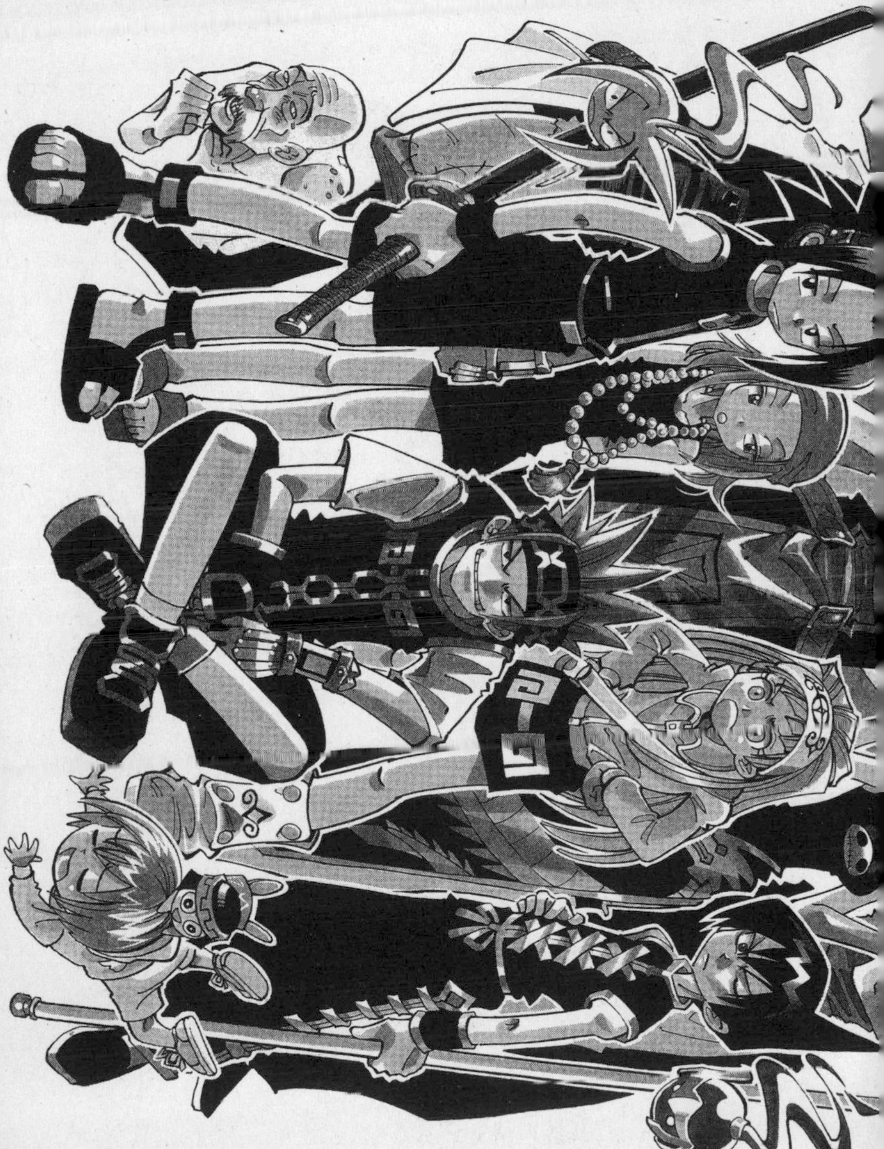

SHAMAN
KING
6

ULTRA HELMET
(HAUTE COUTURE)

READ THIS WAY

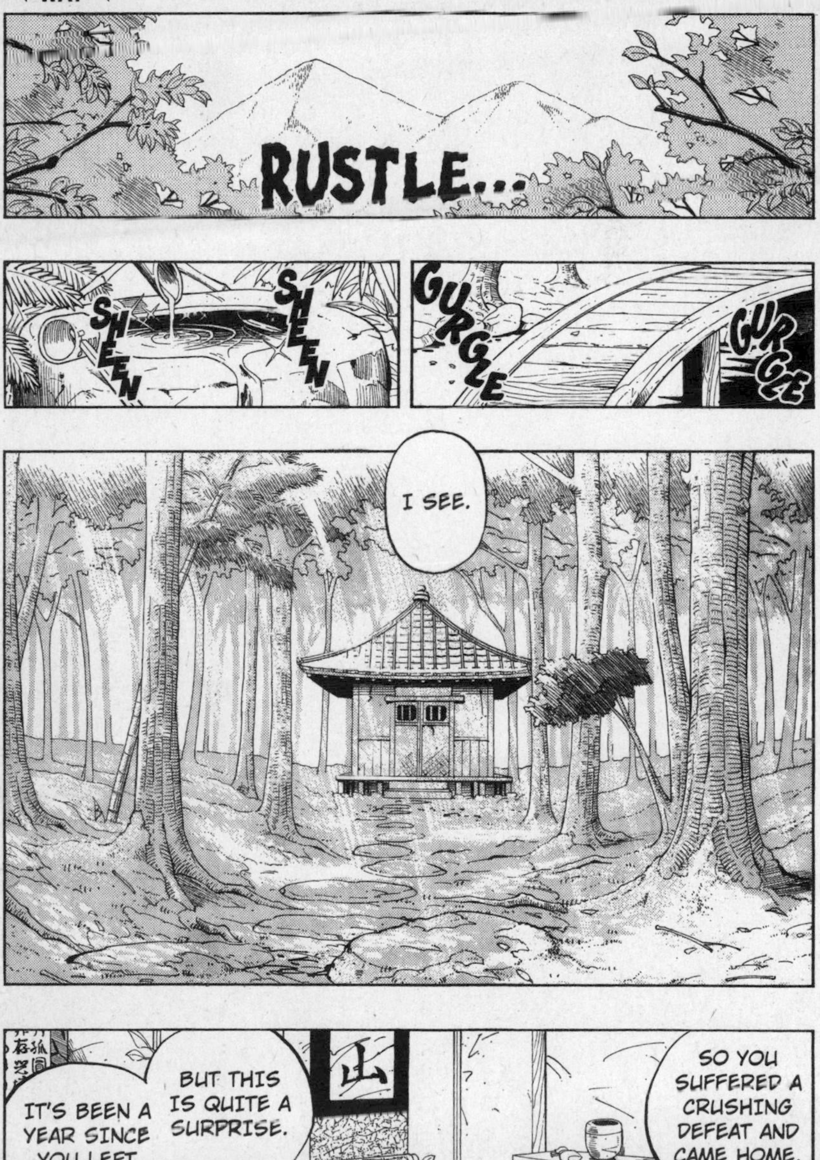
RUSTLE...
GURGLE
GURGLE
SHEEN
SHEEN
I SEE.
SO YOU SUFFERED A CRUSHING DEFEAT AND CAME HOME.
BUT THIS IS QUITE A SURPRISE.
IT'S BEEN A YEAR SINCE YOU LEFT FOR TOKYO...

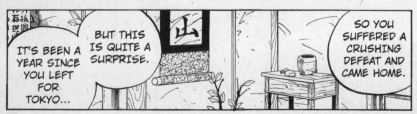

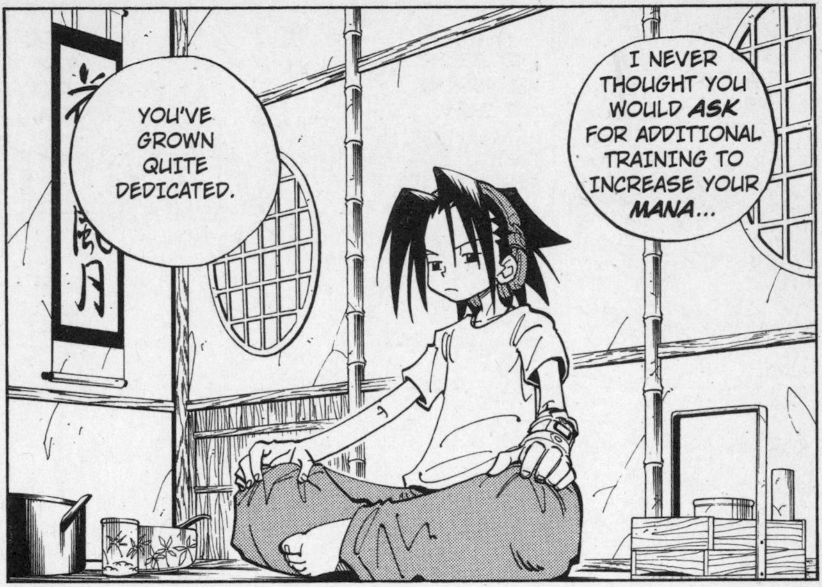
I NEVER THOUGHT YOU WOULD **ASK** FOR ADDITIONAL TRAINING TO INCREASE YOUR ***MANA***...
YOU'VE GROWN QUITE DEDICATED.

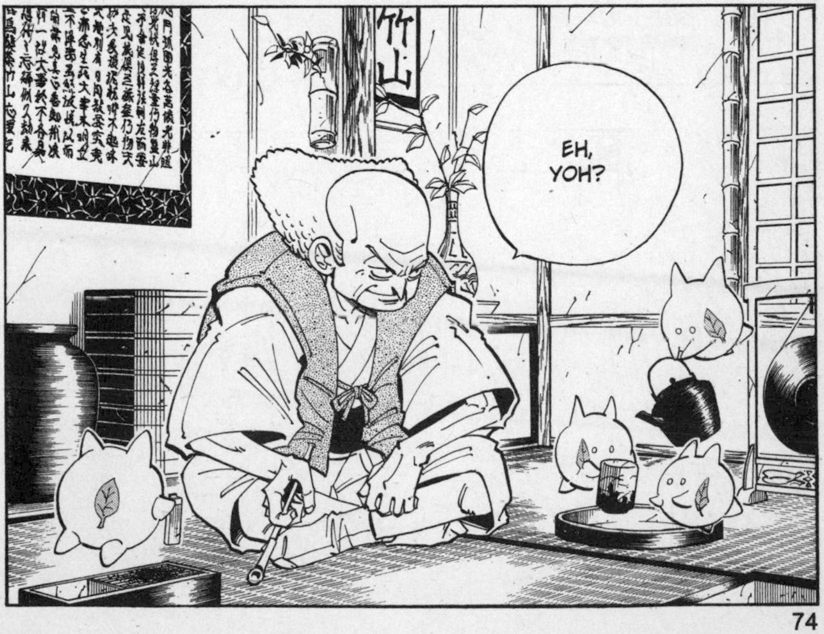
EH, YOH?

READ THIS WAY

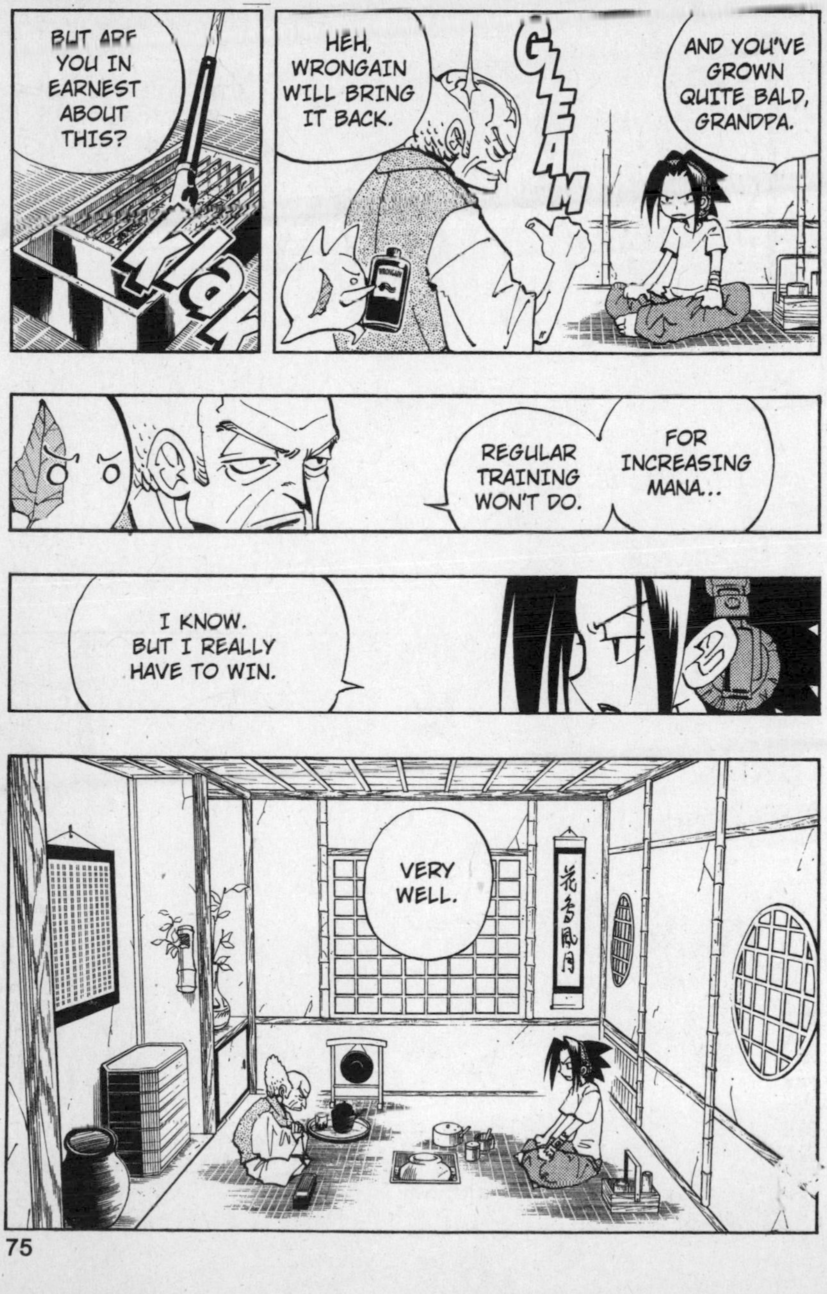

AND YOU'VE GROWN QUITE BALD, GRANDPA.
GLEAM
HEH, WRONGAIN WILL BRING IT BACK.
BUT ARE YOU IN EARNEST ABOUT THIS?
KICK
FOR INCREASING MANA...
REGULAR TRAINING WON'T DO.
I KNOW. BUT I REALLY HAVE TO WIN.
VERY WELL.

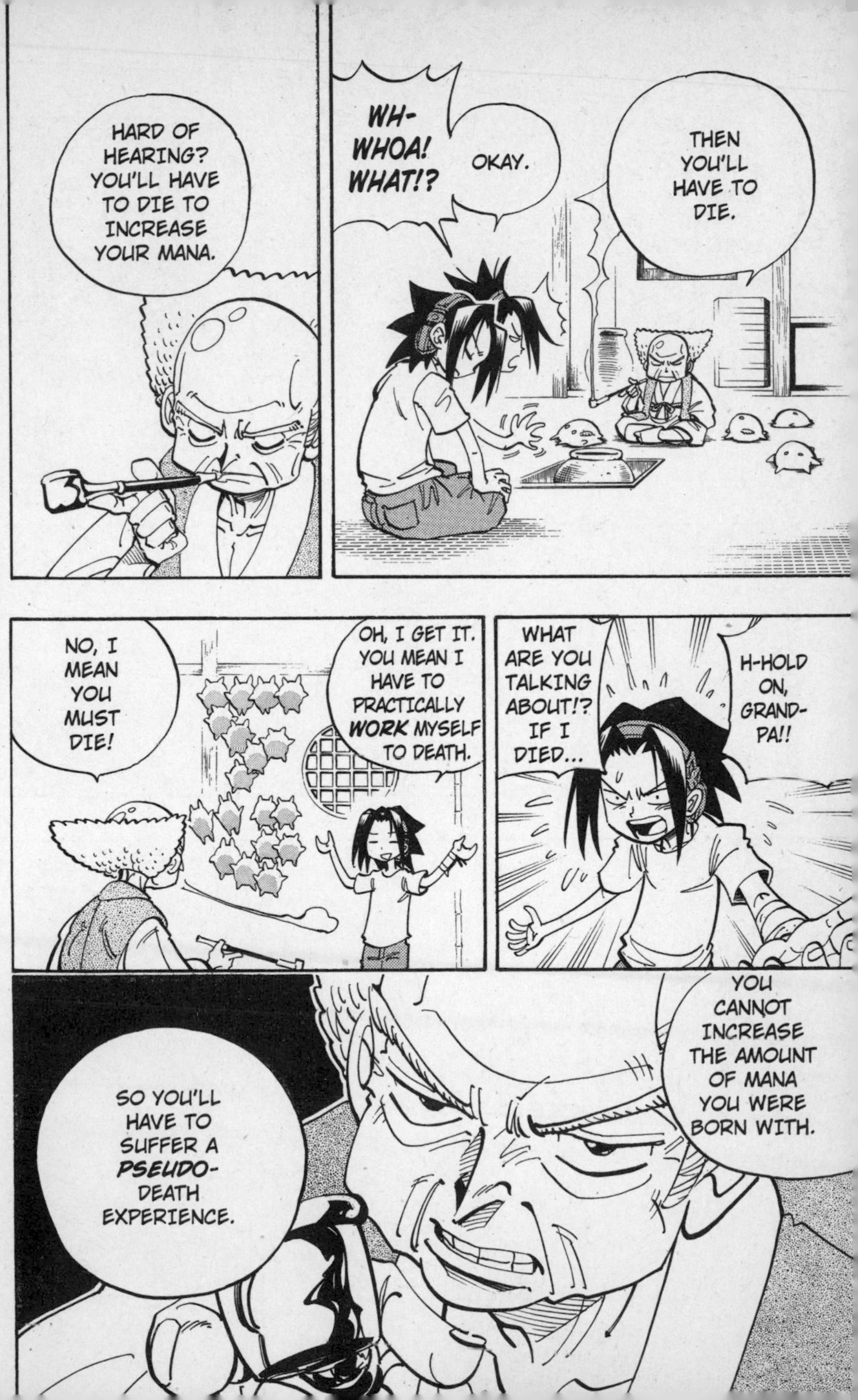
THEN YOU'LL HAVE TO DIE.
OKAY.
WH-WHOA! WHAT!?
HARD OF HEARING? YOU'LL HAVE TO DIE TO INCREASE YOUR MANA.
H-HOLD ON, GRANDPA!!
WHAT ARE YOU TALKING ABOUT!? IF I DIED...
OH, I GET IT. YOU MEAN I HAVE TO PRACTICALLY WORK MYSELF TO DEATH.
NO, I MEAN YOU MUST DIE!
YOU CANNOT INCREASE THE AMOUNT OF MANA YOU WERE BORN WITH.
SO YOU'LL HAVE TO SUFFER A PSEUDO-DEATH EXPERIENCE.

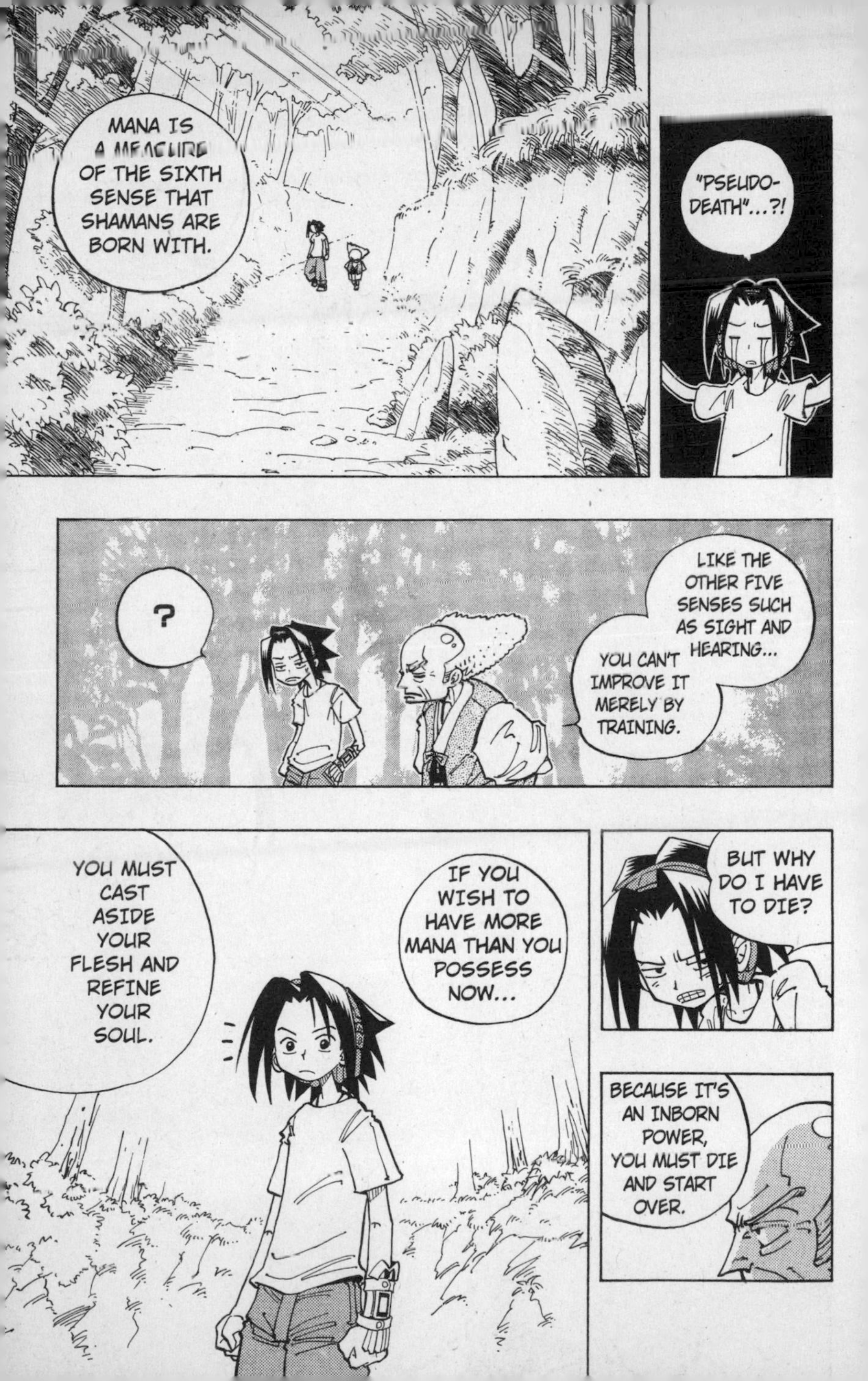
"PSEUDO-DEATH"...?!
MANA IS A MEASURE OF THE SIXTH SENSE THAT SHAMANS ARE BORN WITH.
LIKE THE OTHER FIVE SENSES SUCH AS SIGHT AND HEARING...
YOU CAN'T IMPROVE IT MERELY BY TRAINING.
?
BUT WHY DO I HAVE TO DIE?
BECAUSE IT'S AN INBORN POWER, YOU MUST DIE AND START OVER.
IF YOU WISH TO HAVE MORE MANA THAN YOU POSSESS NOW...
YOU MUST CAST ASIDE YOUR FLESH AND REFINE YOUR SOUL.

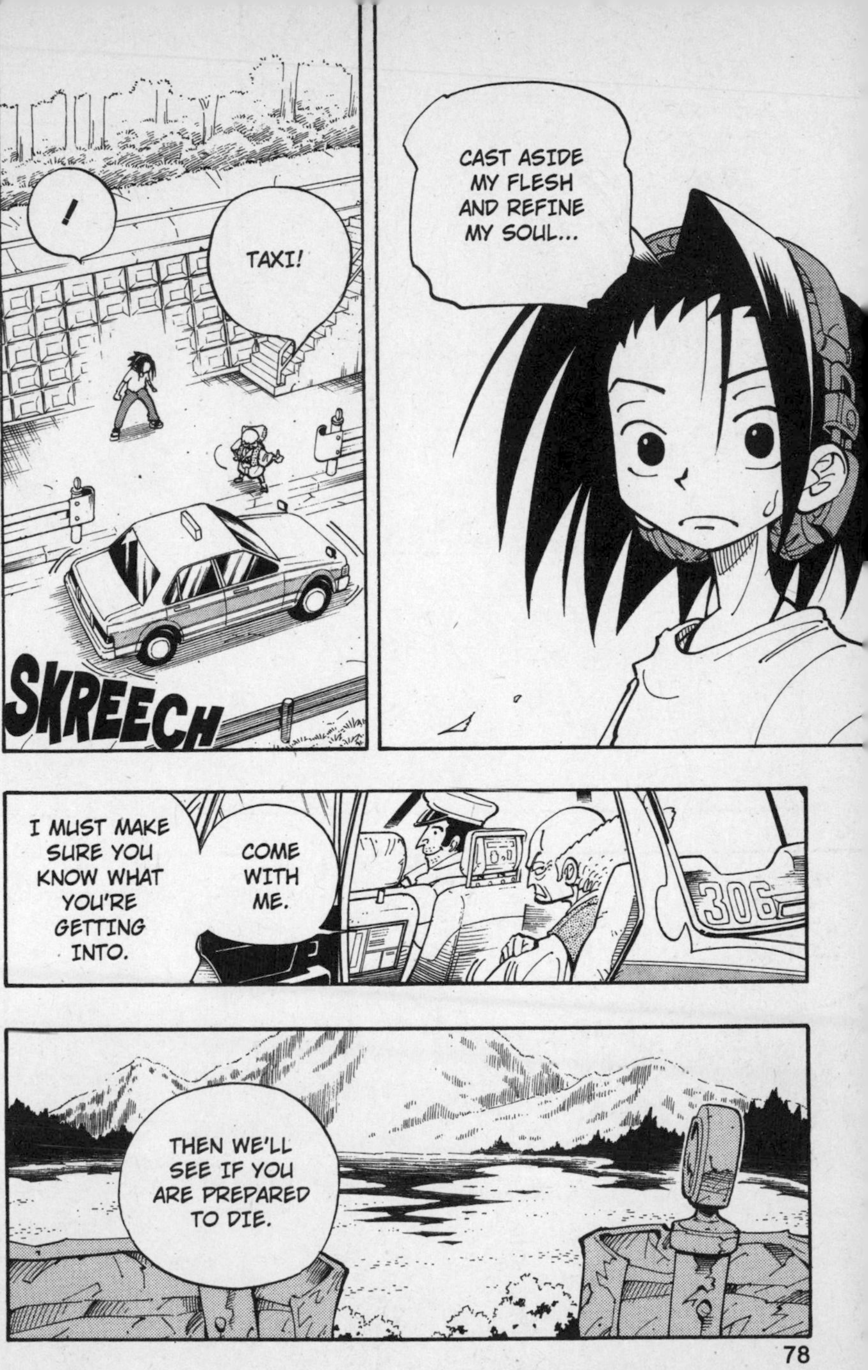
CAST ASIDE MY FLESH AND REFINE MY SOUL...
TAXI!
!
SKREECH
COME WITH ME.
I MUST MAKE SURE YOU KNOW WHAT YOU'RE GETTING INTO.
THEN WE'LL SEE IF YOU ARE PREPARED TO DIE.

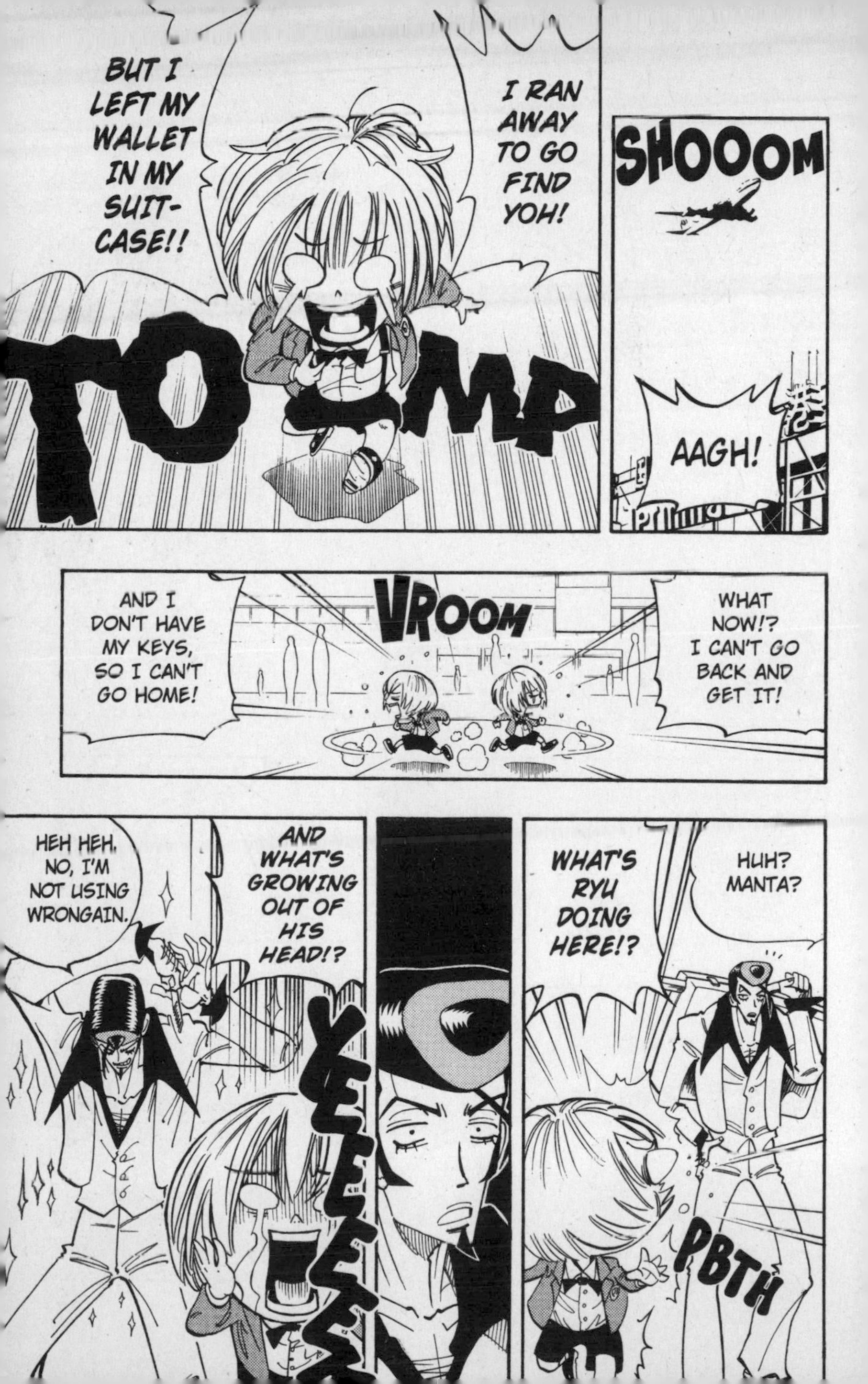
SHOOOM
AAGH!
I RAN AWAY TO GO FIND YOH!
BUT I LEFT MY WALLET IN MY SUIT-CASE!!
TOMP
WHAT NOW!? I CAN'T GO BACK AND GET IT!
VROOM
AND I DON'T HAVE MY KEYS, SO I CAN'T GO HOME!
HUH? MANTA?
WHAT'S RYU DOING HERE!?
PBTH
AND WHAT'S GROWING OUT OF HIS HEAD!?
HEH HEH. NO, I'M NOT USING WRONGAIN.

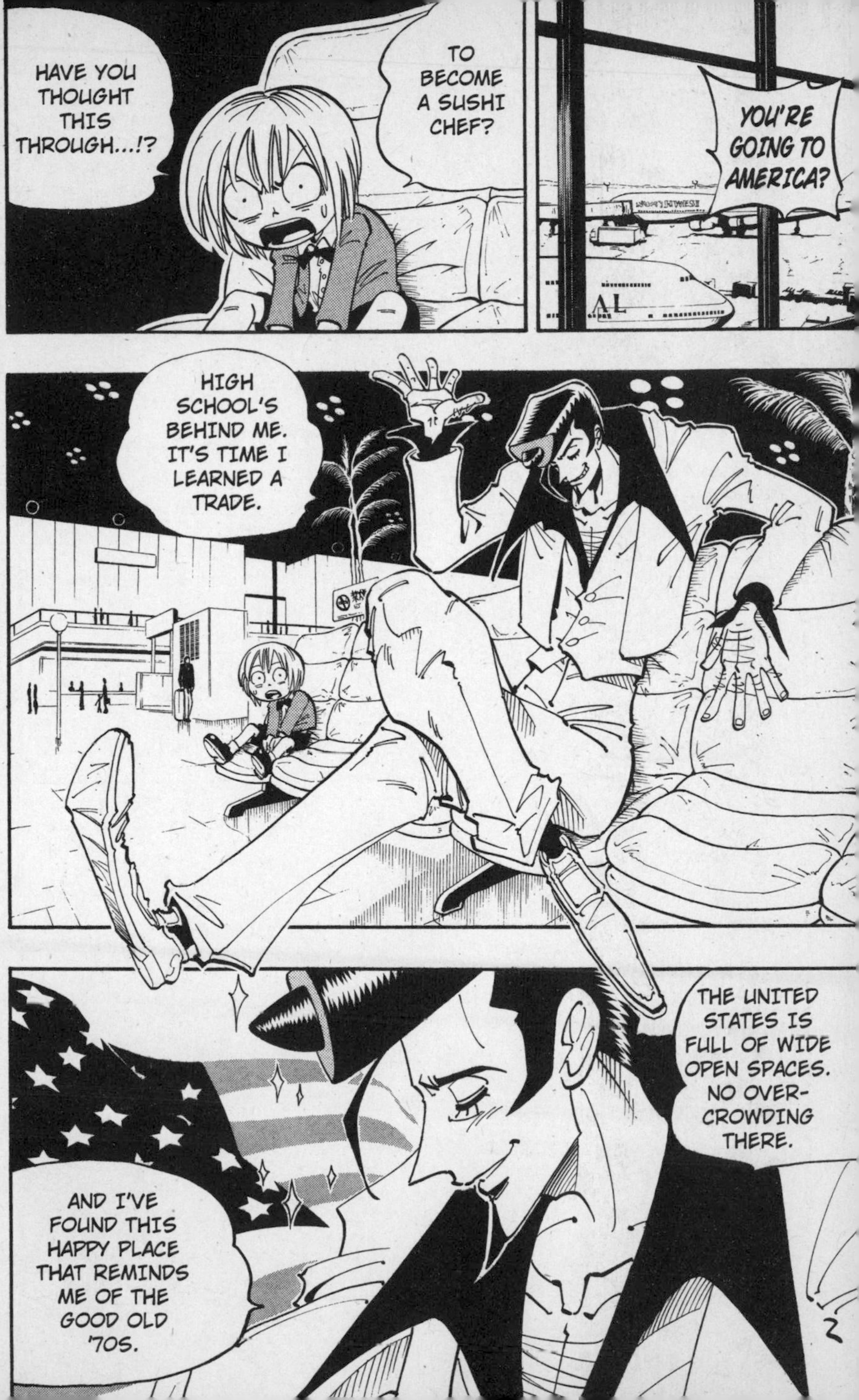
YOU'RE GOING TO AMERICA?
TO BECOME A SUSHI CHEF?
HAVE YOU THOUGHT THIS THROUGH...!?
HIGH SCHOOL'S BEHIND ME. IT'S TIME I LEARNED A TRADE.
THE UNITED STATES IS FULL OF WIDE OPEN SPACES. NO OVER-CROWDING THERE.
AND I'VE FOUND THIS HAPPY PLACE THAT REMINDS ME OF THE GOOD OLD '70S.
2

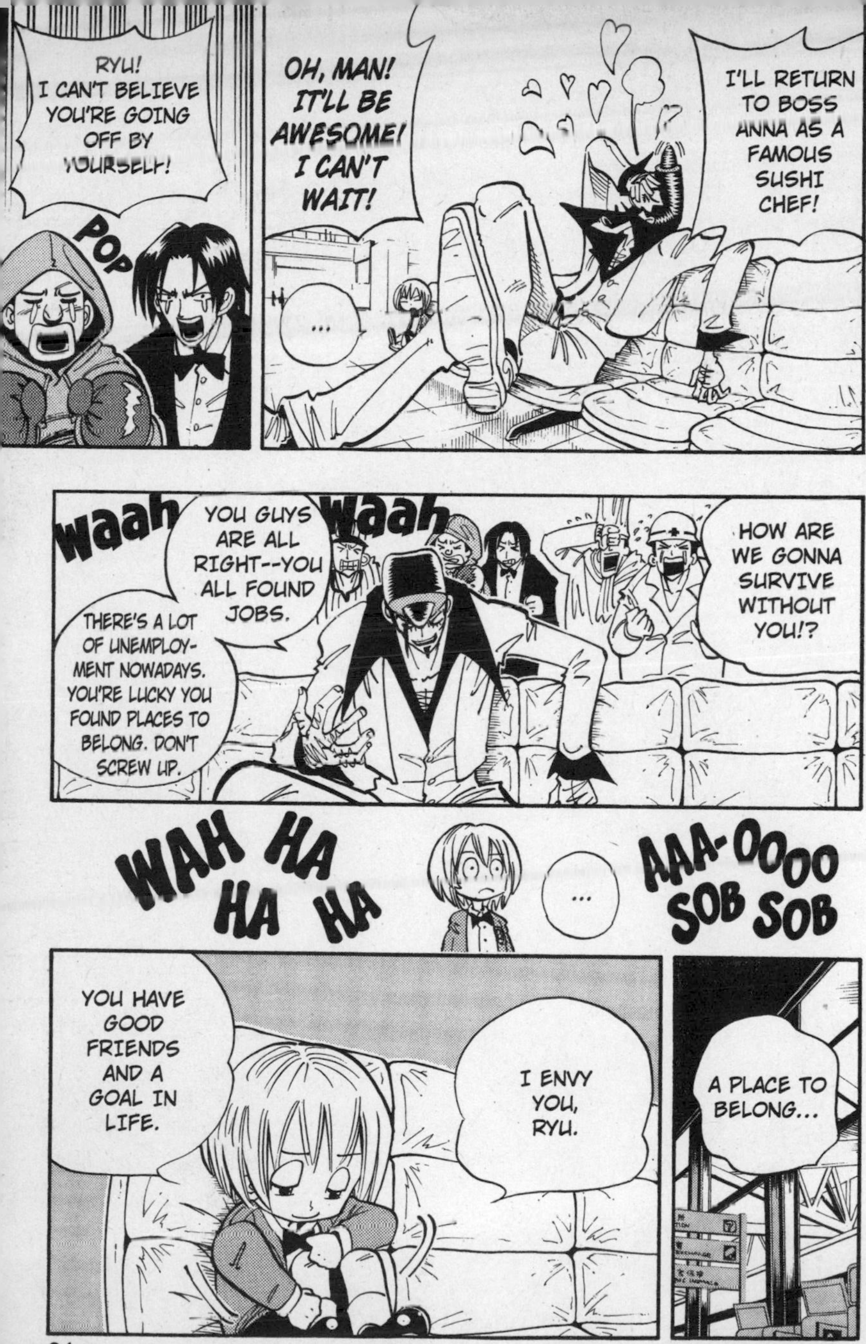
I'LL RETURN TO BOSS ANNA AS A FAMOUS SUSHI CHEF!
OH, MAN! IT'LL BE AWESOME! I CAN'T WAIT!
...
RYU! I CAN'T BELIEVE YOU'RE GOING OFF BY YOURSELF!
POP
HOW ARE WE GONNA SURVIVE WITHOUT YOU!?
waah
YOU GUYS ARE ALL RIGHT--YOU ALL FOUND JOBS.
waah
THERE'S A LOT OF UNEMPLOYMENT NOWADAYS. YOU'RE LUCKY YOU FOUND PLACES TO BELONG. DON'T SCREW UP.
AAA-OOOO SOB SOB
...
WAH HA HA HA HA
A PLACE TO BELONG...
I ENVY YOU, RYU.
YOU HAVE GOOD FRIENDS AND A GOAL IN LIFE.

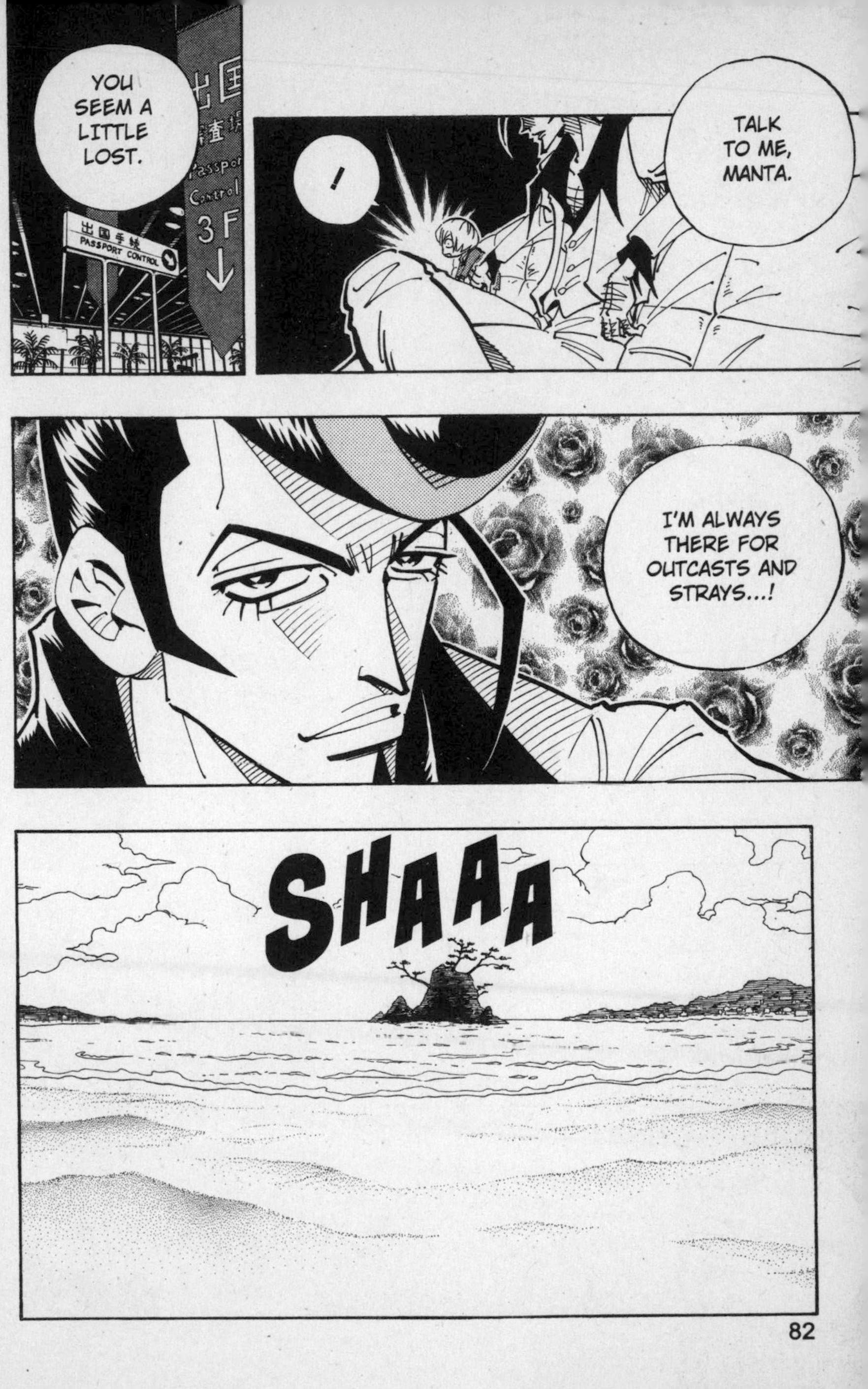
TALK TO ME, MANTA.
!
YOU SEEM A LITTLE LOST.
出国手続
PASSPORT CONTROL
I'M ALWAYS THERE FOR OUTCASTS AND STRAYS...!
SHAAA

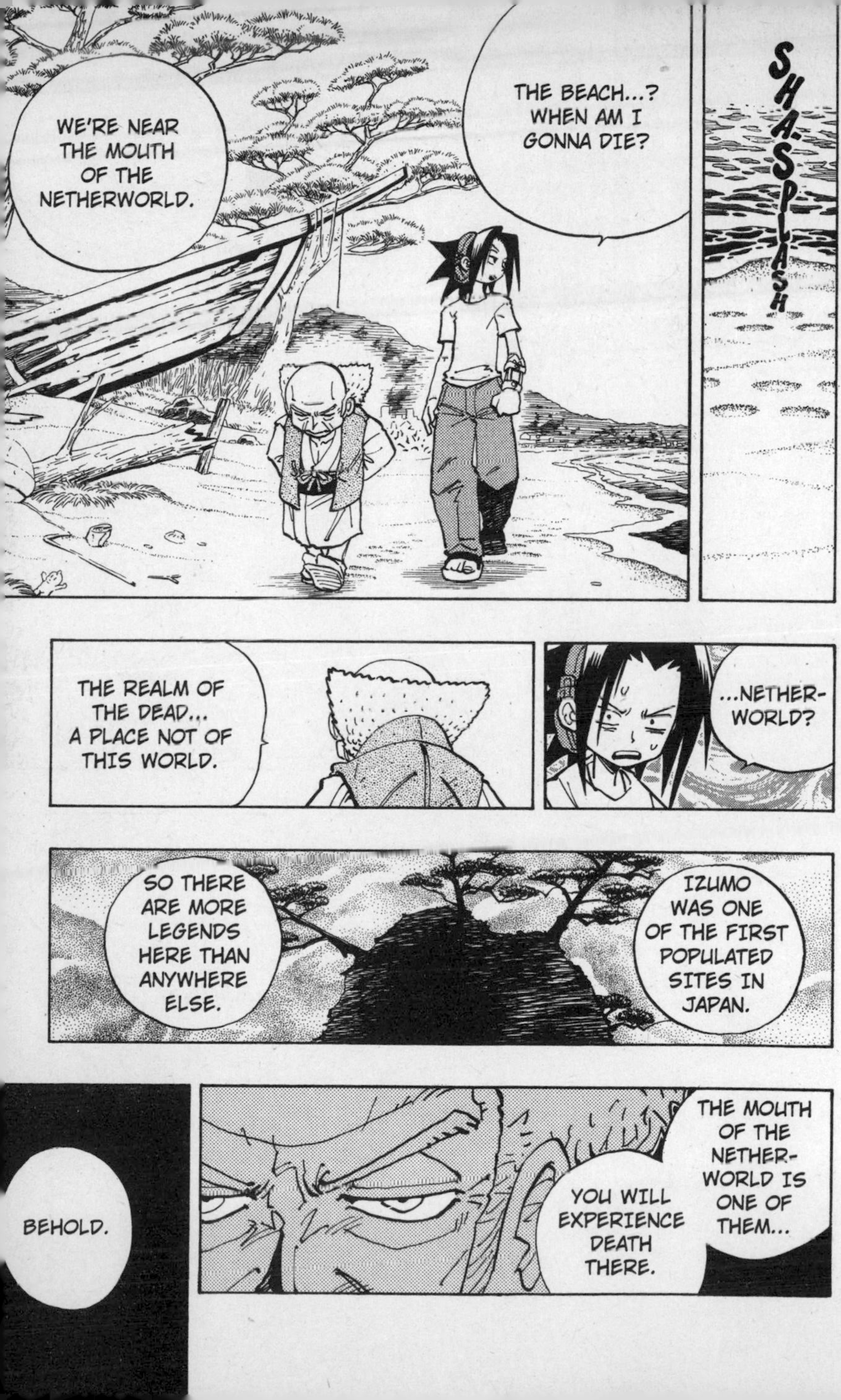

SHA-SPLASH
THE BEACH...? WHEN AM I GONNA DIE?
WE'RE NEAR THE MOUTH OF THE NETHERWORLD.
...NETHER-WORLD?
THE REALM OF THE DEAD... A PLACE NOT OF THIS WORLD.
IZUMO WAS ONE OF THE FIRST POPULATED SITES IN JAPAN.
SO THERE ARE MORE LEGENDS HERE THAN ANYWHERE ELSE.
THE MOUTH OF THE NETHER-WORLD IS ONE OF THEM...
YOU WILL EXPERIENCE DEATH THERE.
BEHOLD.

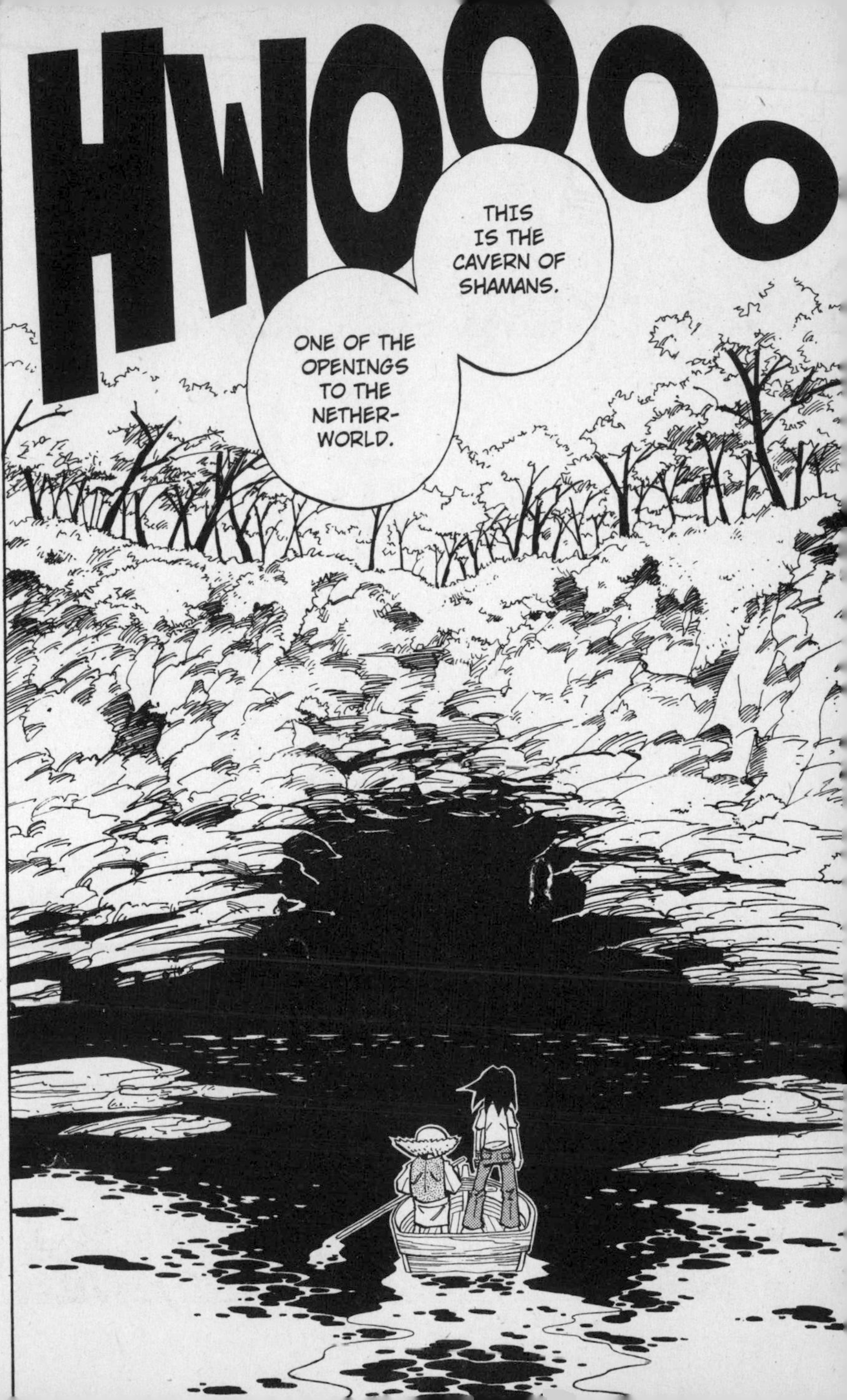
HWOOOO
THIS IS THE CAVERN OF SHAMANS.
ONE OF THE OPENINGS TO THE NETHER-WORLD.

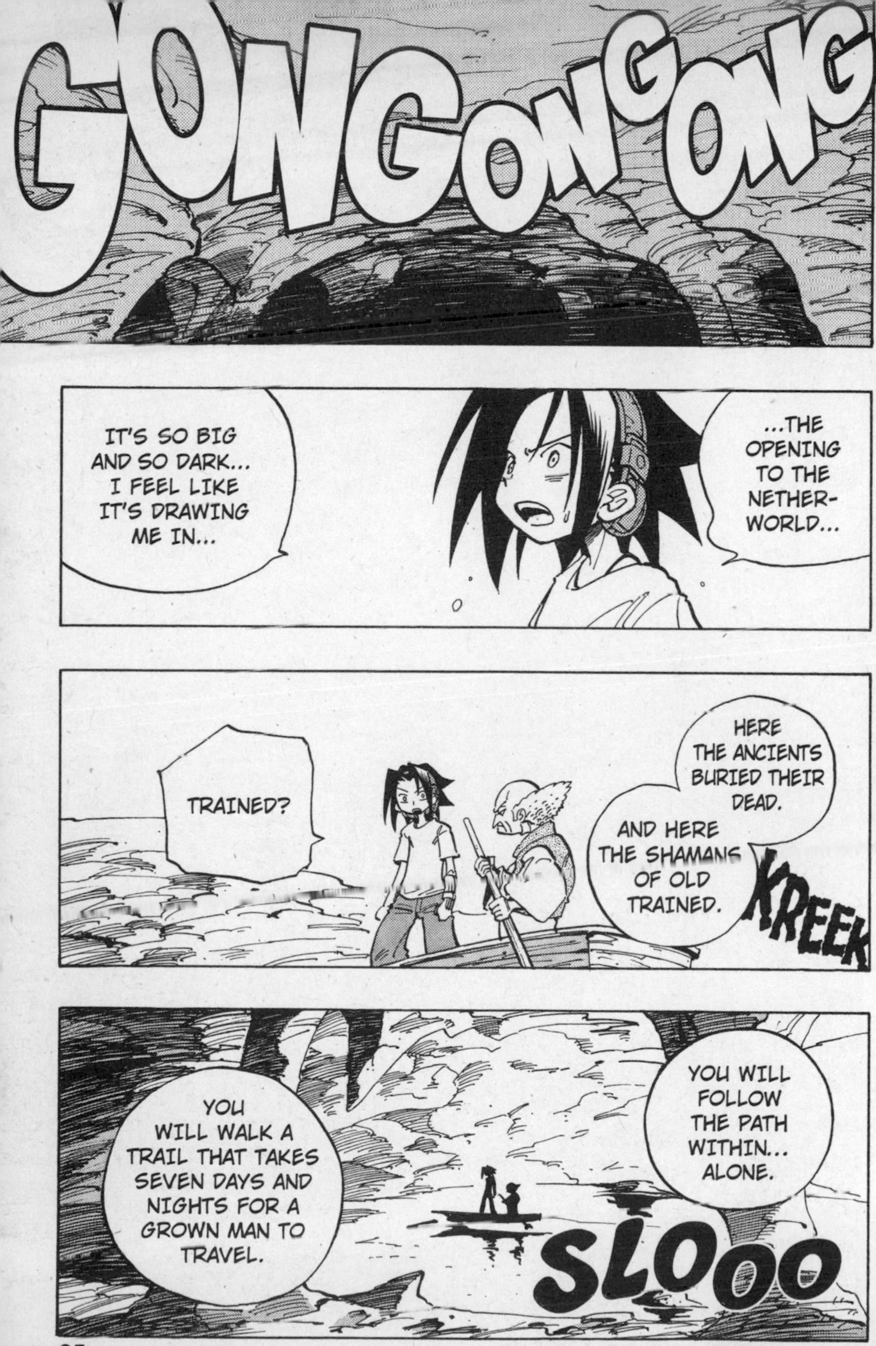
GONGONGONG
...THE OPENING TO THE NETHER-WORLD...
IT'S SO BIG AND SO DARK... I FEEL LIKE IT'S DRAWING ME IN...
HERE THE ANCIENTS BURIED THEIR DEAD.
AND HERE THE SHAMANS OF OLD TRAINED.
KREEK
TRAINED?
YOU WILL FOLLOW THE PATH WITHIN... ALONE.
YOU WILL WALK A TRAIL THAT TAKES SEVEN DAYS AND NIGHTS FOR A GROWN MAN TO TRAVEL.
SLOOO

READ THIS WAY

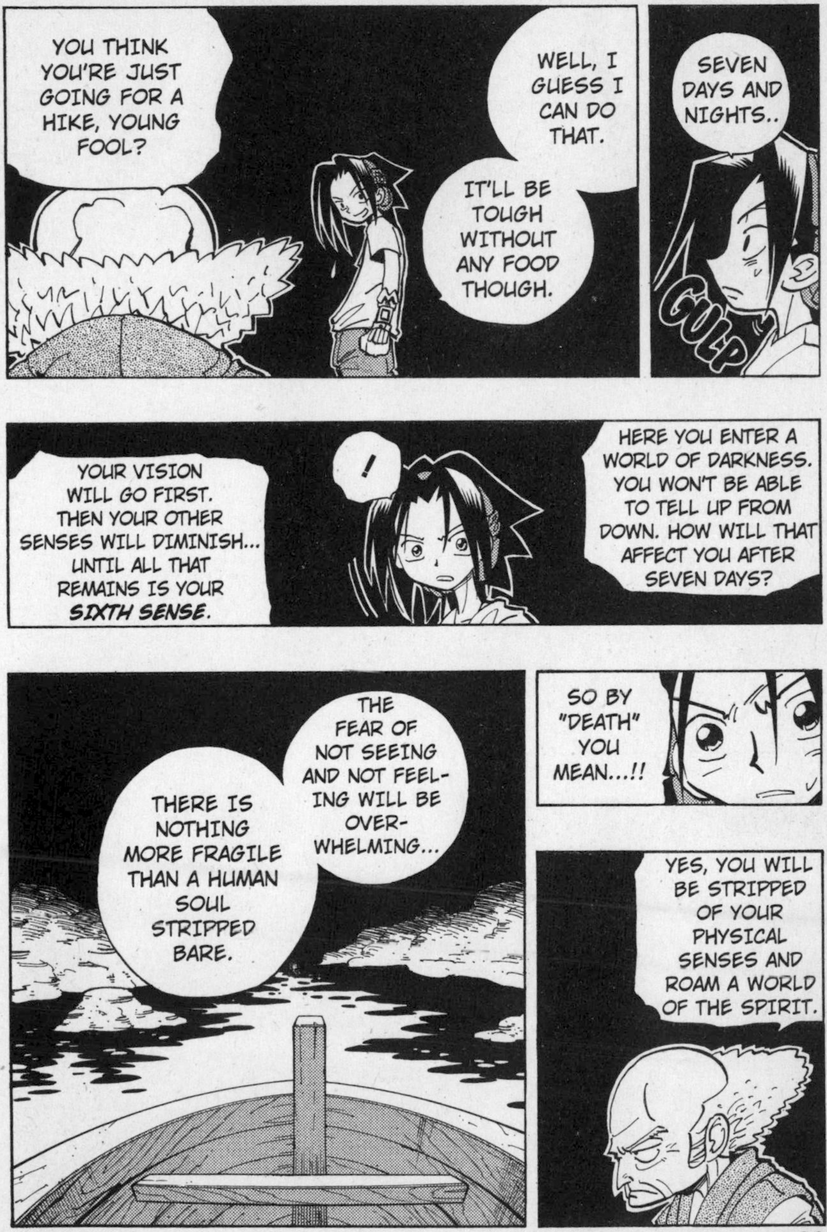
SEVEN DAYS AND NIGHTS..
GULP
WELL, I GUESS I CAN DO THAT.
IT'LL BE TOUGH WITHOUT ANY FOOD THOUGH.
YOU THINK YOU'RE JUST GOING FOR A HIKE, YOUNG FOOL?
HERE YOU ENTER A WORLD OF DARKNESS. YOU WON'T BE ABLE TO TELL UP FROM DOWN. HOW WILL THAT AFFECT YOU AFTER SEVEN DAYS?
!
YOUR VISION WILL GO FIRST. THEN YOUR OTHER SENSES WILL DIMINISH... UNTIL ALL THAT REMAINS IS YOUR *SIXTH SENSE*.
SO BY "DEATH" YOU MEAN...!!
YES, YOU WILL BE STRIPPED OF YOUR PHYSICAL SENSES AND ROAM A WORLD OF THE SPIRIT.
THE FEAR OF NOT SEEING AND NOT FEELING WILL BE OVERWHELMING...
THERE IS NOTHING MORE FRAGILE THAN A HUMAN SOUL STRIPPED BARE.

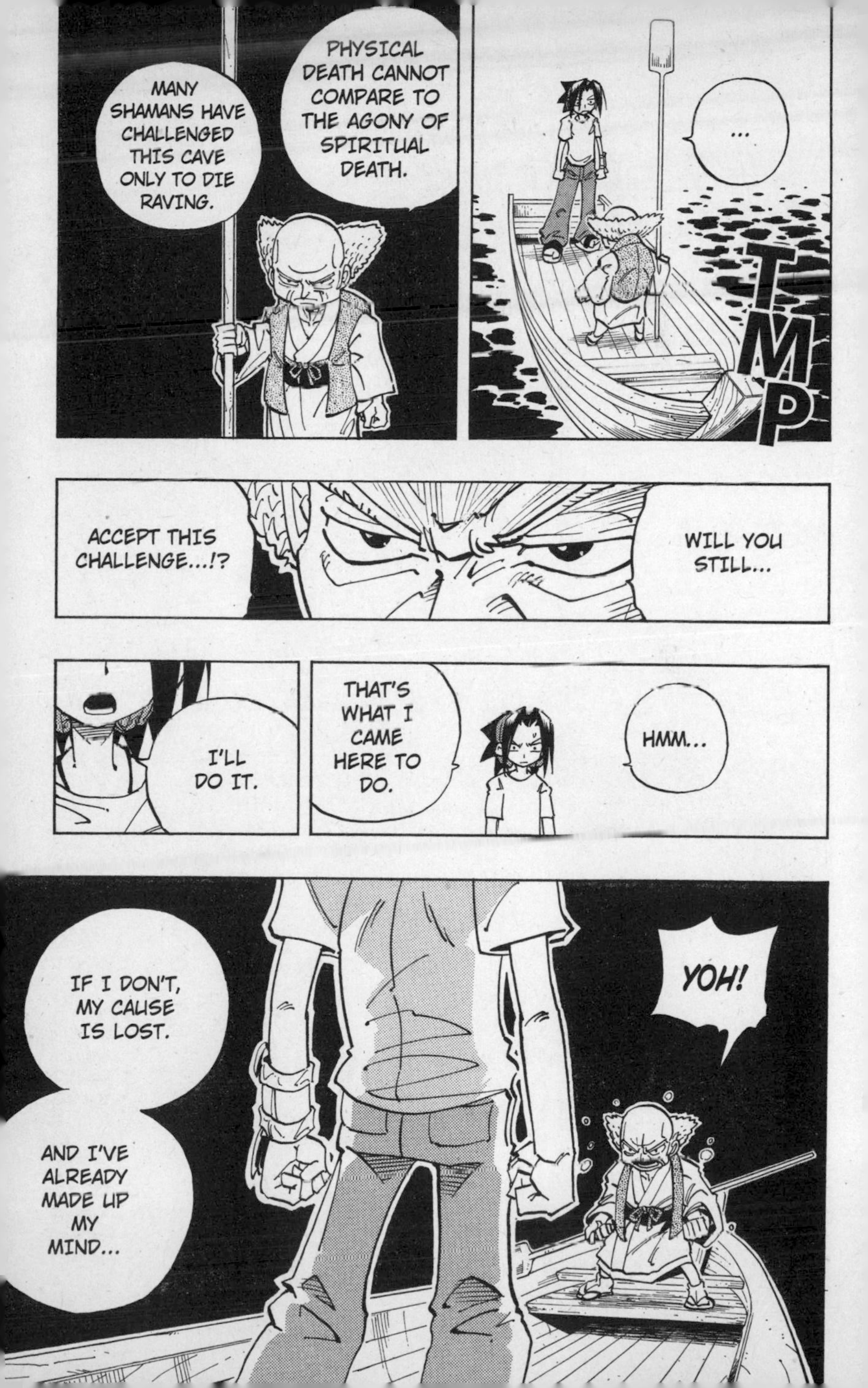
...
TMP
PHYSICAL DEATH CANNOT COMPARE TO THE AGONY OF SPIRITUAL DEATH.
MANY SHAMANS HAVE CHALLENGED THIS CAVE ONLY TO DIE RAVING.
WILL YOU STILL...
ACCEPT THIS CHALLENGE...!?
HMM...
THAT'S WHAT I CAME HERE TO DO.
I'LL DO IT.
YOH!
IF I DON'T, MY CAUSE IS LOST.
AND I'VE ALREADY MADE UP MY MIND...

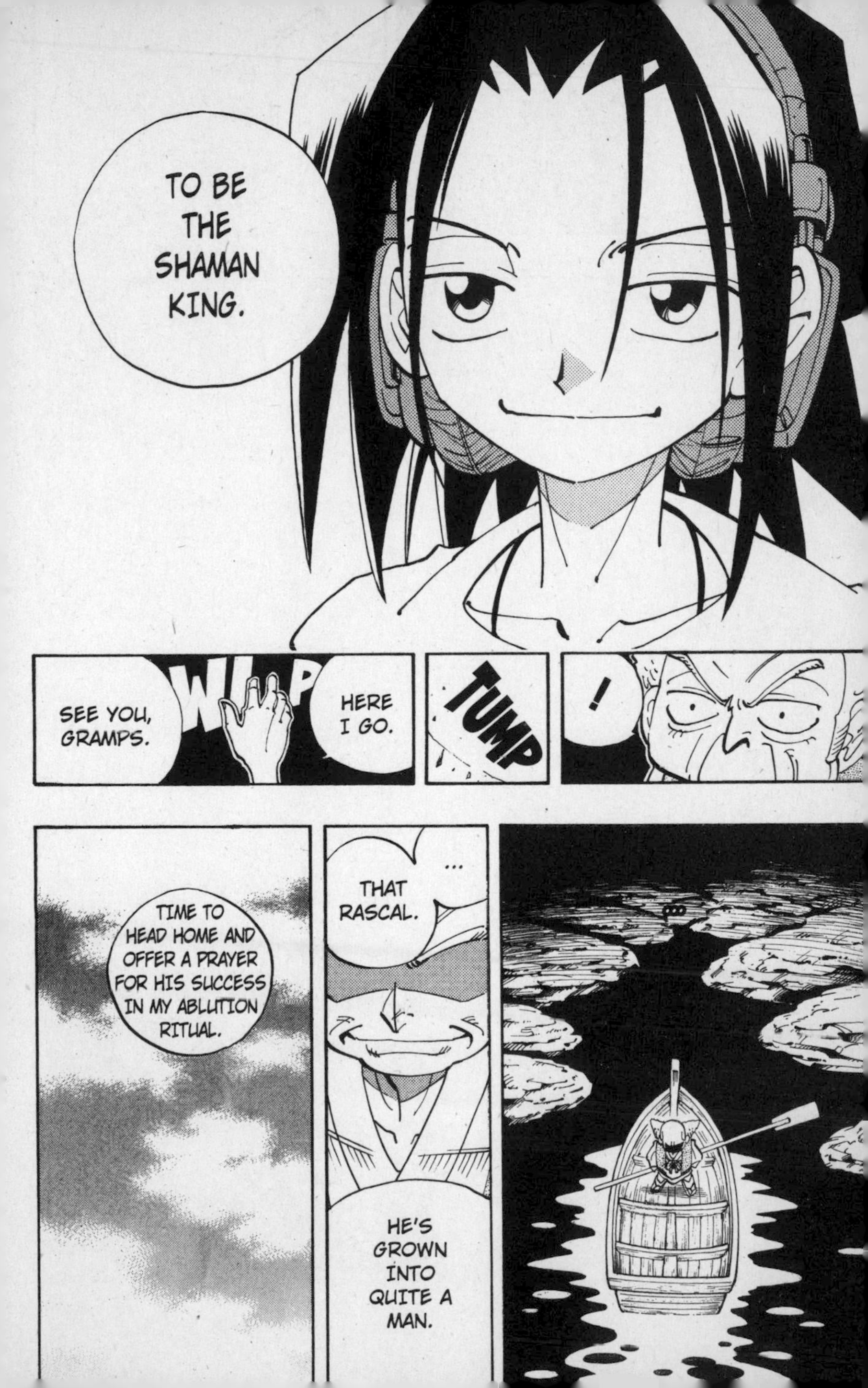
TO BE THE SHAMAN KING.
!
TUMP
HERE I GO.
SEE YOU, GRAMPS.
...
THAT RASCAL.
HE'S GROWN INTO QUITE A MAN.
TIME TO HEAD HOME AND OFFER A PRAYER FOR HIS SUCCESS IN MY ABLUTION RITUAL.

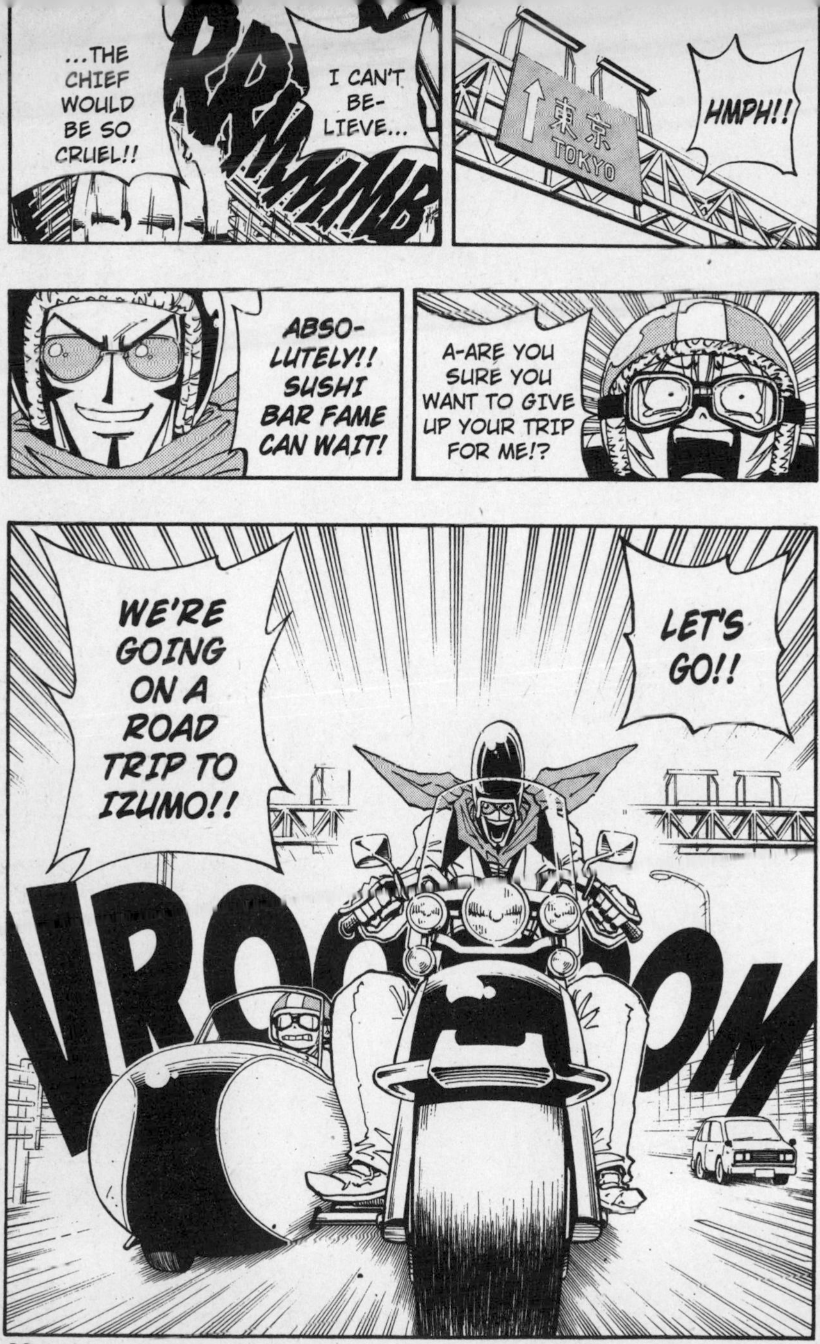

東京
TOKYO
HMPH!!
I CAN'T BE-LIEVE...
...THE CHIEF WOULD BE SO CRUEL!!
BRMMMB
A-ARE YOU SURE YOU WANT TO GIVE UP YOUR TRIP FOR ME!?
ABSO-LUTELY!! SUSHI BAR FAME CAN WAIT!
LET'S GO!!
WE'RE GOING ON A ROAD TRIP TO IZUMO!!
VROOOOM

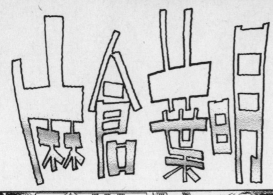

1999
NOV

# YOHMEI ASAKURA

DATE OF BIRTH: JULY 2, 1919
SIGN: CANCER
BLOOD TYPE: O

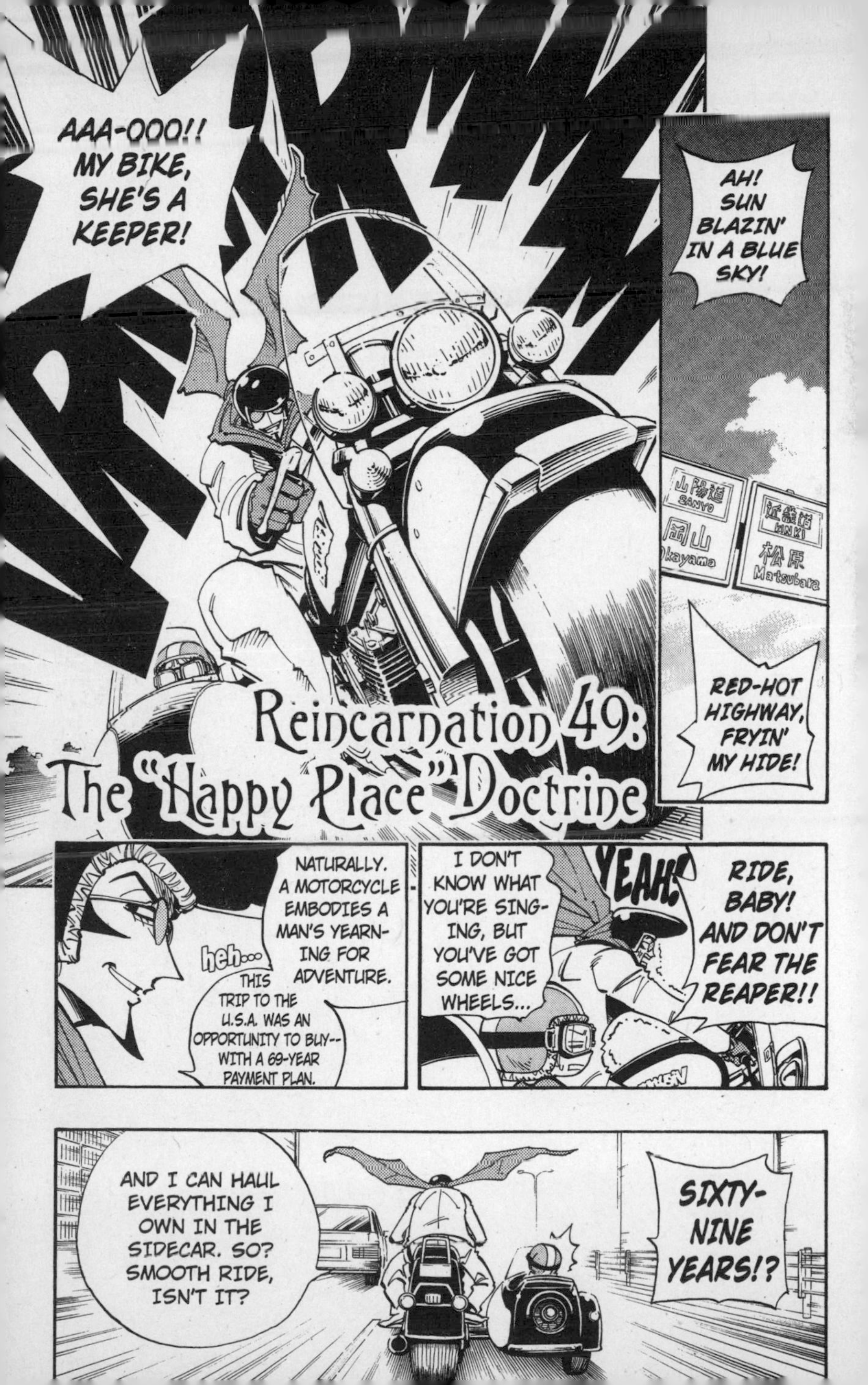
AH! SUN BLAZIN' IN A BLUE SKY!
山陽道 SANYO
岡山 Okayama
近畿道 KINKI
松原 Matsubara
RED-HOT HIGHWAY, FRYIN' MY HIDE!
AAA-OOO!! MY BIKE, SHE'S A KEEPER!
Reincarnation 49: The "Happy Place" Doctrine
YEAH!
RIDE, BABY! AND DON'T FEAR THE REAPER!!
I DON'T KNOW WHAT YOU'RE SING-ING, BUT YOU'VE GOT SOME NICE WHEELS...
NATURALLY. A MOTORCYCLE EMBODIES A MAN'S YEARN-ING FOR ADVENTURE.
heh...
THIS TRIP TO THE U.S.A. WAS AN OPPORTUNITY TO BUY--WITH A 69-YEAR PAYMENT PLAN.
SIXTY-NINE YEARS!?
AND I CAN HAUL EVERYTHING I OWN IN THE SIDECAR. SO? SMOOTH RIDE, ISN'T IT?

READ THIS WAY

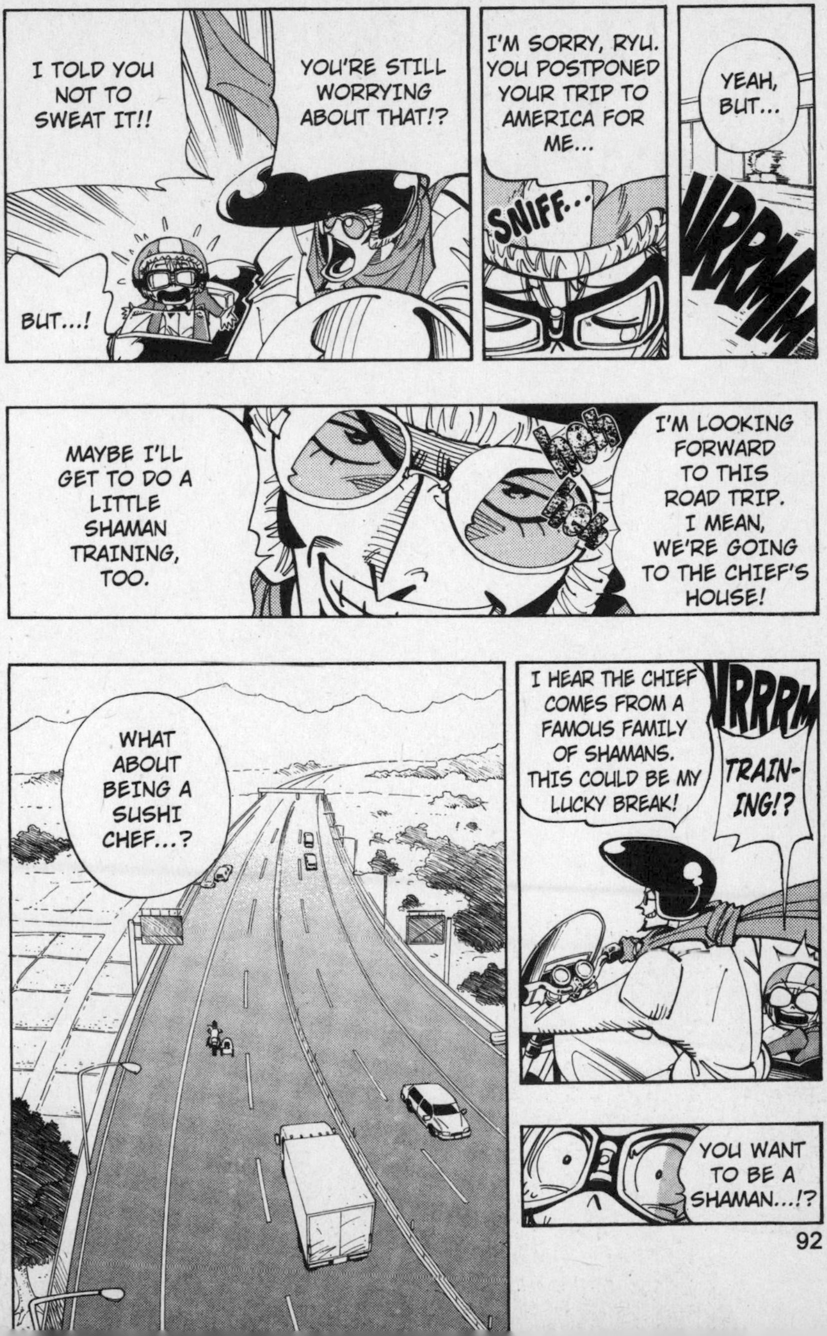

YEAH, BUT...
VRRM
I'M SORRY, RYU. YOU POSTPONED YOUR TRIP TO AMERICA FOR ME...
SNIFF...
YOU'RE STILL WORRYING ABOUT THAT!?
I TOLD YOU NOT TO SWEAT IT!!
BUT...!
I'M LOOKING FORWARD TO THIS ROAD TRIP. I MEAN, WE'RE GOING TO THE CHIEF'S HOUSE!
MAYBE I'LL GET TO DO A LITTLE SHAMAN TRAINING, TOO.
I HEAR THE CHIEF COMES FROM A FAMOUS FAMILY OF SHAMANS. THIS COULD BE MY LUCKY BREAK!
VRRRM
TRAIN-ING!?
YOU WANT TO BE A SHAMAN...!?
WHAT ABOUT BEING A SUSHI CHEF...?

# Reincarnation 49: The "Happy Place" Doctrine

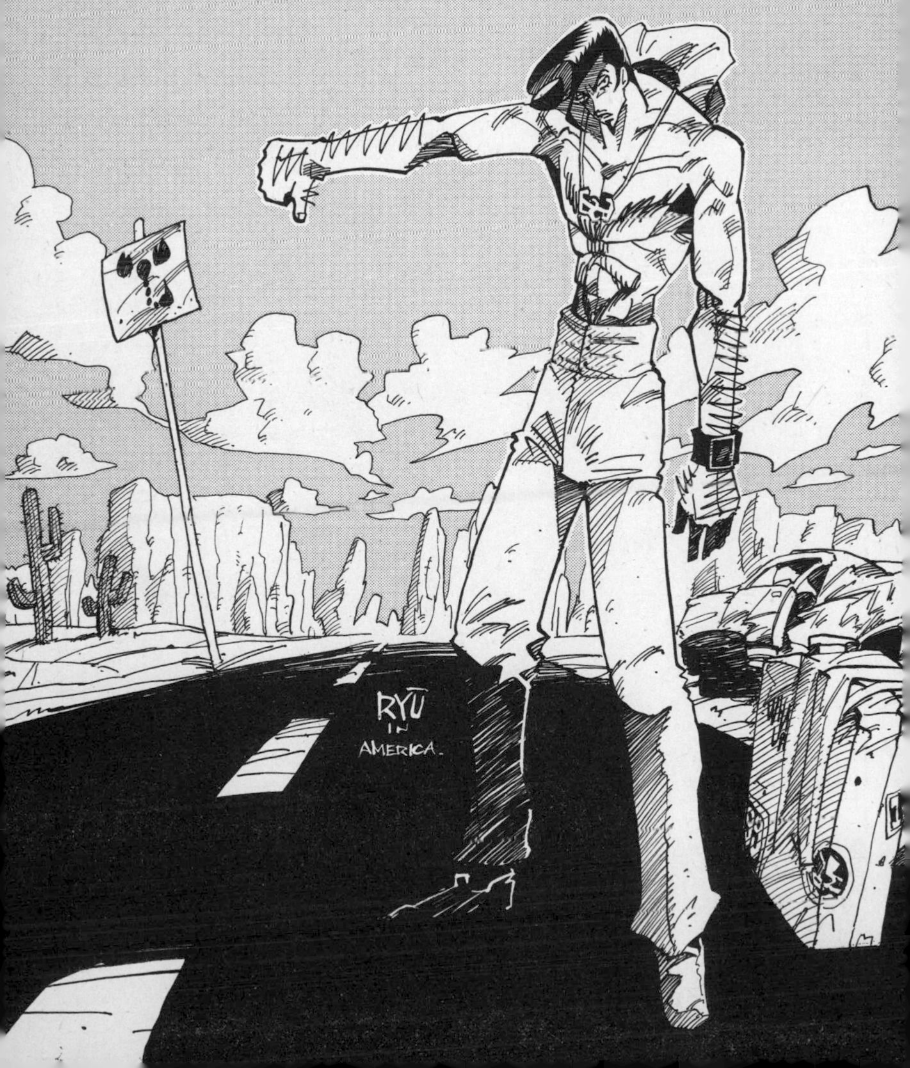
RYU IN AMERICA.

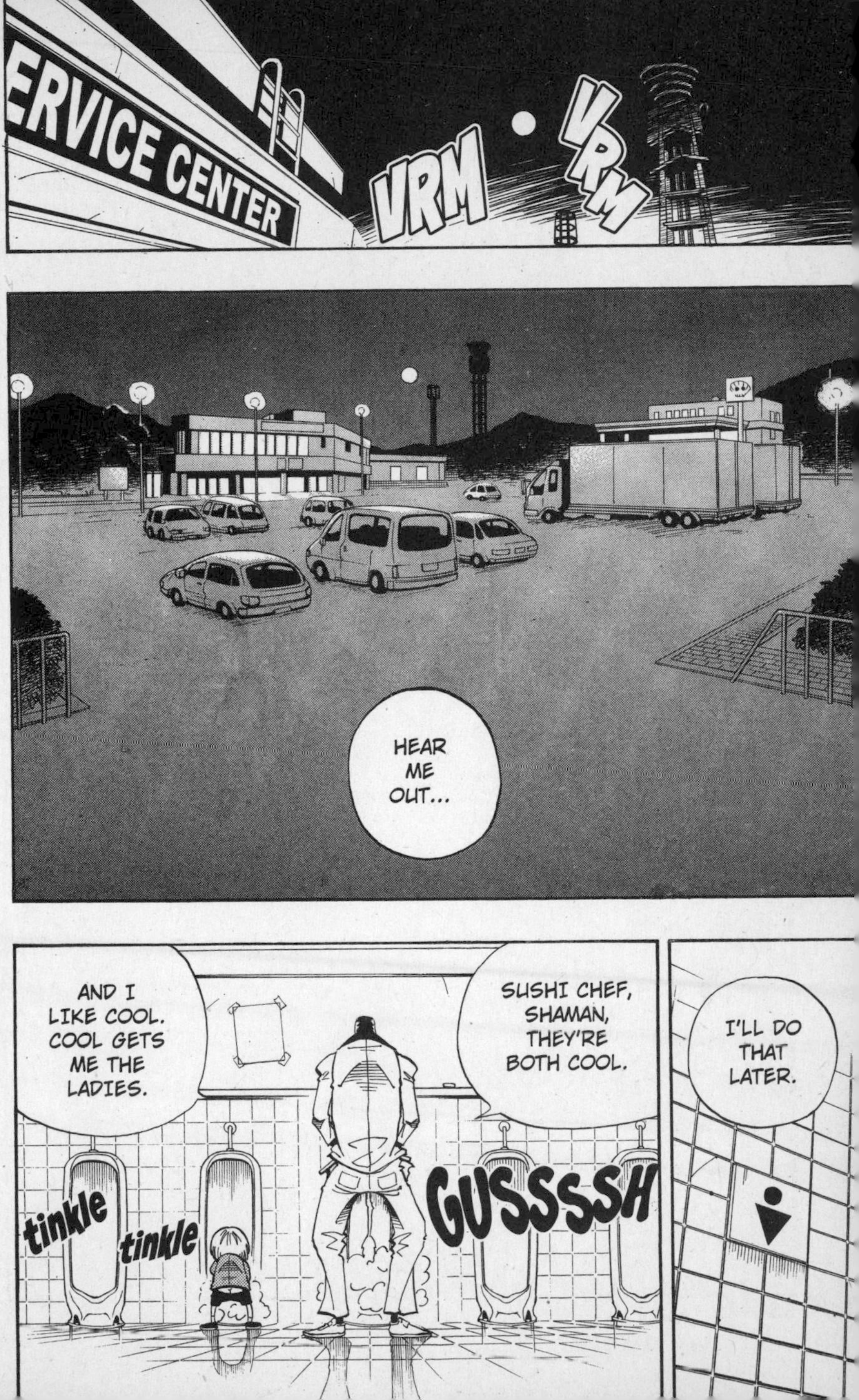
VRM
VRM
ERVICE CENTER
HEAR ME OUT...
I'LL DO THAT LATER.
SUSHI CHEF, SHAMAN, THEY'RE BOTH COOL.
AND I LIKE COOL. COOL GETS ME THE LADIES.
GUSSSSH
tinkle
tinkle

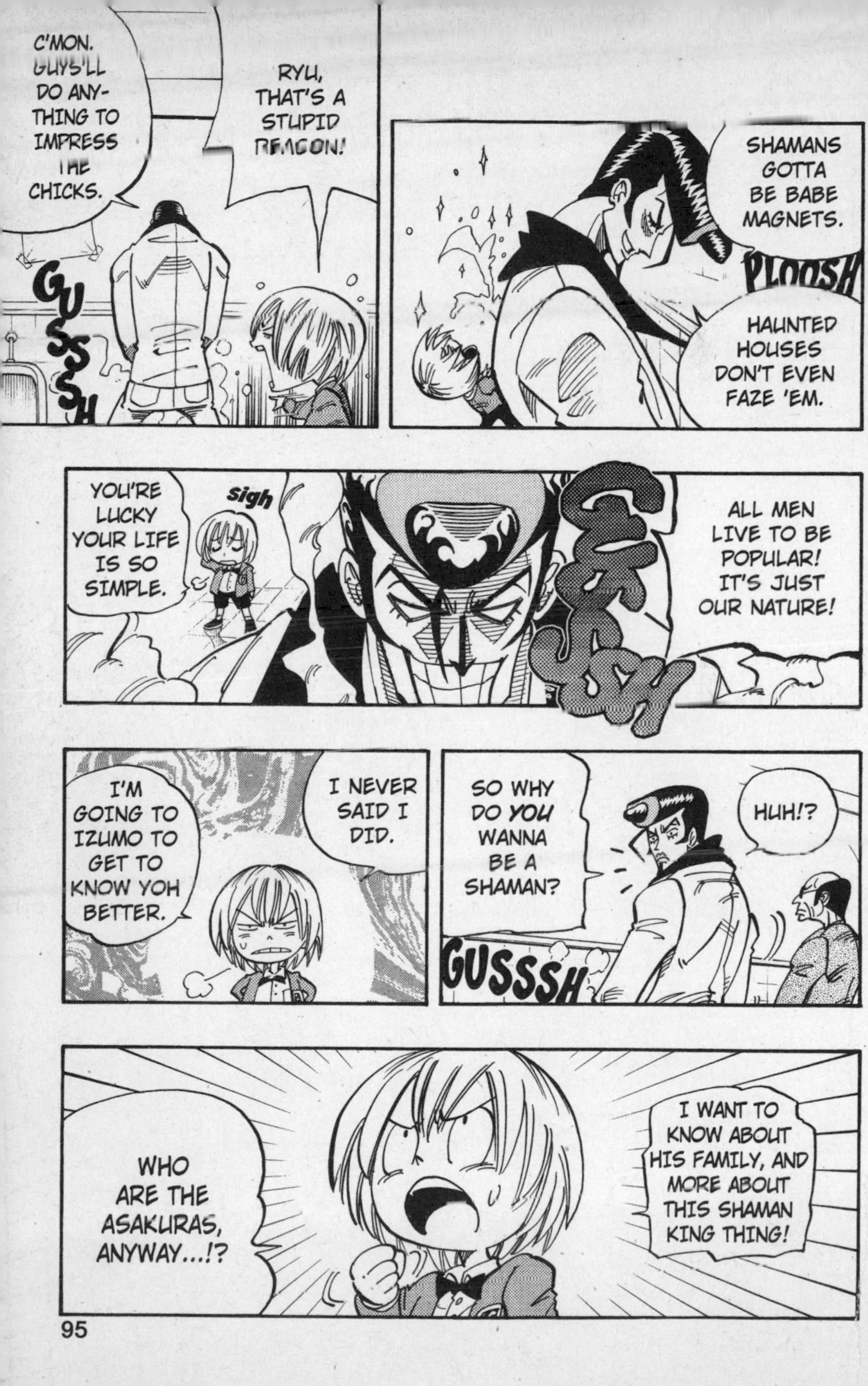
SHAMANS GOTTA BE BABE MAGNETS.
PLOOSH
HAUNTED HOUSES DON'T EVEN FAZE 'EM.
RYU, THAT'S A STUPID REASON!
C'MON. GUYS'LL DO ANYTHING TO IMPRESS THE CHICKS.
GUSSSH
ALL MEN LIVE TO BE POPULAR! IT'S JUST OUR NATURE!
sigh
YOU'RE LUCKY YOUR LIFE IS SO SIMPLE.
HUH!?
SO WHY DO YOU WANNA BE A SHAMAN?
GUSSSH
I NEVER SAID I DID.
I'M GOING TO IZUMO TO GET TO KNOW YOH BETTER.
I WANT TO KNOW ABOUT HIS FAMILY, AND MORE ABOUT THIS SHAMAN KING THING!
WHO ARE THE ASAKURAS, ANYWAY...!?

READ THIS WAY

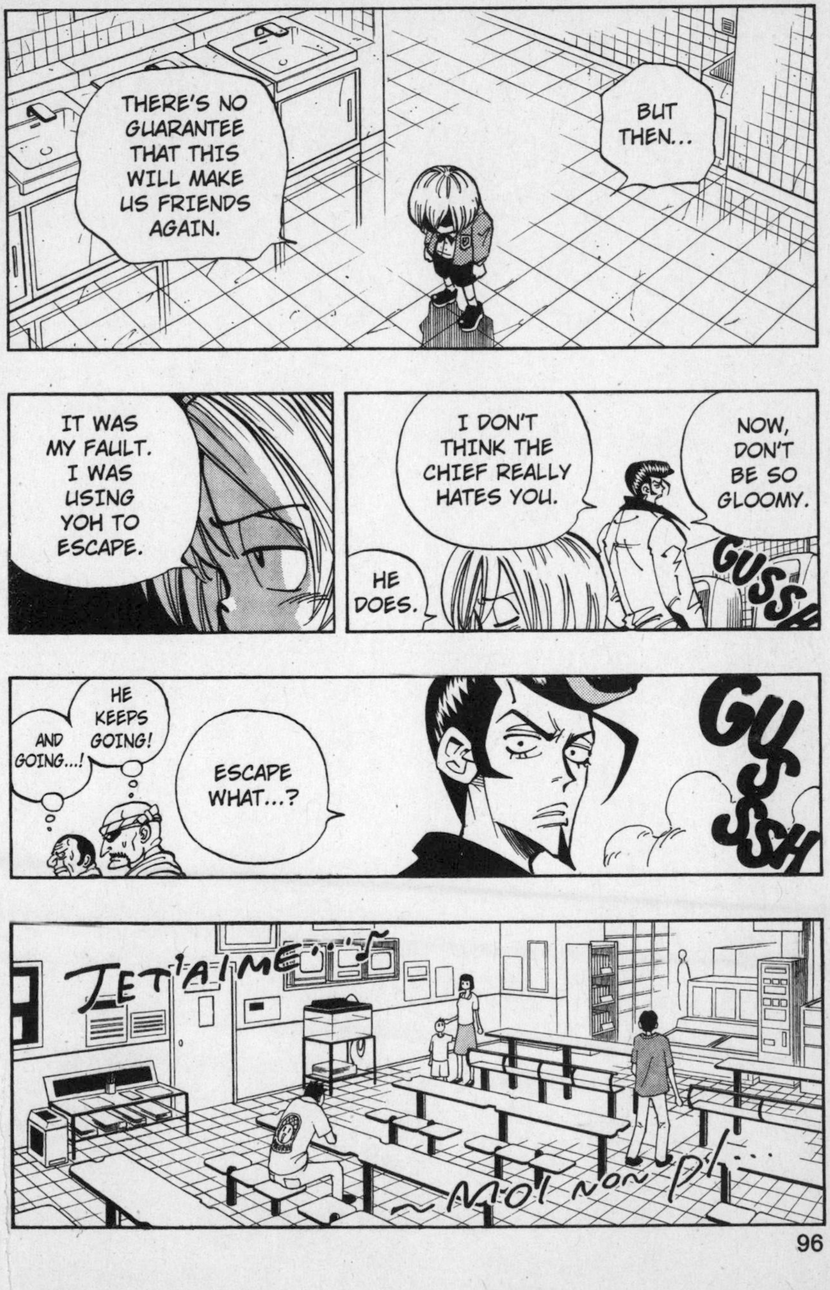

BUT THEN...
THERE'S NO GUARANTEE THAT THIS WILL MAKE US FRIENDS AGAIN.
NOW, DON'T BE SO GLOOMY.
I DON'T THINK THE CHIEF REALLY HATES YOU.
GUSSH
HE DOES.
IT WAS MY FAULT. I WAS USING YOH TO ESCAPE.
GUSSSH
ESCAPE WHAT...?
HE KEEPS GOING!
AND GOING...!
JE T'AIME...♪
~MOI NON PL...

READ THIS WAY

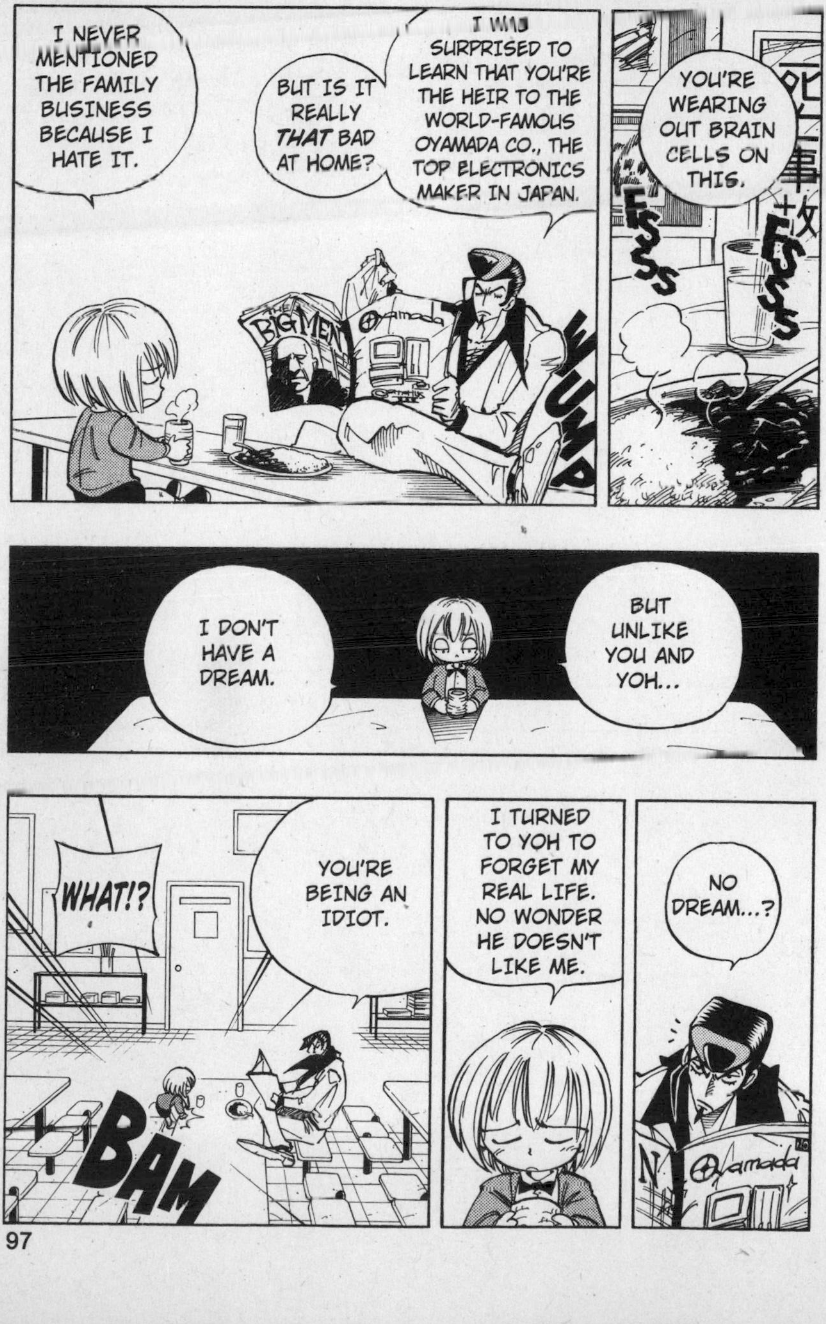
YOU'RE WEARING OUT BRAIN CELLS ON THIS.
FSSS
FSSS
I WAS SURPRISED TO LEARN THAT YOU'RE THE HEIR TO THE WORLD-FAMOUS OYAMADA CO., THE TOP ELECTRONICS MAKER IN JAPAN.
BUT IS IT REALLY *THAT* BAD AT HOME?
I NEVER MENTIONED THE FAMILY BUSINESS BECAUSE I HATE IT.
WUMP
BIG MEN
Oyamada
BUT UNLIKE YOU AND YOH...
I DON'T HAVE A DREAM.
NO DREAM...?
Oyamada
I TURNED TO YOH TO FORGET MY REAL LIFE. NO WONDER HE DOESN'T LIKE ME.
YOU'RE BEING AN IDIOT.
WHAT!?
BAM

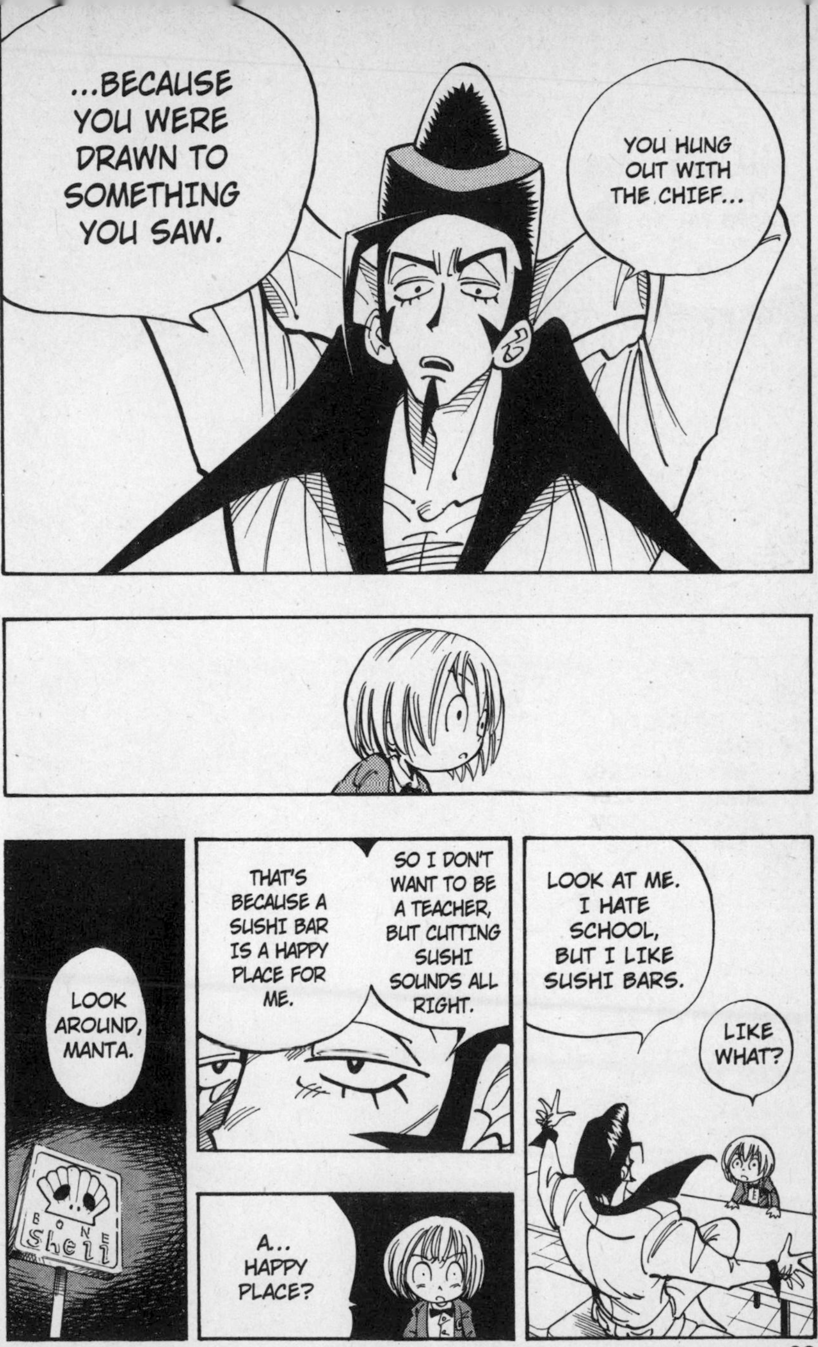
YOU HUNG OUT WITH THE CHIEF...
...BECAUSE YOU WERE DRAWN TO SOMETHING YOU SAW.
LOOK AT ME. I HATE SCHOOL, BUT I LIKE SUSHI BARS.
LIKE WHAT?
SO I DON'T WANT TO BE A TEACHER, BUT CUTTING SUSHI SOUNDS ALL RIGHT.
THAT'S BECAUSE A SUSHI BAR IS A HAPPY PLACE FOR ME.
A... HAPPY PLACE?
LOOK AROUND, MANTA.
BONE
Shell

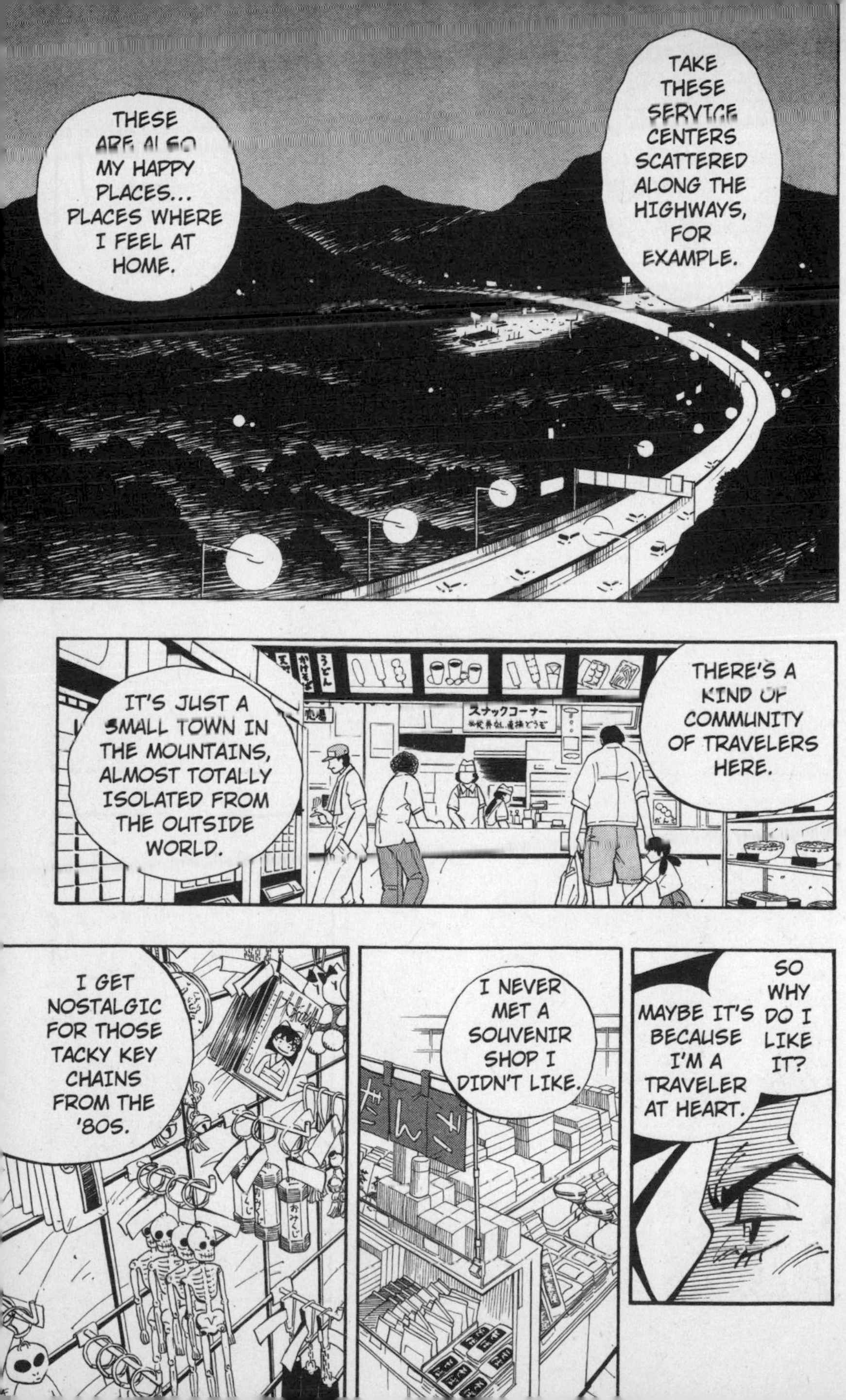
TAKE THESE SERVICE CENTERS SCATTERED ALONG THE HIGHWAYS, FOR EXAMPLE.
THESE ARE ALSO MY HAPPY PLACES... PLACES WHERE I FEEL AT HOME.
THERE'S A KIND OF COMMUNITY OF TRAVELERS HERE.
スナックコーナー
IT'S JUST A SMALL TOWN IN THE MOUNTAINS, ALMOST TOTALLY ISOLATED FROM THE OUTSIDE WORLD.
SO WHY DO I LIKE IT?
MAYBE IT'S BECAUSE I'M A TRAVELER AT HEART.
I NEVER MET A SOUVENIR SHOP I DIDN'T LIKE.
I GET NOSTALGIC FOR THOSE TACKY KEY CHAINS FROM THE '80S.

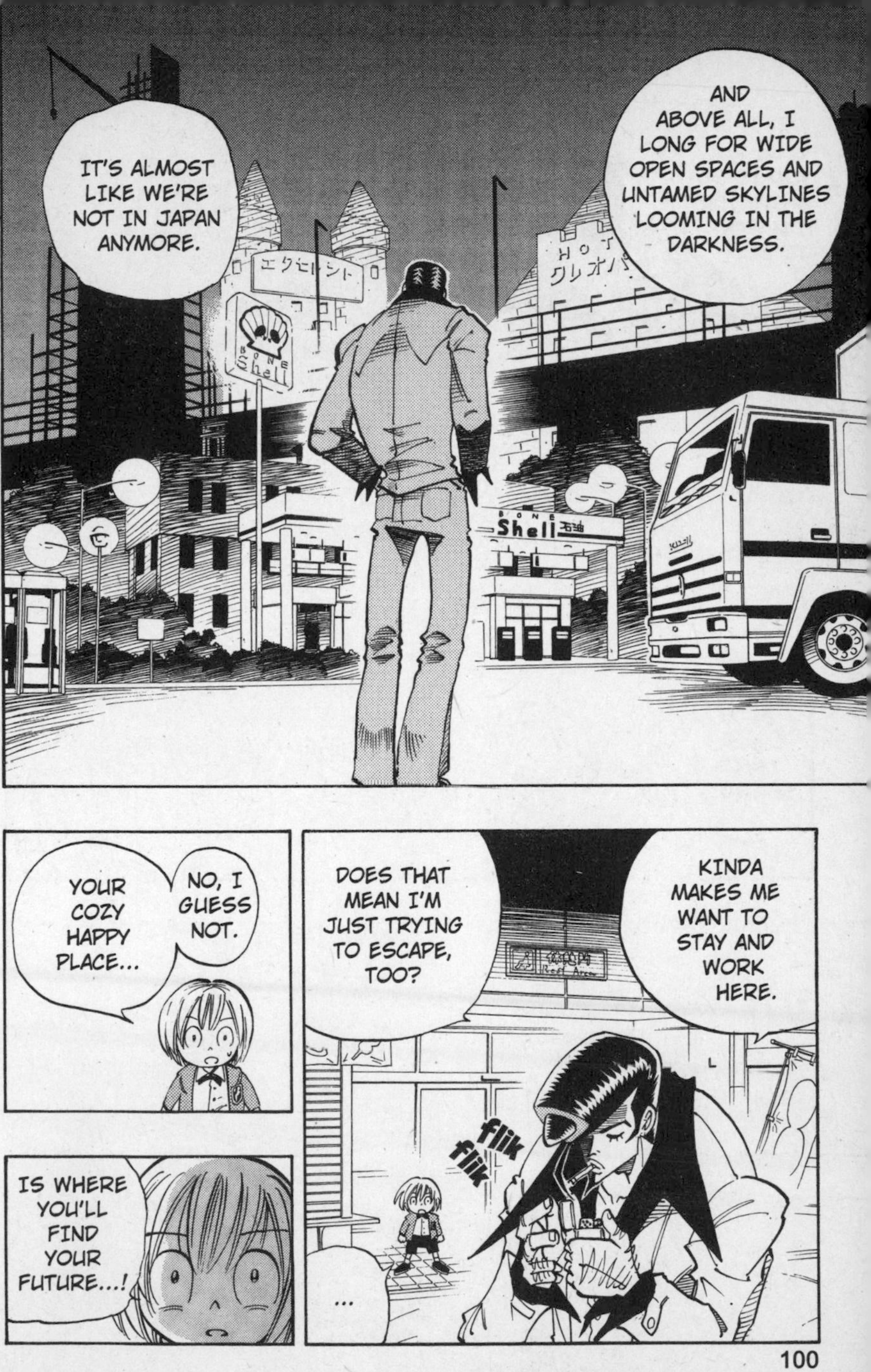
AND ABOVE ALL, I LONG FOR WIDE OPEN SPACES AND UNTAMED SKYLINES LOOMING IN THE DARKNESS.
IT'S ALMOST LIKE WE'RE NOT IN JAPAN ANYMORE.
BONE Shell
BONE Shell
KINDA MAKES ME WANT TO STAY AND WORK HERE.
DOES THAT MEAN I'M JUST TRYING TO ESCAPE, TOO?
flik
flik
...
NO, I GUESS NOT.
YOUR COZY HAPPY PLACE...
IS WHERE YOU'LL FIND YOUR FUTURE...!

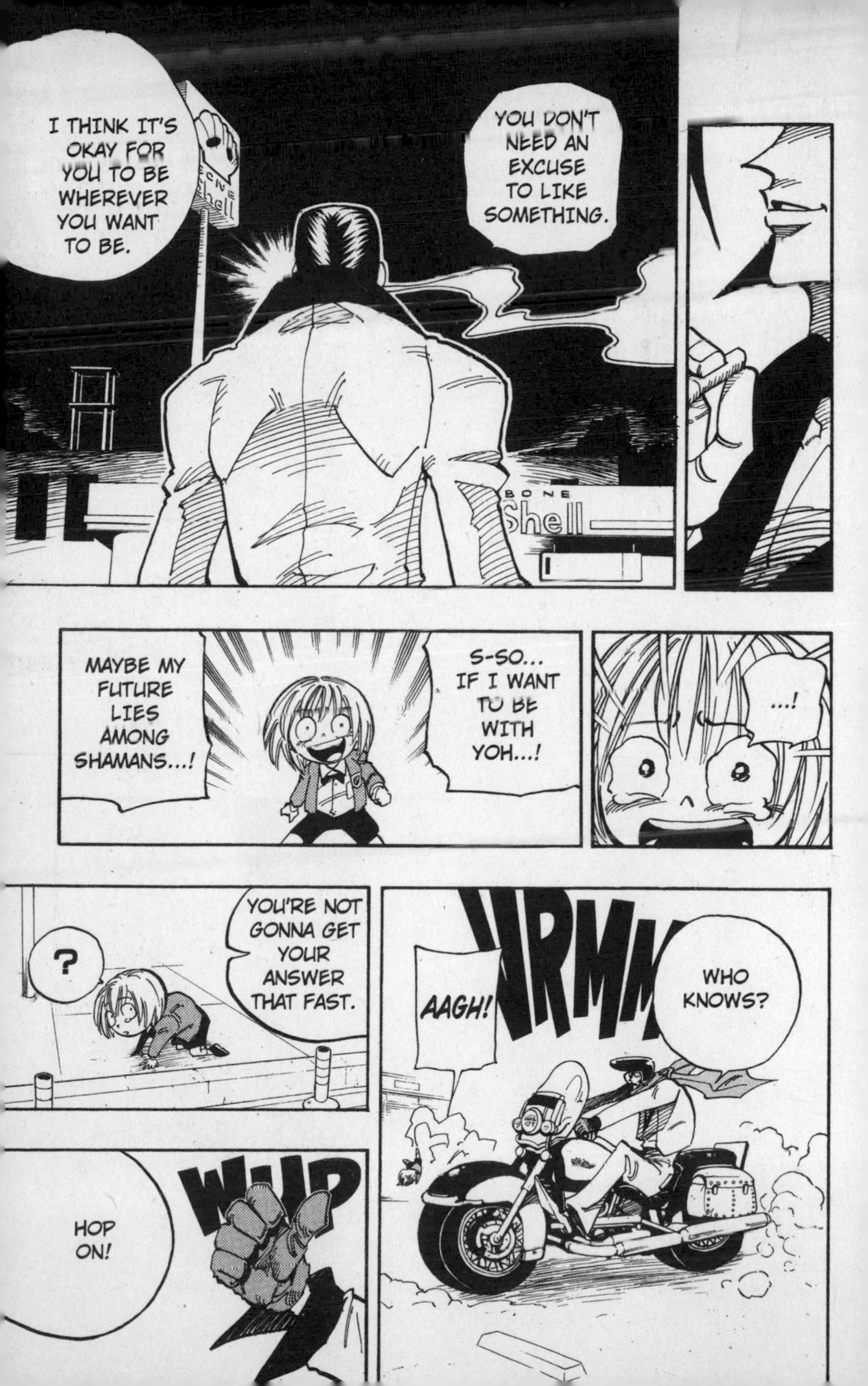
YOU DON'T NEED AN EXCUSE TO LIKE SOMETHING.
I THINK IT'S OKAY FOR YOU TO BE WHEREVER YOU WANT TO BE.
BONE Shell
...!
S-SO... IF I WANT TO BE WITH YOH...!
MAYBE MY FUTURE LIES AMONG SHAMANS...!
VRMM
WHO KNOWS?
AAGH!
YOU'RE NOT GONNA GET YOUR ANSWER THAT FAST.
?
WHUP
HOP ON!

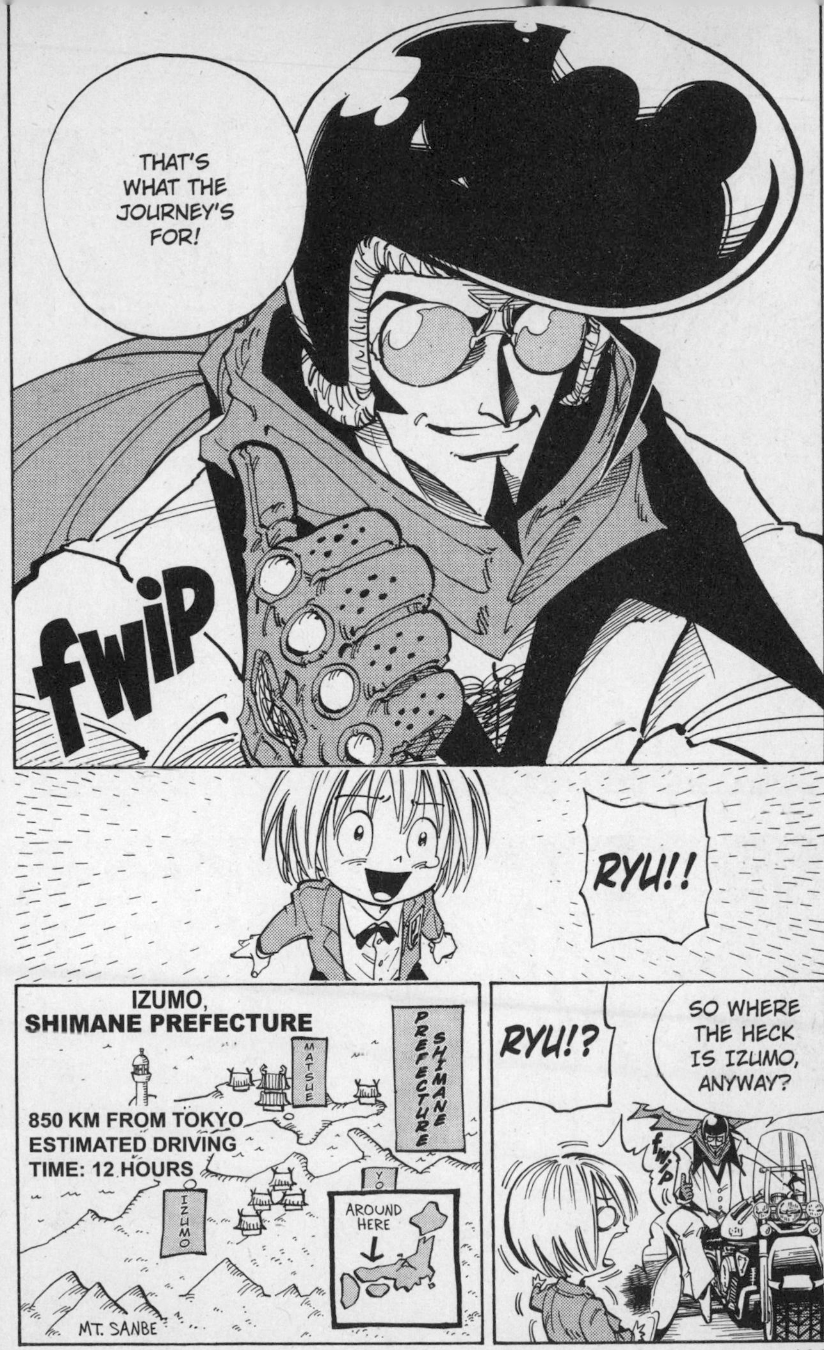
THAT'S WHAT THE JOURNEY'S FOR!
fwip
RYU!!
SO WHERE THE HECK IS IZUMO, ANYWAY?
RYU!?
fwip
IZUMO, SHIMANE PREFECTURE
SHIMANE PREFECTURE
MATSUE
850 KM FROM TOKYO
ESTIMATED DRIVING TIME: 12 HOURS
YO
IZUMO
AROUND HERE
MT. SANBE

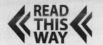

READ THIS WAY

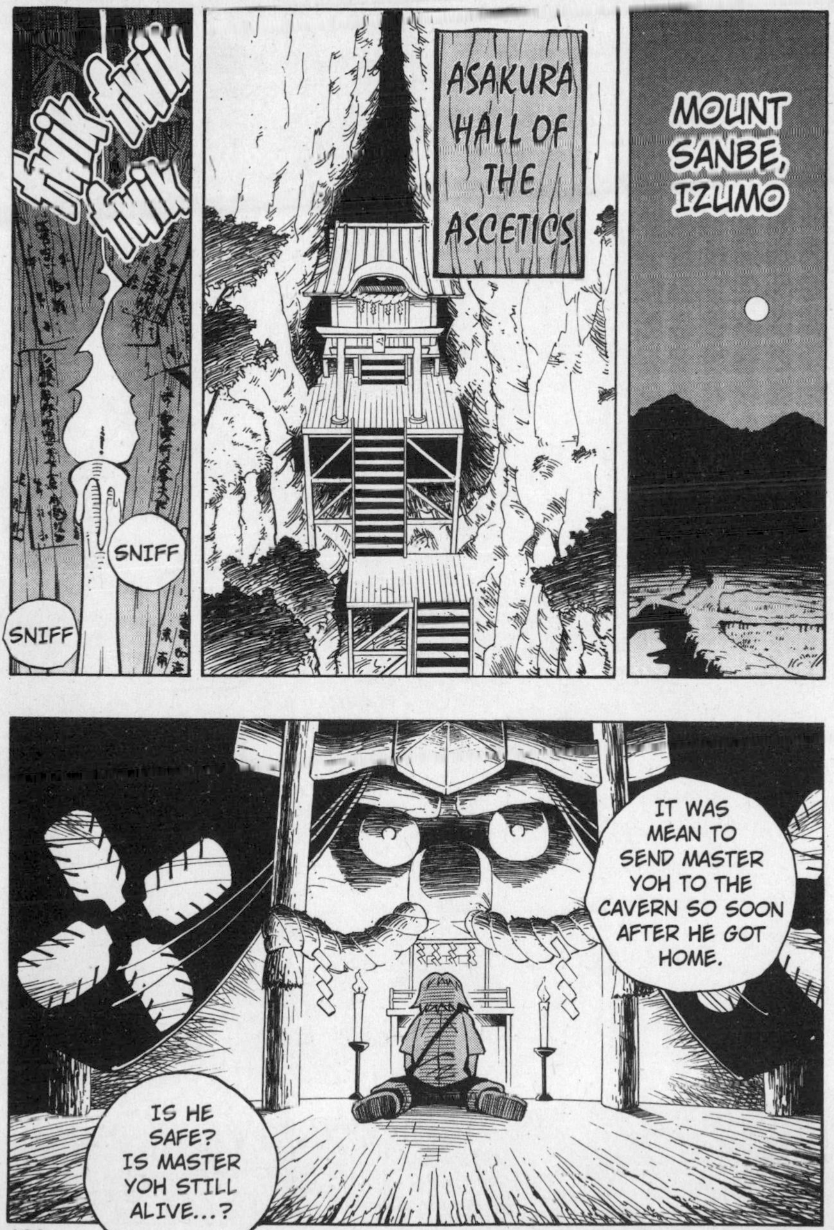
MOUNT SANBE, IZUMO
ASAKURA HALL OF THE ASCETICS
fwik fwik fwik
SNIFF
SNIFF
IT WAS MEAN TO SEND MASTER YOH TO THE CAVERN SO SOON AFTER HE GOT HOME.
IS HE SAFE? IS MASTER YOH STILL ALIVE...?

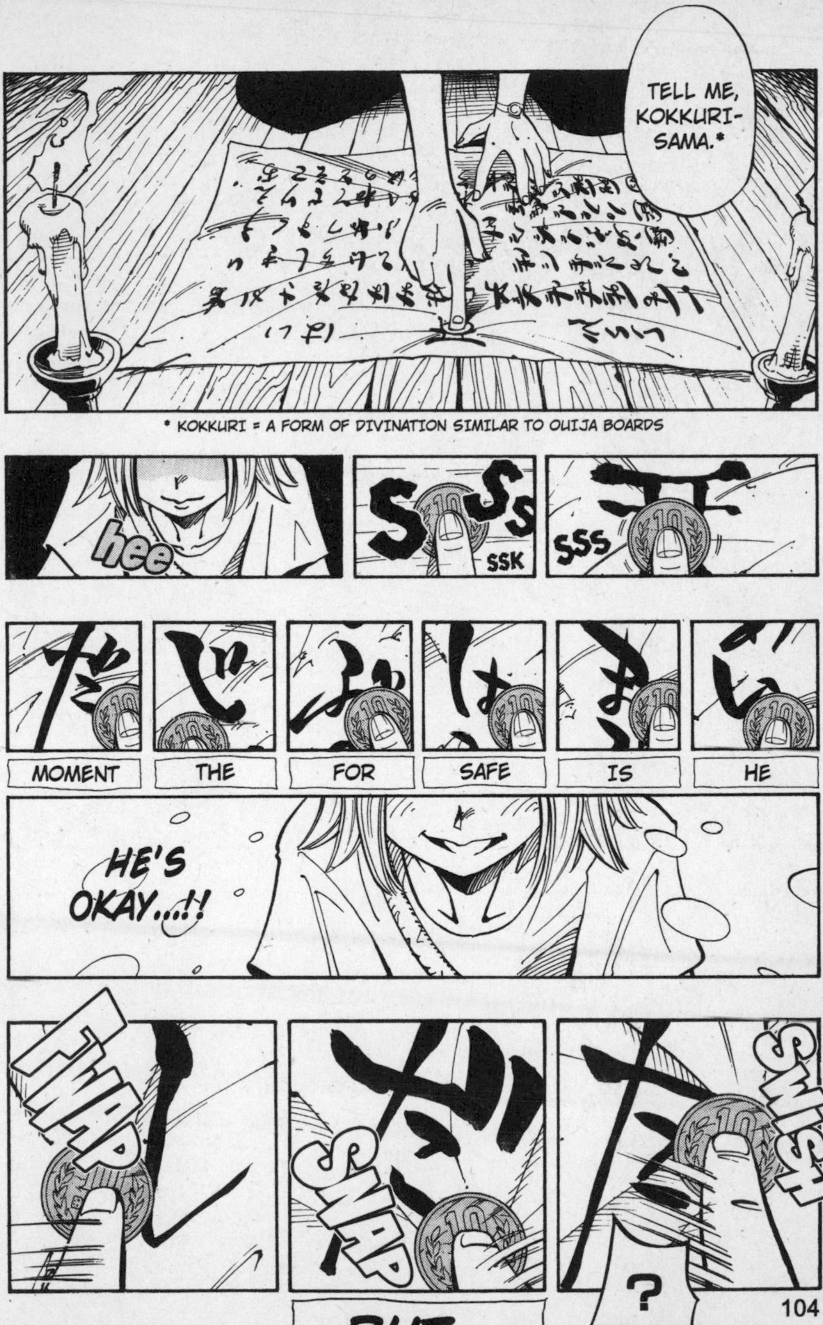
TELL ME, KOKKURI-SAMA.*
* KOKKURI = A FORM OF DIVINATION SIMILAR TO OUIJA BOARDS
SSS
S
S
S
SSK
hee
HE
IS
SAFE
FOR
THE
MOMENT
HE'S OKAY...!!
SWISH
?
SNAP
FWAP
BUT...

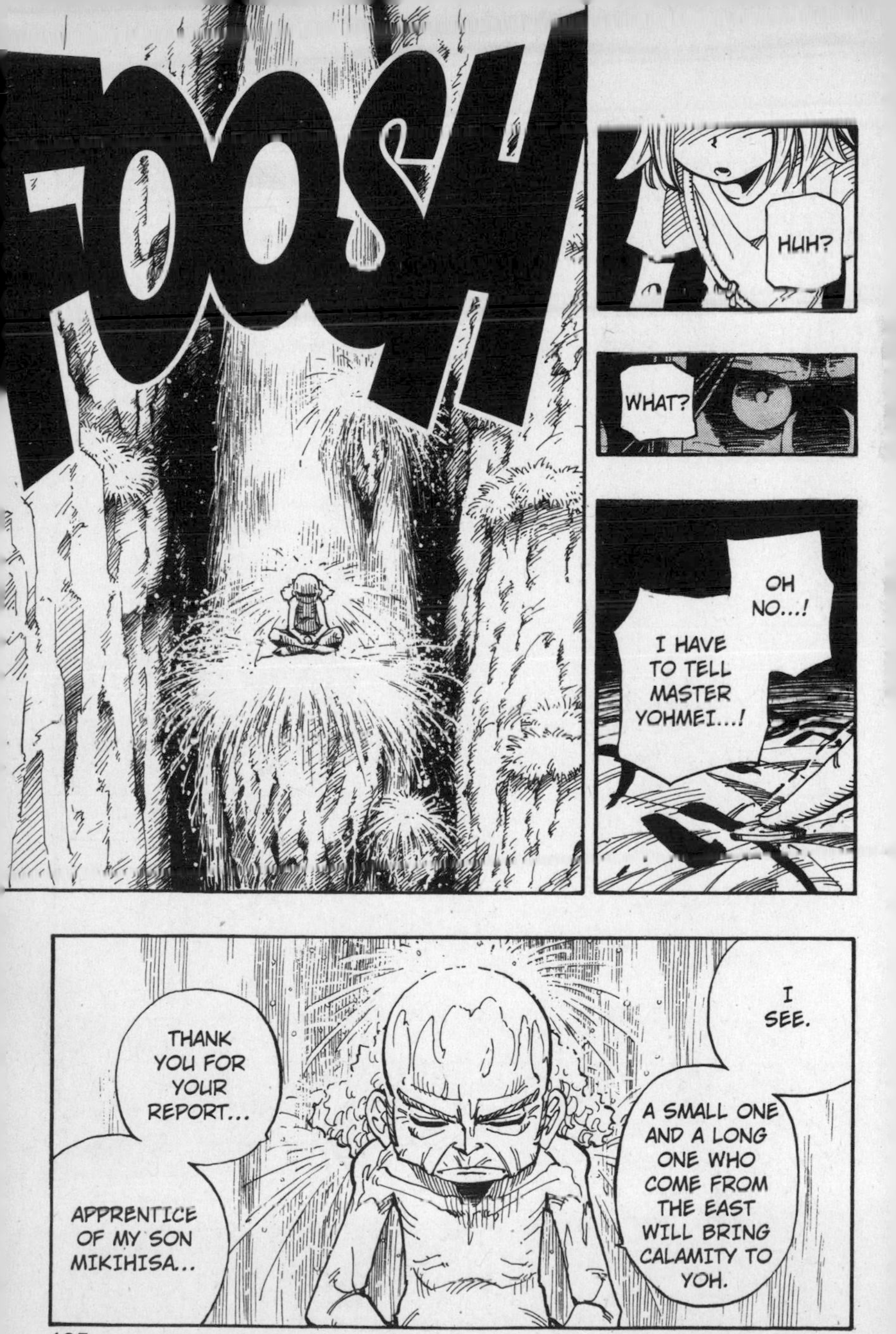
HUH?
WHAT?
OH NO...!
I HAVE TO TELL MASTER YOHMEI...!
FOOSH!!
I SEE.
A SMALL ONE AND A LONG ONE WHO COME FROM THE EAST WILL BRING CALAMITY TO YOH.
THANK YOU FOR YOUR REPORT...
APPRENTICE OF MY SON MIKIHISA...

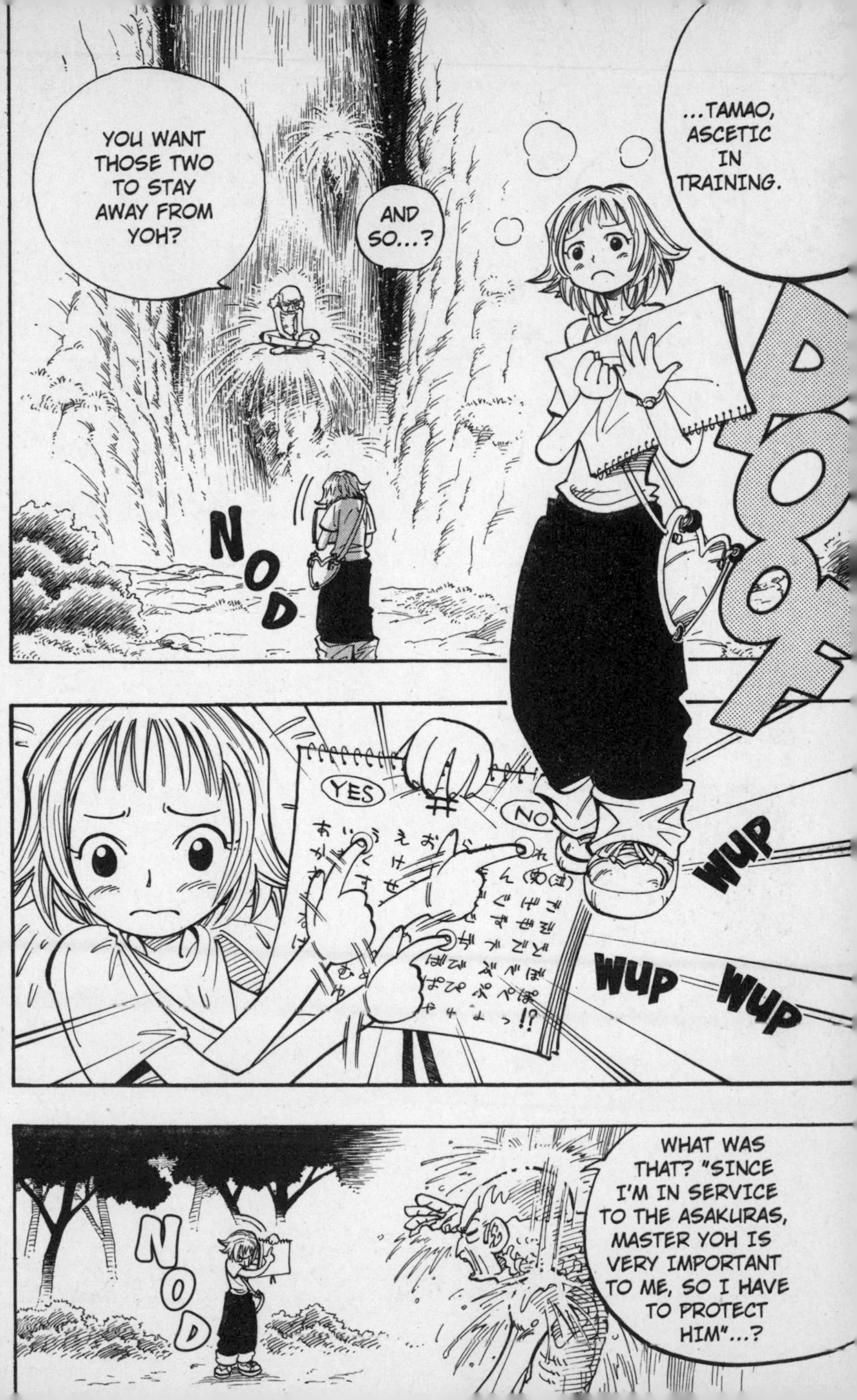
...TAMAO, ASCETIC IN TRAINING.
POOF
YOU WANT THOSE TWO TO STAY AWAY FROM YOH?
AND SO...?
NOD
YES
NO
WUP
WUP
WUP
WHAT WAS THAT? "SINCE I'M IN SERVICE TO THE ASAKURAS, MASTER YOH IS VERY IMPORTANT TO ME, SO I HAVE TO PROTECT HIM"...?
NOD

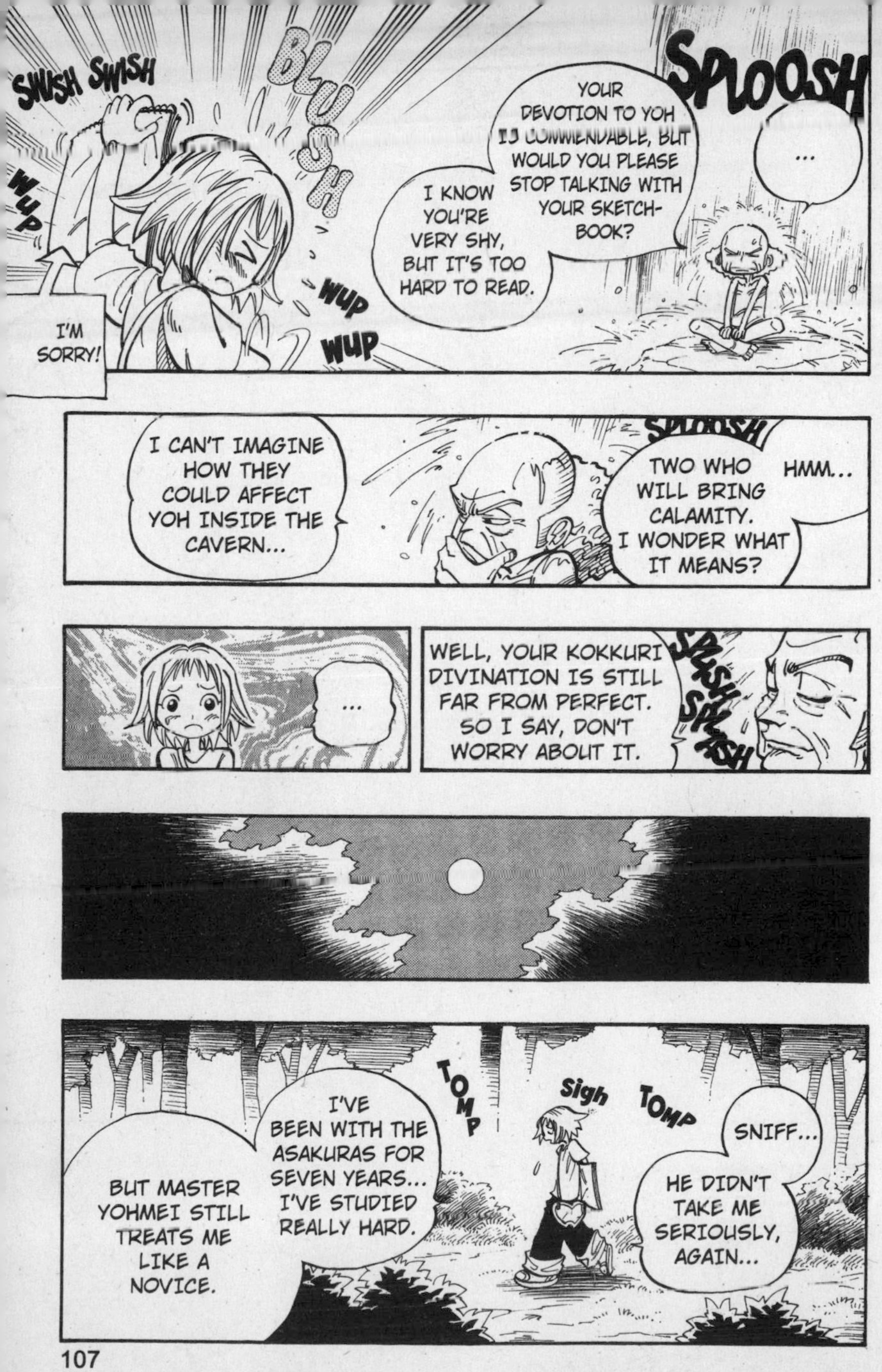
SPLOOSH
...
YOUR DEVOTION TO YOH IS COMMENDABLE, BUT WOULD YOU PLEASE STOP TALKING WITH YOUR SKETCHBOOK?
I KNOW YOU'RE VERY SHY, BUT IT'S TOO HARD TO READ.
BLUSH
SWISH SWISH
WUP
WUP
WUP
I'M SORRY!
SPLOOSH
HMM...
TWO WHO WILL BRING CALAMITY. I WONDER WHAT IT MEANS?
I CAN'T IMAGINE HOW THEY COULD AFFECT YOH INSIDE THE CAVERN...
SPLISH SPLISH
WELL, YOUR KOKKURI DIVINATION IS STILL FAR FROM PERFECT. SO I SAY, DON'T WORRY ABOUT IT.
...
SNIFF...
HE DIDN'T TAKE ME SERIOUSLY, AGAIN...
TOMP
Sigh
TOMP
I'VE BEEN WITH THE ASAKURAS FOR SEVEN YEARS... I'VE STUDIED REALLY HARD.
BUT MASTER YOHMEI STILL TREATS ME LIKE A NOVICE.

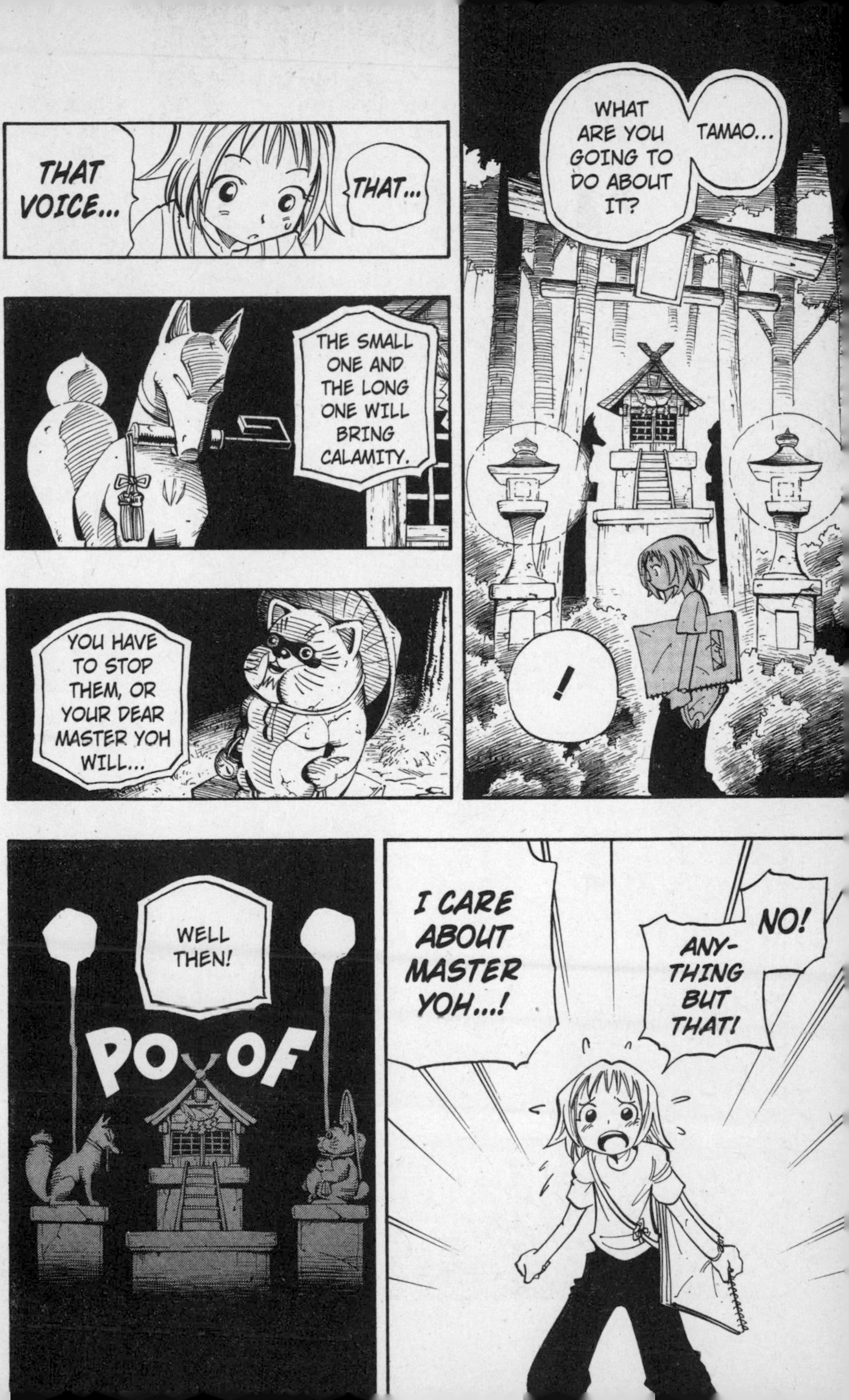
TAMAO...
WHAT ARE YOU GOING TO DO ABOUT IT?
!
THAT...
THAT VOICE...
THE SMALL ONE AND THE LONG ONE WILL BRING CALAMITY.
YOU HAVE TO STOP THEM, OR YOUR DEAR MASTER YOH WILL...
NO!
ANY-THING BUT THAT!
I CARE ABOUT MASTER YOH...!
WELL THEN!
POOF

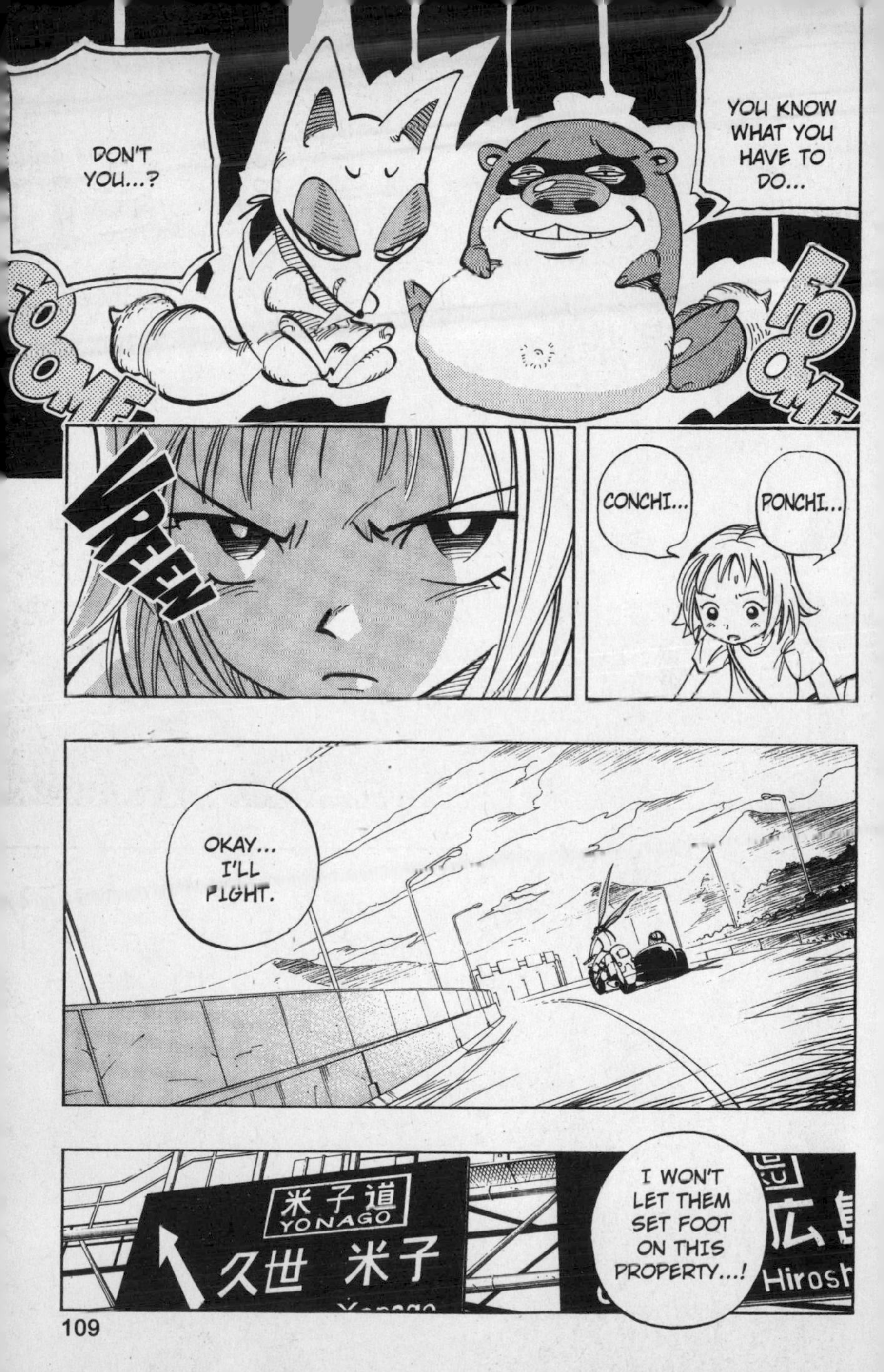
YOU KNOW WHAT YOU HAVE TO DO...
DON'T YOU...?
FOOMF
FOOMF
PONCHI...
CONCHI...
VREEN
OKAY... I'LL FIGHT.
I WON'T LET THEM SET FOOT ON THIS PROPERTY...!
米子道
YONAGO
久世 米子

SHAMAN
KING
**6**

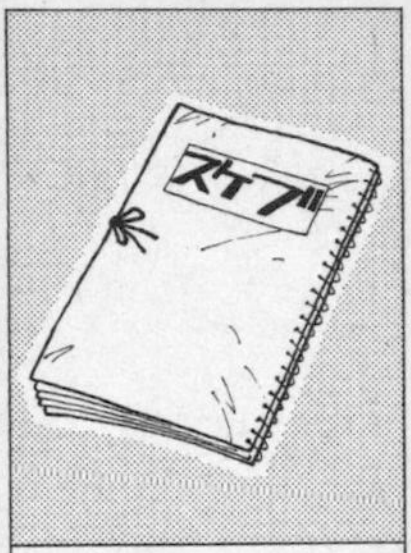
スケブ

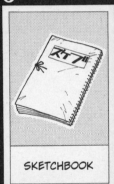

SKETCHBOOK

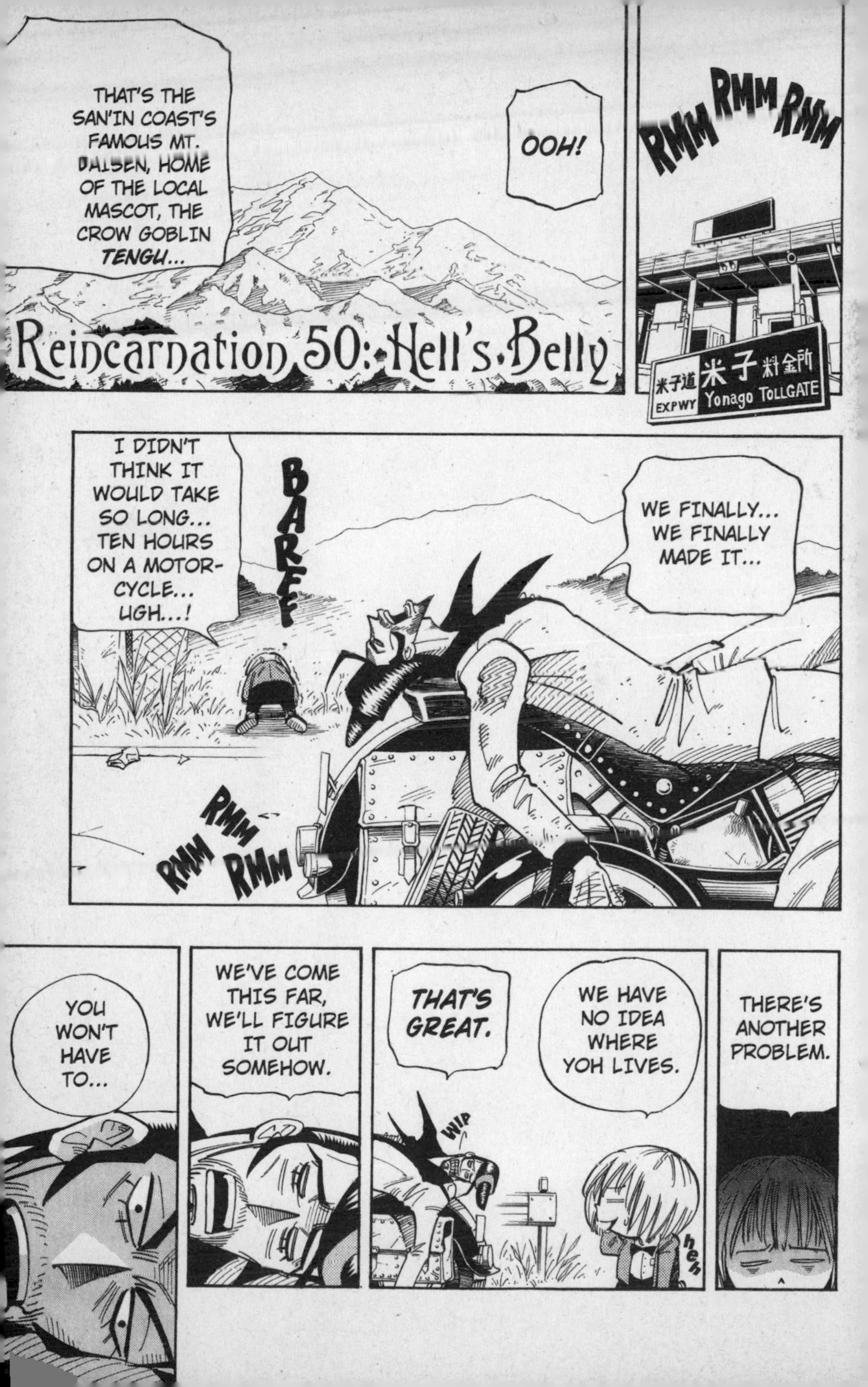
RMM RMM RMM
米子道
EXPWY
米子 料金所
Yonago TOLLGATE
OOH!
THAT'S THE SAN'IN COAST'S FAMOUS MT. DAISEN, HOME OF THE LOCAL MASCOT, THE CROW GOBLIN TENGU...
Reincarnation 50: Hell's Belly
WE FINALLY... WE FINALLY MADE IT...
BARFF
I DIDN'T THINK IT WOULD TAKE SO LONG... TEN HOURS ON A MOTOR-CYCLE... UGH...!
RMM RMM RMM
THERE'S ANOTHER PROBLEM.
WE HAVE NO IDEA WHERE YOH LIVES.
THAT'S GREAT.
WIP
WE'VE COME THIS FAR, WE'LL FIGURE IT OUT SOMEHOW.
YOU WON'T HAVE TO...

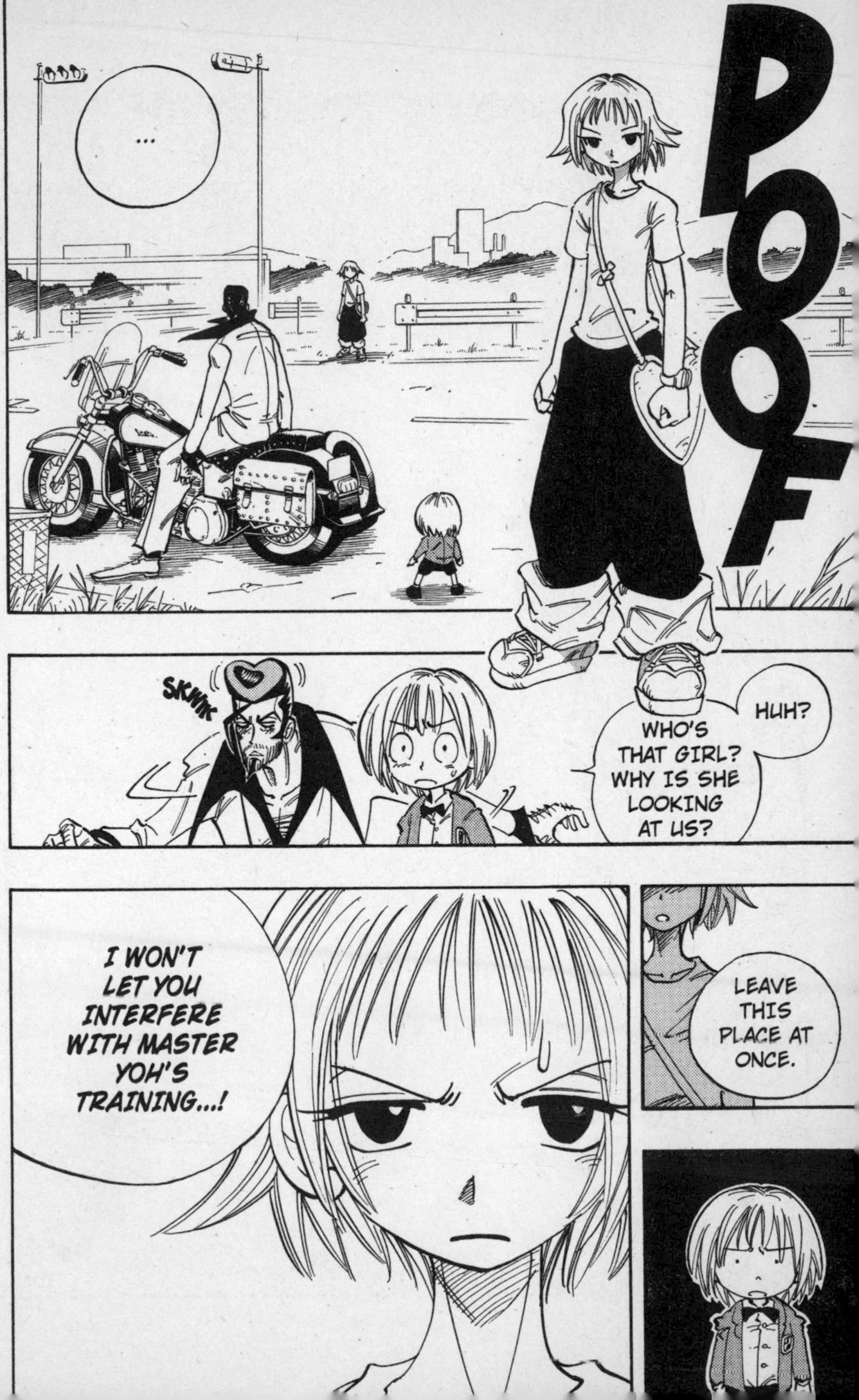
POOF
...
SKWIK
HUH?
WHO'S THAT GIRL? WHY IS SHE LOOKING AT US?
LEAVE THIS PLACE AT ONCE.
I WON'T LET YOU INTERFERE WITH MASTER YOH'S TRAINING...!

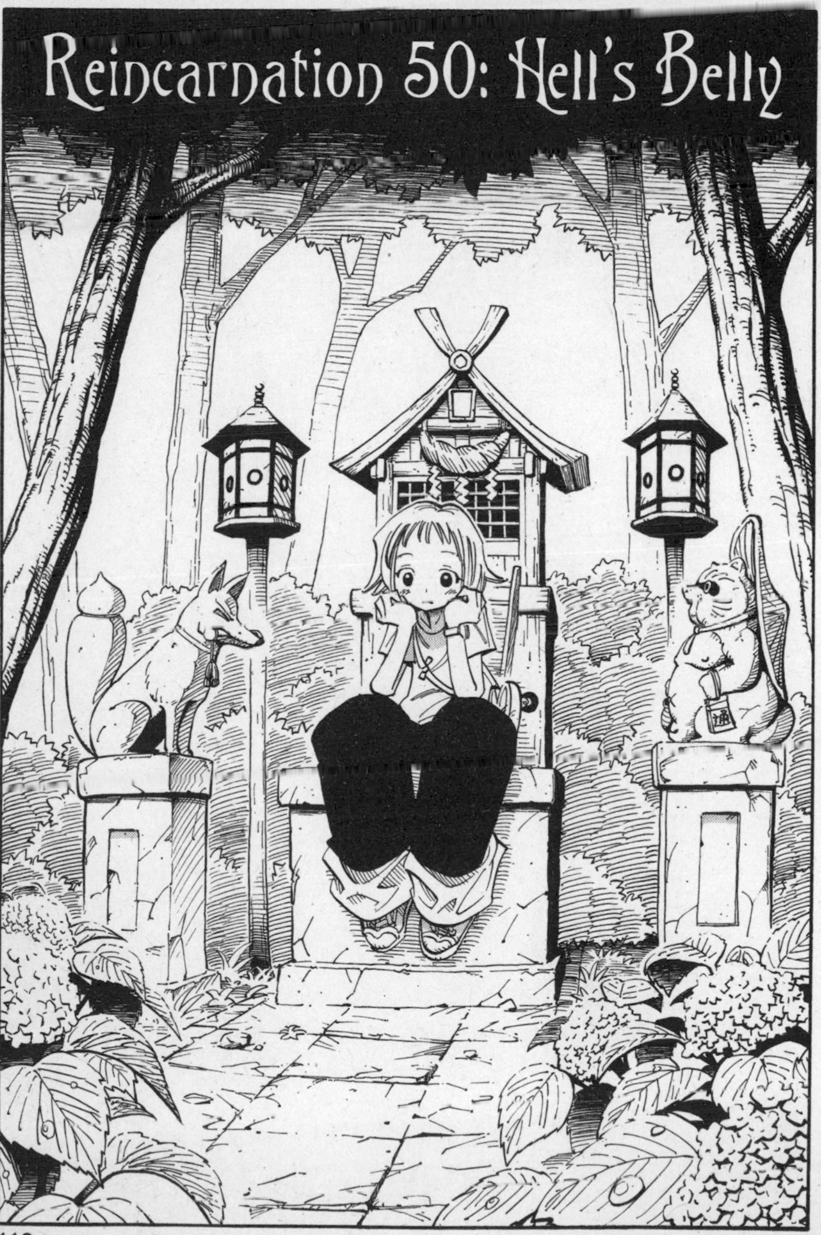
Reincarnation 50: Hell's Belly

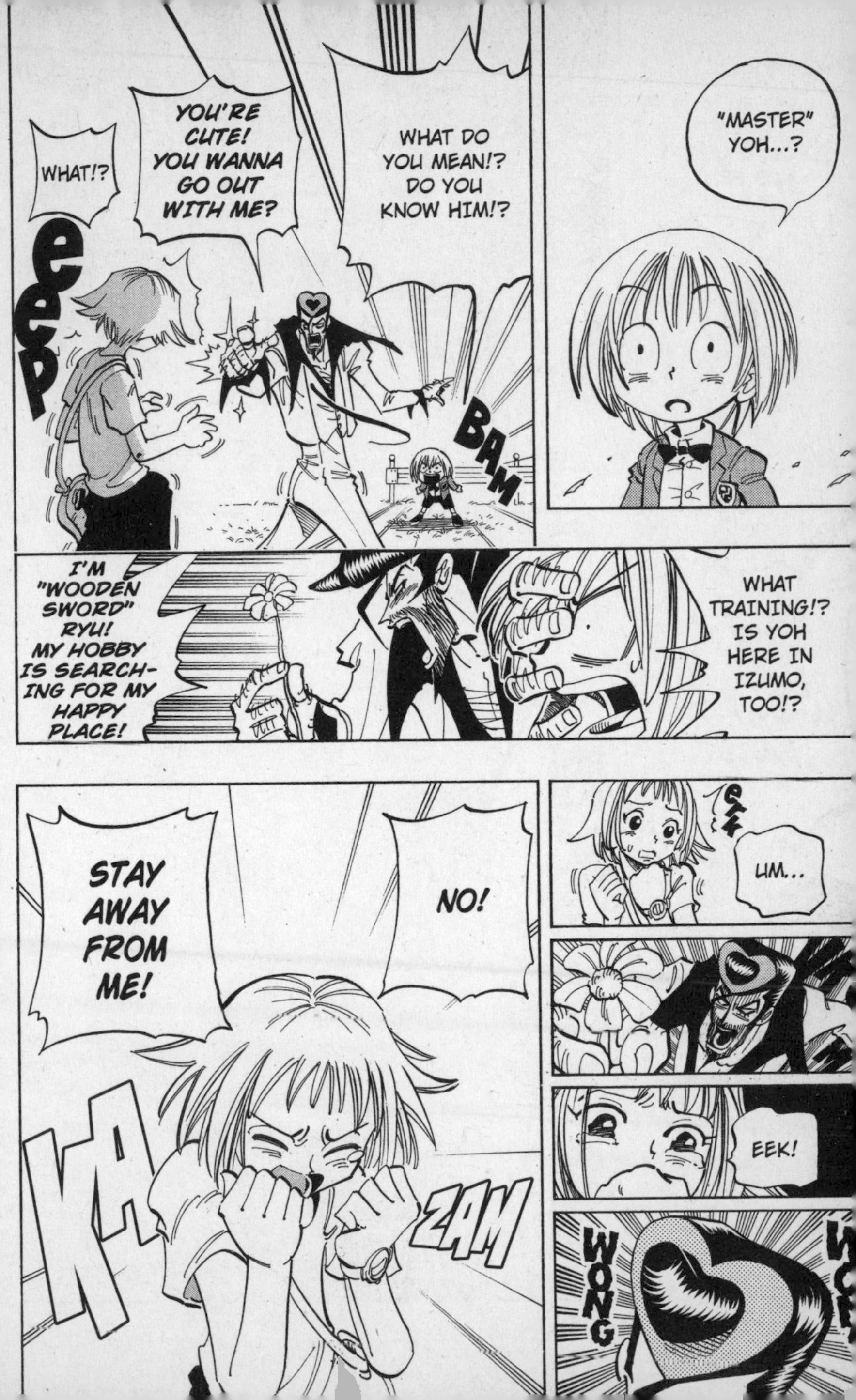

"MASTER" YOH...?
WHAT DO YOU MEAN!? DO YOU KNOW HIM!?
YOU'RE CUTE! YOU WANNA GO OUT WITH ME?
WHAT!?
BAM
PEEP
WHAT TRAINING!? IS YOH HERE IN IZUMO, TOO!?
I'M "WOODEN SWORD" RYU! MY HOBBY IS SEARCH-ING FOR MY HAPPY PLACE!
EEK
UM...
EEK!
WONG
WONG
NO!
STAY AWAY FROM ME!
ZAM
KA

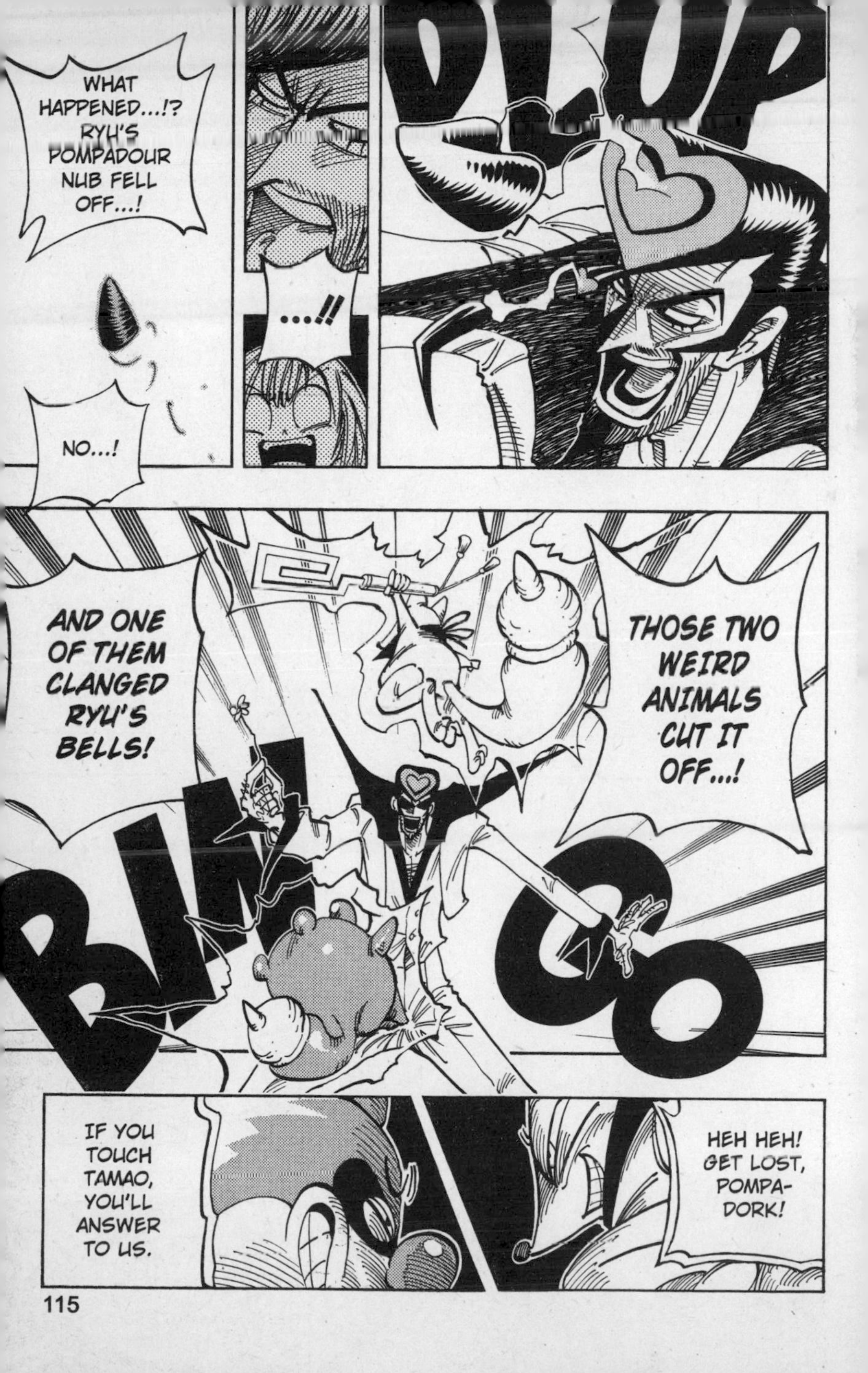
...!!
WHAT HAPPENED...!? RYU'S POMPADOUR NUB FELL OFF...!
NO...!
THOSE TWO WEIRD ANIMALS CUT IT OFF...!
AND ONE OF THEM CLANGED RYU'S BELLS!
HEH HEH! GET LOST, POMPA-DORK!
IF YOU TOUCH TAMAO, YOU'LL ANSWER TO US.

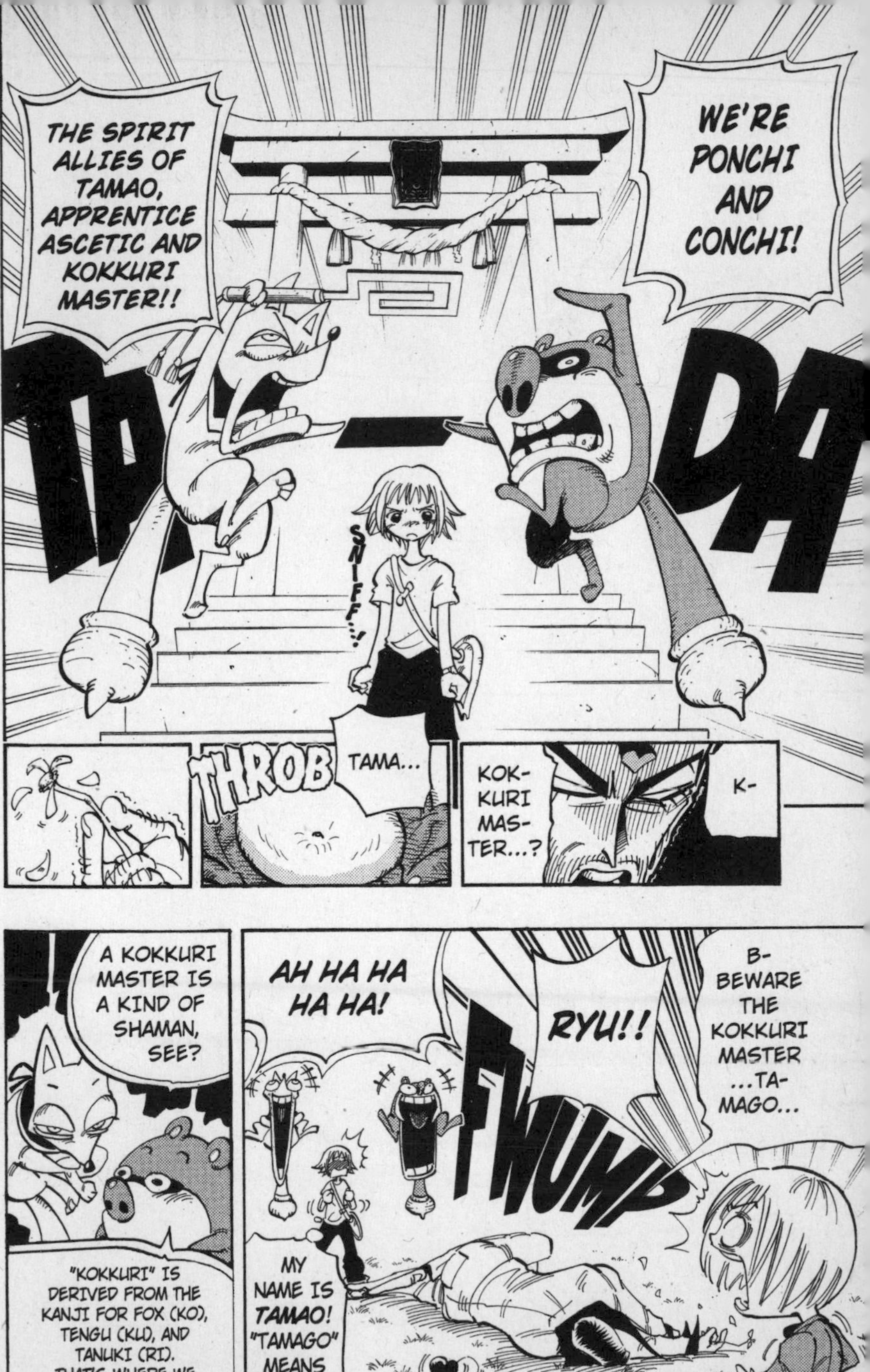
WE'RE PONCHI AND CONCHI!
THE SPIRIT ALLIES OF TAMAO, APPRENTICE ASCETIC AND KOKKURI MASTER!!
DA — DA
SNIFF...!
K-
KOK-KURI MAS-TER...?
TAMA...
THROB
B-BEWARE THE KOKKURI MASTER ...TA-MAGO...
RYU!!
FWUMP
AH HA HA HA HA!
MY NAME IS TAMAO! "TAMAGO" MEANS "EGG"...!
TUMBLE
A KOKKURI MASTER IS A KIND OF SHAMAN, SEE?
"KOKKURI" IS DERIVED FROM THE KANJI FOR FOX (KO), TENGU (KU), AND TANUKI (RI). THAT'S WHERE WE GET OUR POWERS!

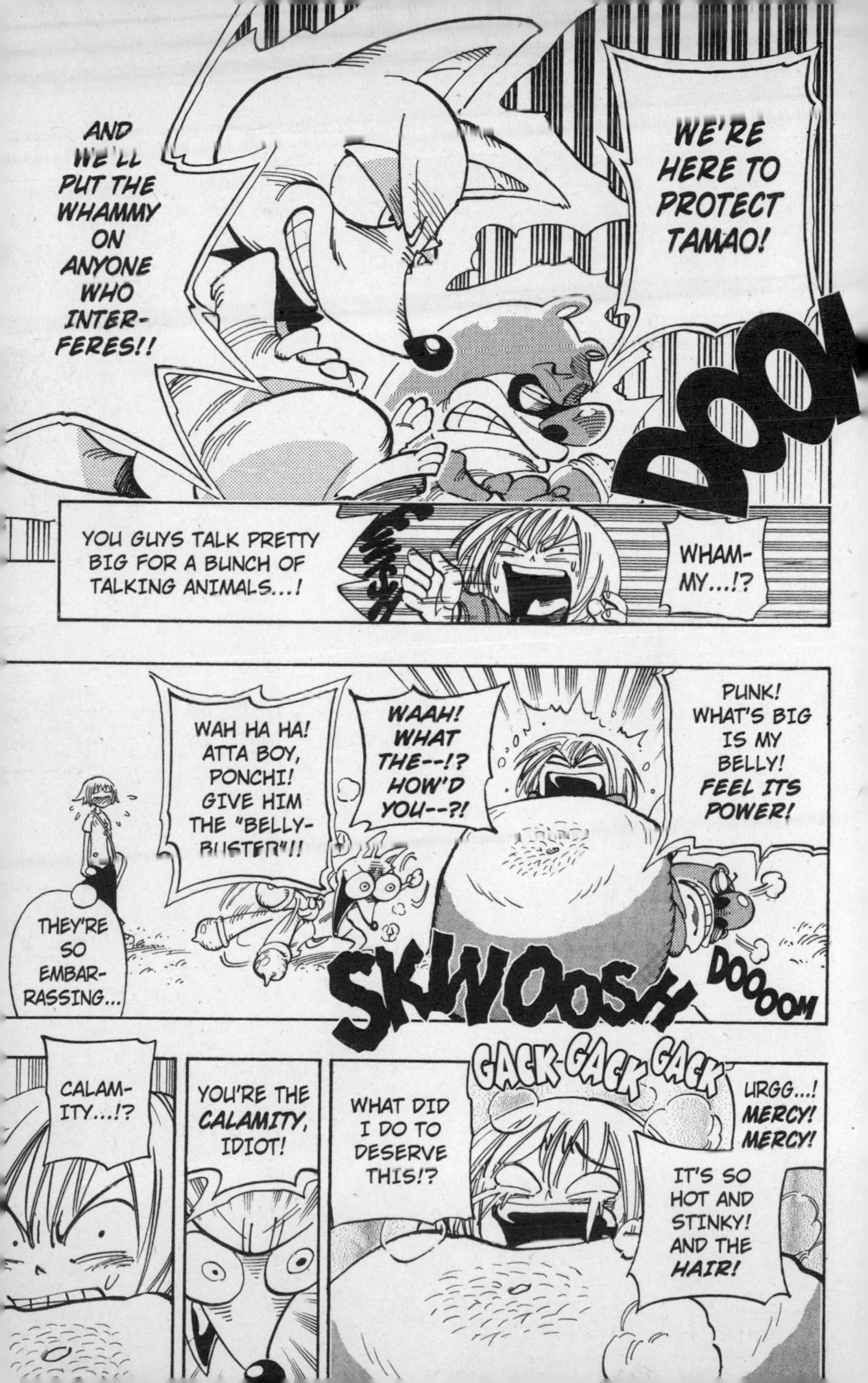
WE'RE HERE TO PROTECT TAMAO!
AND WE'LL PUT THE WHAMMY ON ANYONE WHO INTERFERES!!
WHAMMY...!?
YOU GUYS TALK PRETTY BIG FOR A BUNCH OF TALKING ANIMALS...!
PUNK! WHAT'S BIG IS MY BELLY! FEEL ITS POWER!
WAAH! WHAT THE--!? HOW'D YOU--?!
WAH HA HA! ATTA BOY, PONCHI! GIVE HIM THE "BELLY-BUSTER"!!
THEY'RE SO EMBARRASSING...
SKWOOSH
DOOOOOM
GACK-GACK GACK
URGG...! MERCY! MERCY!
IT'S SO HOT AND STINKY! AND THE HAIR!
WHAT DID I DO TO DESERVE THIS!?
YOU'RE THE CALAMITY, IDIOT!
CALAMITY...!?

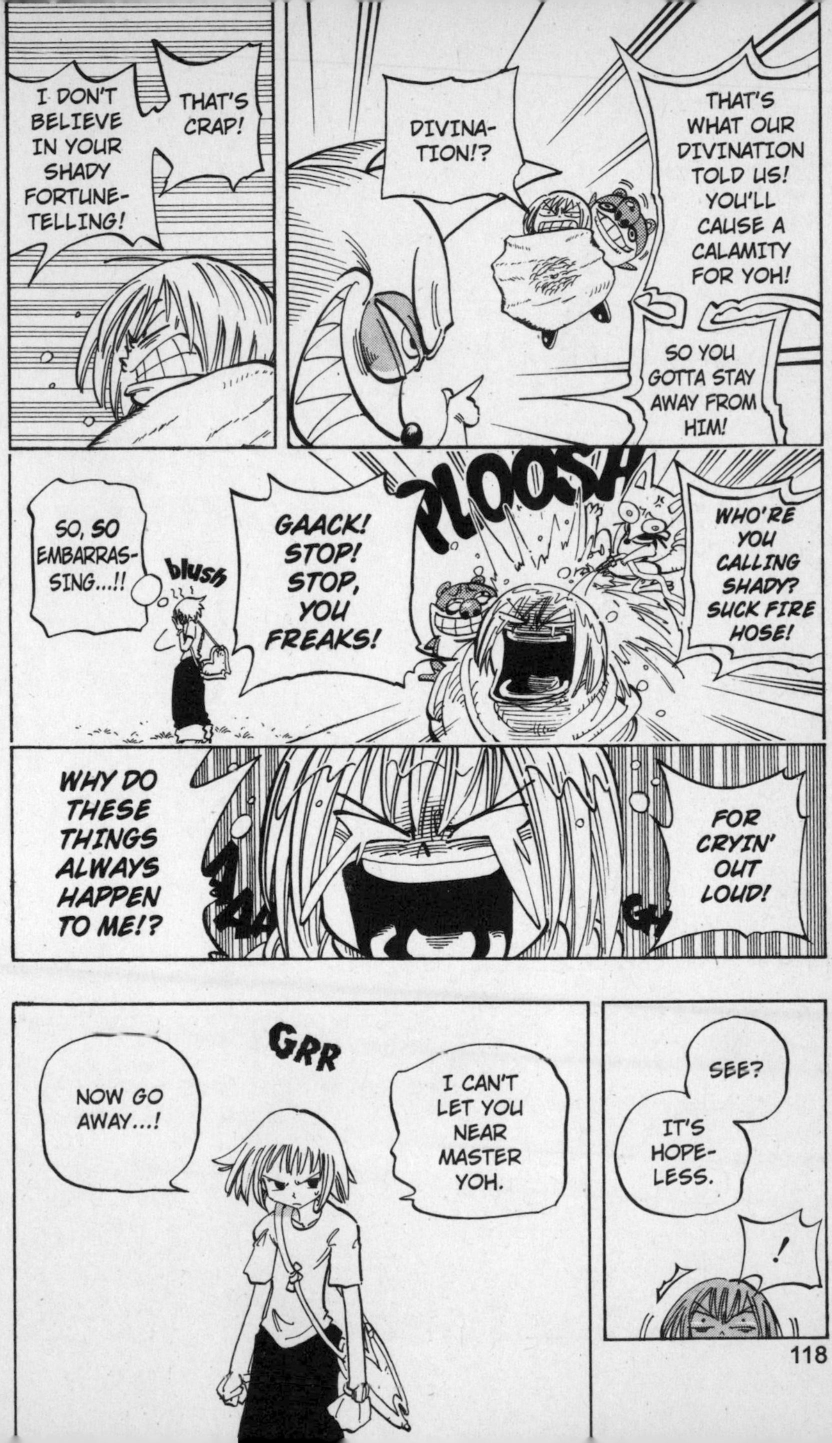
THAT'S WHAT OUR DIVINATION TOLD US! YOU'LL CAUSE A CALAMITY FOR YOH!
DIVINATION!?
SO YOU GOTTA STAY AWAY FROM HIM!
THAT'S CRAP!
I DON'T BELIEVE IN YOUR SHADY FORTUNE-TELLING!
WHO'RE YOU CALLING SHADY? SUCK FIRE HOSE!
PLOOSH
GAACK! STOP! STOP, YOU FREAKS!
SO, SO EMBARRASSING...!!
blush
FOR CRYIN' OUT LOUD!
GH
AAA
WHY DO THESE THINGS ALWAYS HAPPEN TO ME!?
SEE?
IT'S HOPELESS.
!
I CAN'T LET YOU NEAR MASTER YOH.
GRR
NOW GO AWAY...!

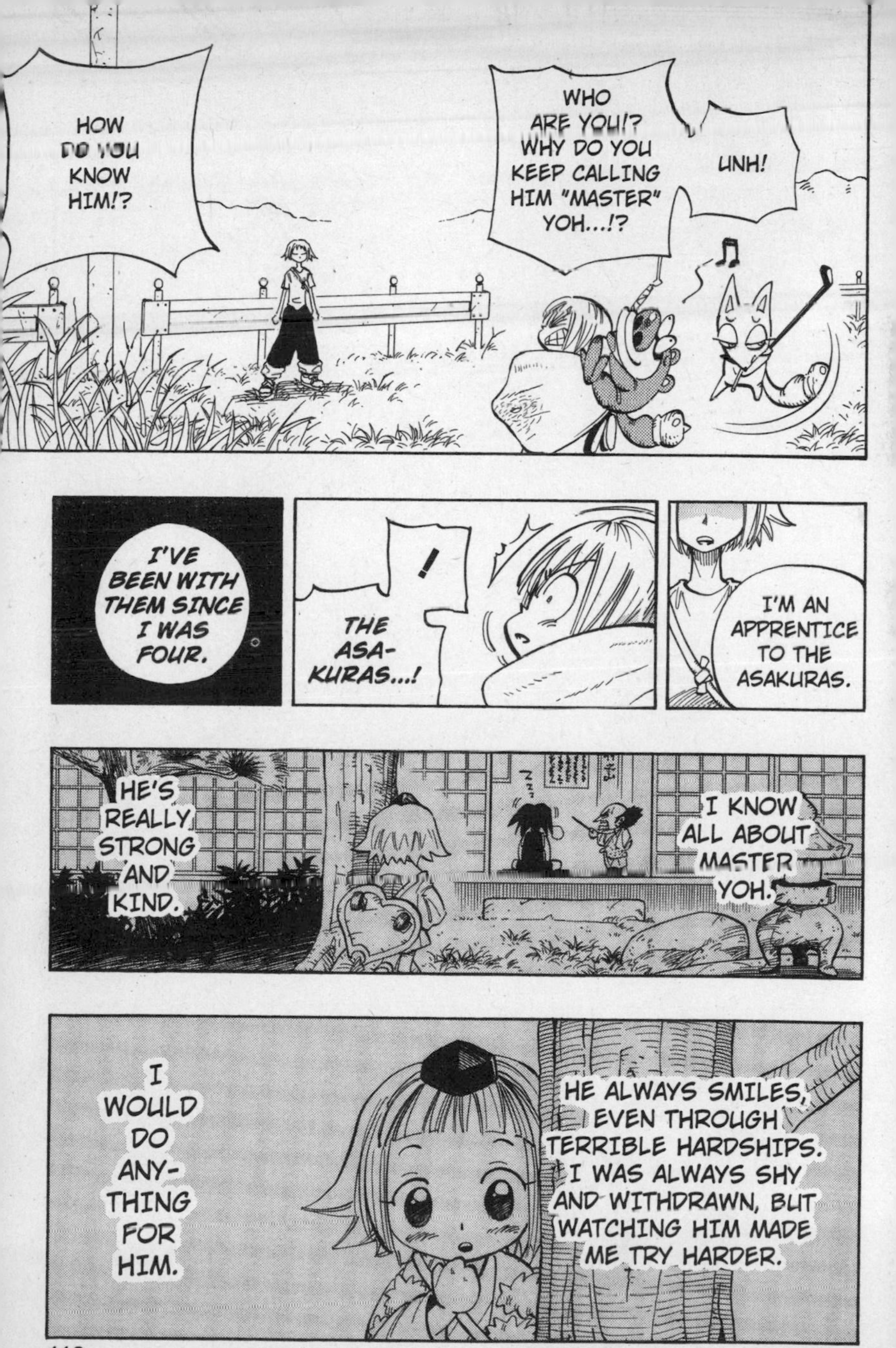

UNH!
WHO ARE YOU!? WHY DO YOU KEEP CALLING HIM "MASTER" YOH...!?
HOW DO YOU KNOW HIM!?
I'M AN APPRENTICE TO THE ASAKURAS.
!
THE ASA-KURAS...!
I'VE BEEN WITH THEM SINCE I WAS FOUR.
I KNOW ALL ABOUT MASTER YOH.
HE'S REALLY STRONG AND KIND.
HE ALWAYS SMILES, EVEN THROUGH TERRIBLE HARDSHIPS. I WAS ALWAYS SHY AND WITHDRAWN, BUT WATCHING HIM MADE ME TRY HARDER.
I WOULD DO ANY-THING FOR HIM.

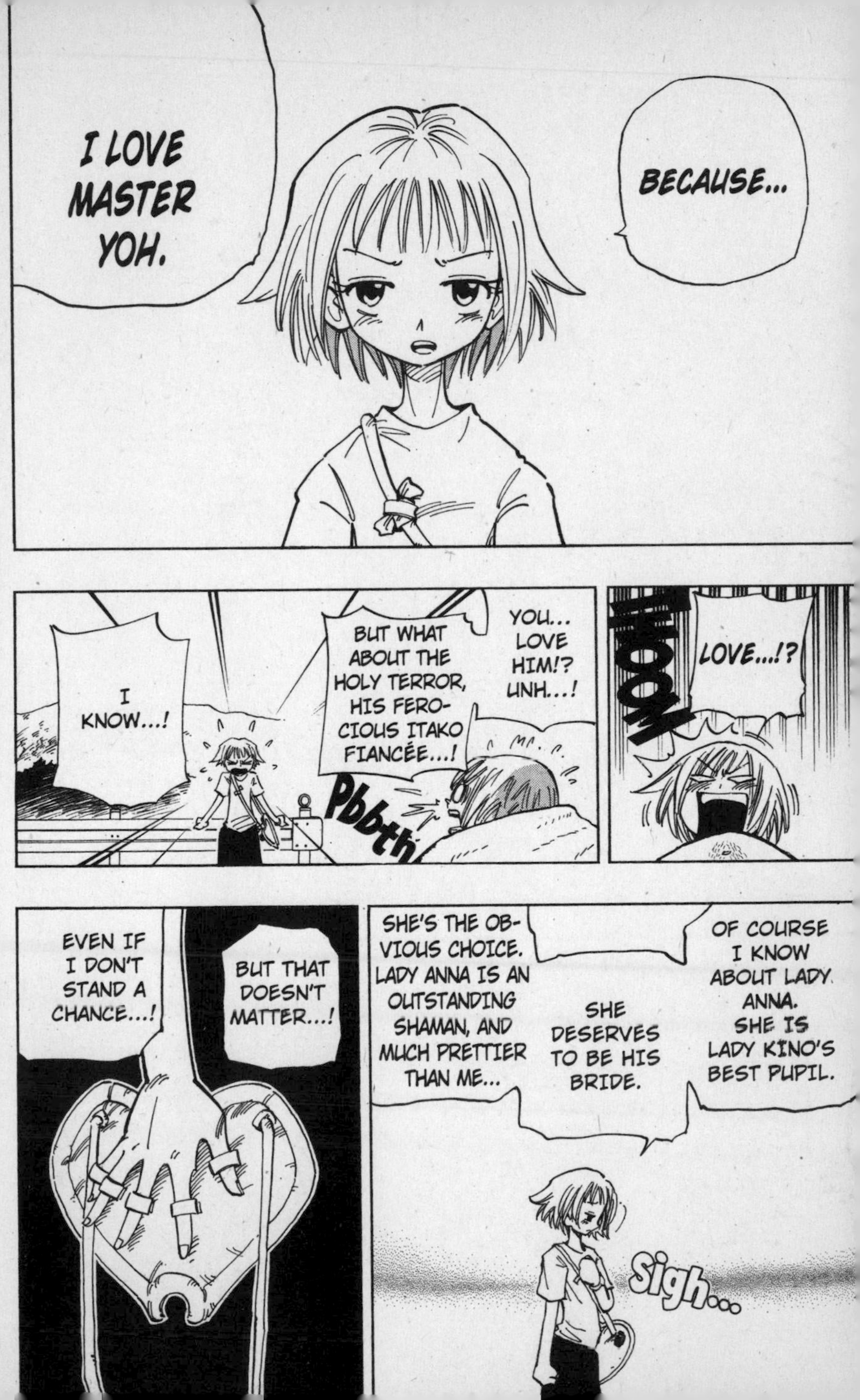
BECAUSE...
I LOVE MASTER YOH.
WOOM
LOVE...!?
YOU... LOVE HIM!? UNH...!
BUT WHAT ABOUT THE HOLY TERROR, HIS FERO-CIOUS ITAKO FIANCÉE...!
Pbbth
I KNOW...!
OF COURSE I KNOW ABOUT LADY ANNA. SHE IS LADY KINO'S BEST PUPIL.
SHE DESERVES TO BE HIS BRIDE.
SHE'S THE OB-VIOUS CHOICE. LADY ANNA IS AN OUTSTANDING SHAMAN, AND MUCH PRETTIER THAN ME...
Sigh...
BUT THAT DOESN'T MATTER...!
EVEN IF I DON'T STAND A CHANCE...!

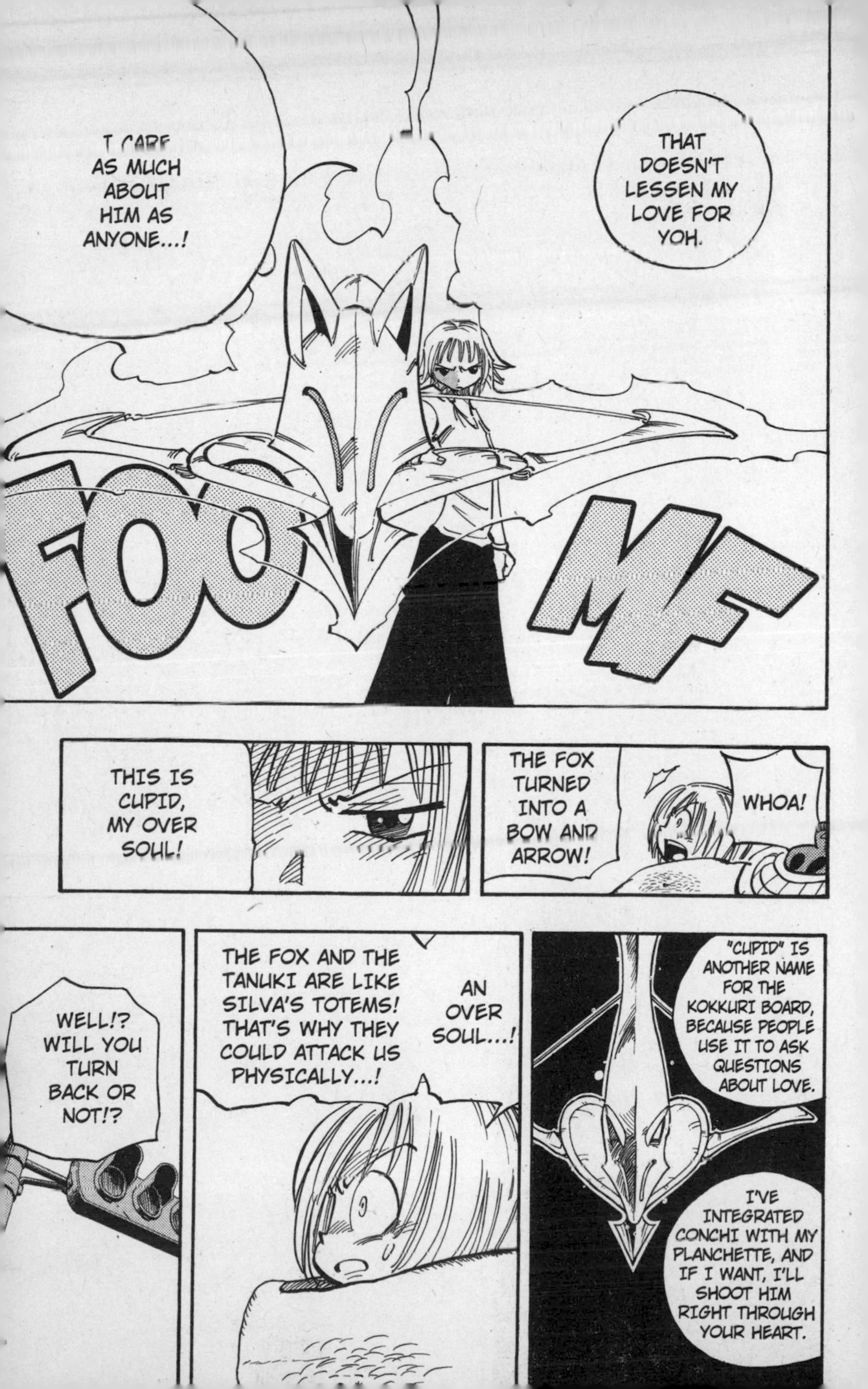
THAT DOESN'T LESSEN MY LOVE FOR YOH.
I CARE AS MUCH ABOUT HIM AS ANYONE...!
FOOMF
WHOA!
THE FOX TURNED INTO A BOW AND ARROW!
THIS IS CUPID, MY OVER SOUL!
"CUPID" IS ANOTHER NAME FOR THE KOKKURI BOARD, BECAUSE PEOPLE USE IT TO ASK QUESTIONS ABOUT LOVE.
I'VE INTEGRATED CONCHI WITH MY PLANCHETTE, AND IF I WANT, I'LL SHOOT HIM RIGHT THROUGH YOUR HEART.
AN OVER SOUL...!
THE FOX AND THE TANUKI ARE LIKE SILVA'S TOTEMS! THAT'S WHY THEY COULD ATTACK US PHYSICALLY...!
WELL!? WILL YOU TURN BACK OR NOT!?

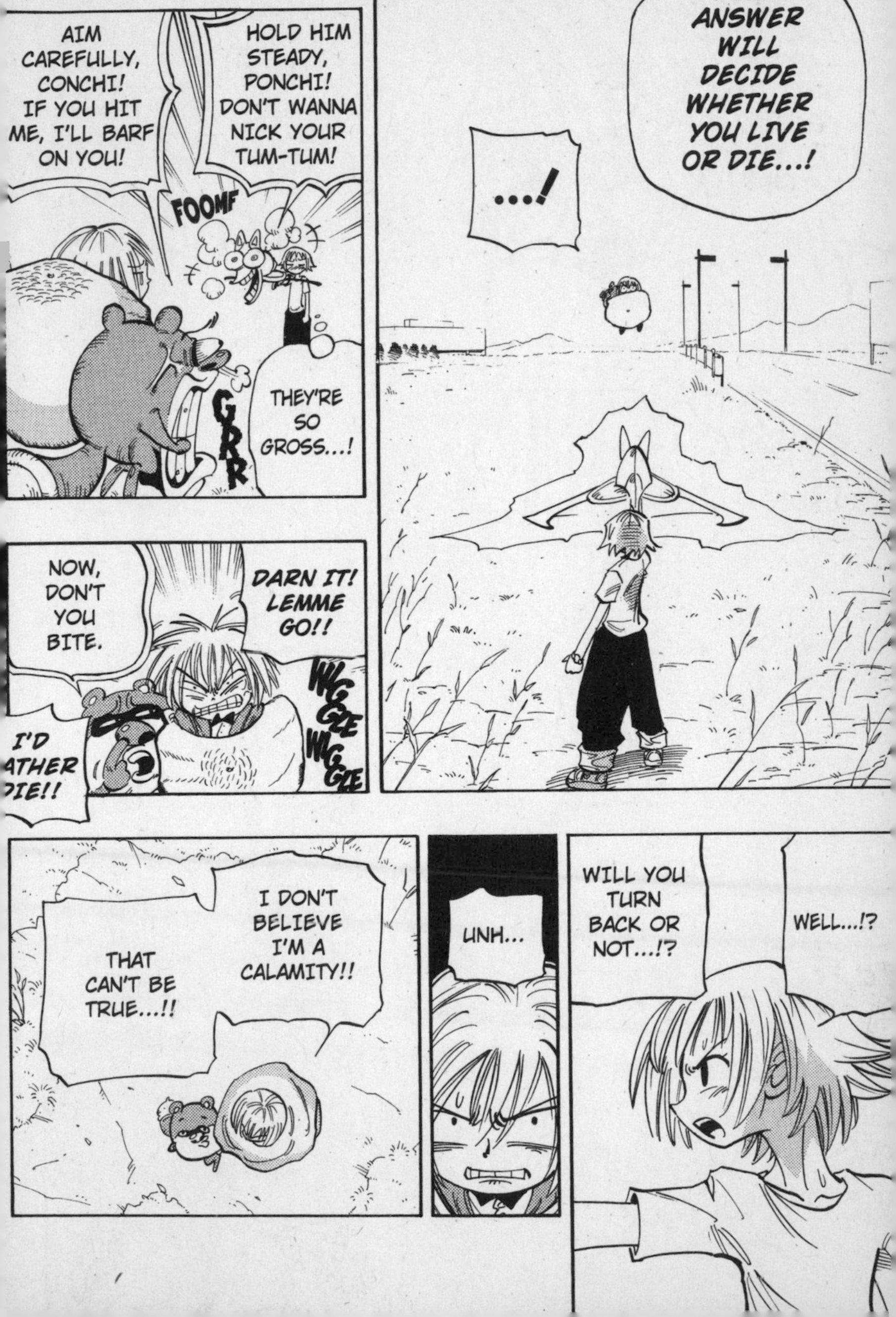
YOUR ANSWER WILL DECIDE WHETHER YOU LIVE OR DIE...!
...!
HOLD HIM STEADY, PONCHI! DON'T WANNA NICK YOUR TUM-TUM!
AIM CAREFULLY, CONCHI! IF YOU HIT ME, I'LL BARF ON YOU!
FOOMF
THEY'RE SO GROSS...!
GRR
DARN IT! LEMME GO!!
NOW, DON'T YOU BITE.
WIGGLE WIGGLE
I'D ATHER DIE!!
WELL...!?
WILL YOU TURN BACK OR NOT...!?
UNH...
I DON'T BELIEVE I'M A CALAMITY!!
THAT CAN'T BE TRUE...!!

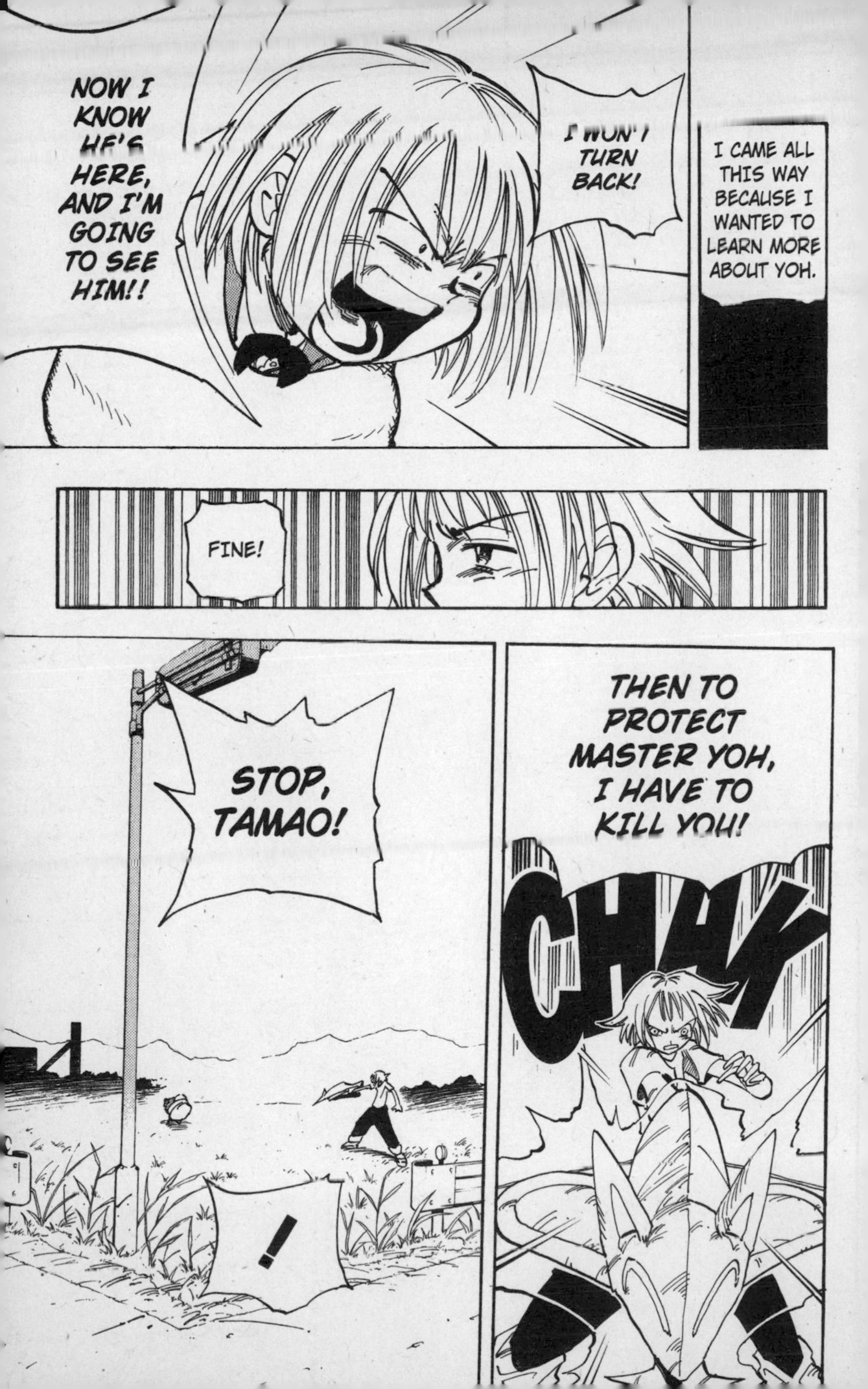
I CAME ALL THIS WAY BECAUSE I WANTED TO LEARN MORE ABOUT YOH.
I WON'T TURN BACK!
NOW I KNOW HE'S HERE, AND I'M GOING TO SEE HIM!!
FINE!
THEN TO PROTECT MASTER YOH, I HAVE TO KILL YOH!
CHK
STOP, TAMAO!
!

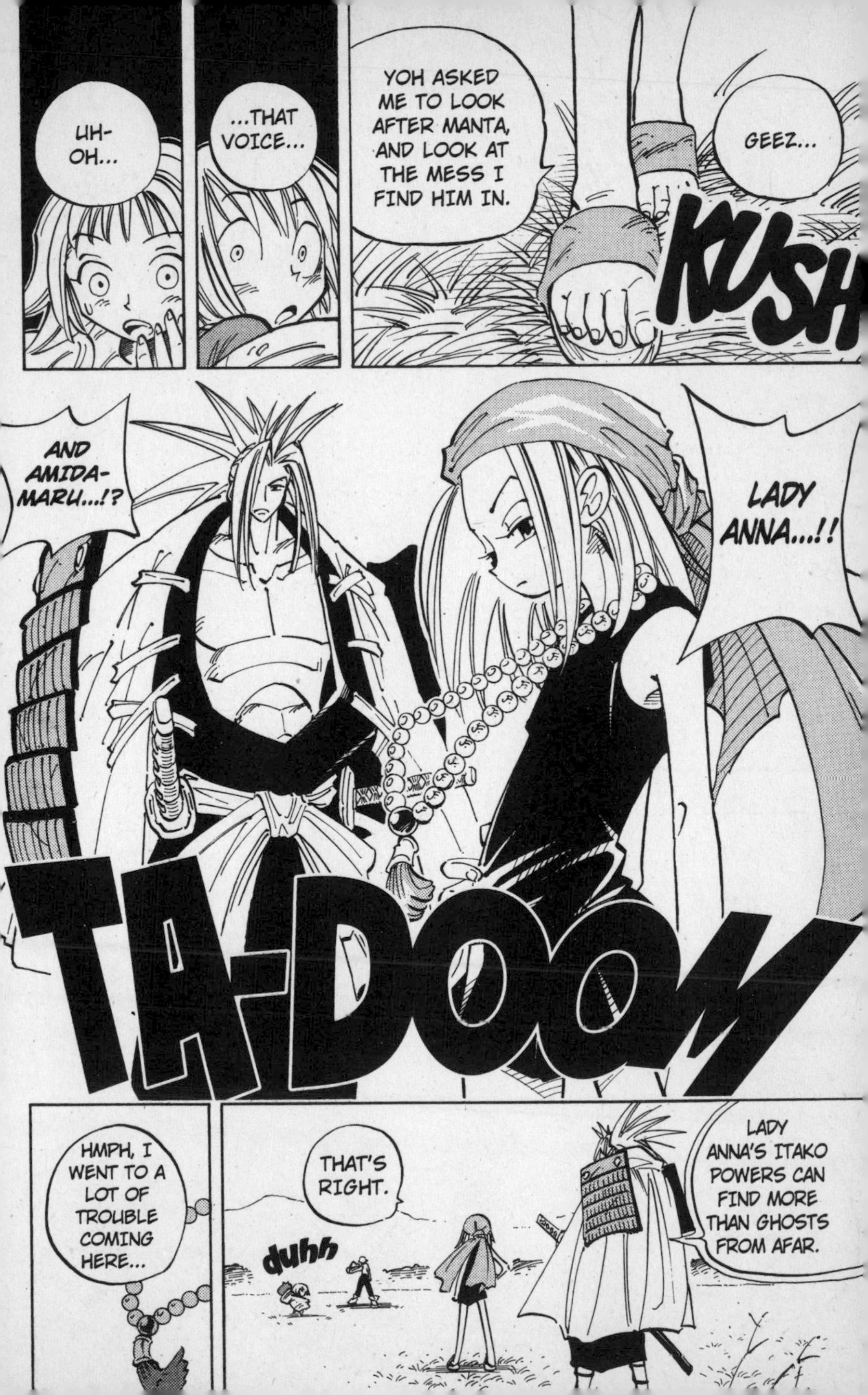
GEEZ...
KUSH
YOH ASKED ME TO LOOK AFTER MANTA, AND LOOK AT THE MESS I FIND HIM IN.
...THAT VOICE...
UH-OH...
LADY ANNA...!!
AND AMIDA-MARU...!?
TA-DOOM
LADY ANNA'S ITAKO POWERS CAN FIND MORE THAN GHOSTS FROM AFAR.
THAT'S RIGHT.
duhh
HMPH, I WENT TO A LOT OF TROUBLE COMING HERE...

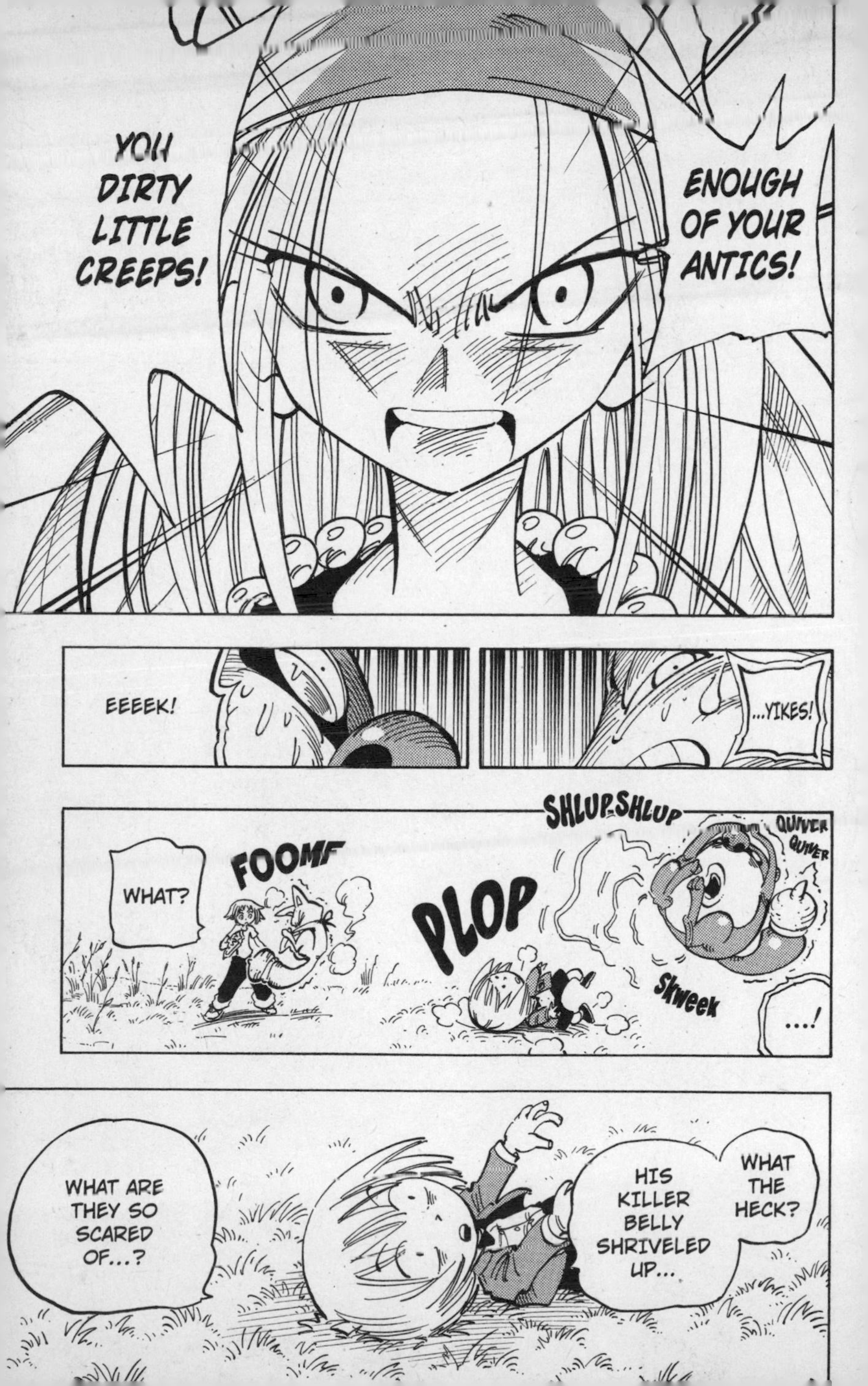
ENOUGH OF YOUR ANTICS!
YOU DIRTY LITTLE CREEPS!
...YIKES!
EEEEK!
QUIVER QUIVER
SHLUP SHLUP
...!
Skweek
PLOP
FOOMF
WHAT?
WHAT THE HECK?
HIS KILLER BELLY SHRIVELED UP...
WHAT ARE THEY SO SCARED OF...?

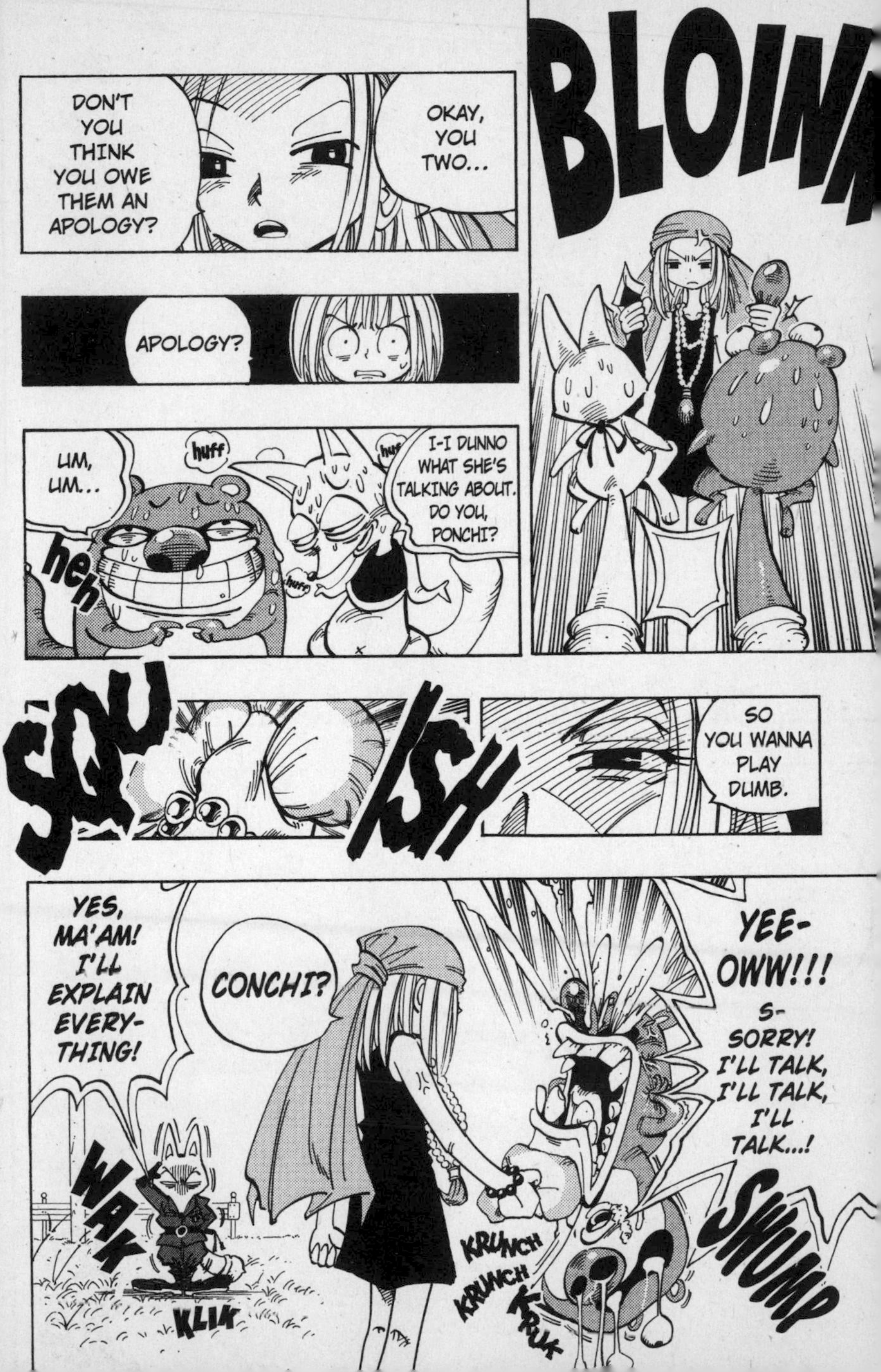
BLOINK
OKAY, YOU TWO...
DON'T YOU THINK YOU OWE THEM AN APOLOGY?
APOLOGY?
I-I DUNNO WHAT SHE'S TALKING ABOUT. DO YOU, PONCHI?
huff
huff
UM, UM...
heh
SO YOU WANNA PLAY DUMB.
SQUISH
YEE-OWW!!!
S-SORRY! I'LL TALK, I'LL TALK, I'LL TALK...!
SHUMP
CONCHI?
YES, MA'AM! I'LL EXPLAIN EVERY-THING!
KRUNCH
KRUNCH
KRUK
WAK
KLIK

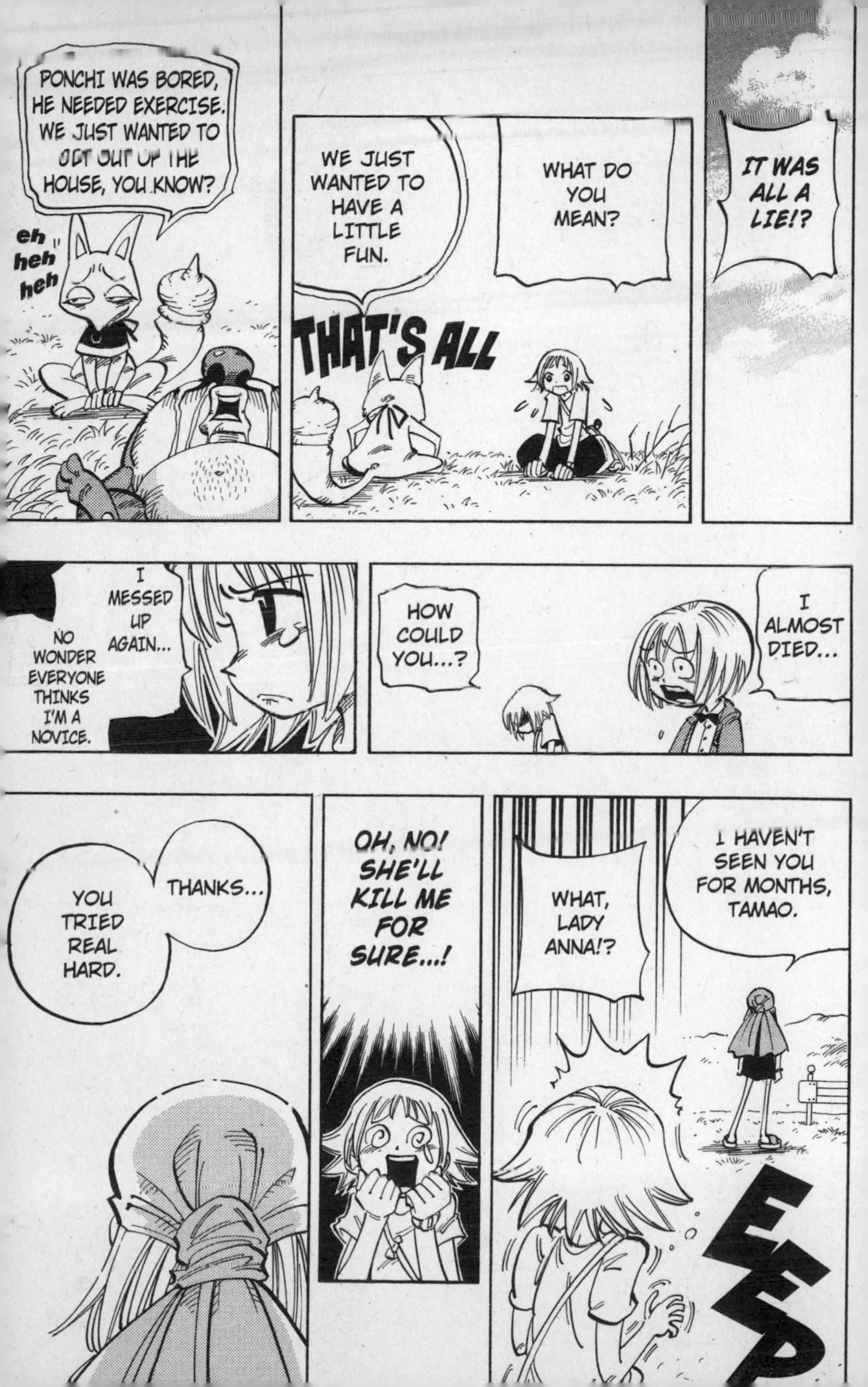
IT WAS ALL A LIE!?
WHAT DO YOU MEAN?
WE JUST WANTED TO HAVE A LITTLE FUN.
THAT'S ALL
PONCHI WAS BORED, HE NEEDED EXERCISE. WE JUST WANTED TO GET OUT OF THE HOUSE, YOU KNOW?
eh heh heh
I ALMOST DIED...
HOW COULD YOU...?
I MESSED UP AGAIN...
NO WONDER EVERYONE THINKS I'M A NOVICE.
I HAVEN'T SEEN YOU FOR MONTHS, TAMAO.
WHAT, LADY ANNA!?
EEP
OH, NO! SHE'LL KILL ME FOR SURE...!
THANKS...
YOU TRIED REAL HARD.

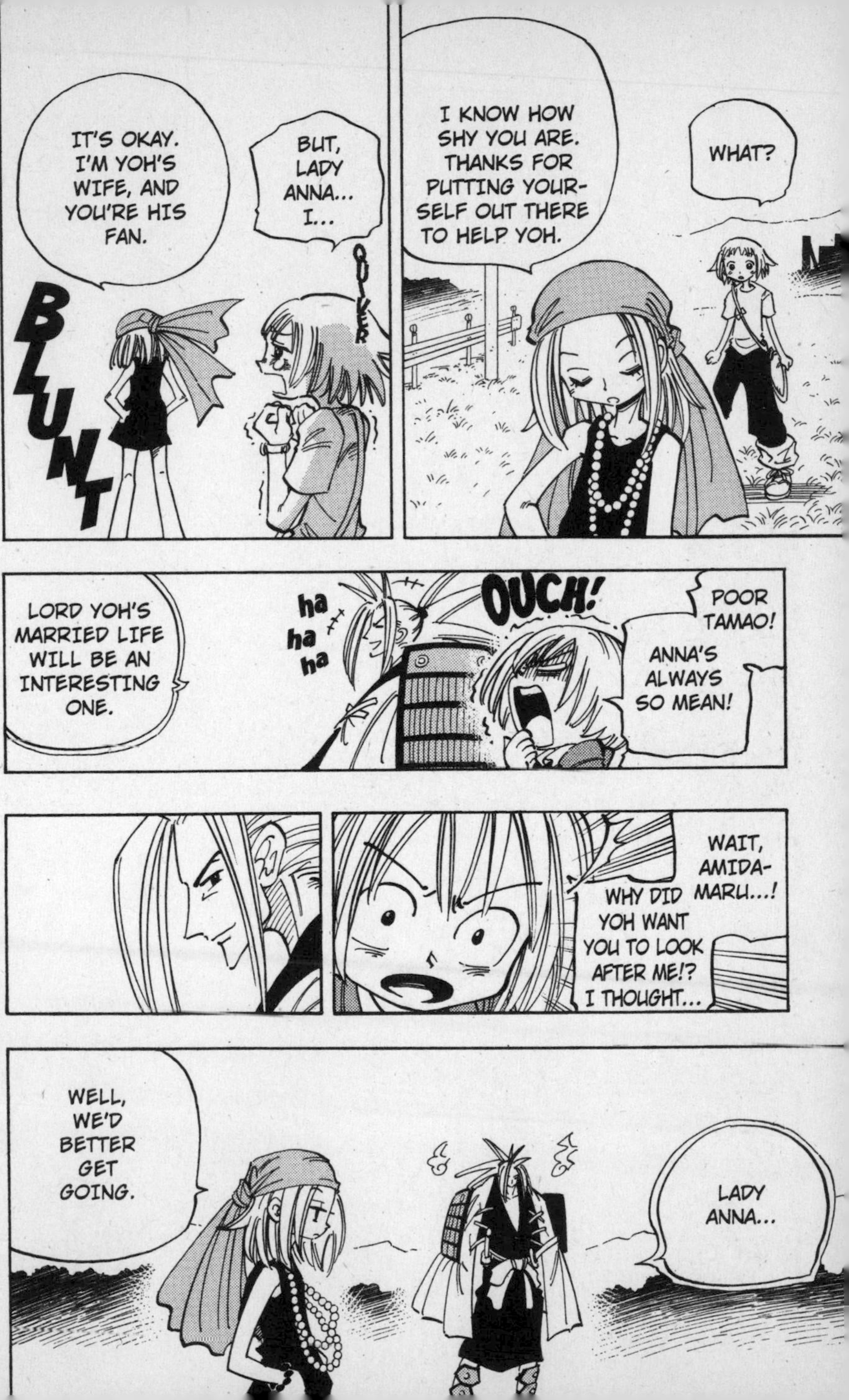
WHAT?
I KNOW HOW SHY YOU ARE. THANKS FOR PUTTING YOURSELF OUT THERE TO HELP YOH.
BUT, LADY ANNA... I...
QUIVER
IT'S OKAY. I'M YOH'S WIFE, AND YOU'RE HIS FAN.
BLUNT
POOR TAMAO!
ANNA'S ALWAYS SO MEAN!
OUCH!
ha ha ha
LORD YOH'S MARRIED LIFE WILL BE AN INTERESTING ONE.
WAIT, AMIDA-MARU...!
WHY DID YOH WANT YOU TO LOOK AFTER ME!? I THOUGHT...
LADY ANNA...
WELL, WE'D BETTER GET GOING.

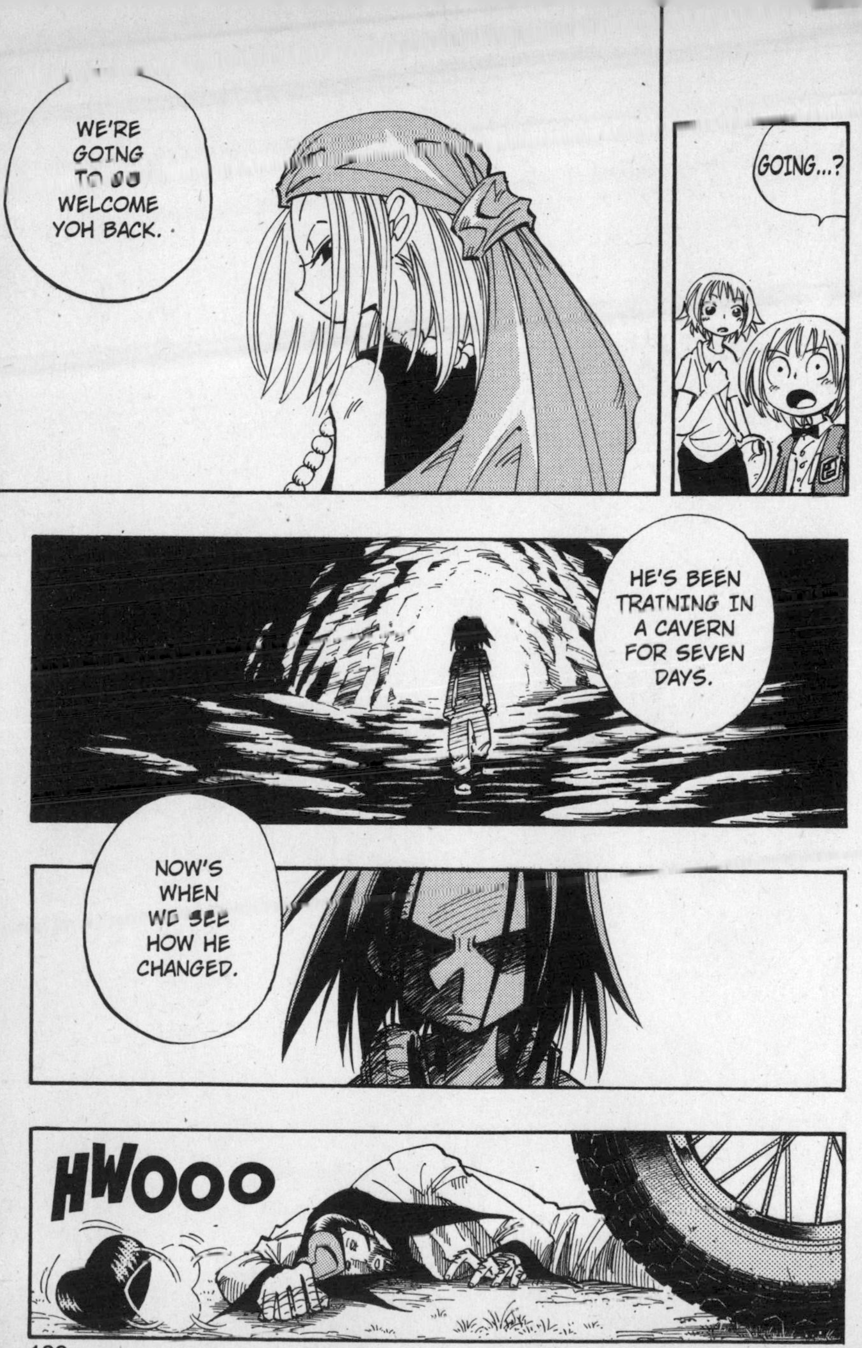
GOING...?
WE'RE GOING TO GO WELCOME YOH BACK.
HE'S BEEN TRAINING IN A CAVERN FOR SEVEN DAYS.
NOW'S WHEN WE SEE HOW HE CHANGED.
HWOOO

## SHAMAN KING CHARACTER FILE No.27

# 玉村たまお

1999
NOV.

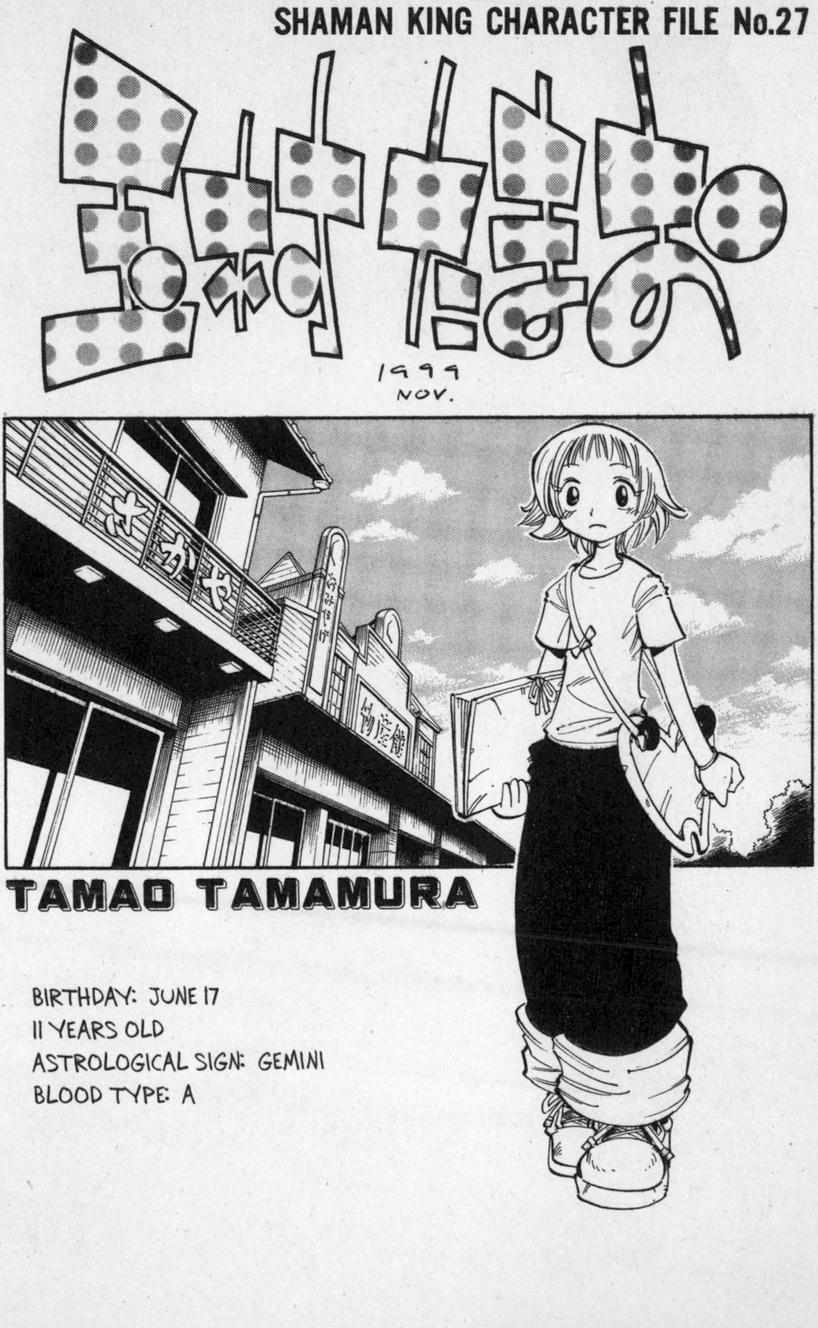

**TAMAO TAMAMURA**

BIRTHDAY: JUNE 17
11 YEARS OLD
ASTROLOGICAL SIGN: GEMINI
BLOOD TYPE: A

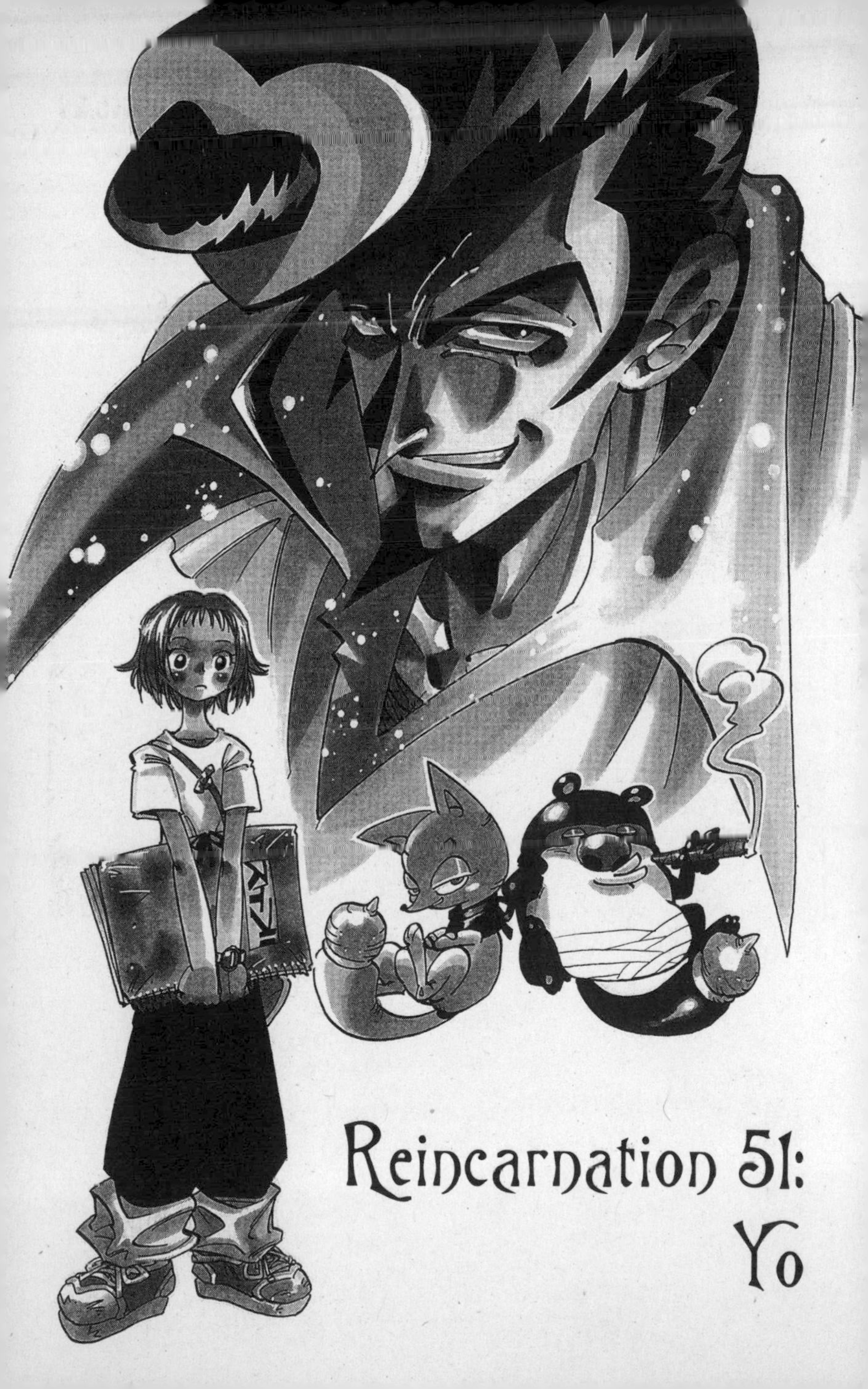

# Reincarnation 51: Yo

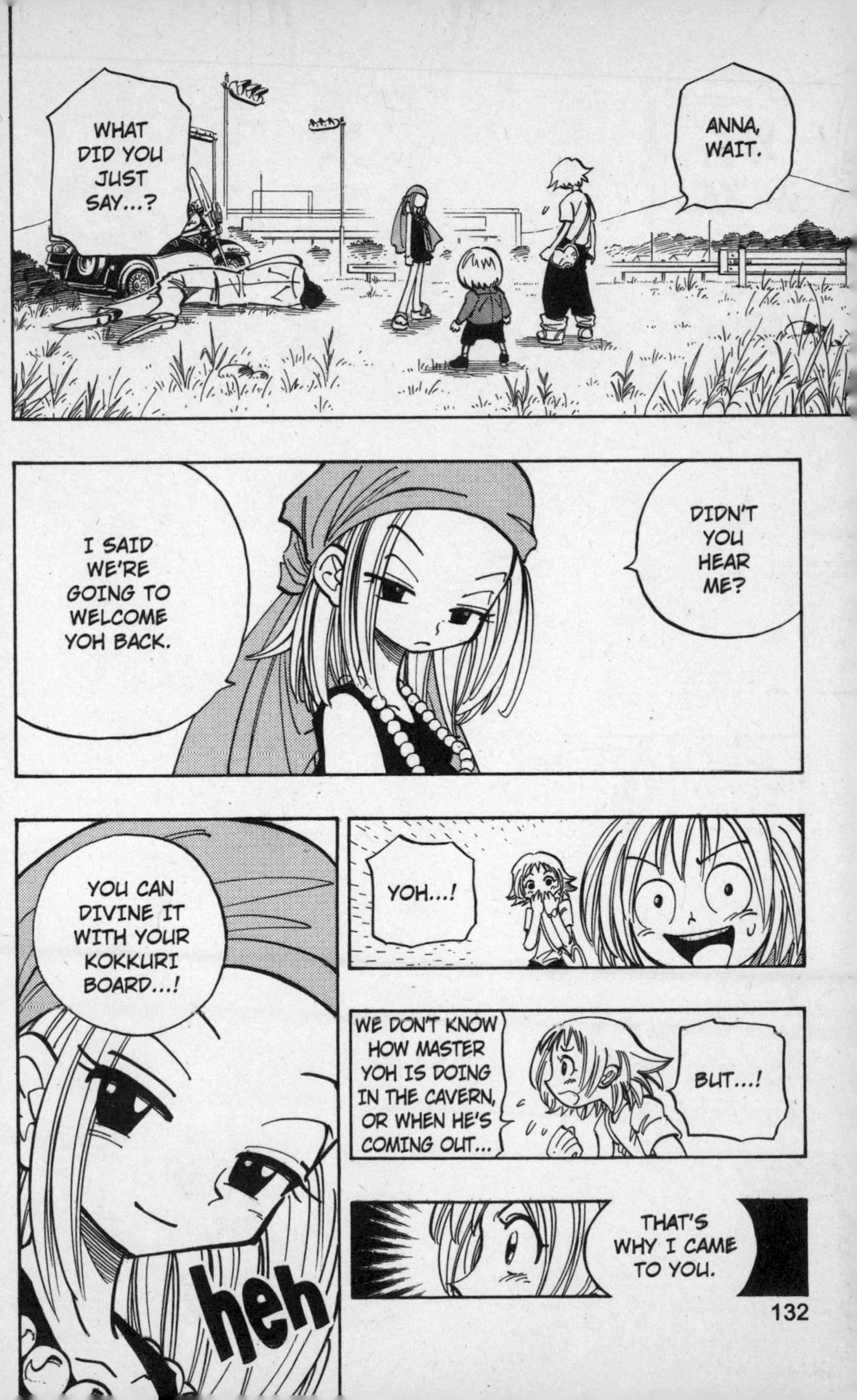
ANNA, WAIT.
WHAT DID YOU JUST SAY...?
DIDN'T YOU HEAR ME?
I SAID WE'RE GOING TO WELCOME YOH BACK.
YOH...!
BUT...!
WE DON'T KNOW HOW MASTER YOH IS DOING IN THE CAVERN, OR WHEN HE'S COMING OUT...
THAT'S WHY I CAME TO YOU.
YOU CAN DIVINE IT WITH YOUR KOKKURI BOARD...!
heh

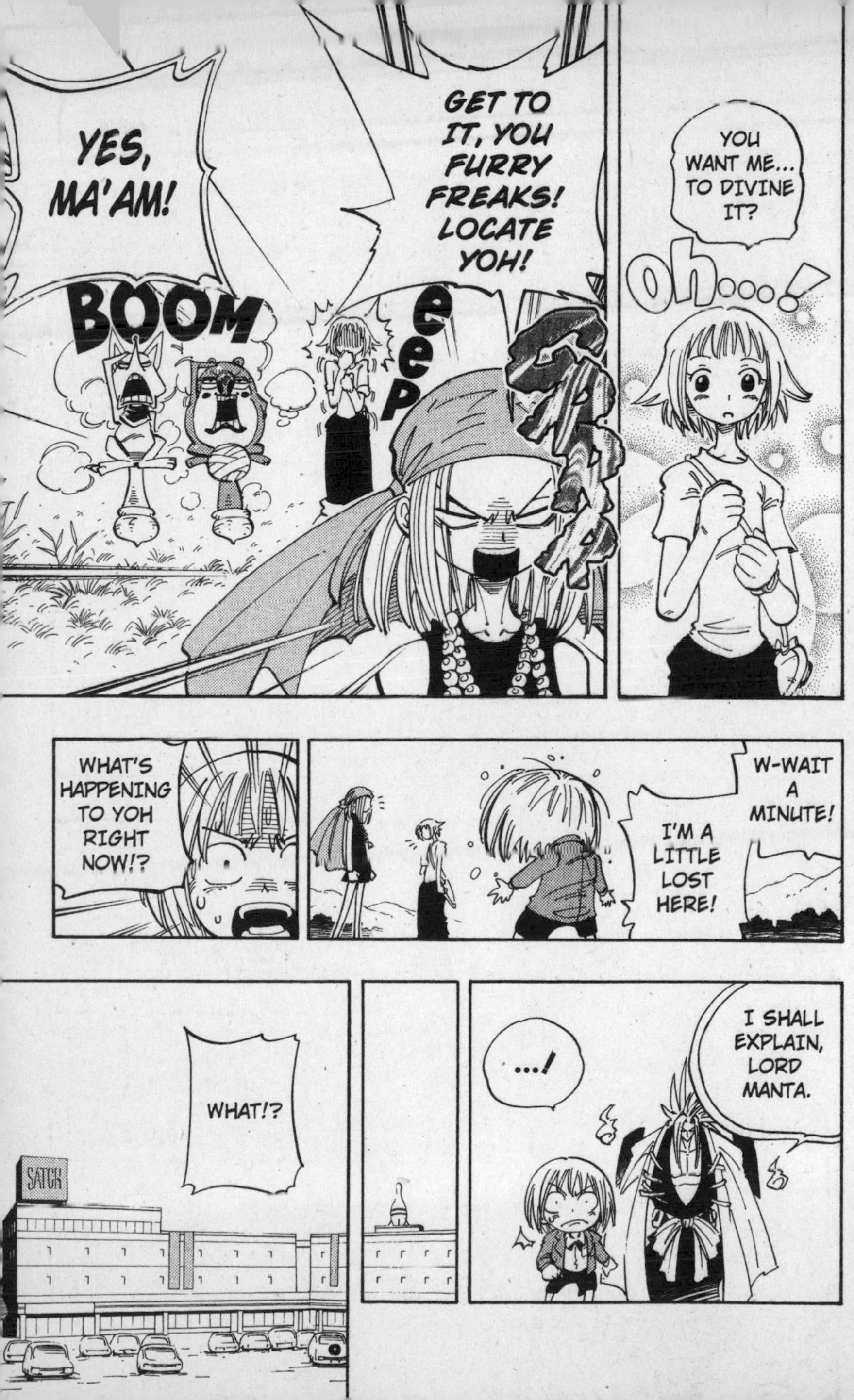
YOU WANT ME... TO DIVINE IT?
oh...!
GET TO IT, YOU FURRY FREAKS! LOCATE YOH!
eep
YES, MA'AM!
BOOM
W-WAIT A MINUTE!
I'M A LITTLE LOST HERE!
WHAT'S HAPPENING TO YOH RIGHT NOW!?
I SHALL EXPLAIN, LORD MANTA.
...!
WHAT!?
SATCH

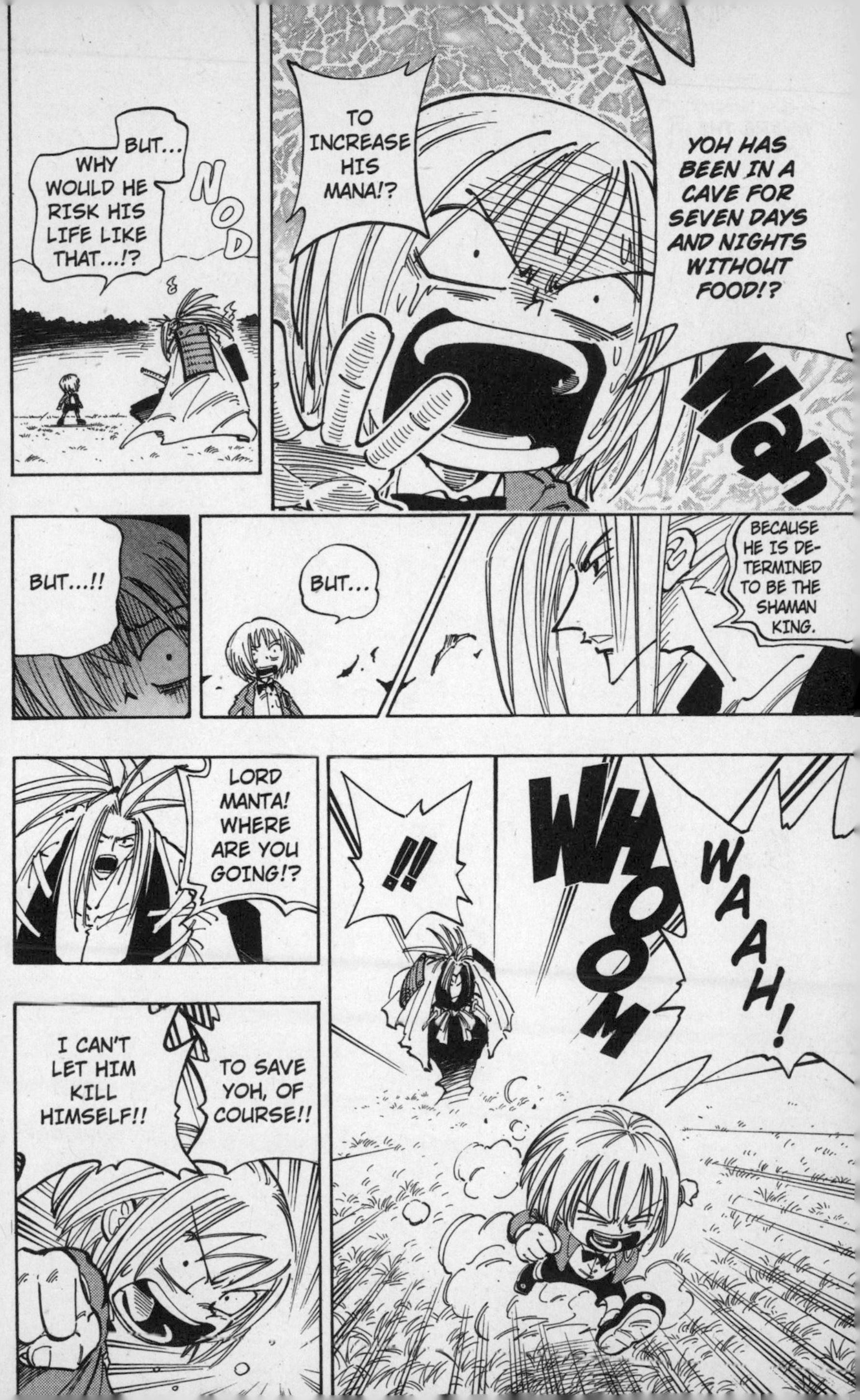
YOH HAS BEEN IN A CAVE FOR SEVEN DAYS AND NIGHTS WITHOUT FOOD!?
TO INCREASE HIS MANA!?
WAH
NOD
BUT... WHY WOULD HE RISK HIS LIFE LIKE THAT...!?
BECAUSE HE IS DETERMINED TO BE THE SHAMAN KING.
BUT...
BUT...!!
WAAAH!
WHOOOM
!!
LORD MANTA! WHERE ARE YOU GOING!?
TO SAVE YOH, OF COURSE!!
I CAN'T LET HIM KILL HIMSELF!!

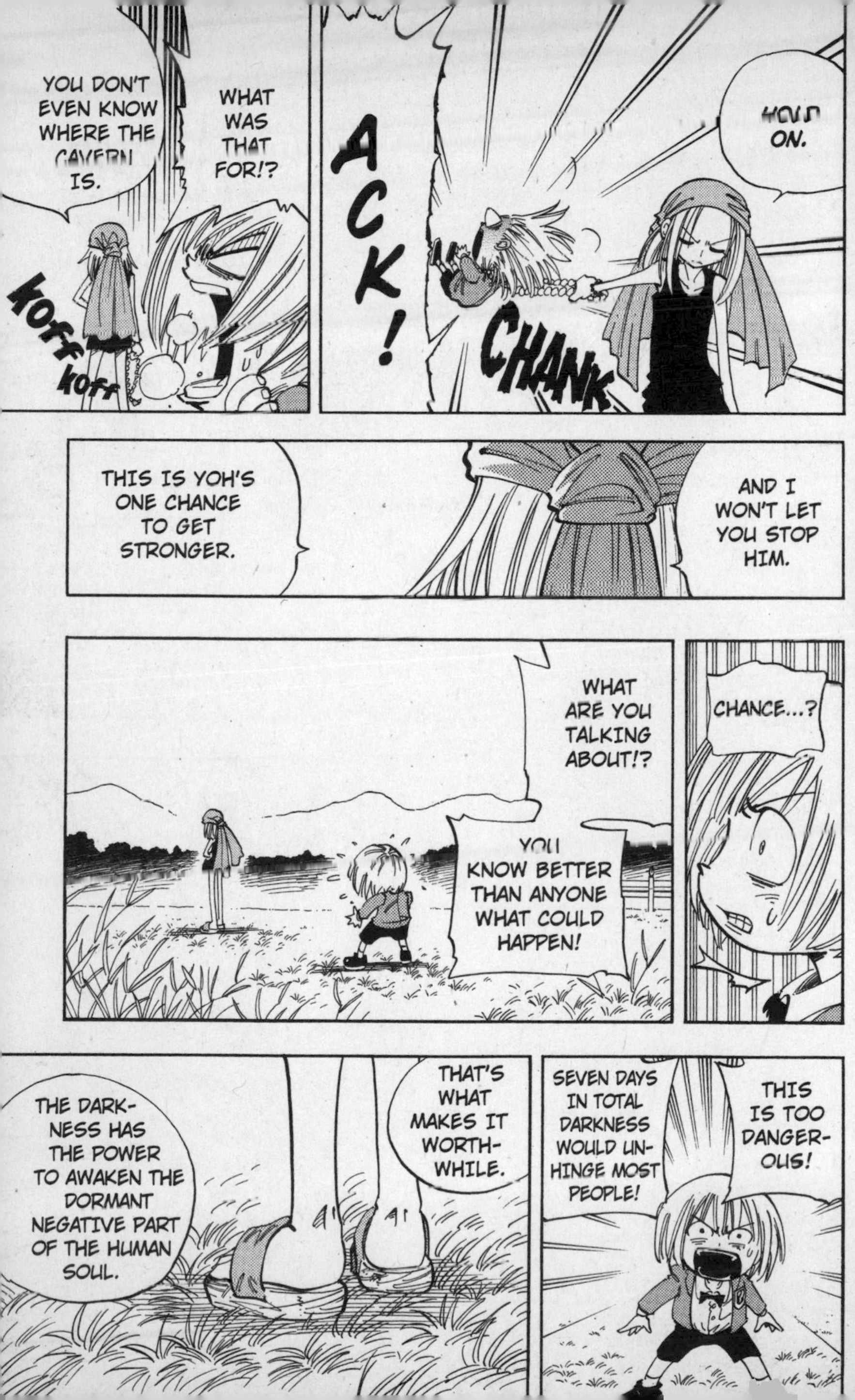
ON.
ACK!
CHANK
WHAT WAS THAT FOR!?
YOU DON'T EVEN KNOW WHERE THE CAVERN IS.
KOFF KOFF
THIS IS YOH'S ONE CHANCE TO GET STRONGER.
AND I WON'T LET YOU STOP HIM.
CHANCE...?
WHAT ARE YOU TALKING ABOUT!?
YOU KNOW BETTER THAN ANYONE WHAT COULD HAPPEN!
THIS IS TOO DANGER-OUS!
SEVEN DAYS IN TOTAL DARKNESS WOULD UN-HINGE MOST PEOPLE!
THAT'S WHAT MAKES IT WORTH-WHILE.
THE DARK-NESS HAS THE POWER TO AWAKEN THE DORMANT NEGATIVE PART OF THE HUMAN SOUL.

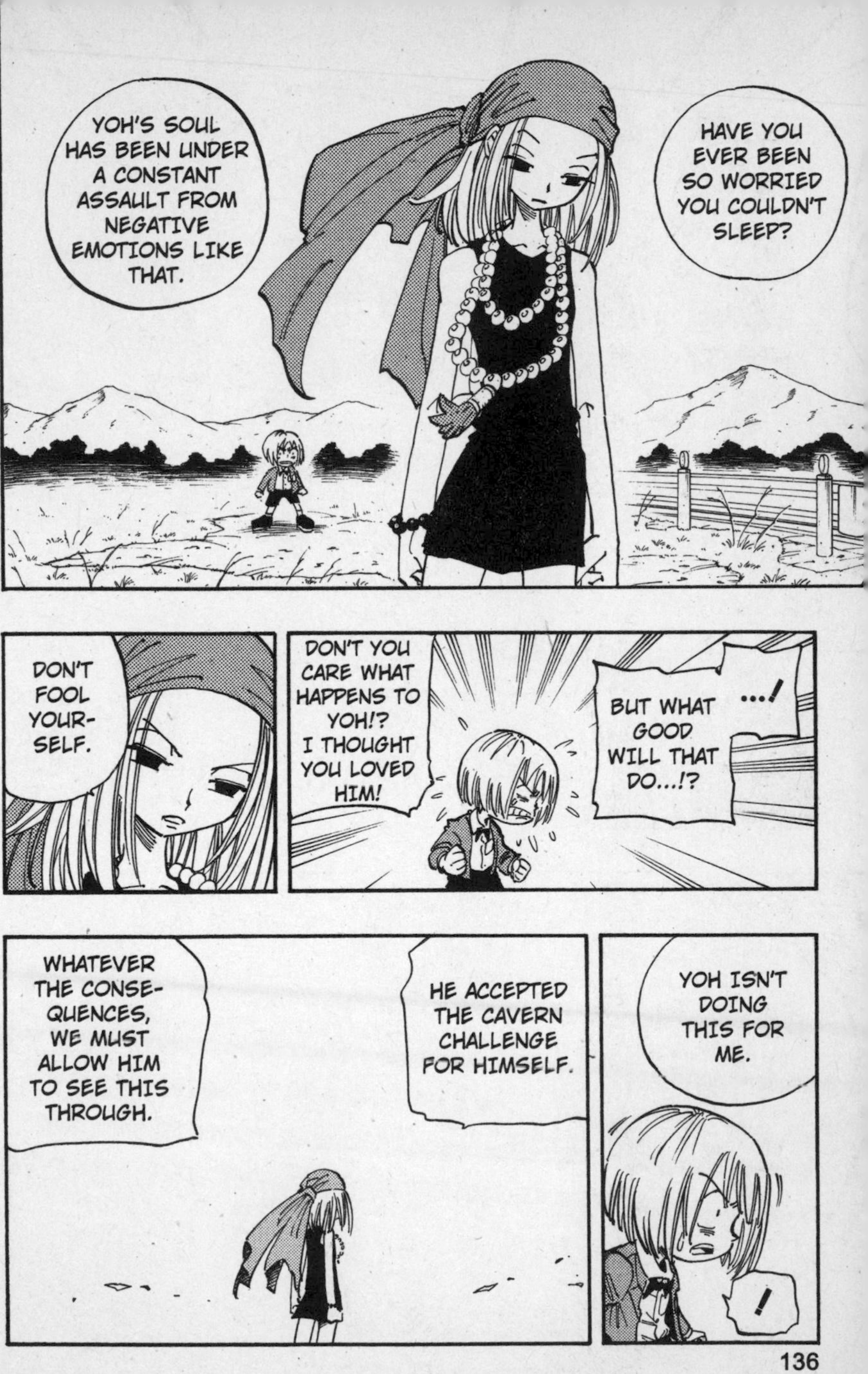
HAVE YOU EVER BEEN SO WORRIED YOU COULDN'T SLEEP?
YOH'S SOUL HAS BEEN UNDER A CONSTANT ASSAULT FROM NEGATIVE EMOTIONS LIKE THAT.
...!
BUT WHAT GOOD WILL THAT DO...!?
DON'T YOU CARE WHAT HAPPENS TO YOH!? I THOUGHT YOU LOVED HIM!
DON'T FOOL YOUR-SELF.
YOH ISN'T DOING THIS FOR ME.
!
HE ACCEPTED THE CAVERN CHALLENGE FOR HIMSELF.
WHATEVER THE CONSE-QUENCES, WE MUST ALLOW HIM TO SEE THIS THROUGH.

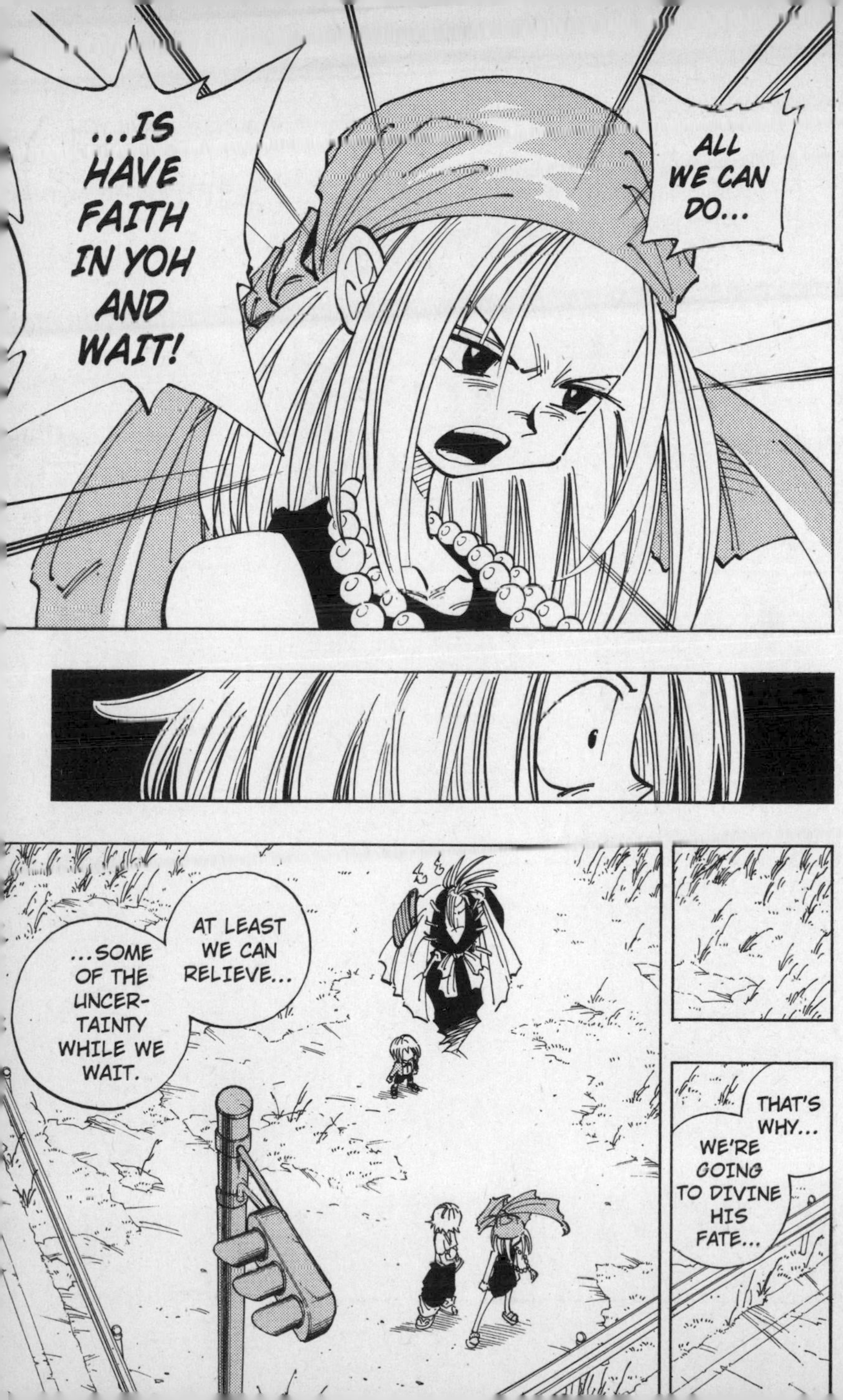
ALL WE CAN DO...
...IS HAVE FAITH IN YOH AND WAIT!
THAT'S WHY... WE'RE GOING TO DIVINE HIS FATE...
AT LEAST WE CAN RELIEVE...
...SOME OF THE UNCER-TAINTY WHILE WE WAIT.

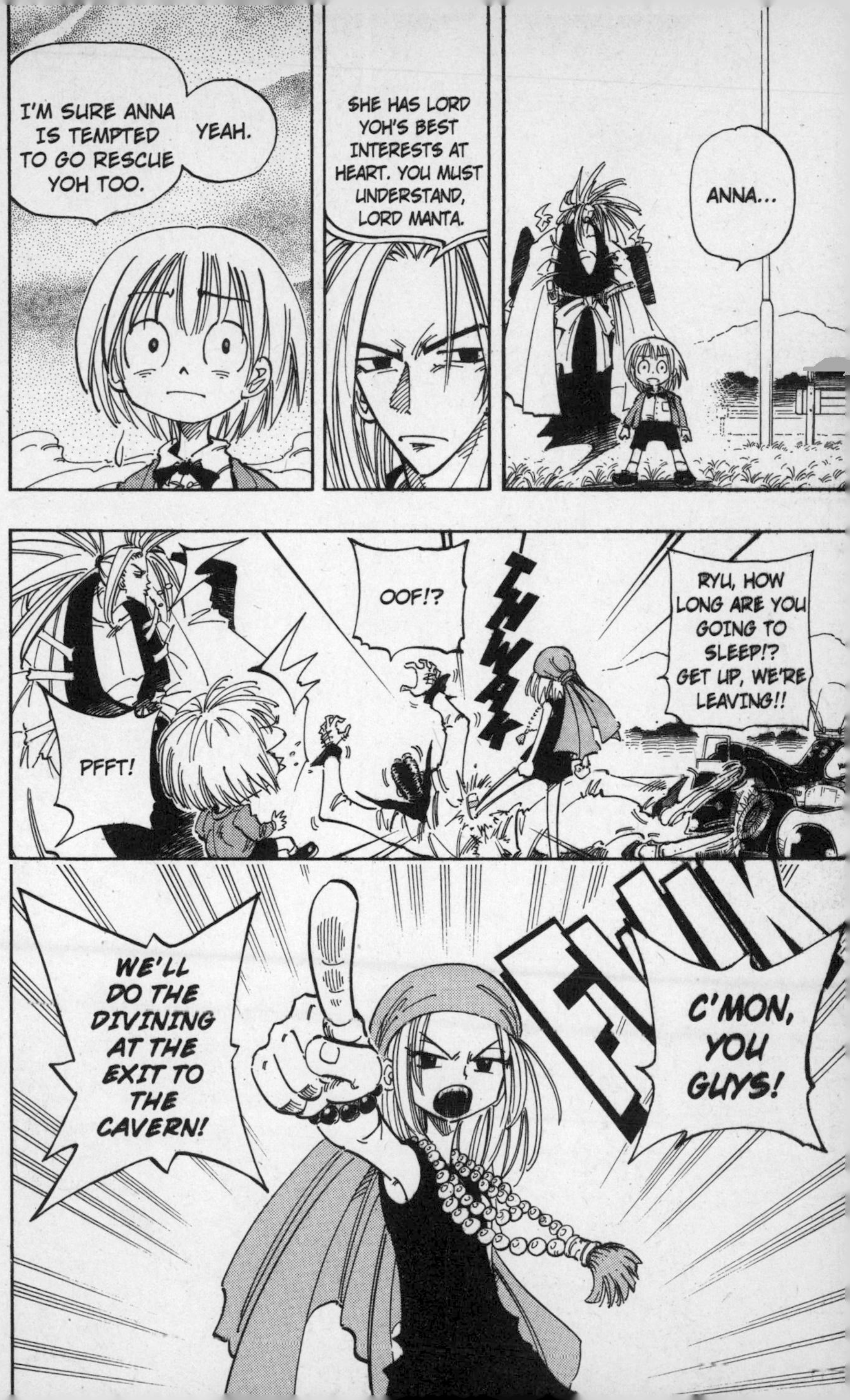
ANNA...
SHE HAS LORD YOH'S BEST INTERESTS AT HEART. YOU MUST UNDERSTAND, LORD MANTA.
YEAH.
I'M SURE ANNA IS TEMPTED TO GO RESCUE YOH TOO.
RYU, HOW LONG ARE YOU GOING TO SLEEP!? GET UP, WE'RE LEAVING!!
THWAK
OOF!?
PFFT!
C'MON, YOU GUYS!
WE'LL DO THE DIVINING AT THE EXIT TO THE CAVERN!

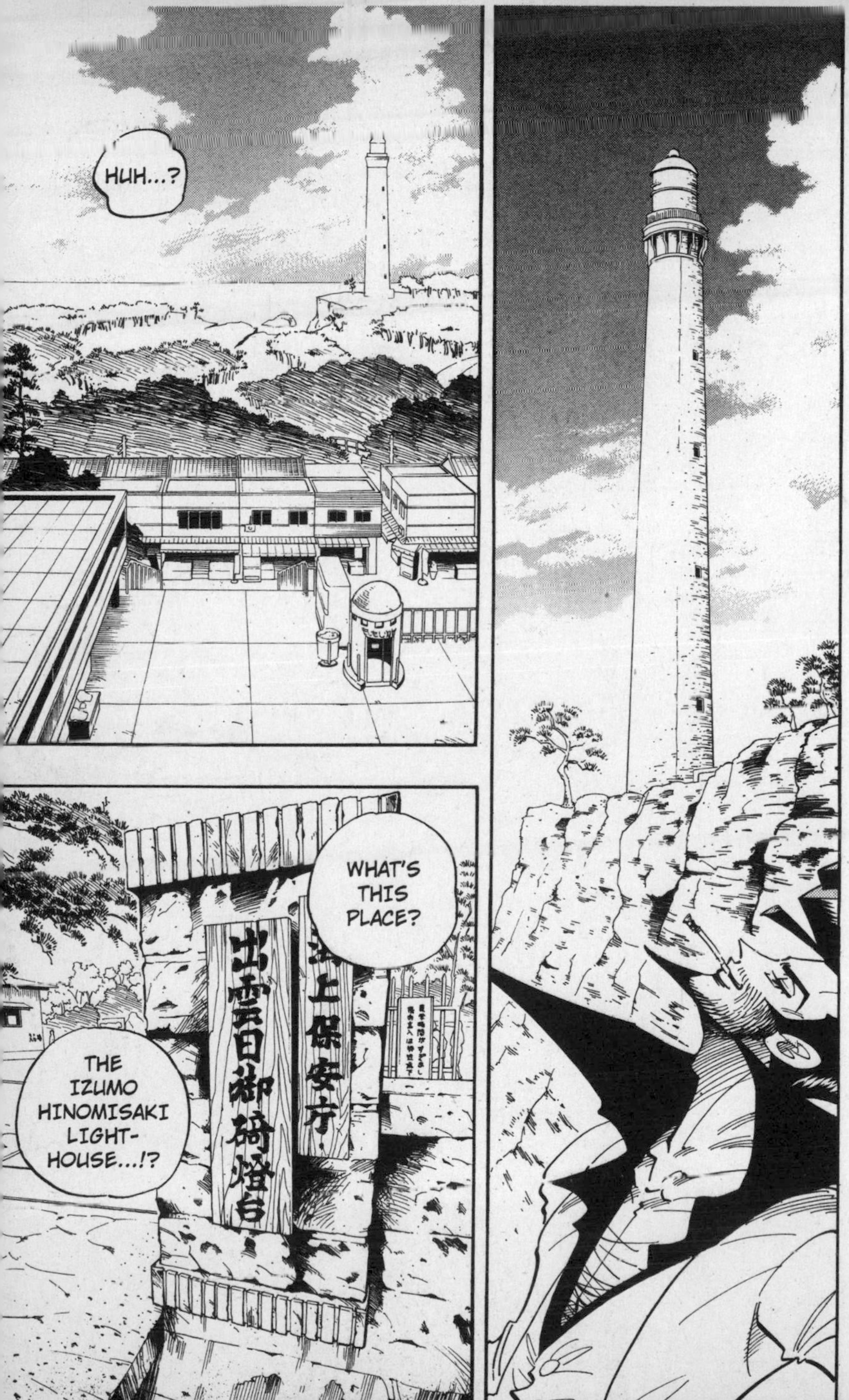
HUH...?
WHAT'S THIS PLACE?
出雲日御碕燈台
上保安庁
THE IZUMO HINOMISAKI LIGHT-HOUSE...!?

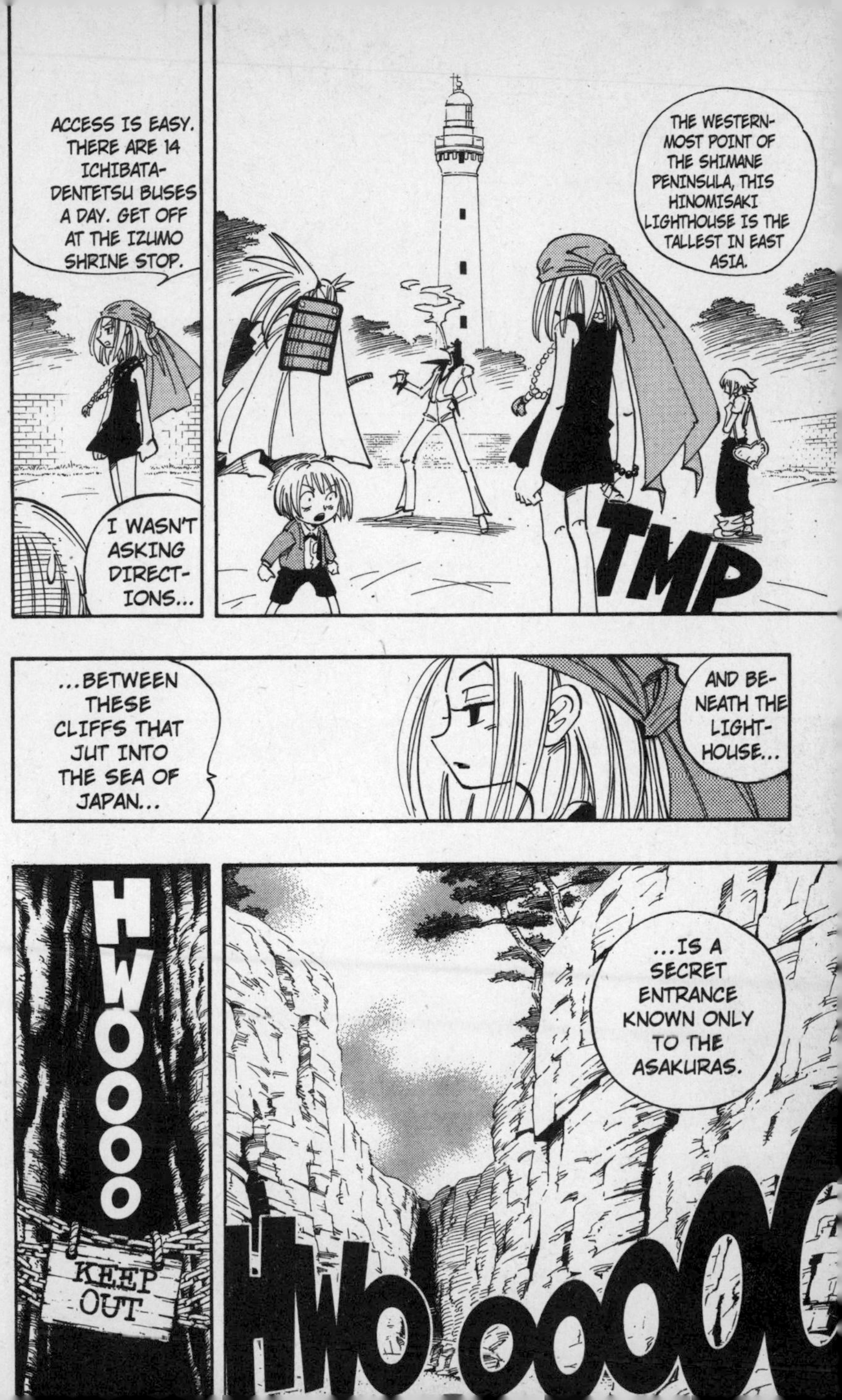
THE WESTERN-MOST POINT OF THE SHIMANE PENINSULA, THIS HINOMISAKI LIGHTHOUSE IS THE TALLEST IN EAST ASIA.
TMP
ACCESS IS EASY. THERE ARE 14 ICHIBATA-DENTETSU BUSES A DAY. GET OFF AT THE IZUMO SHRINE STOP.
I WASN'T ASKING DIRECT-IONS...
AND BE-NEATH THE LIGHT-HOUSE...
...BETWEEN THESE CLIFFS THAT JUT INTO THE SEA OF JAPAN...
...IS A SECRET ENTRANCE KNOWN ONLY TO THE ASAKURAS.
HWOOOOO
HWOOOO
KEEP OUT

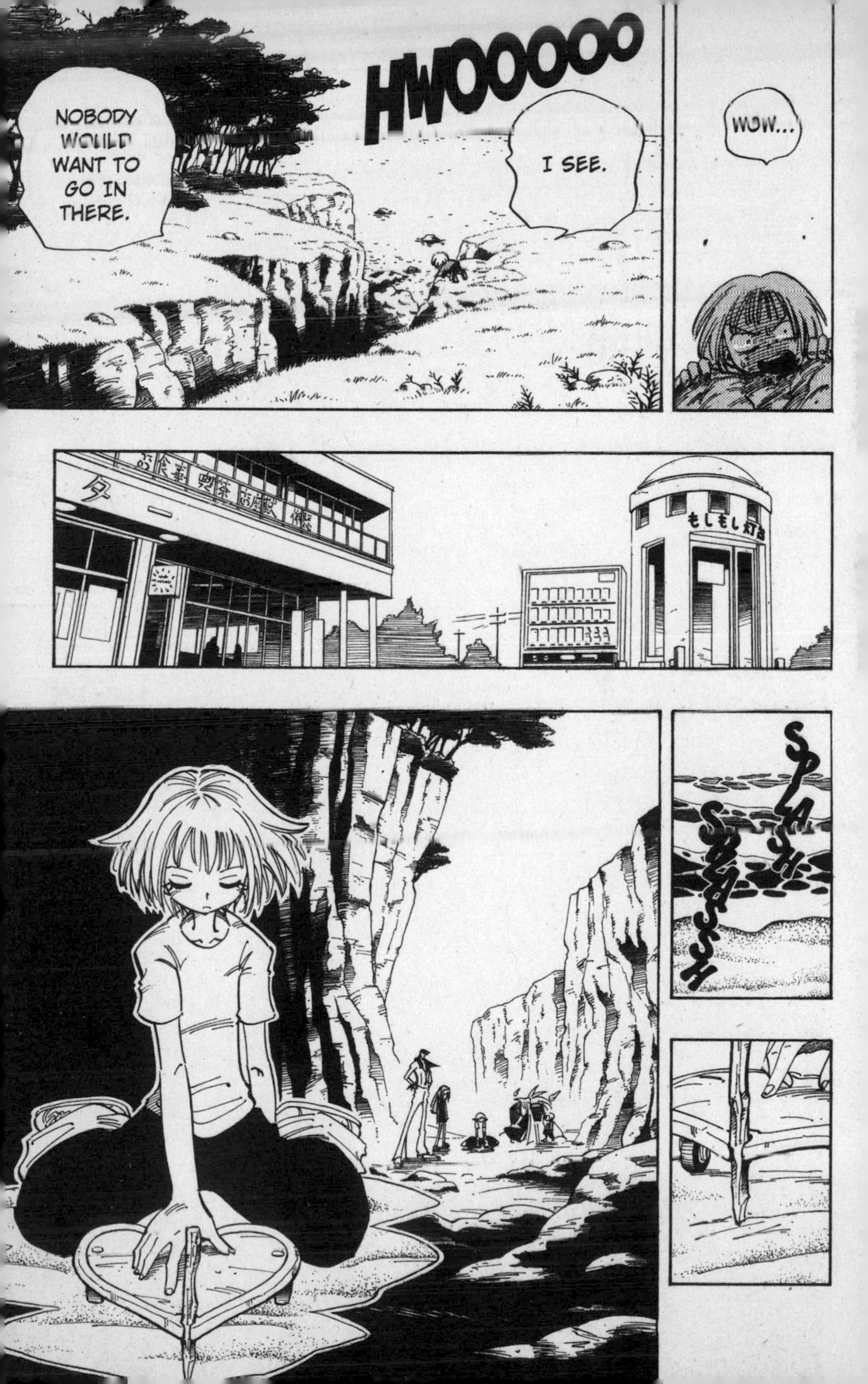
WOW...
HWOOOOO
I SEE.
NOBODY WOULD WANT TO GO IN THERE.
もしもし灯台
SPLASH
SPLASSH

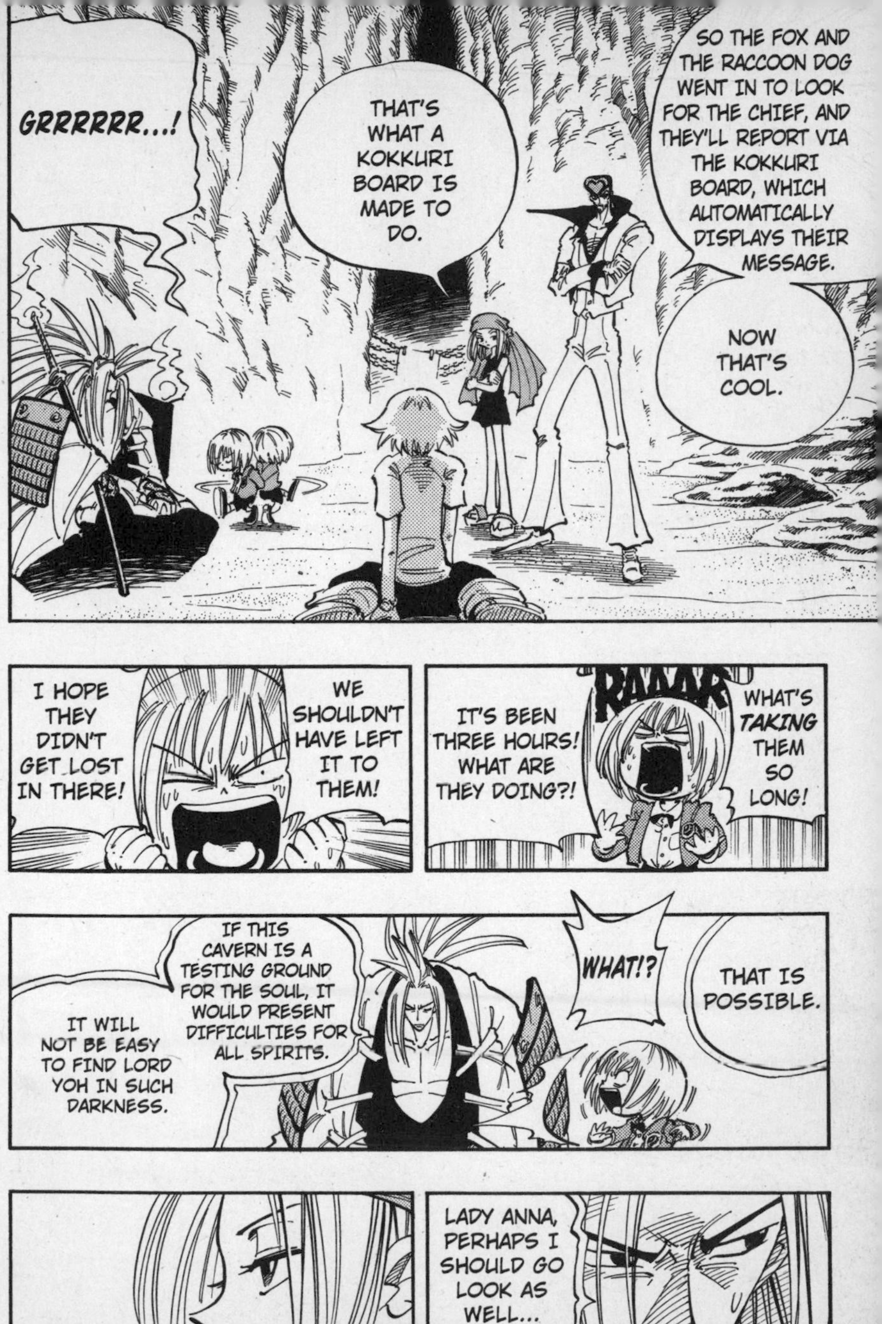

SO THE FOX AND THE RACCOON DOG WENT IN TO LOOK FOR THE CHIEF, AND THEY'LL REPORT VIA THE KOKKURI BOARD, WHICH AUTOMATICALLY DISPLAYS THEIR MESSAGE.
NOW THAT'S COOL.
THAT'S WHAT A KOKKURI BOARD IS MADE TO DO.
GRRRRRR...!
RAAAR
WHAT'S TAKING THEM SO LONG!
IT'S BEEN THREE HOURS! WHAT ARE THEY DOING?!
WE SHOULDN'T HAVE LEFT IT TO THEM!
I HOPE THEY DIDN'T GET LOST IN THERE!
THAT IS POSSIBLE.
WHAT!?
IF THIS CAVERN IS A TESTING GROUND FOR THE SOUL, IT WOULD PRESENT DIFFICULTIES FOR ALL SPIRITS.
IT WILL NOT BE EASY TO FIND LORD YOH IN SUCH DARKNESS.
LADY ANNA, PERHAPS I SHOULD GO LOOK AS WELL...

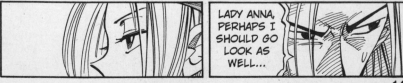

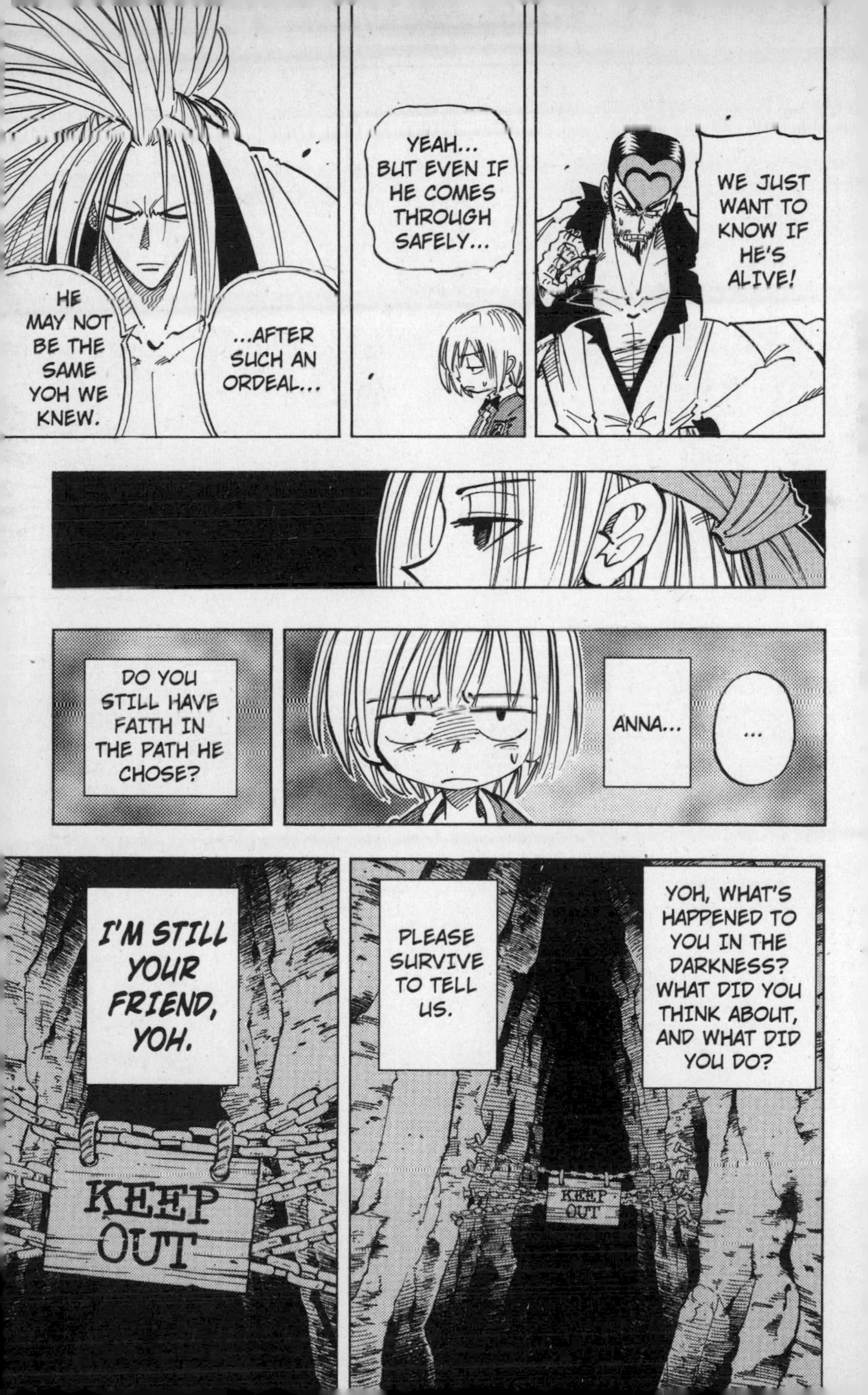
WE JUST WANT TO KNOW IF HE'S ALIVE!
YEAH... BUT EVEN IF HE COMES THROUGH SAFELY...
...AFTER SUCH AN ORDEAL...
HE MAY NOT BE THE SAME YOH WE KNEW.
...
ANNA...
DO YOU STILL HAVE FAITH IN THE PATH HE CHOSE?
YOH, WHAT'S HAPPENED TO YOU IN THE DARKNESS? WHAT DID YOU THINK ABOUT, AND WHAT DID YOU DO?
PLEASE SURVIVE TO TELL US.
KEEP OUT
*I'M STILL YOUR FRIEND, YOH.*
KEEP OUT

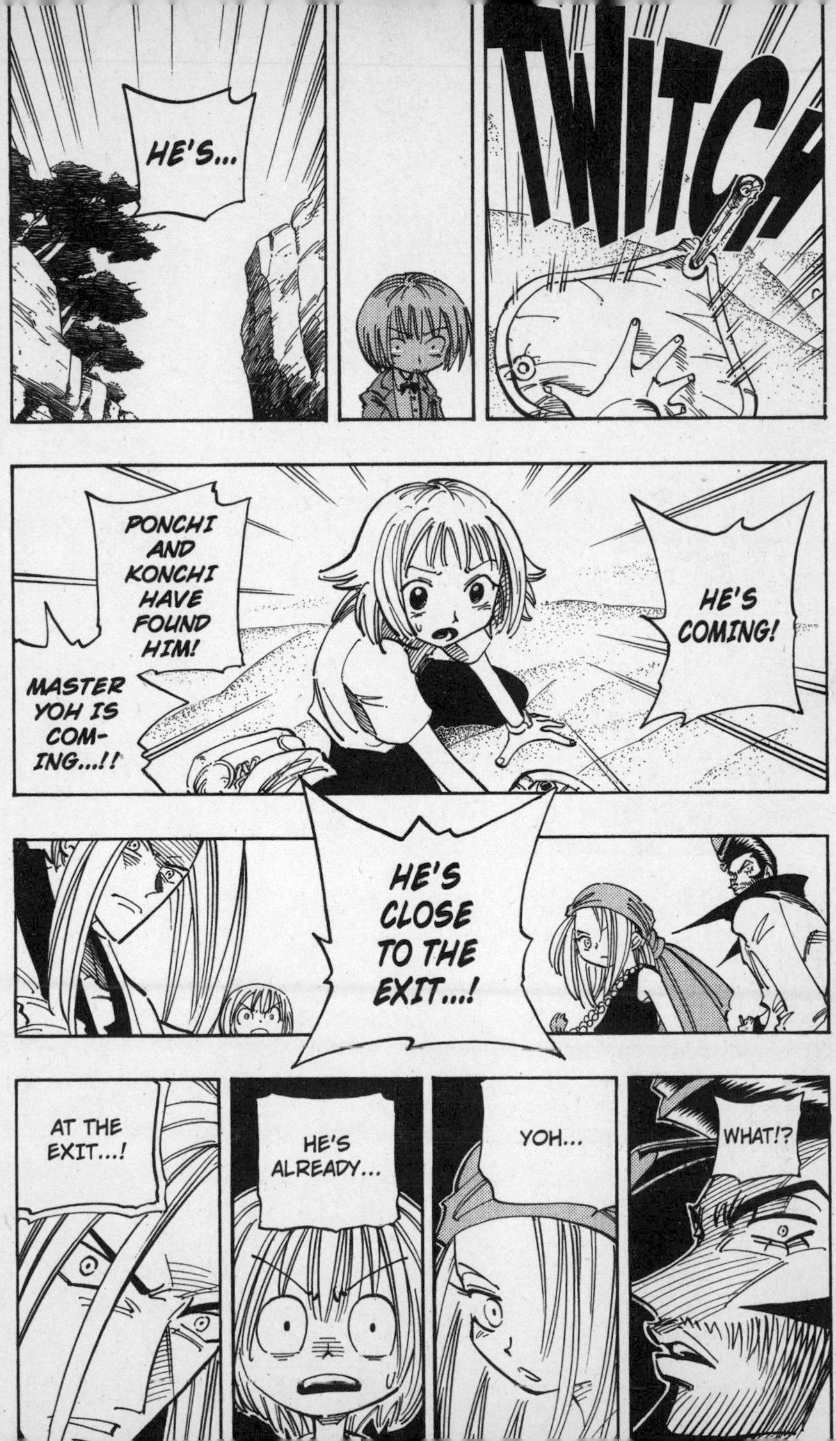

TWITCH
HE'S...
HE'S COMING!
PONCHI AND KONCHI HAVE FOUND HIM!
MASTER YOH IS COM-ING...!!
HE'S CLOSE TO THE EXIT...!
WHAT!?
YOH...
HE'S ALREADY...
AT THE EXIT...!

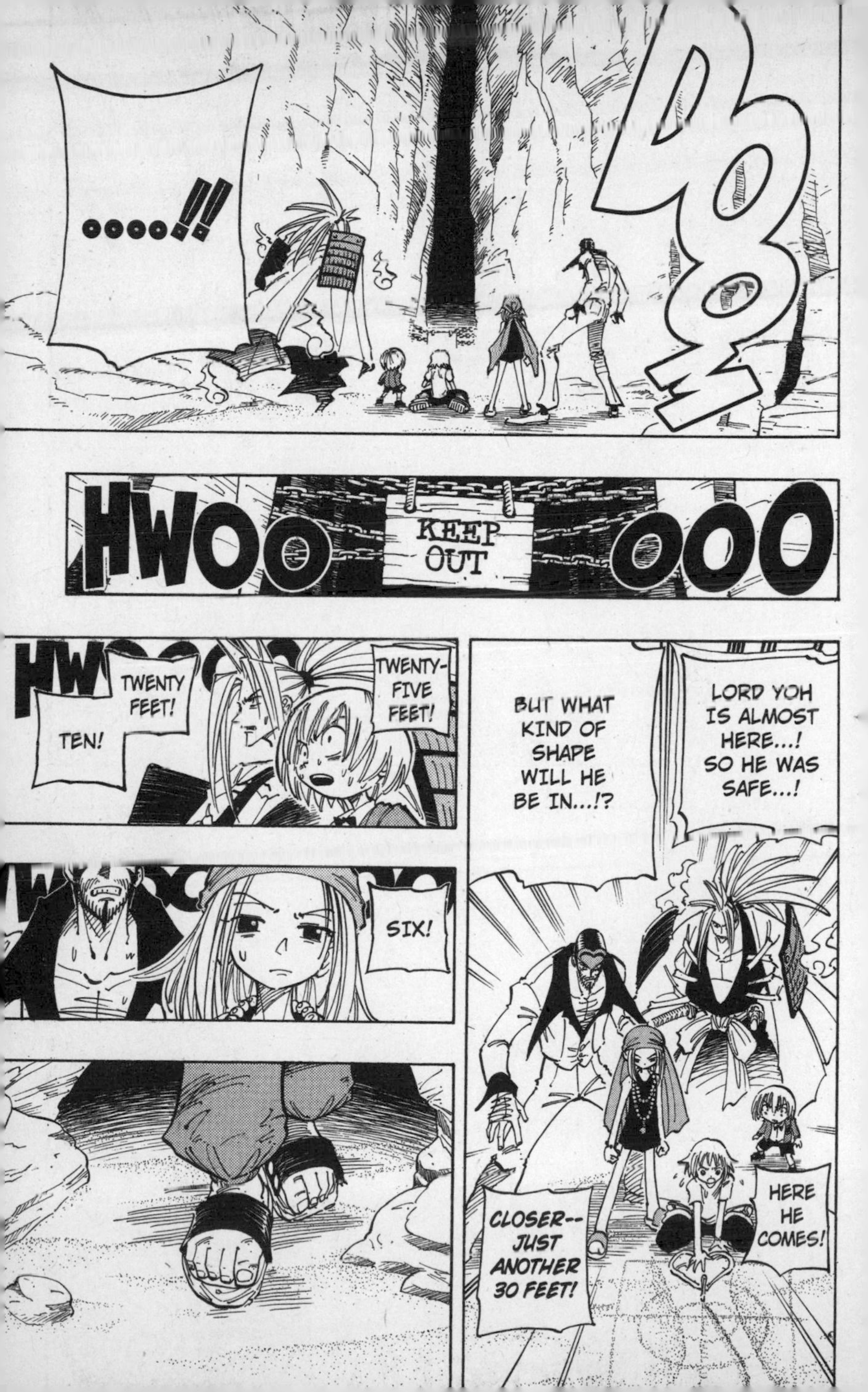

DOOM
....!!
HWOO
KEEP OUT
OOO
LORD YOH IS ALMOST HERE...! SO HE WAS SAFE...!
BUT WHAT KIND OF SHAPE WILL HE BE IN...!?
TWENTY-FIVE FEET!
TWENTY FEET!
TEN!
HERE HE COMES!
CLOSER-- JUST ANOTHER 30 FEET!
SIX!

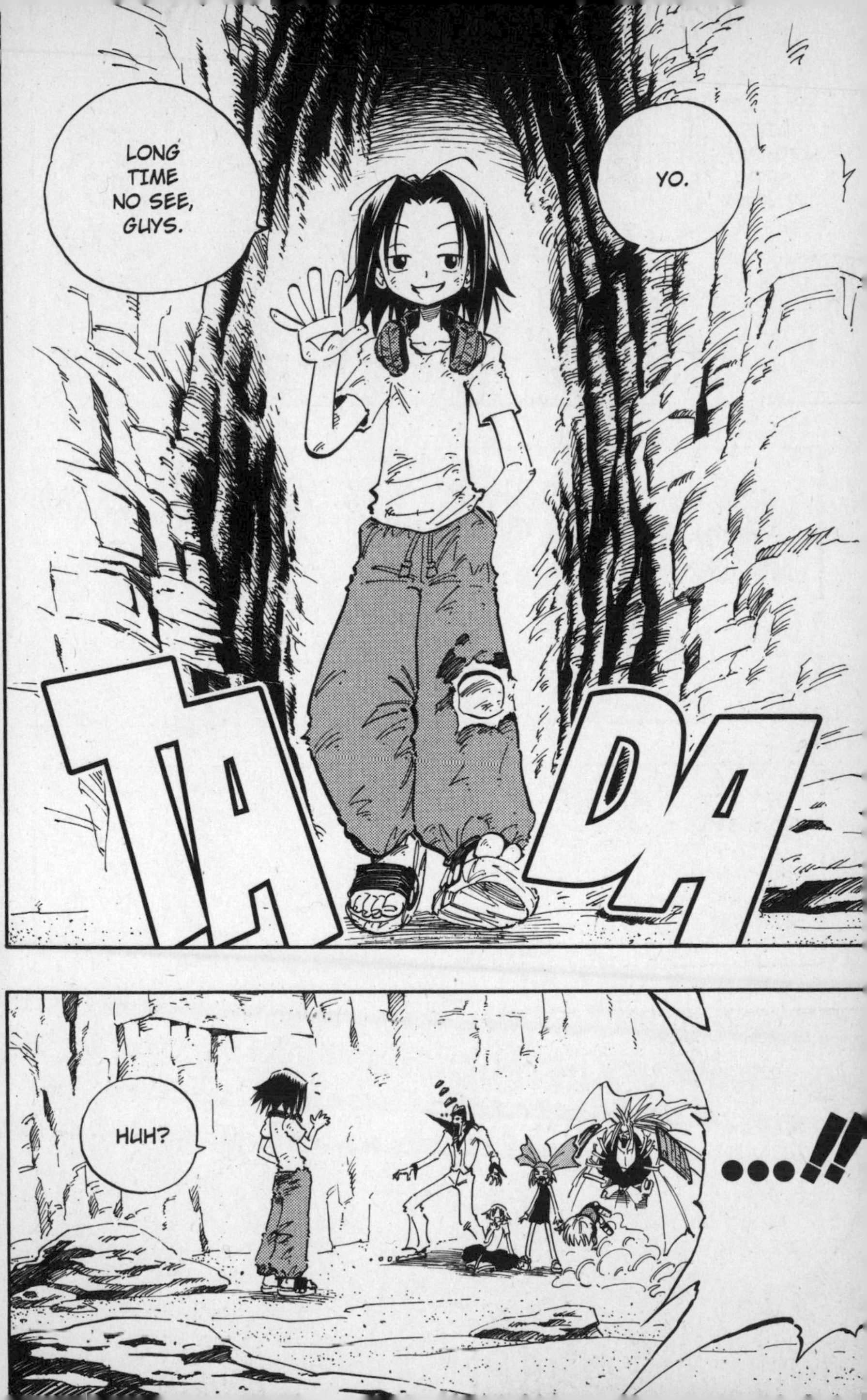
YO.
LONG TIME NO SEE, GUYS.
TADA
...!!
HUH?

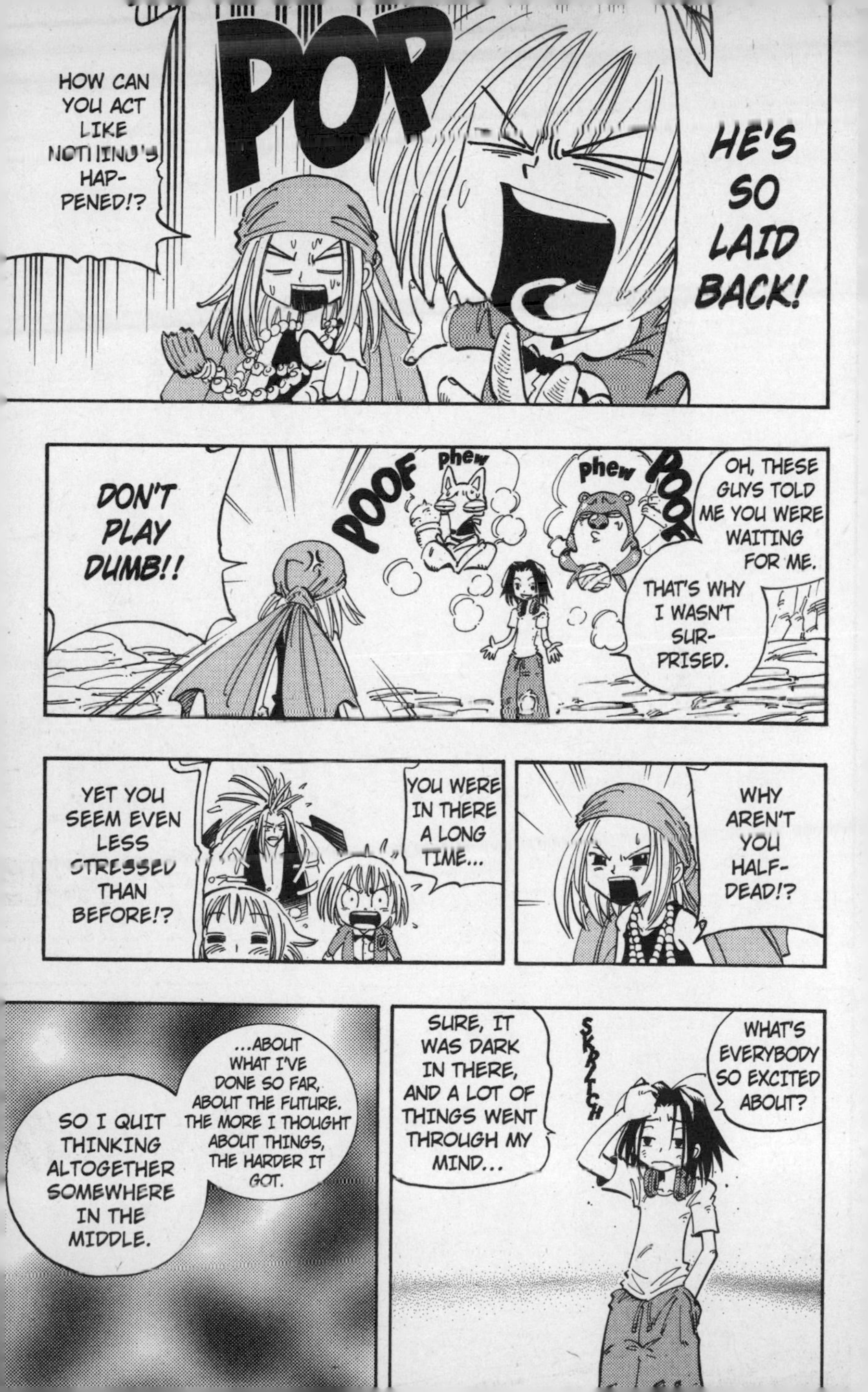
HE'S SO LAID BACK!
POP
HOW CAN YOU ACT LIKE NOTHING'S HAP-PENED!?
OH, THESE GUYS TOLD ME YOU WERE WAITING FOR ME.
POOF
phew
phew
POOF
THAT'S WHY I WASN'T SUR-PRISED.
DON'T PLAY DUMB!!
WHY AREN'T YOU HALF-DEAD!?
YOU WERE IN THERE A LONG TIME...
YET YOU SEEM EVEN LESS STRESSED THAN BEFORE!?
WHAT'S EVERYBODY SO EXCITED ABOUT?
SKRITCH
SURE, IT WAS DARK IN THERE, AND A LOT OF THINGS WENT THROUGH MY MIND...
...ABOUT WHAT I'VE DONE SO FAR, ABOUT THE FUTURE. THE MORE I THOUGHT ABOUT THINGS, THE HARDER IT GOT.
SO I QUIT THINKING ALTOGETHER SOMEWHERE IN THE MIDDLE.

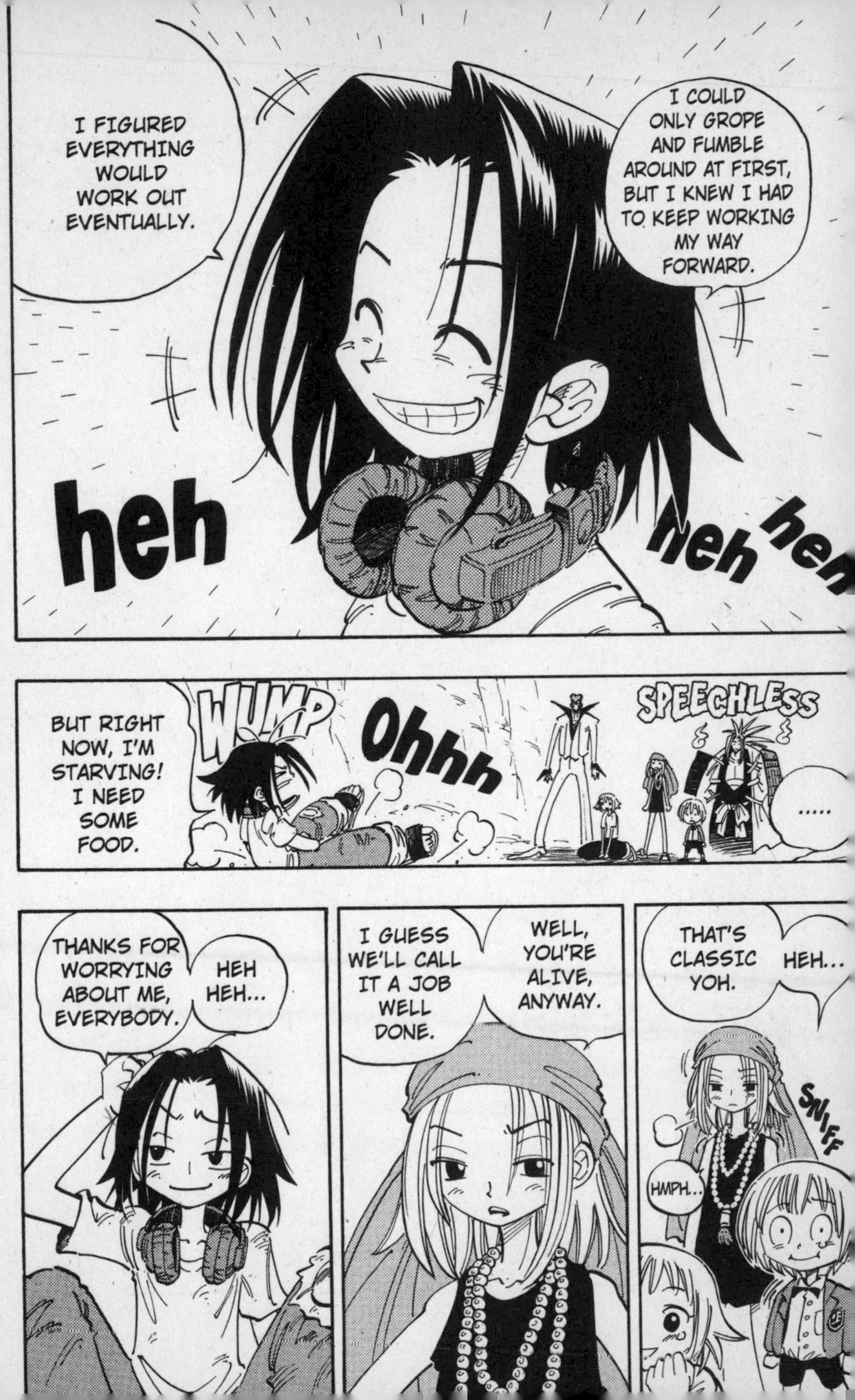
I COULD ONLY GROPE AND FUMBLE AROUND AT FIRST, BUT I KNEW I HAD TO KEEP WORKING MY WAY FORWARD.
I FIGURED EVERYTHING WOULD WORK OUT EVENTUALLY.
heh heh
heh
SPEECHLESS
.....
Ohhh
WUMP
BUT RIGHT NOW, I'M STARVING! I NEED SOME FOOD.
HEH...
THAT'S CLASSIC YOH.
SNIFF
HMPH...
WELL, YOU'RE ALIVE, ANYWAY.
I GUESS WE'LL CALL IT A JOB WELL DONE.
HEH HEH...
THANKS FOR WORRYING ABOUT ME, EVERYBODY.

READ THIS WAY

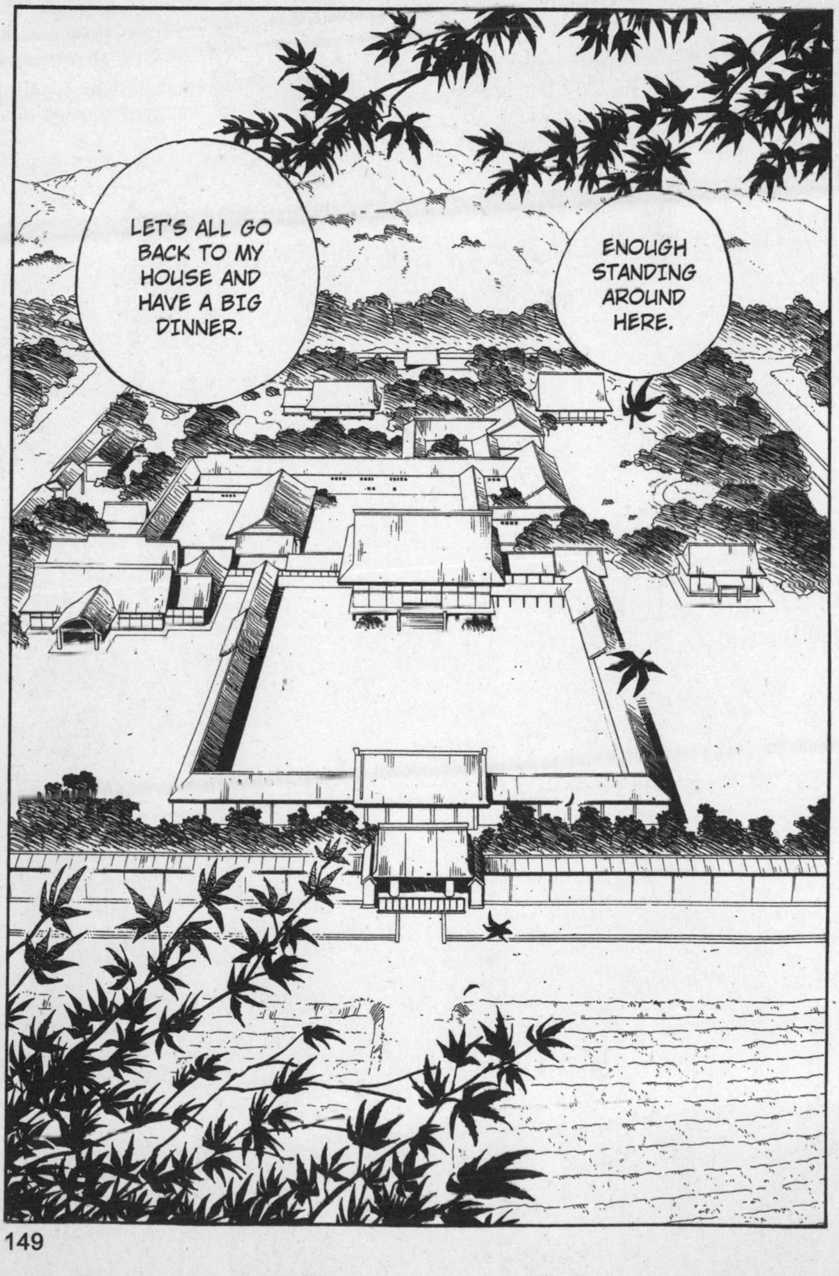
ENOUGH STANDING AROUND HERE.
LET'S ALL GO BACK TO MY HOUSE AND HAVE A BIG DINNER.

SHAMAN
KING
**6**

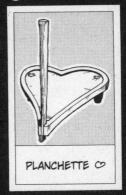

PLANCHETTE ∽

# Reincarnation 52: Progress

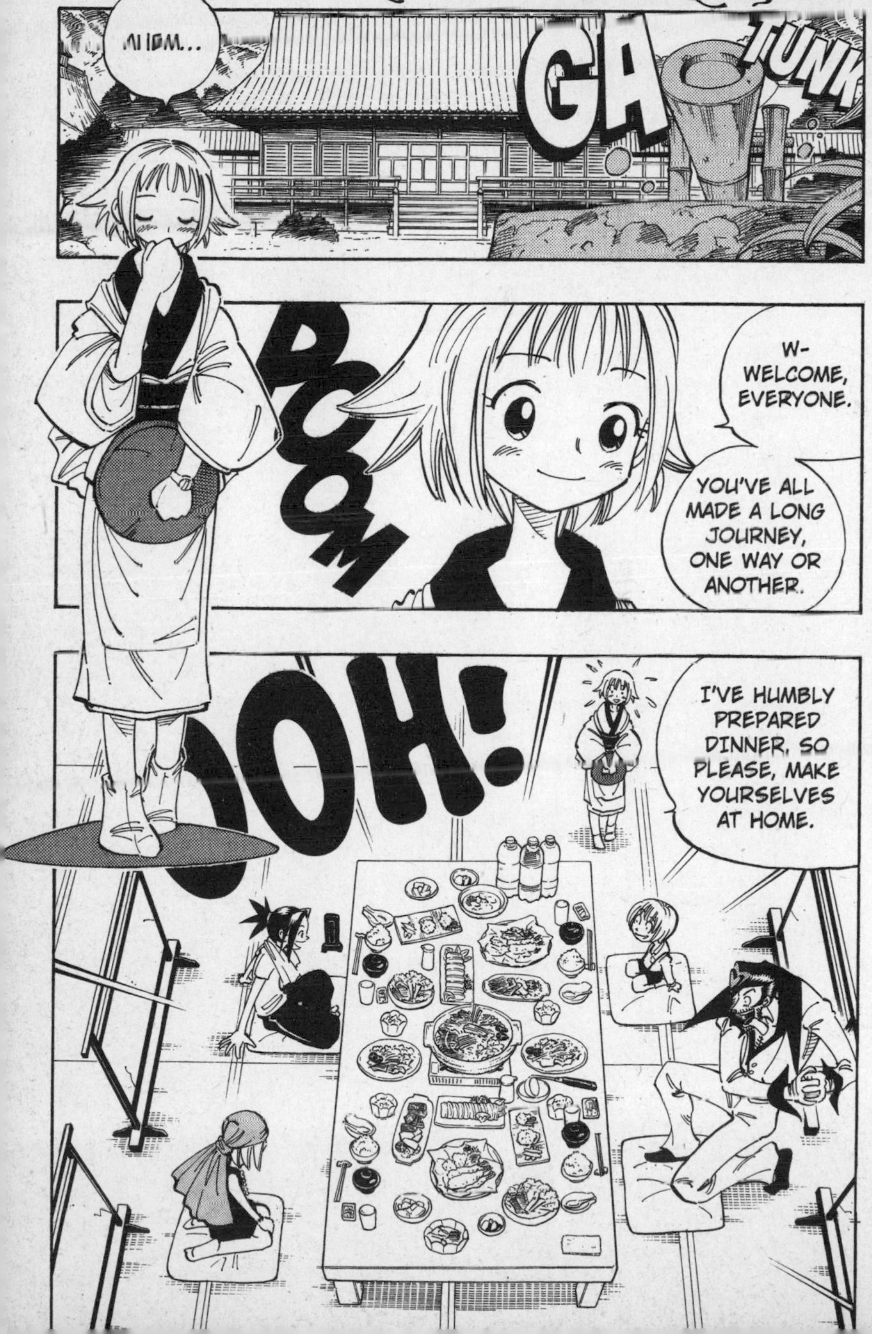
GA TUNK
AHEM...
W-WELCOME, EVERYONE.
YOU'VE ALL MADE A LONG JOURNEY, ONE WAY OR ANOTHER.
BOOM
I'VE HUMBLY PREPARED DINNER, SO PLEASE, MAKE YOURSELVES AT HOME.
OOH!

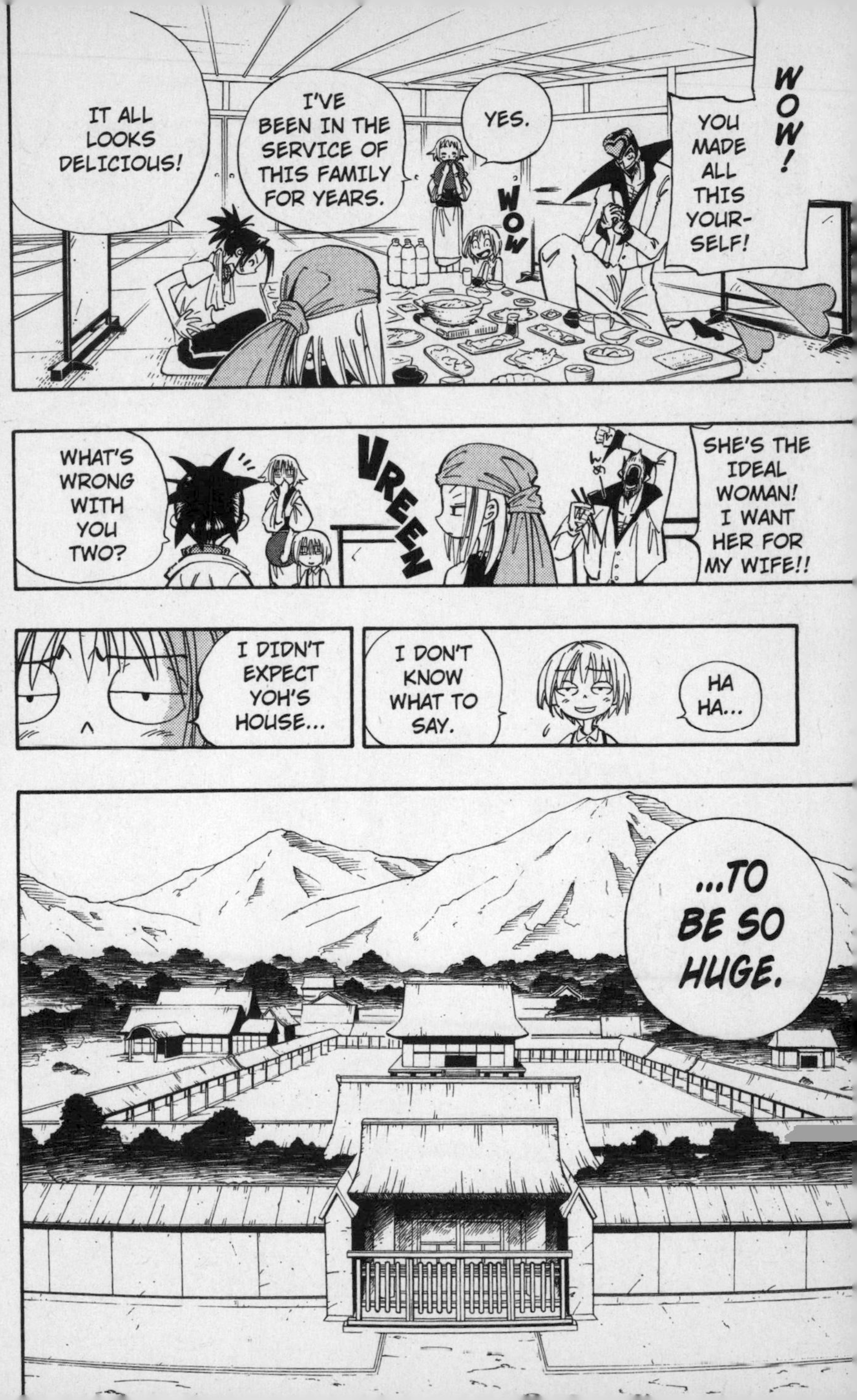
WOW!
YOU MADE ALL THIS YOURSELF!
WOW
YES.
I'VE BEEN IN THE SERVICE OF THIS FAMILY FOR YEARS.
IT ALL LOOKS DELICIOUS!
SHE'S THE IDEAL WOMAN! I WANT HER FOR MY WIFE!!
VREEN
WHAT'S WRONG WITH YOU TWO?
HA HA...
I DON'T KNOW WHAT TO SAY.
I DIDN'T EXPECT YOH'S HOUSE...
...TO BE SO HUGE.

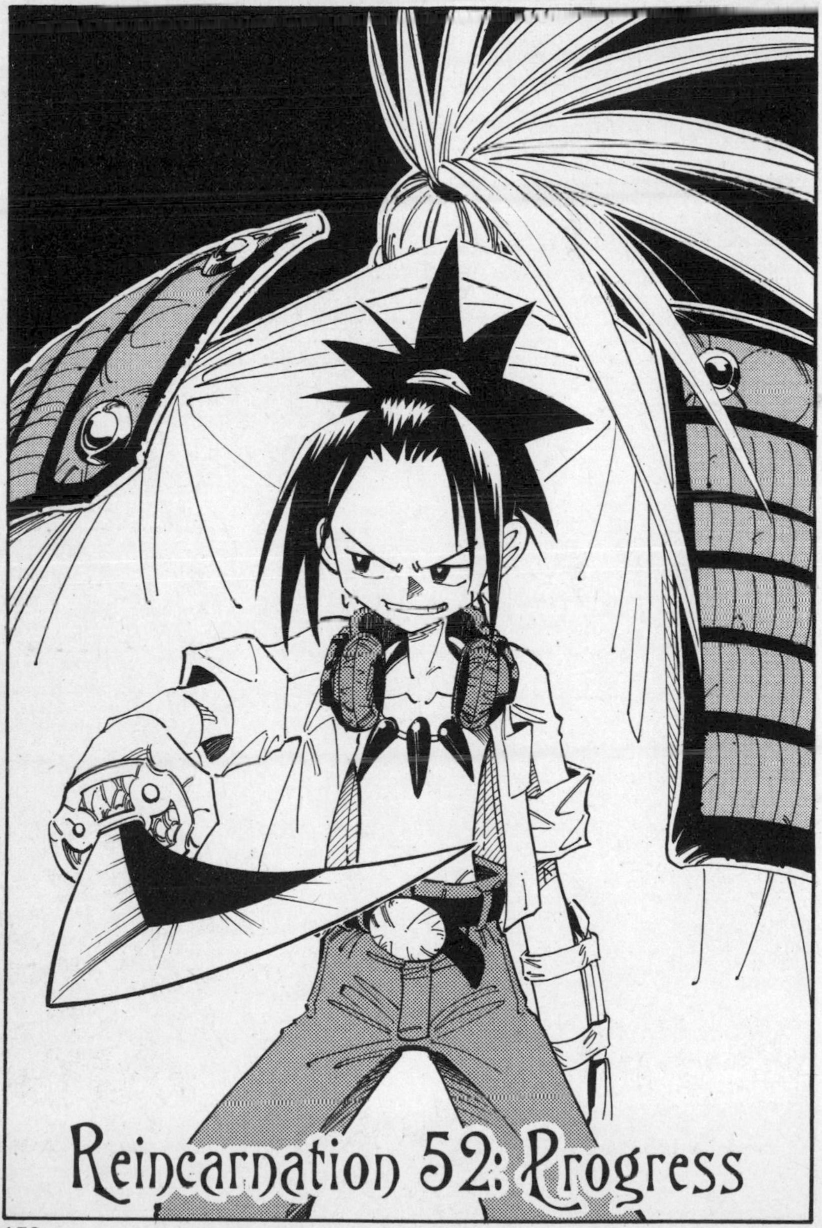
Reincarnation 52: Progress

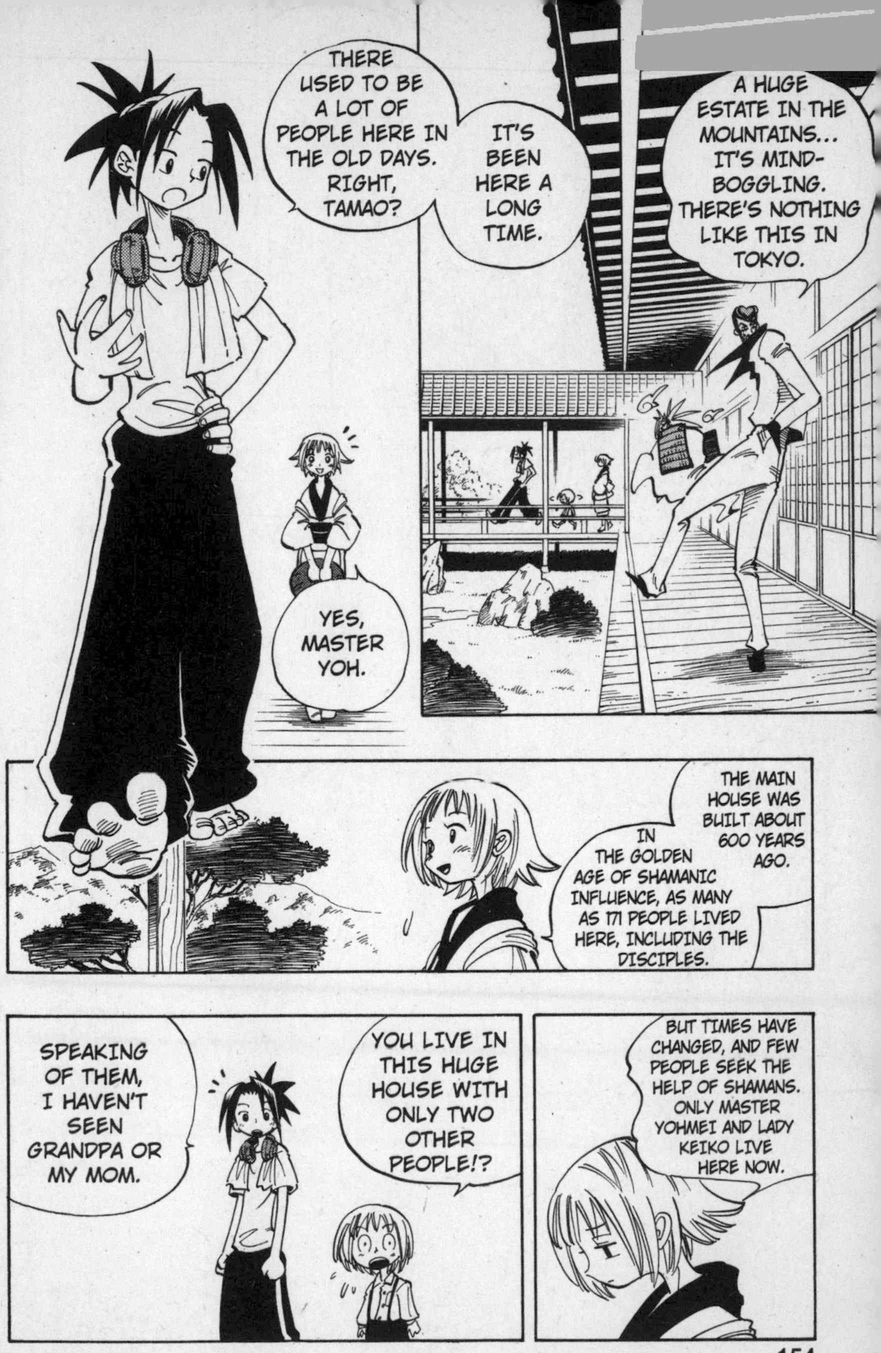
A HUGE ESTATE IN THE MOUNTAINS... IT'S MIND-BOGGLING. THERE'S NOTHING LIKE THIS IN TOKYO.
IT'S BEEN HERE A LONG TIME.
THERE USED TO BE A LOT OF PEOPLE HERE IN THE OLD DAYS. RIGHT, TAMAO?
YES, MASTER YOH.
THE MAIN HOUSE WAS BUILT ABOUT 600 YEARS AGO.
IN THE GOLDEN AGE OF SHAMANIC INFLUENCE, AS MANY AS 171 PEOPLE LIVED HERE, INCLUDING THE DISCIPLES.
BUT TIMES HAVE CHANGED, AND FEW PEOPLE SEEK THE HELP OF SHAMANS. ONLY MASTER YOHMEI AND LADY KEIKO LIVE HERE NOW.
YOU LIVE IN THIS HUGE HOUSE WITH ONLY TWO OTHER PEOPLE!?
SPEAKING OF THEM, I HAVEN'T SEEN GRANDPA OR MY MOM.

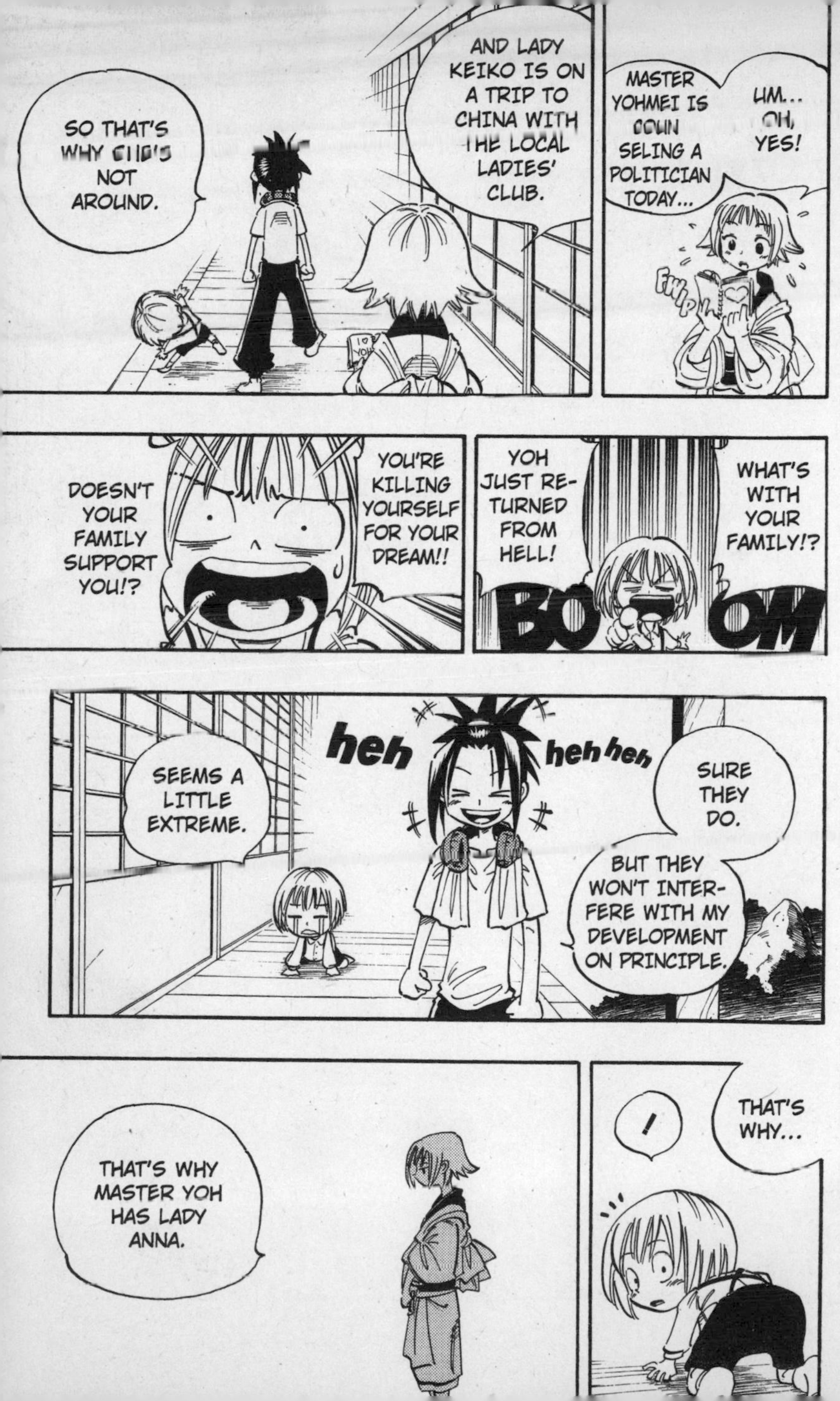
UM... OH, YES!
MASTER YOHMEI IS COUNSELING A POLITICIAN TODAY...
FWIP
AND LADY KEIKO IS ON A TRIP TO CHINA WITH THE LOCAL LADIES' CLUB.
SO THAT'S WHY SHE'S NOT AROUND.
WHAT'S WITH YOUR FAMILY!?
YOH JUST RE-TURNED FROM HELL!
BOOM
YOU'RE KILLING YOURSELF FOR YOUR DREAM!!
DOESN'T YOUR FAMILY SUPPORT YOU!?
SURE THEY DO.
heh heh heh
BUT THEY WON'T INTER-FERE WITH MY DEVELOPMENT ON PRINCIPLE.
SEEMS A LITTLE EXTREME.
THAT'S WHY...
!
THAT'S WHY MASTER YOH HAS LADY ANNA.

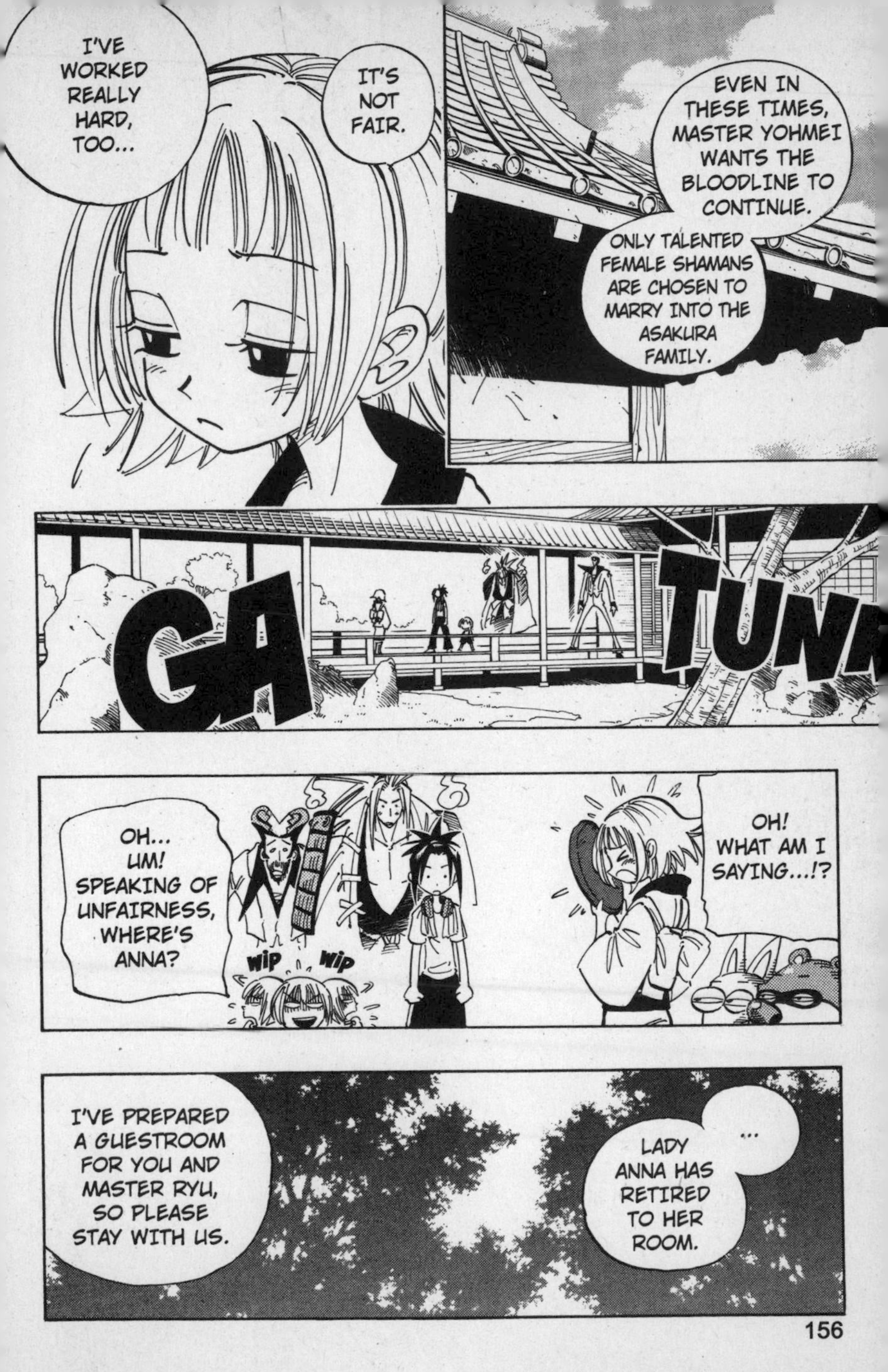
EVEN IN THESE TIMES, MASTER YOHMEI WANTS THE BLOODLINE TO CONTINUE.
ONLY TALENTED FEMALE SHAMANS ARE CHOSEN TO MARRY INTO THE ASAKURA FAMILY.
IT'S NOT FAIR.
I'VE WORKED REALLY HARD, TOO...
CA TUNK
OH! WHAT AM I SAYING...!?
OH... UM! SPEAKING OF UNFAIRNESS, WHERE'S ANNA?
wip
wip
...
LADY ANNA HAS RETIRED TO HER ROOM.
I'VE PREPARED A GUESTROOM FOR YOU AND MASTER RYU, SO PLEASE STAY WITH US.

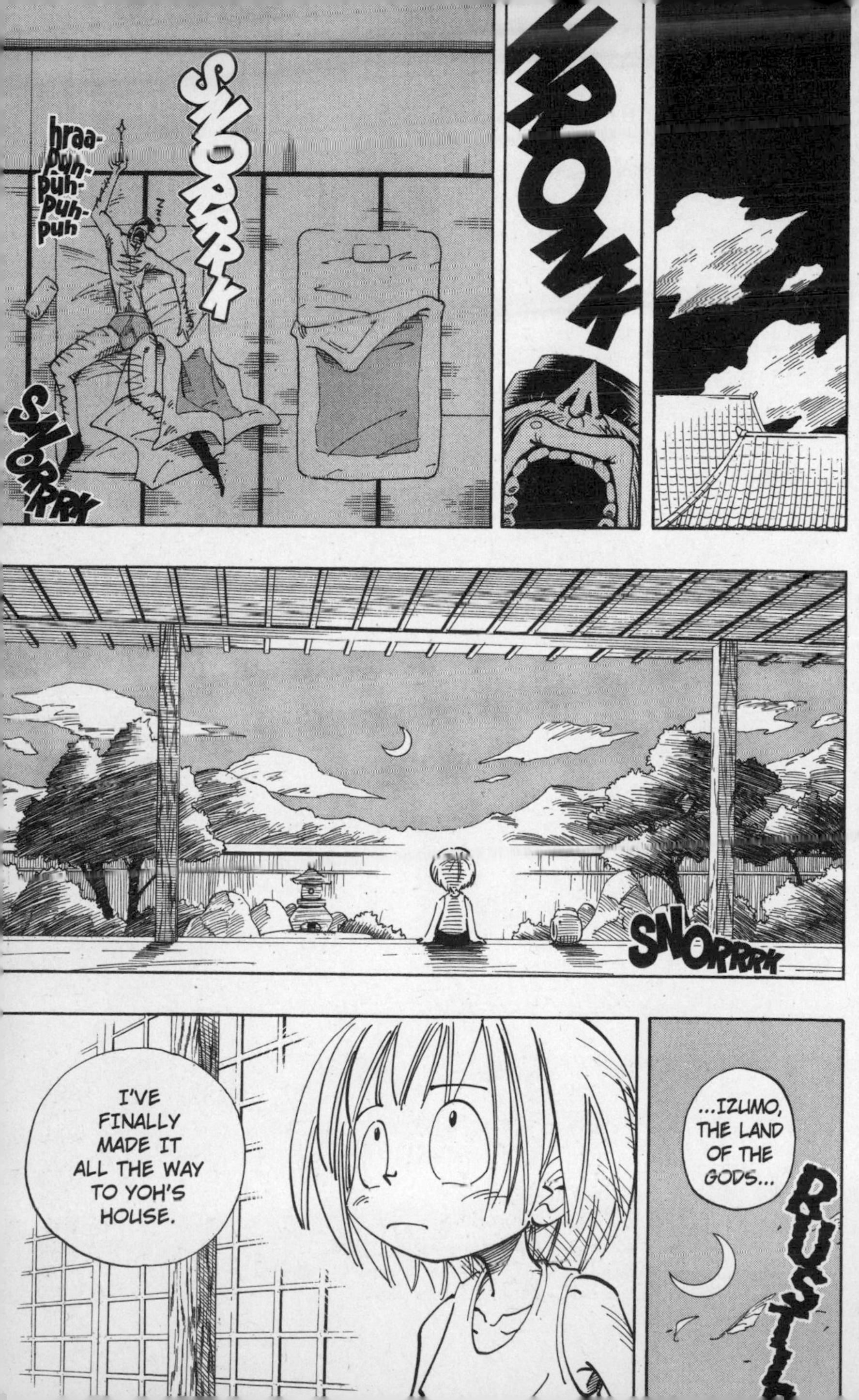
HRONK
SNORRRK
hraa-puh-puh-puh-puh
SNORRRK
SNORRRK
...IZUMO, THE LAND OF THE GODS...
RUSTL
I'VE FINALLY MADE IT ALL THE WAY TO YOH'S HOUSE.

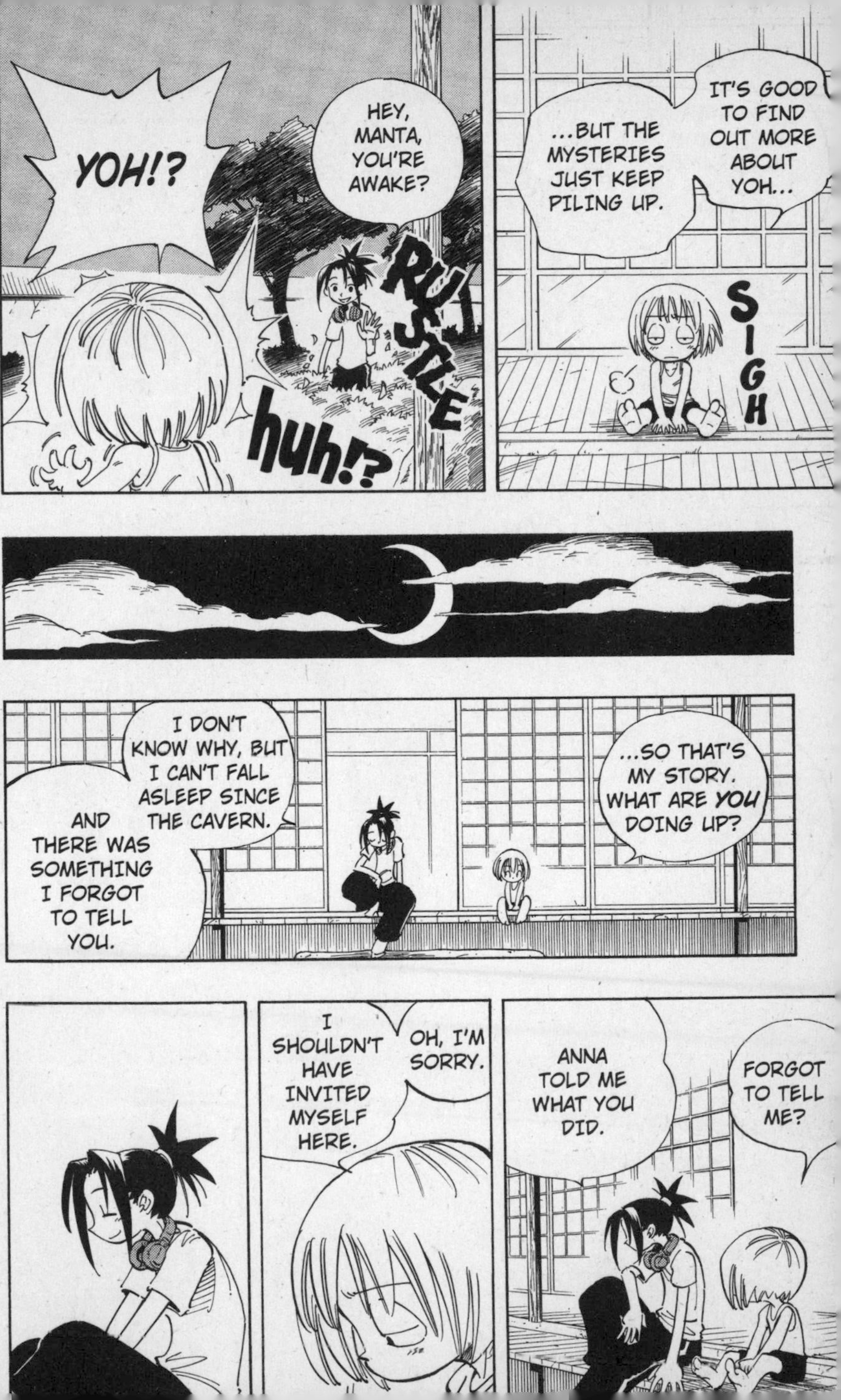
IT'S GOOD TO FIND OUT MORE ABOUT YOH...
...BUT THE MYSTERIES JUST KEEP PILING UP.
SIGH
HEY, MANTA, YOU'RE AWAKE?
RUSTLE
huh!?
YOH!?
...SO THAT'S MY STORY. WHAT ARE YOU DOING UP?
I DON'T KNOW WHY, BUT I CAN'T FALL ASLEEP SINCE THE CAVERN.
AND THERE WAS SOMETHING I FORGOT TO TELL YOU.
FORGOT TO TELL ME?
ANNA TOLD ME WHAT YOU DID.
OH, I'M SORRY.
I SHOULDN'T HAVE INVITED MYSELF HERE.

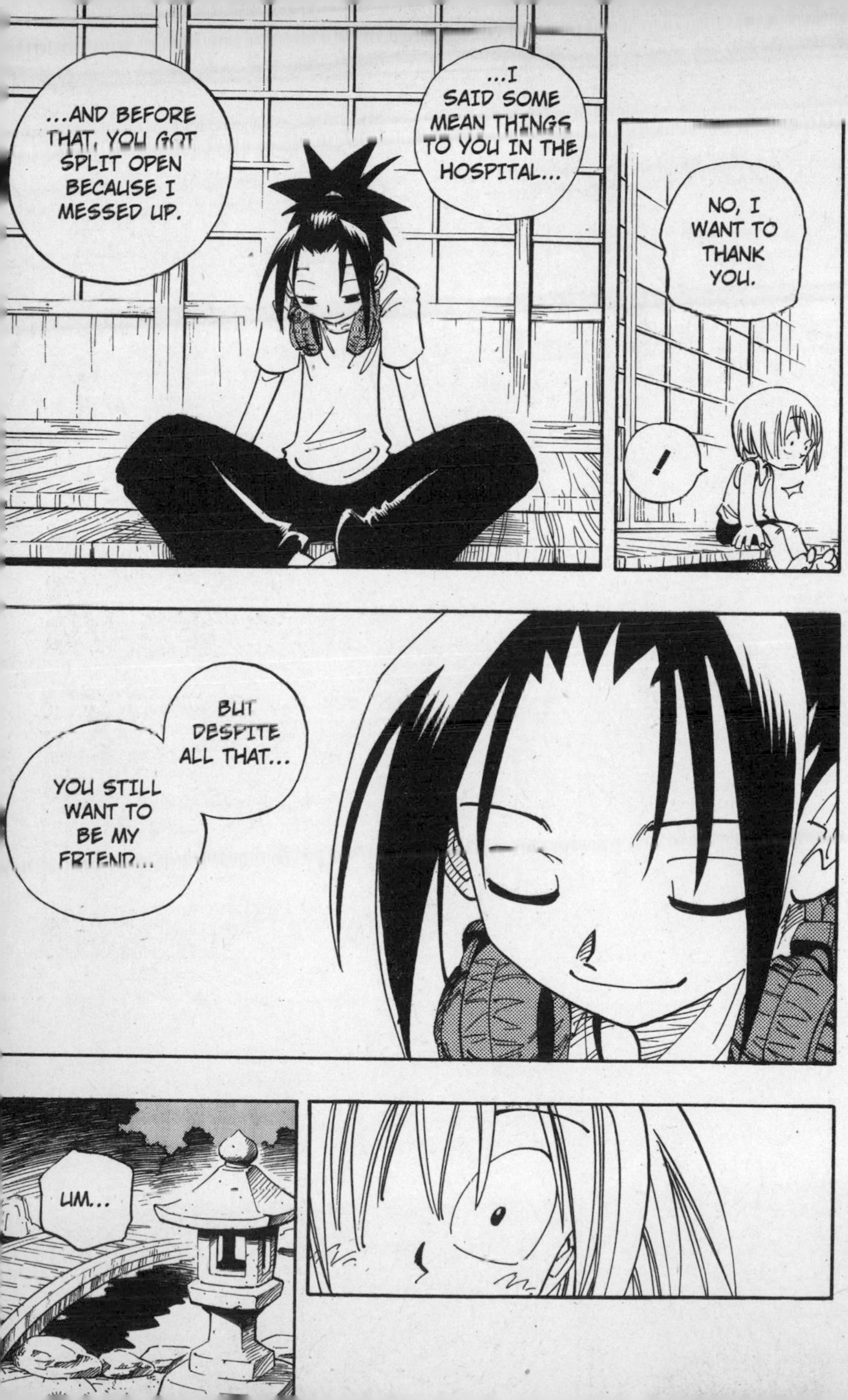
NO, I WANT TO THANK YOU.
!
...I SAID SOME MEAN THINGS TO YOU IN THE HOSPITAL...
...AND BEFORE THAT, YOU GOT SPLIT OPEN BECAUSE I MESSED UP.
BUT DESPITE ALL THAT...
YOU STILL WANT TO BE MY FRIEND...
UM...

READ THIS WAY

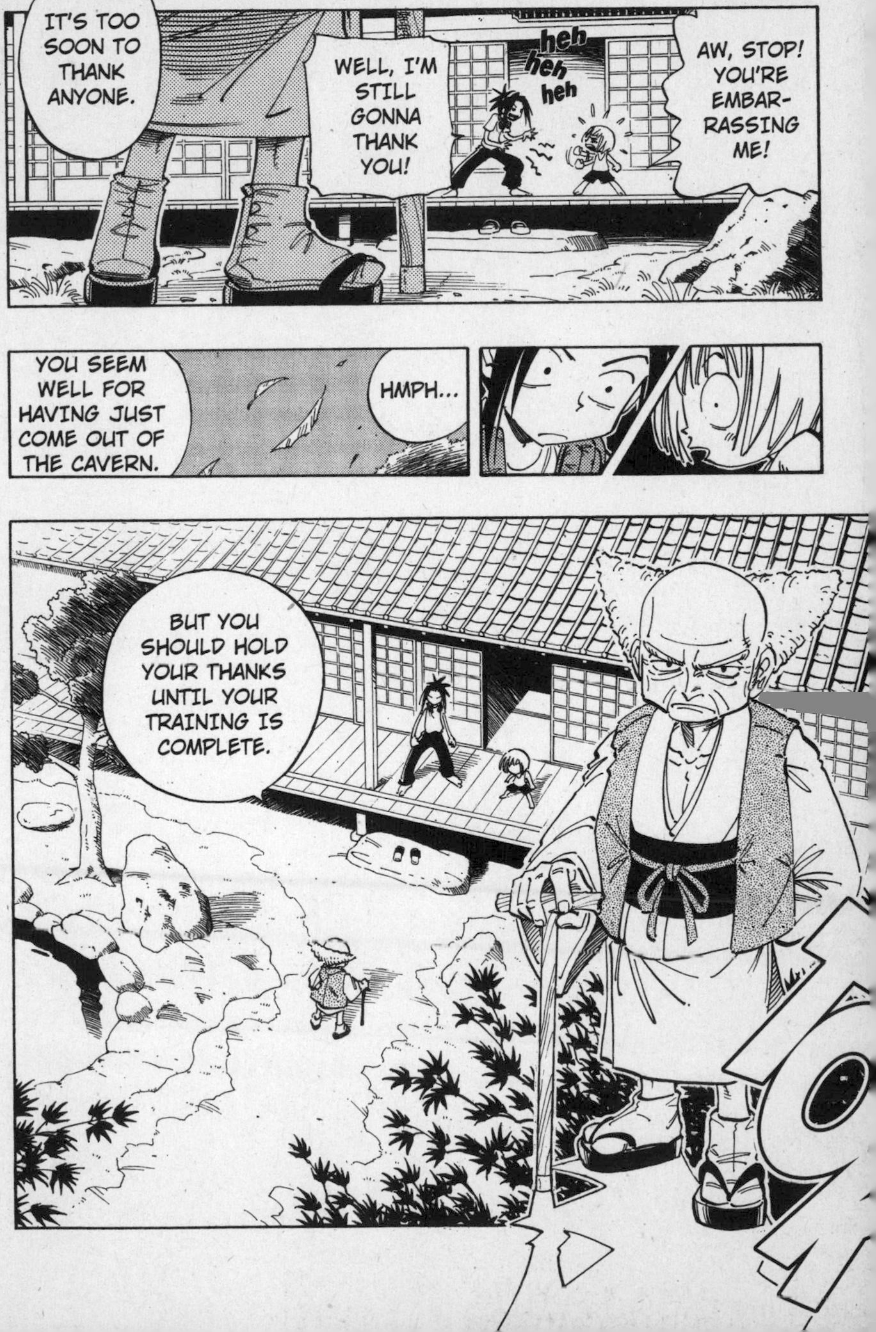
AW, STOP! YOU'RE EMBAR-RASSING ME!
heh heh heh
WELL, I'M STILL GONNA THANK YOU!
IT'S TOO SOON TO THANK ANYONE.
HMPH...
YOU SEEM WELL FOR HAVING JUST COME OUT OF THE CAVERN.
BUT YOU SHOULD HOLD YOUR THANKS UNTIL YOUR TRAINING IS COMPLETE.

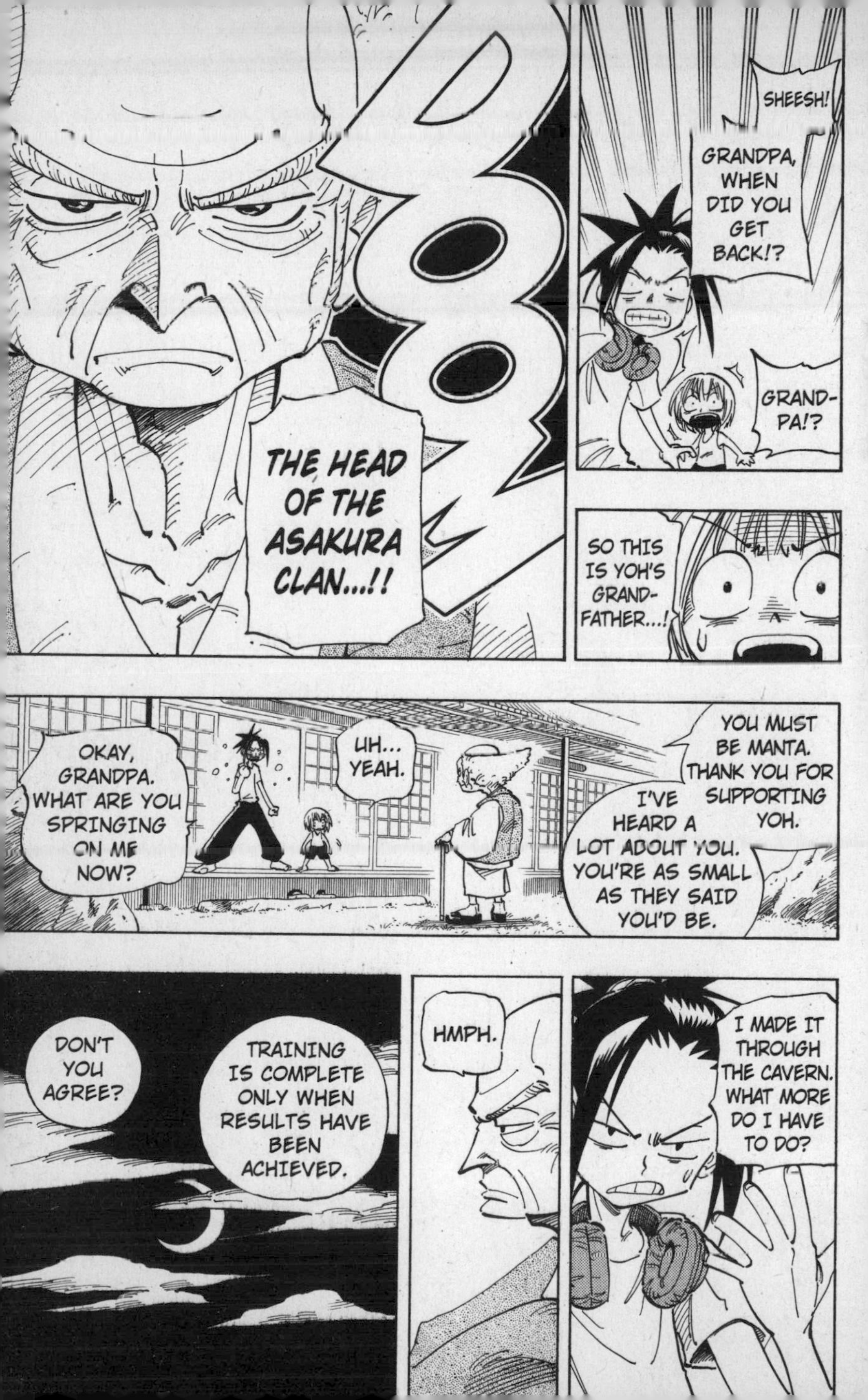
SHEESH!
GRANDPA, WHEN DID YOU GET BACK!?
GRAND-PA!?
SO THIS IS YOH'S GRAND-FATHER...!
THE HEAD OF THE ASAKURA CLAN...!!
YOU MUST BE MANTA. THANK YOU FOR SUPPORTING YOH.
I'VE HEARD A LOT ABOUT YOU. YOU'RE AS SMALL AS THEY SAID YOU'D BE.
UH... YEAH.
OKAY, GRANDPA. WHAT ARE YOU SPRINGING ON ME NOW?
I MADE IT THROUGH THE CAVERN. WHAT MORE DO I HAVE TO DO?
HMPH.
TRAINING IS COMPLETE ONLY WHEN RESULTS HAVE BEEN ACHIEVED.
DON'T YOU AGREE?

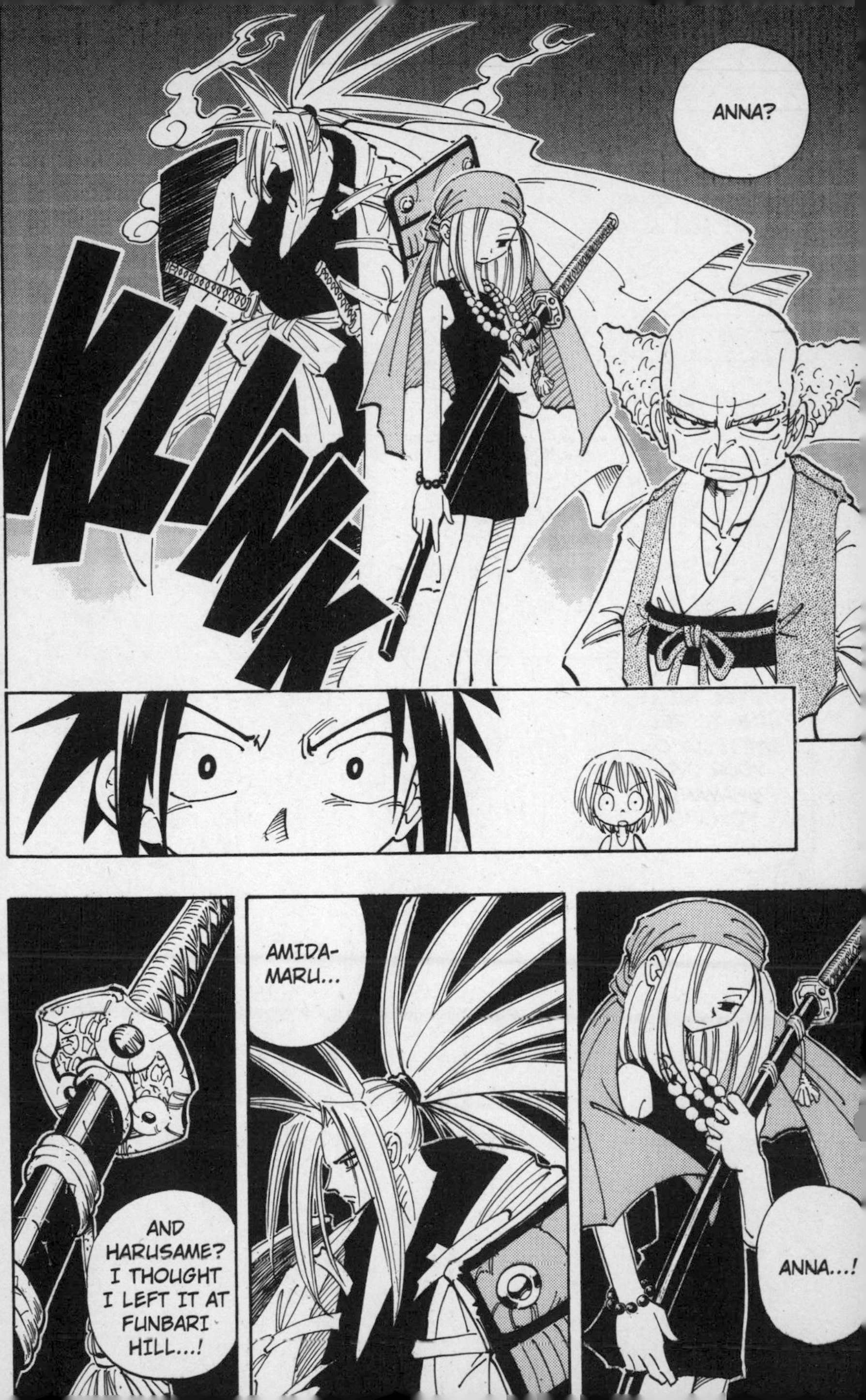
ANNA?
ANNA...!
AMIDA-MARU...
AND HARUSAME? I THOUGHT I LEFT IT AT FUNBARI HILL...!

READ THIS WAY

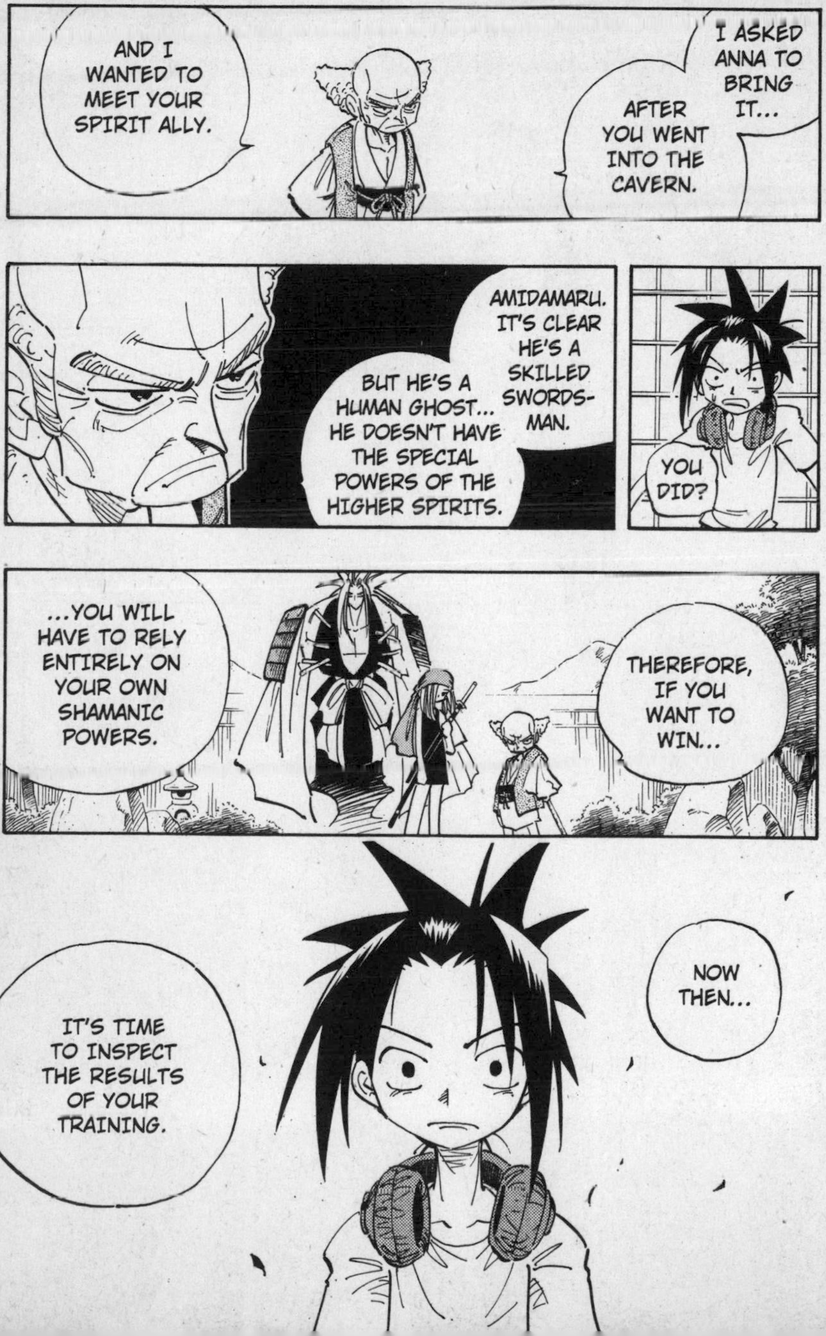
I ASKED ANNA TO BRING IT...
AFTER YOU WENT INTO THE CAVERN.
AND I WANTED TO MEET YOUR SPIRIT ALLY.
YOU DID?
AMIDAMARU. IT'S CLEAR HE'S A SKILLED SWORDS-MAN.
BUT HE'S A HUMAN GHOST... HE DOESN'T HAVE THE SPECIAL POWERS OF THE HIGHER SPIRITS.
THEREFORE, IF YOU WANT TO WIN...
...YOU WILL HAVE TO RELY ENTIRELY ON YOUR OWN SHAMANIC POWERS.
NOW THEN...
IT'S TIME TO INSPECT THE RESULTS OF YOUR TRAINING.

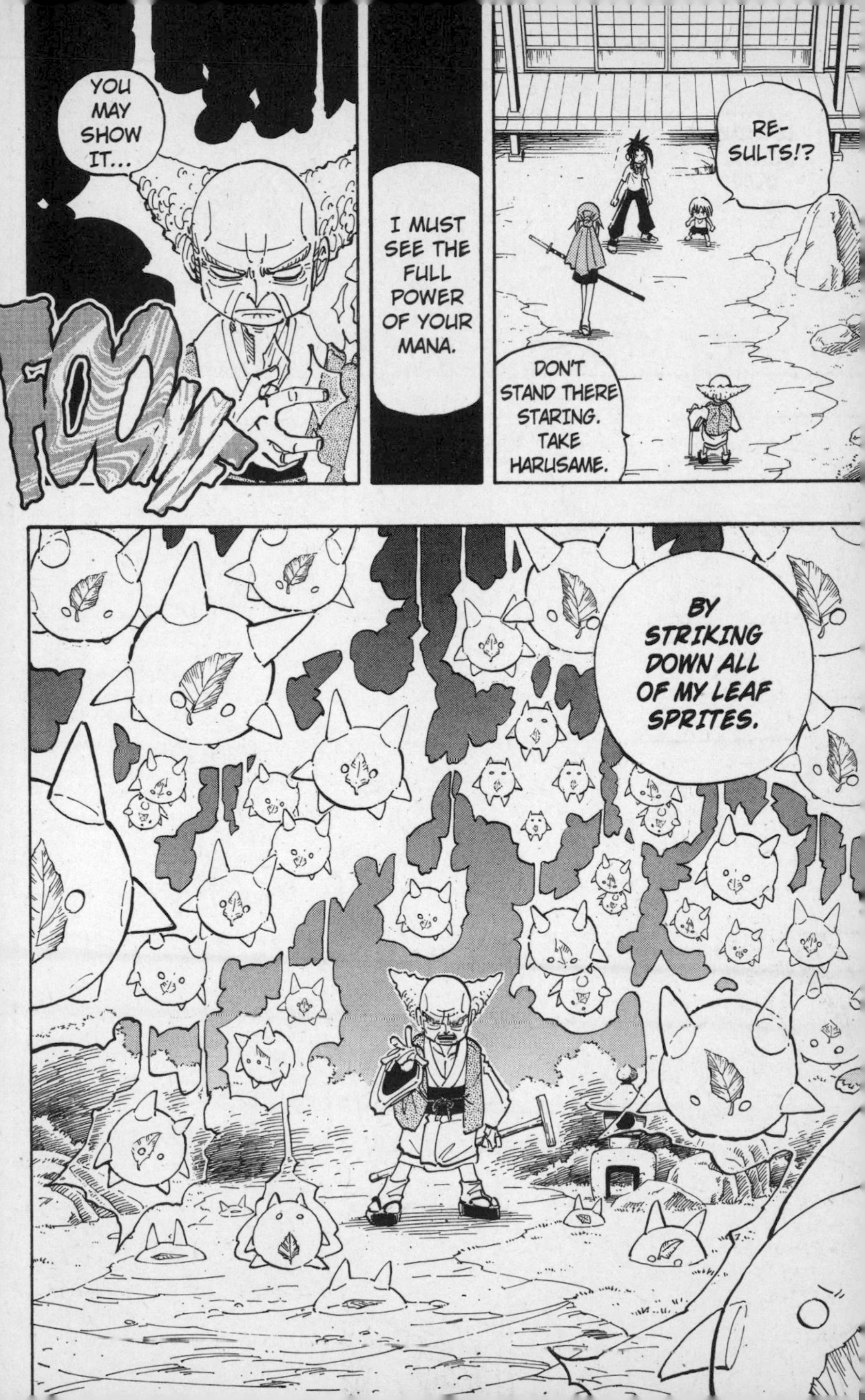
RE-SULTS!?
DON'T STAND THERE STARING. TAKE HARUSAME.
I MUST SEE THE FULL POWER OF YOUR MANA.
YOU MAY SHOW IT...
FOOM
BY STRIKING DOWN ALL OF MY LEAF SPRITES.

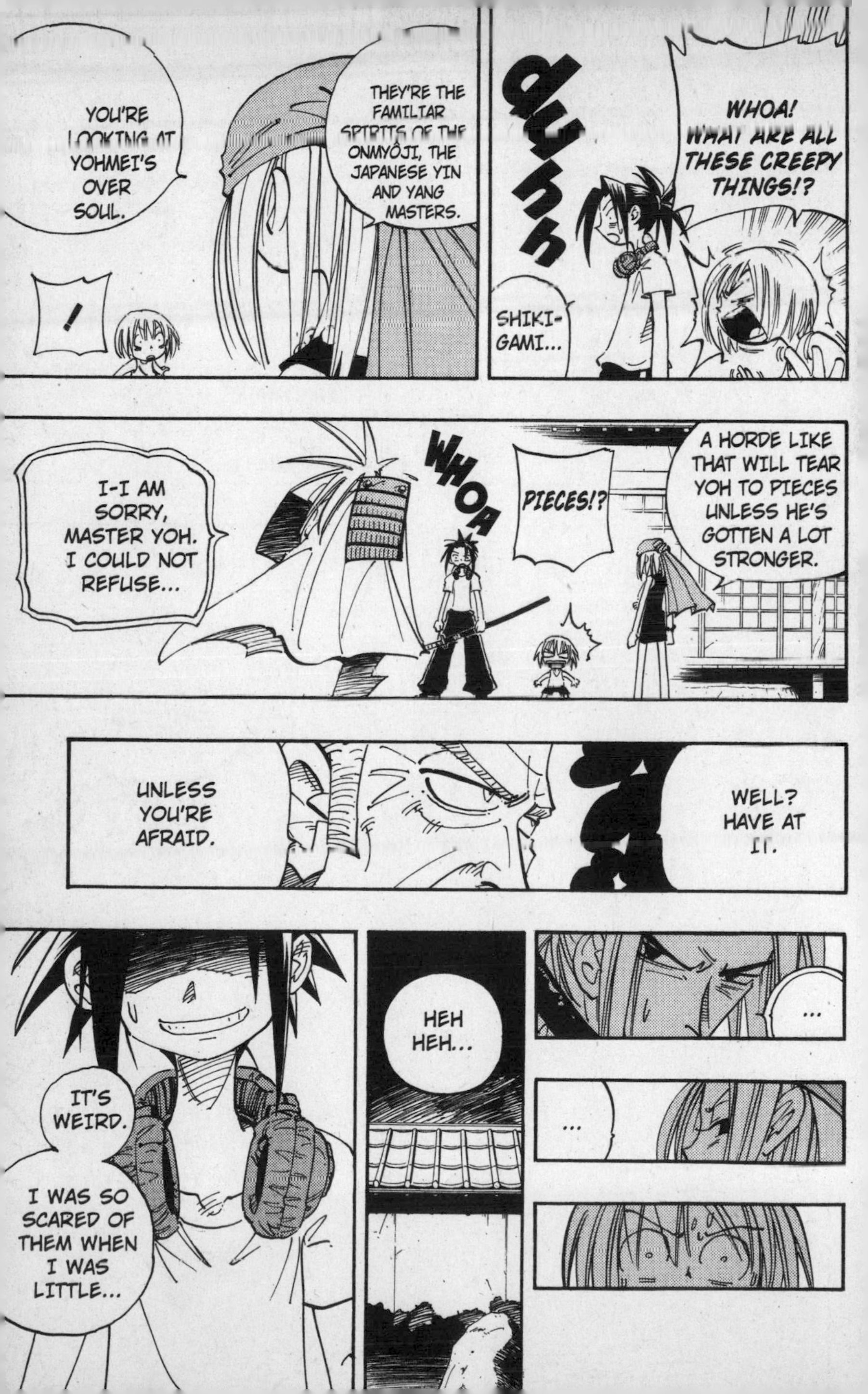
WHOA! WHAT ARE ALL THESE CREEPY THINGS!?
dunh
SHIKI-GAMI...
THEY'RE THE FAMILIAR SPIRITS OF THE ONMYÔJI, THE JAPANESE YIN AND YANG MASTERS.
YOU'RE LOOKING AT YOHMEI'S OVER SOUL.
!
A HORDE LIKE THAT WILL TEAR YOH TO PIECES UNLESS HE'S GOTTEN A LOT STRONGER.
PIECES!?
WHOA
I-I AM SORRY, MASTER YOH. I COULD NOT REFUSE...
WELL? HAVE AT IT.
UNLESS YOU'RE AFRAID.
...
...
HEH HEH...
IT'S WEIRD.
I WAS SO SCARED OF THEM WHEN I WAS LITTLE...

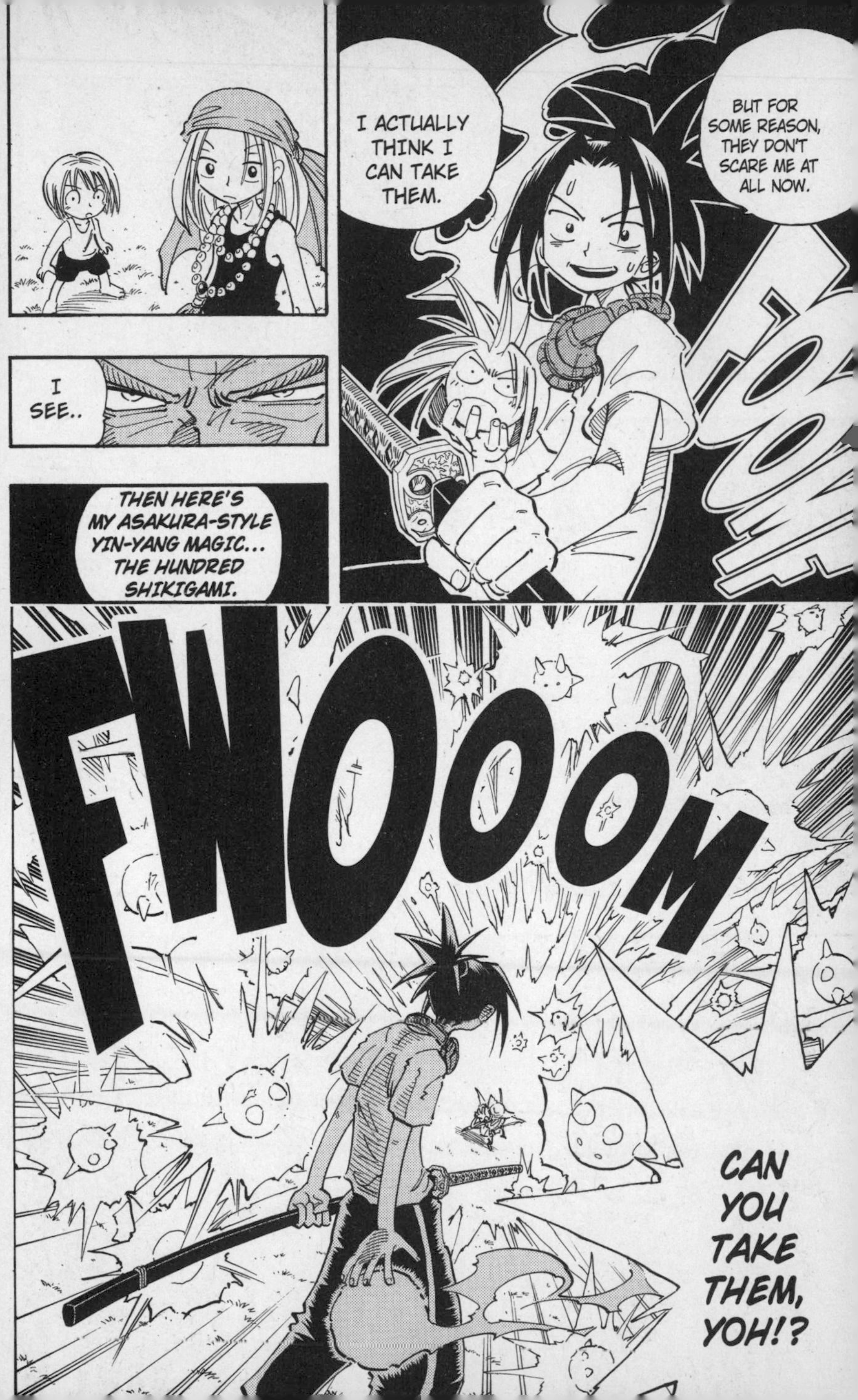
BUT FOR SOME REASON, THEY DON'T SCARE ME AT ALL NOW.
I ACTUALLY THINK I CAN TAKE THEM.
I SEE..
THEN HERE'S MY ASAKURA-STYLE YIN-YANG MAGIC... THE HUNDRED SHIKIGAMI.
FWOOOM
CAN YOU TAKE THEM, YOH!?

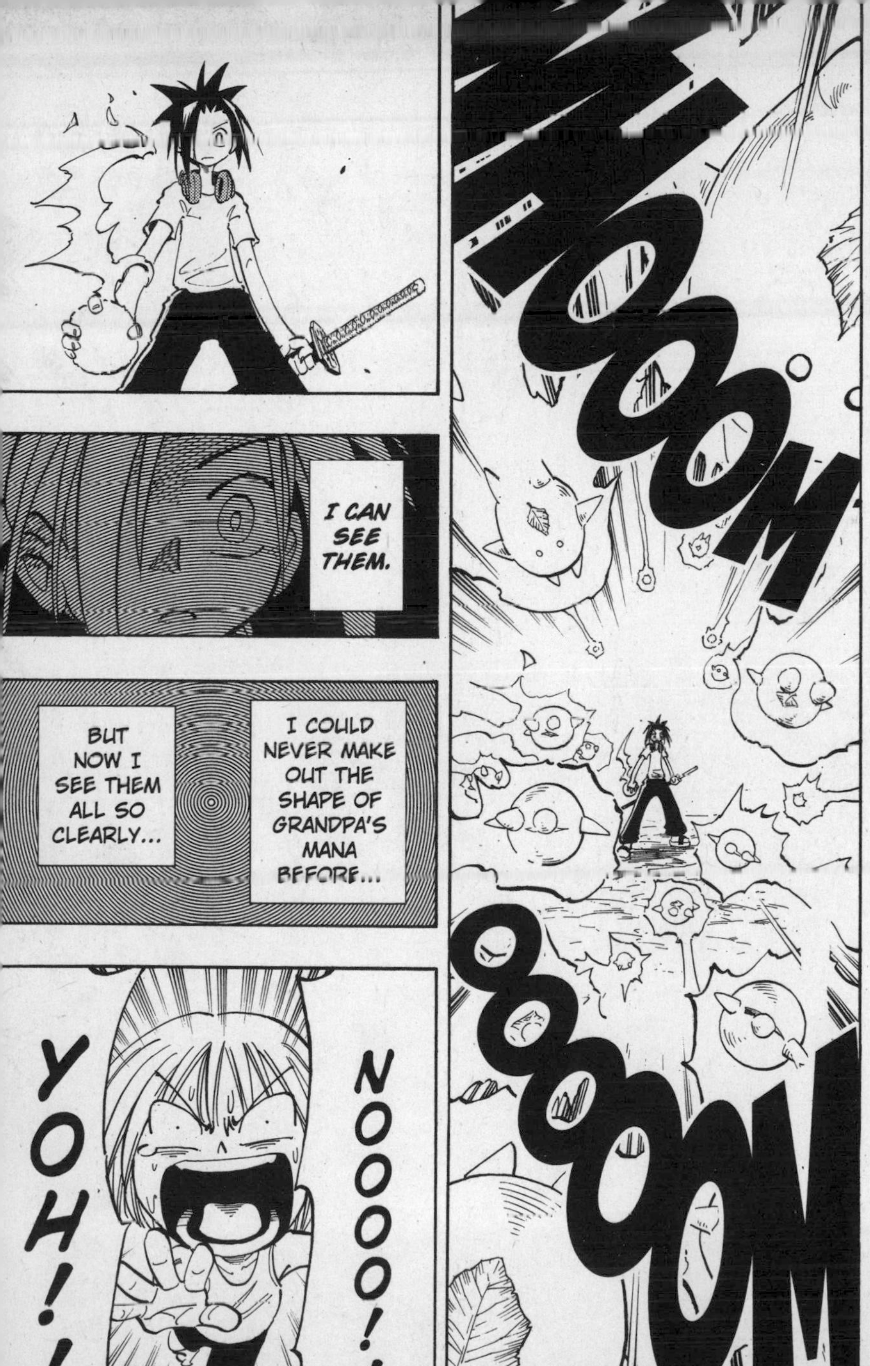
OOOOM
OOOOOOM
I CAN SEE THEM.
I COULD NEVER MAKE OUT THE SHAPE OF GRANDPA'S MANA BEFORE...
BUT NOW I SEE THEM ALL SO CLEARLY...
NOOOO!!
YOH!!!

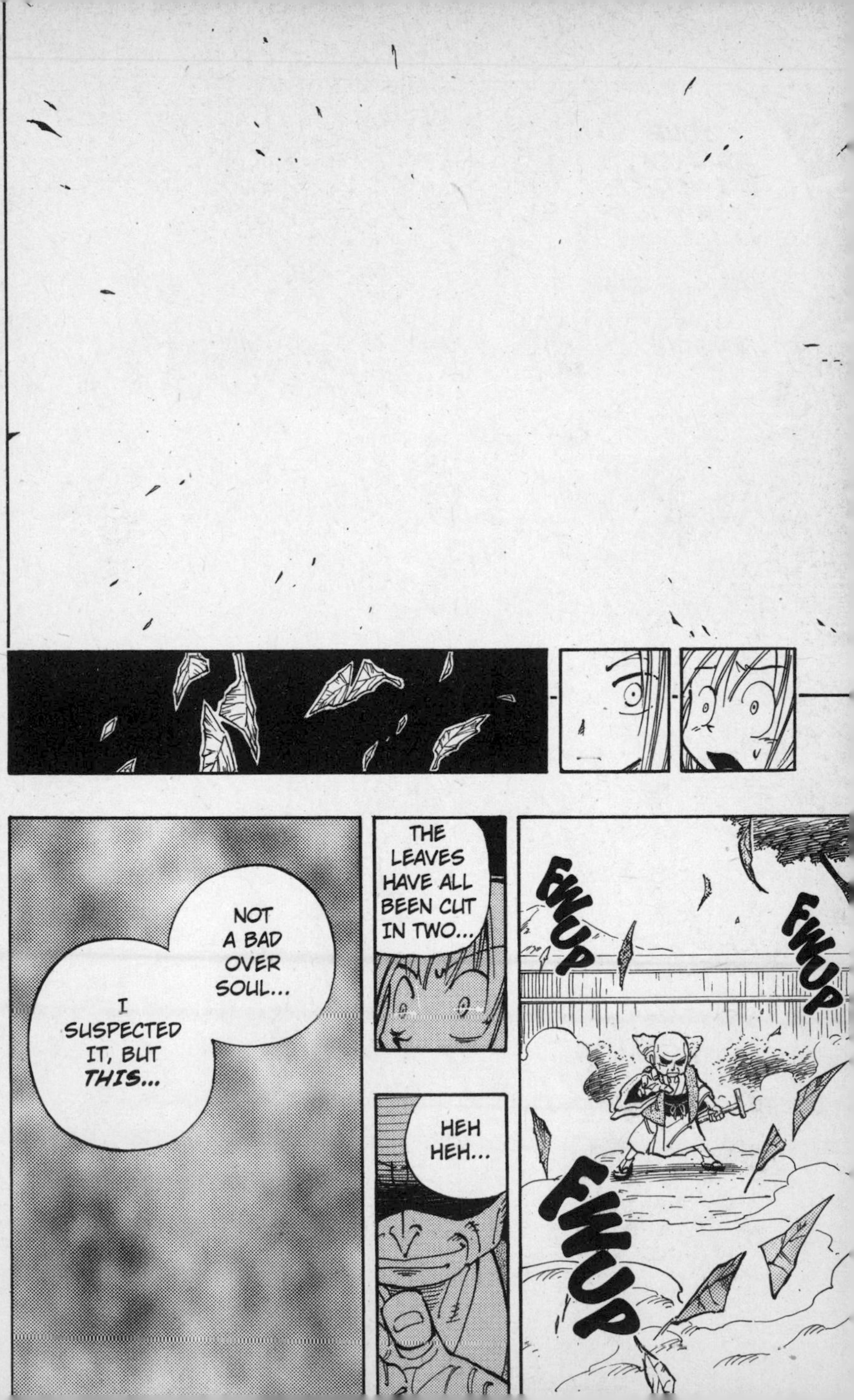
FWUP
FWUP
FWUP
THE LEAVES HAVE ALL BEEN CUT IN TWO...
HEH HEH...
NOT A BAD OVER SOUL...
I SUSPECTED IT, BUT *THIS...*

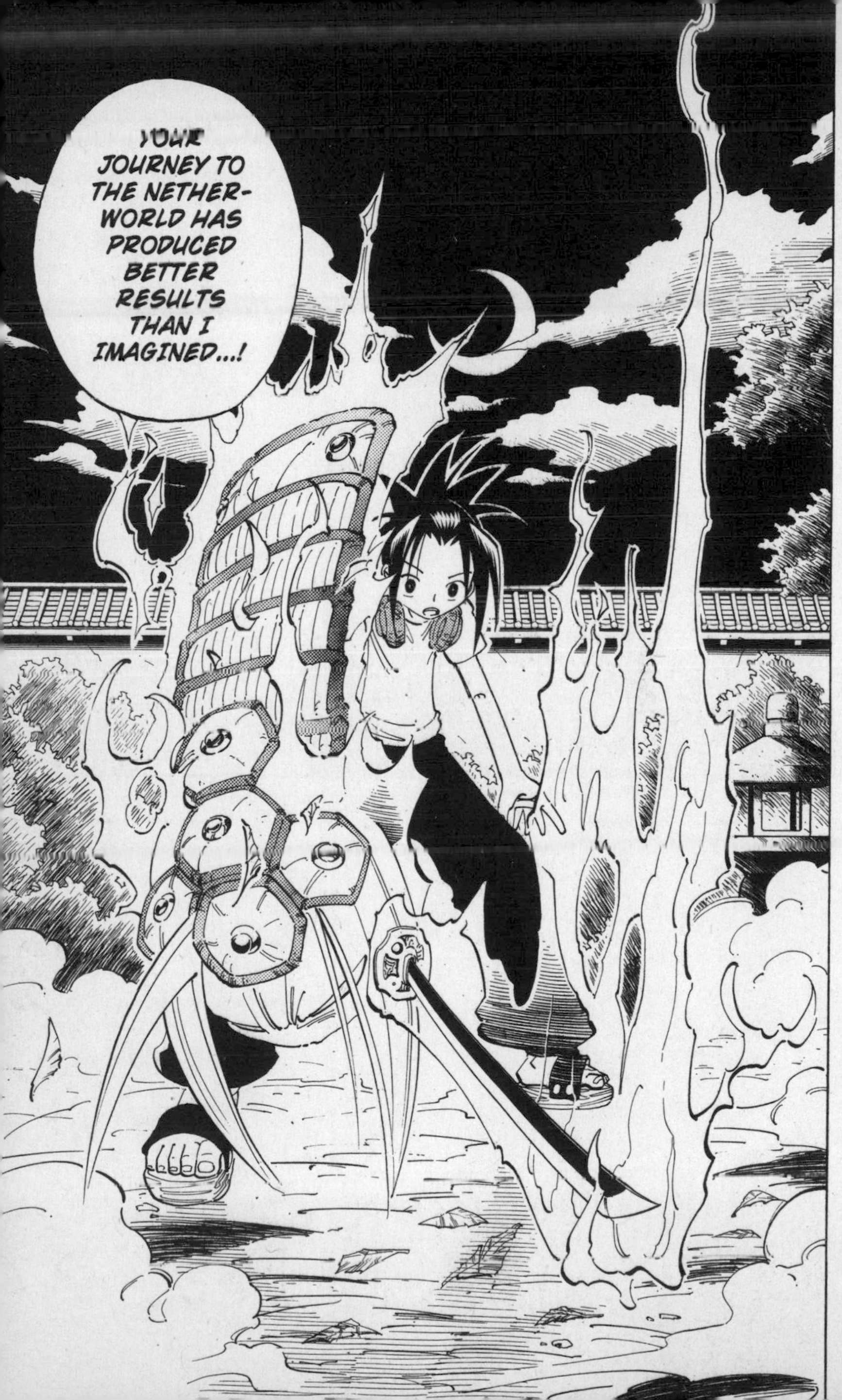
YOUR JOURNEY TO THE NETHER-WORLD HAS PRODUCED BETTER RESULTS THAN I IMAGINED...!

SHAMAN KING CHARACTER FILE No.28

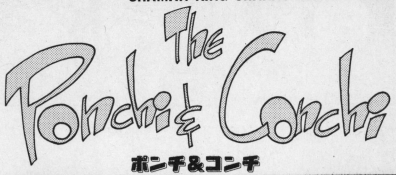

# The Ponchi & Conchi

ポンチ＆コンチ

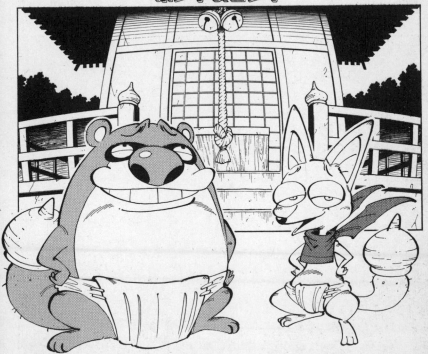

DATA UNKNOWN

# Reincarnation 53: Two Tough Ghosts

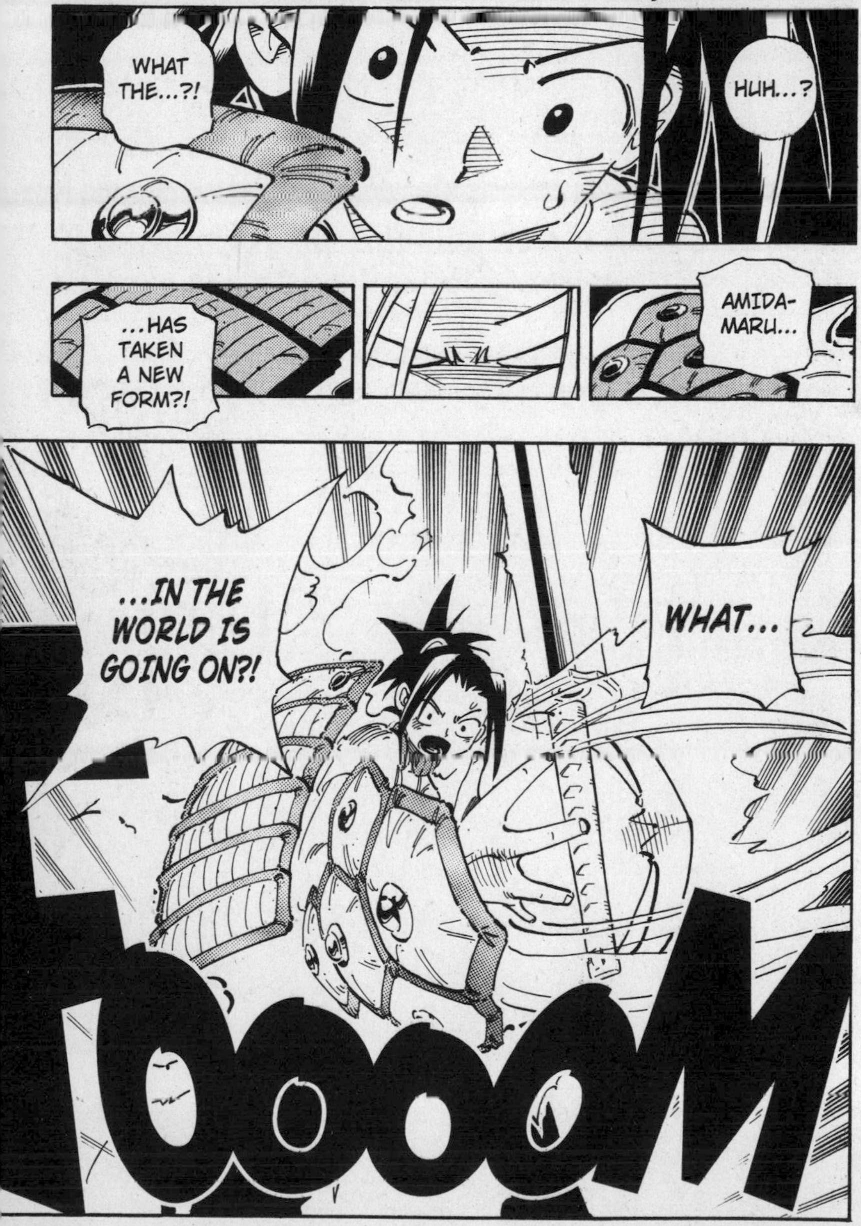
HUH...?
WHAT THE...?!
AMIDA-MARU...
...HAS TAKEN A NEW FORM?!
WHAT...
...IN THE WORLD IS GOING ON?!

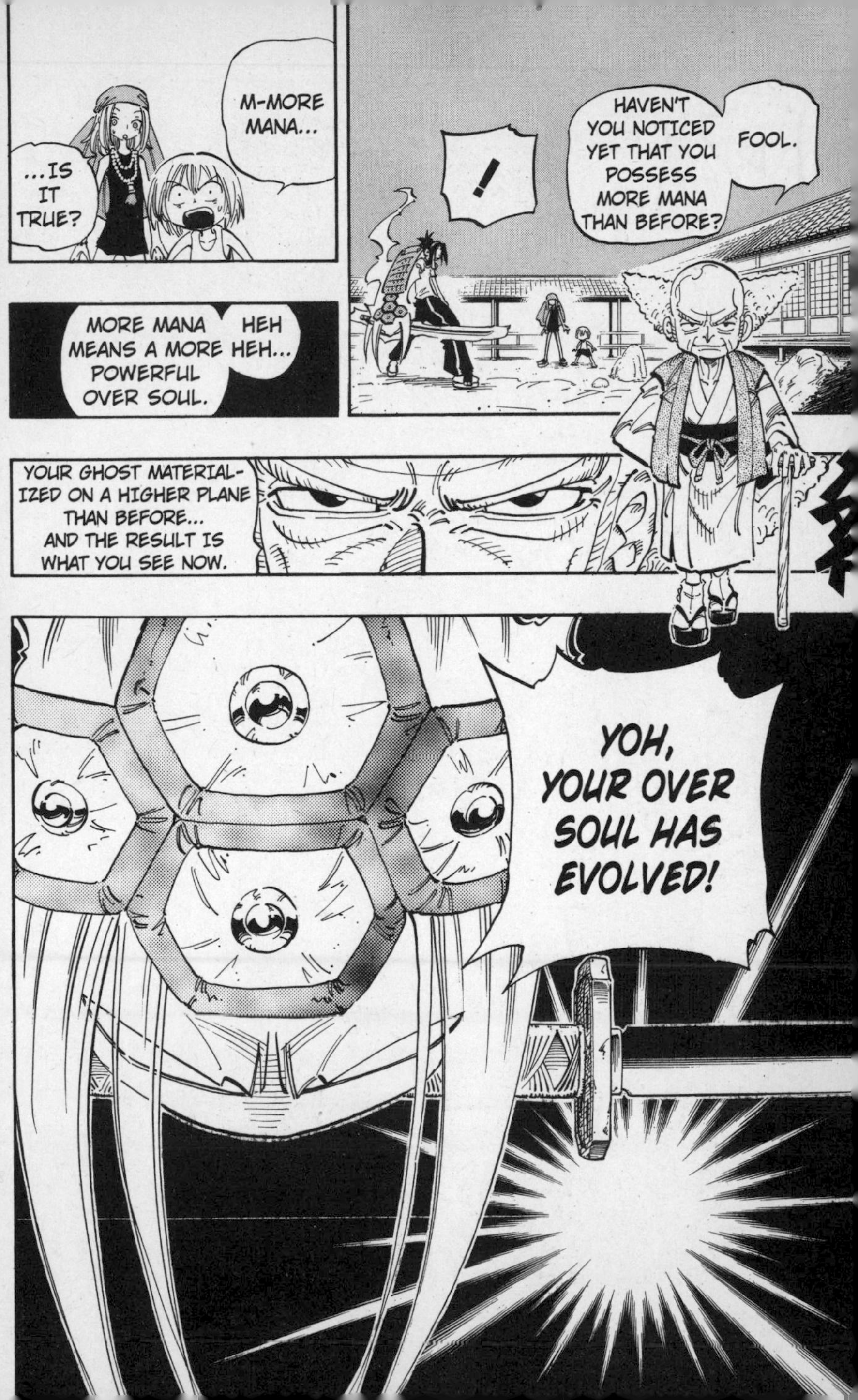
HAVEN'T YOU NOTICED YET THAT YOU POSSESS MORE MANA THAN BEFORE?
FOOL.
!
M-MORE MANA...
...IS IT TRUE?
HEH HEH...
MORE MANA MEANS A MORE POWERFUL OVER SOUL.
YOUR GHOST MATERIALIZED ON A HIGHER PLANE THAN BEFORE... AND THE RESULT IS WHAT YOU SEE NOW.
YOH, YOUR OVER SOUL HAS EVOLVED!

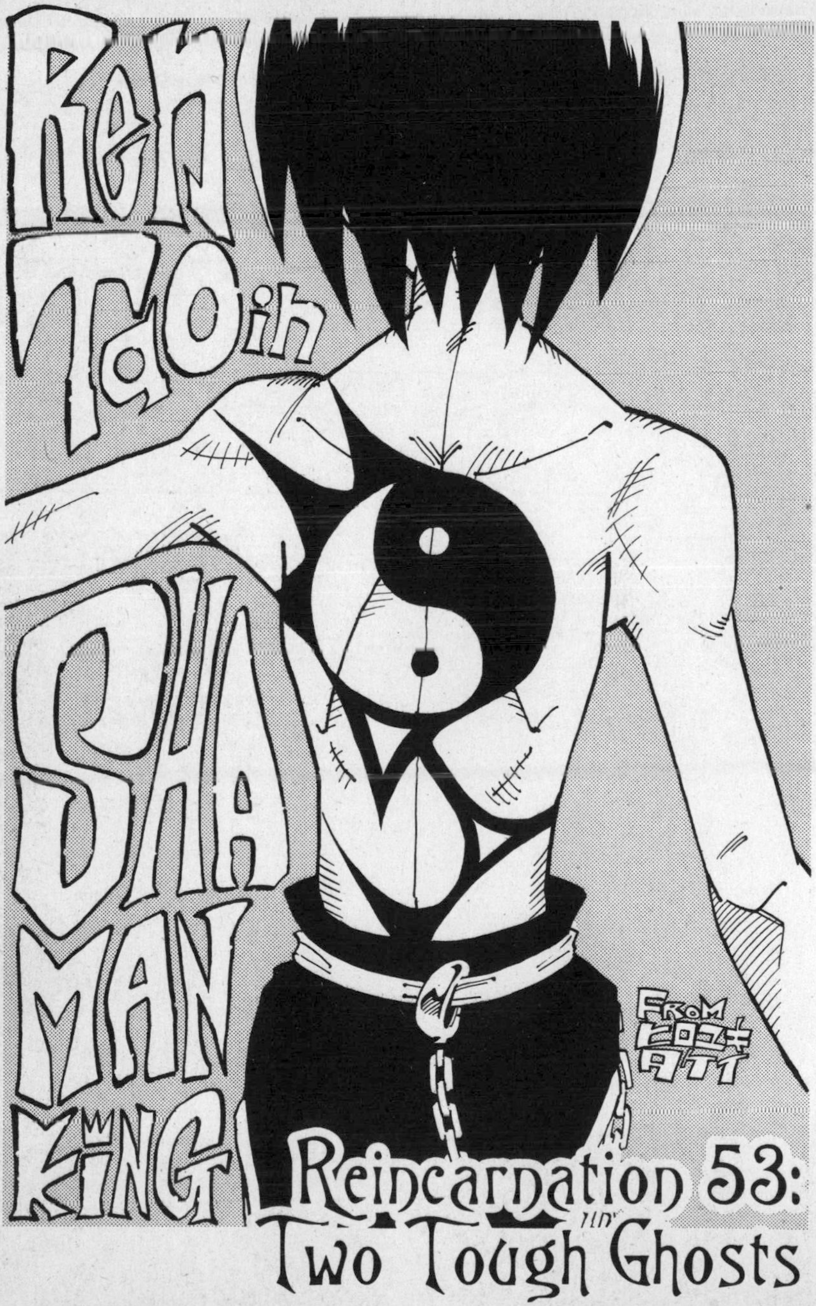
Ren Tao in
SHAMAN KING
FROM ヒロユキ タケイ
Reincarnation 53:
Two Tough Ghosts

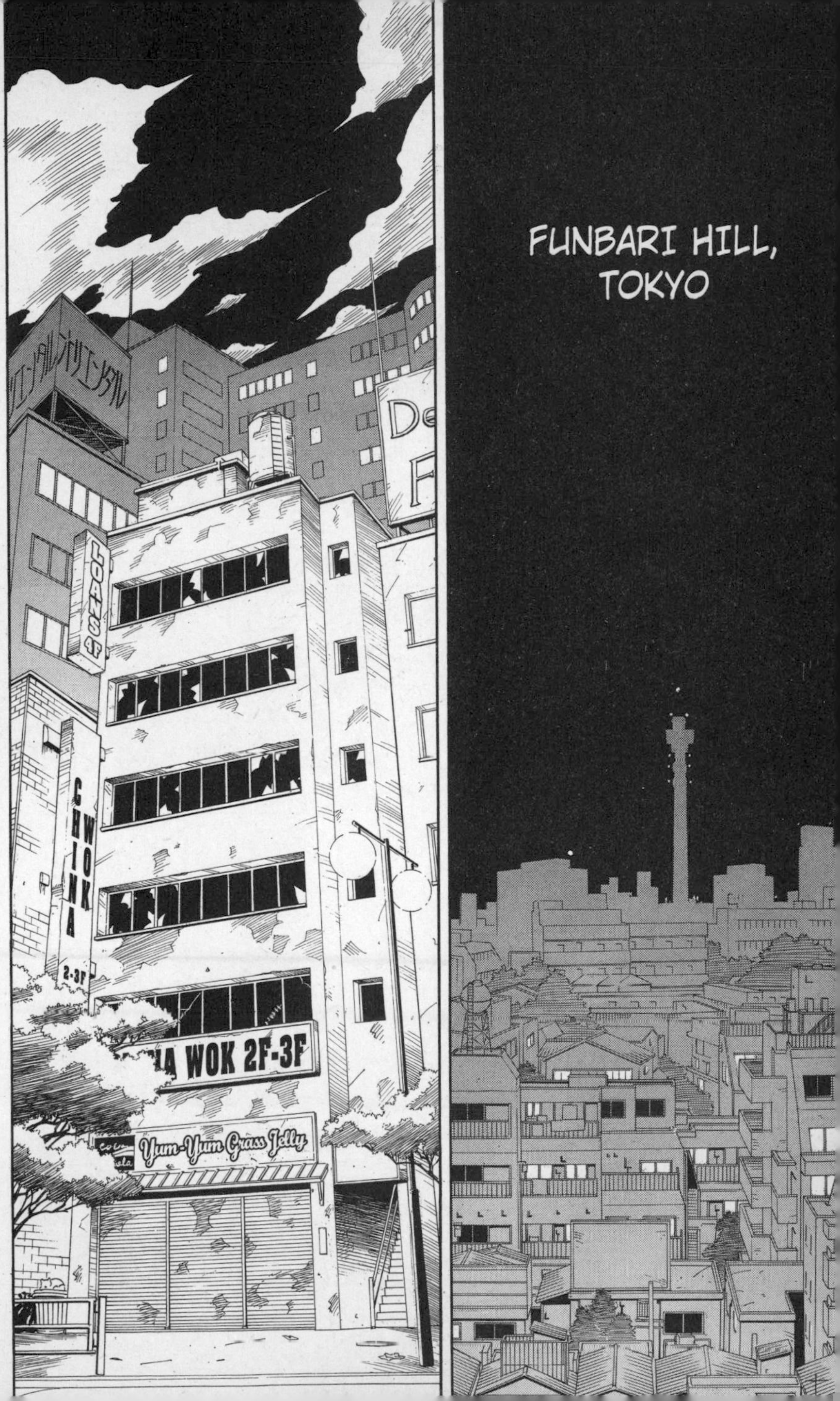

FUNBARI HILL, TOKYO
LOANS 4F
CHINA WOK
2-3F
WOK 2F-3F
Yum-Yum Grass Jelly

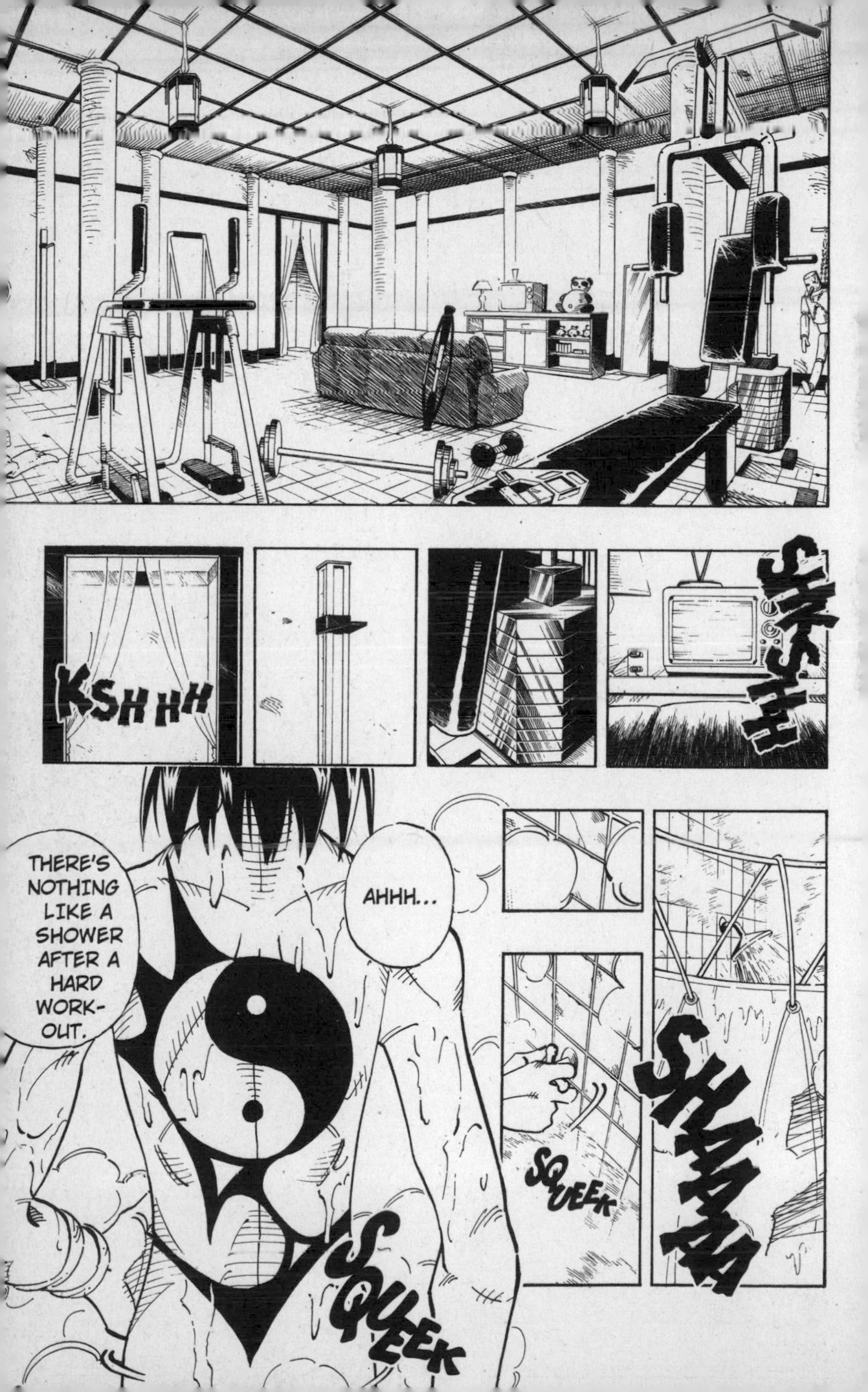
SHSH
KSHHHH
SHAAAA
SQUEEK
AHHH...
THERE'S NOTHING LIKE A SHOWER AFTER A HARD WORK-OUT.
SQUEEK

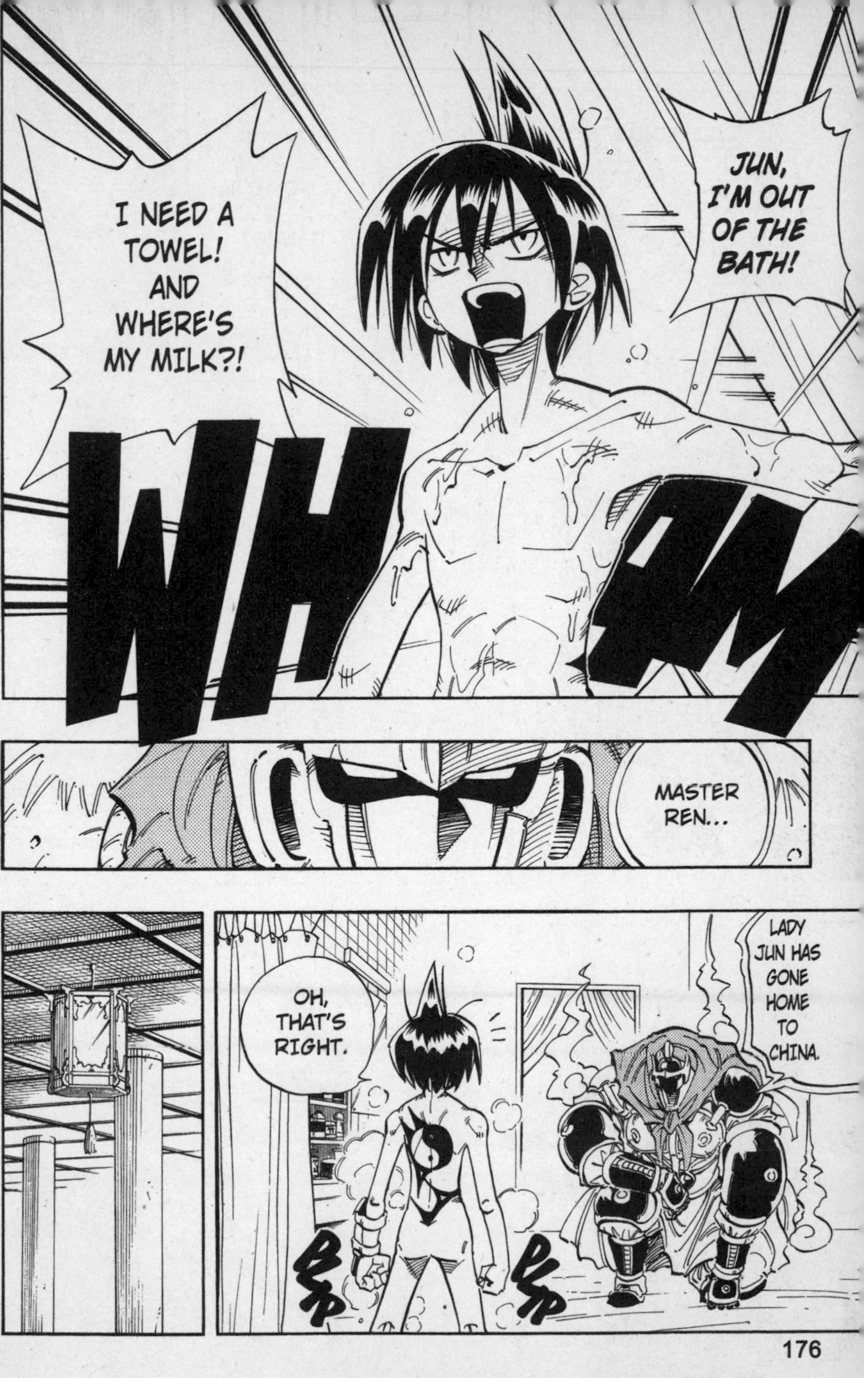

JUN, I'M OUT OF THE BATH!
I NEED A TOWEL! AND WHERE'S MY MILK?!
WHAM
MASTER REN...
LADY JUN HAS GONE HOME TO CHINA.
OH, THAT'S RIGHT.

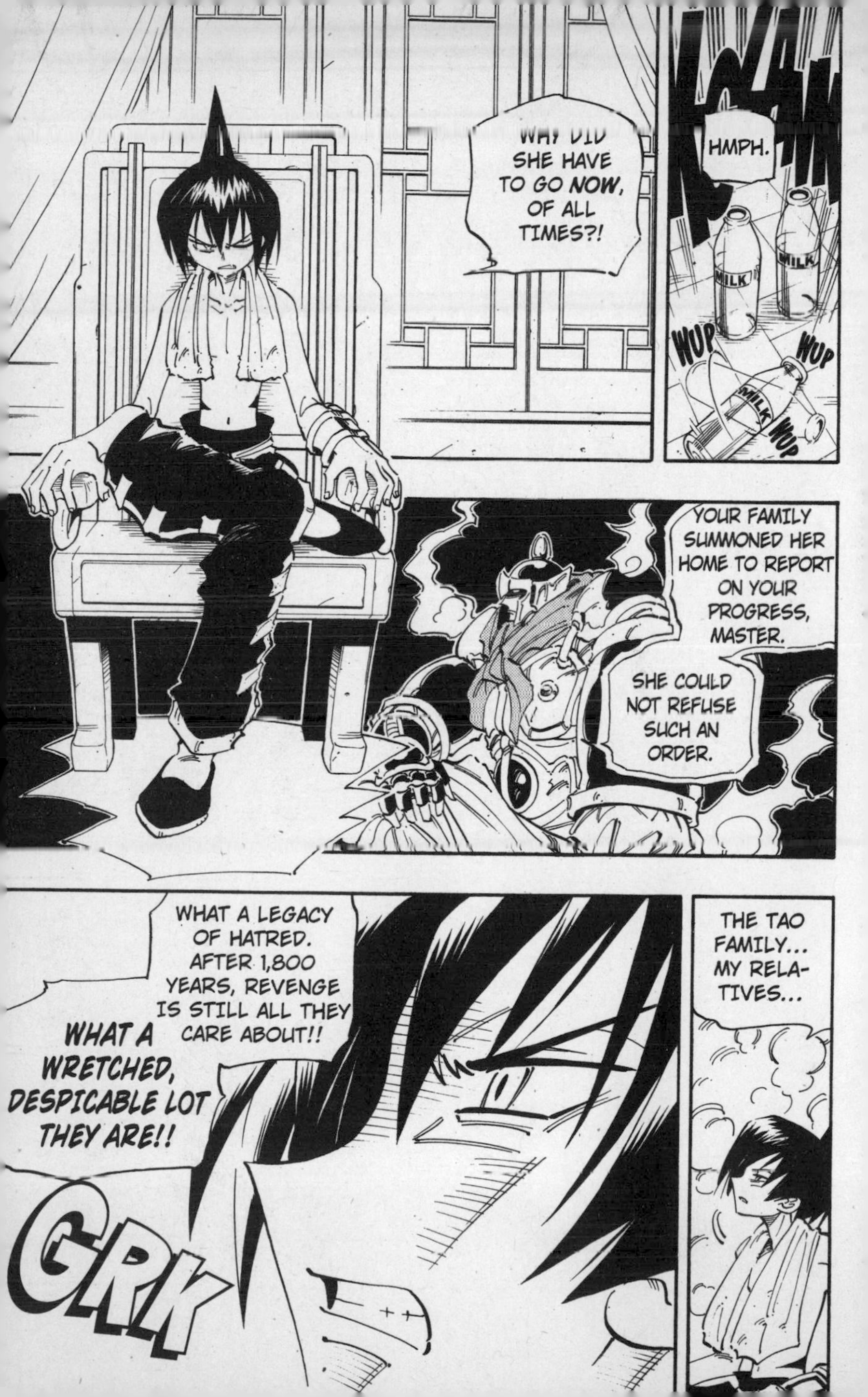
HMPH.
WUP
WUP
WUP
WHY DID SHE HAVE TO GO NOW, OF ALL TIMES?!
YOUR FAMILY SUMMONED HER HOME TO REPORT ON YOUR PROGRESS, MASTER.
SHE COULD NOT REFUSE SUCH AN ORDER.
THE TAO FAMILY... MY RELATIVES...
WHAT A LEGACY OF HATRED. AFTER 1,800 YEARS, REVENGE IS STILL ALL THEY CARE ABOUT!!
WHAT A WRETCHED, DESPICABLE LOT THEY ARE!!
GRK

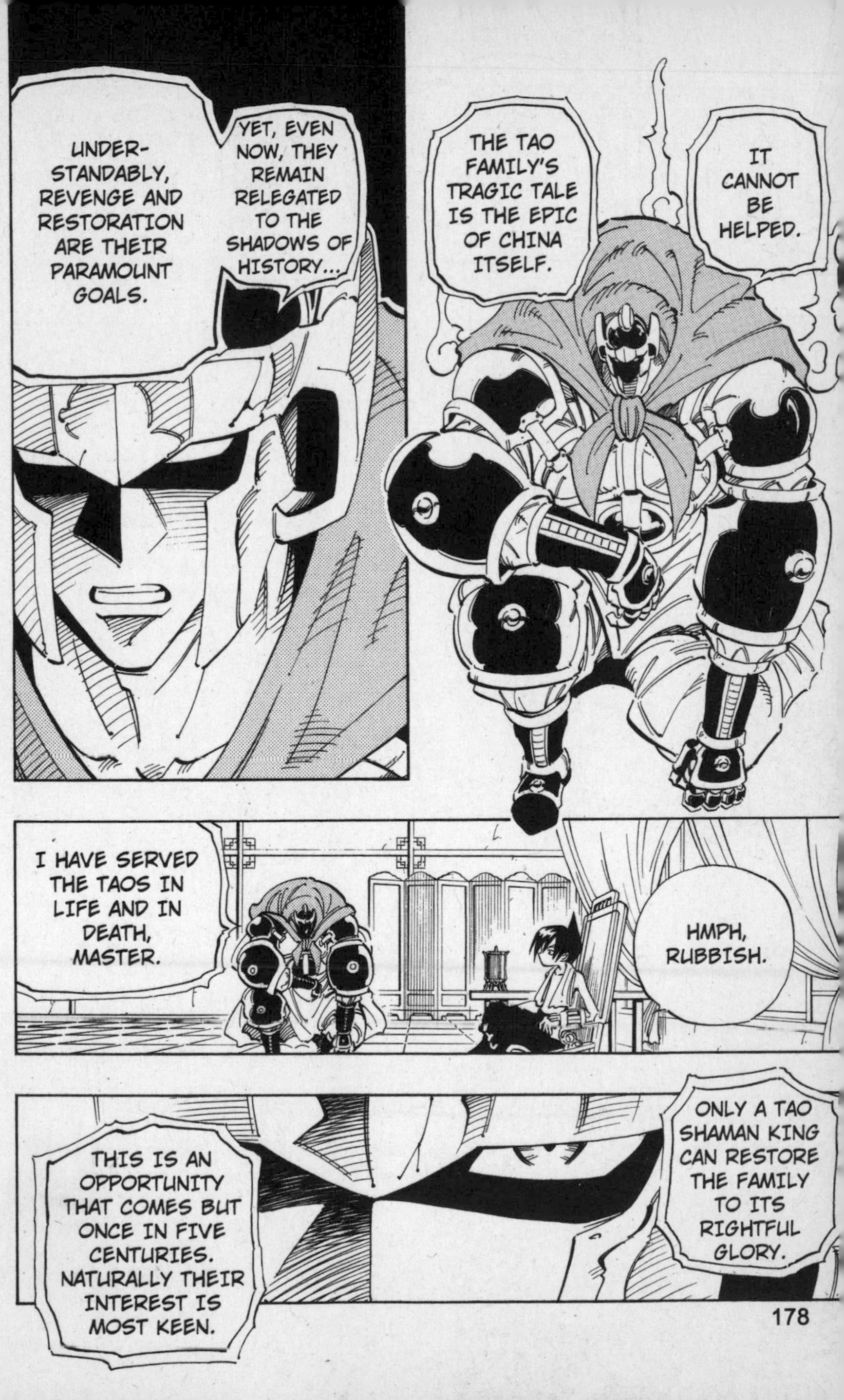
IT CANNOT BE HELPED.
THE TAO FAMILY'S TRAGIC TALE IS THE EPIC OF CHINA ITSELF.
YET, EVEN NOW, THEY REMAIN RELEGATED TO THE SHADOWS OF HISTORY...
UNDER-STANDABLY, REVENGE AND RESTORATION ARE THEIR PARAMOUNT GOALS.
HMPH, RUBBISH.
I HAVE SERVED THE TAOS IN LIFE AND IN DEATH, MASTER.
ONLY A TAO SHAMAN KING CAN RESTORE THE FAMILY TO ITS RIGHTFUL GLORY.
THIS IS AN OPPORTUNITY THAT COMES BUT ONCE IN FIVE CENTURIES. NATURALLY THEIR INTEREST IS MOST KEEN.

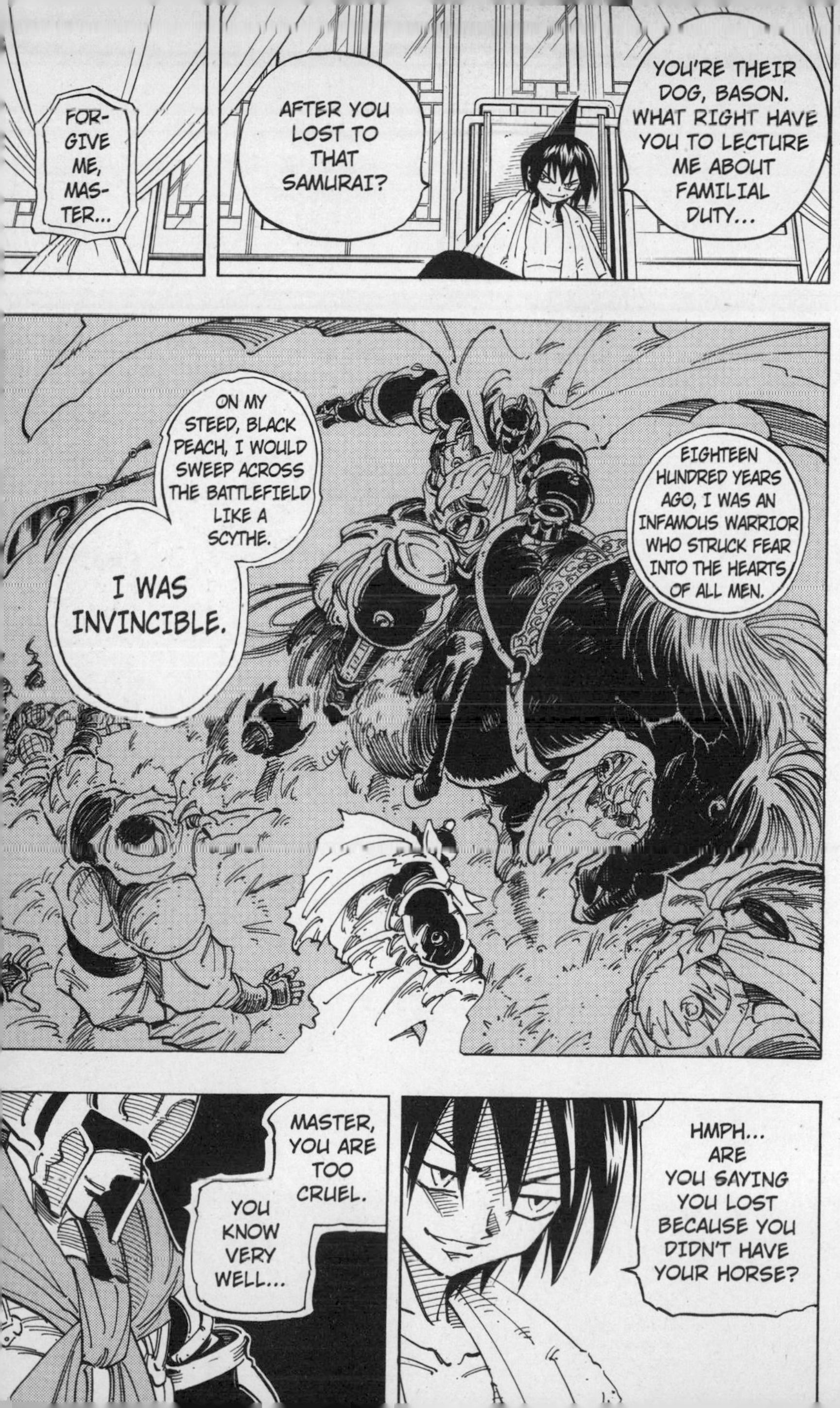
YOU'RE THEIR DOG, BASON. WHAT RIGHT HAVE YOU TO LECTURE ME ABOUT FAMILIAL DUTY...
AFTER YOU LOST TO THAT SAMURAI?
FOR-GIVE ME, MAS-TER...
EIGHTEEN HUNDRED YEARS AGO, I WAS AN INFAMOUS WARRIOR WHO STRUCK FEAR INTO THE HEARTS OF ALL MEN.
ON MY STEED, BLACK PEACH, I WOULD SWEEP ACROSS THE BATTLEFIELD LIKE A SCYTHE.
I WAS INVINCIBLE.
HMPH... ARE YOU SAYING YOU LOST BECAUSE YOU DIDN'T HAVE YOUR HORSE?
MASTER, YOU ARE TOO CRUEL.
YOU KNOW VERY WELL...

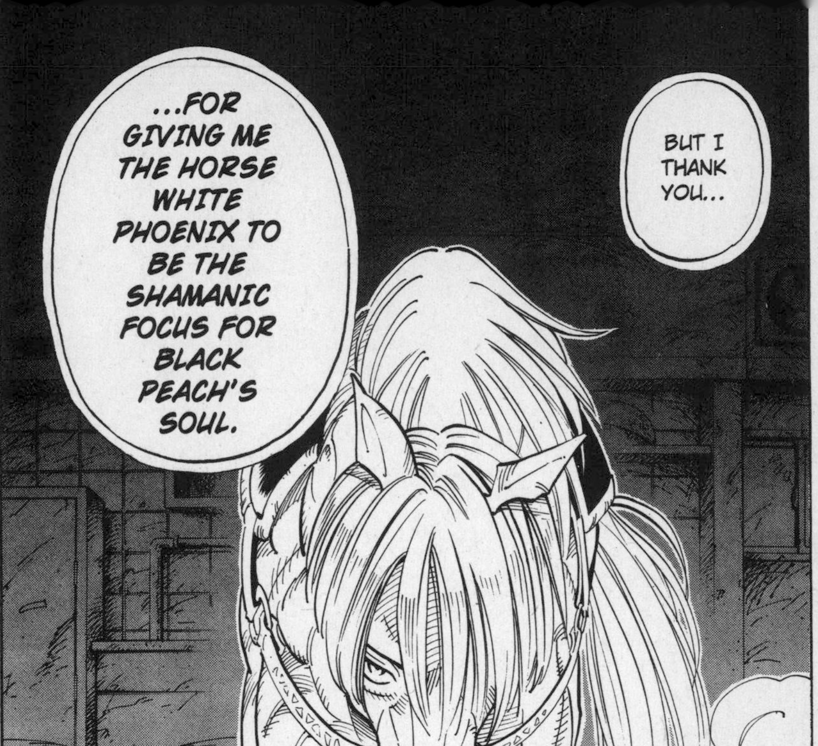
BUT I THANK YOU...
...FOR GIVING ME THE HORSE WHITE PHOENIX TO BE THE SHAMANIC FOCUS FOR BLACK PEACH'S SOUL.
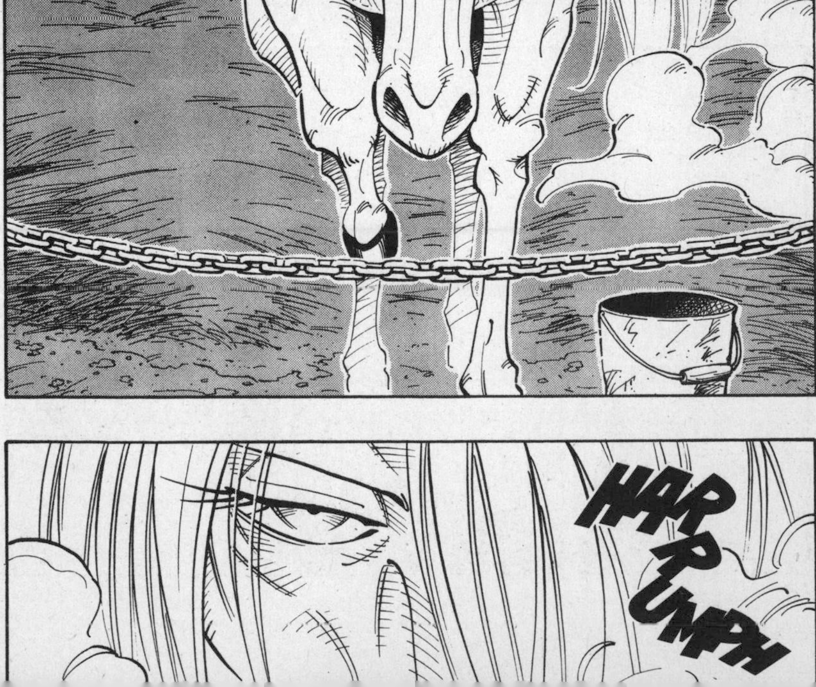
HARRUMPH

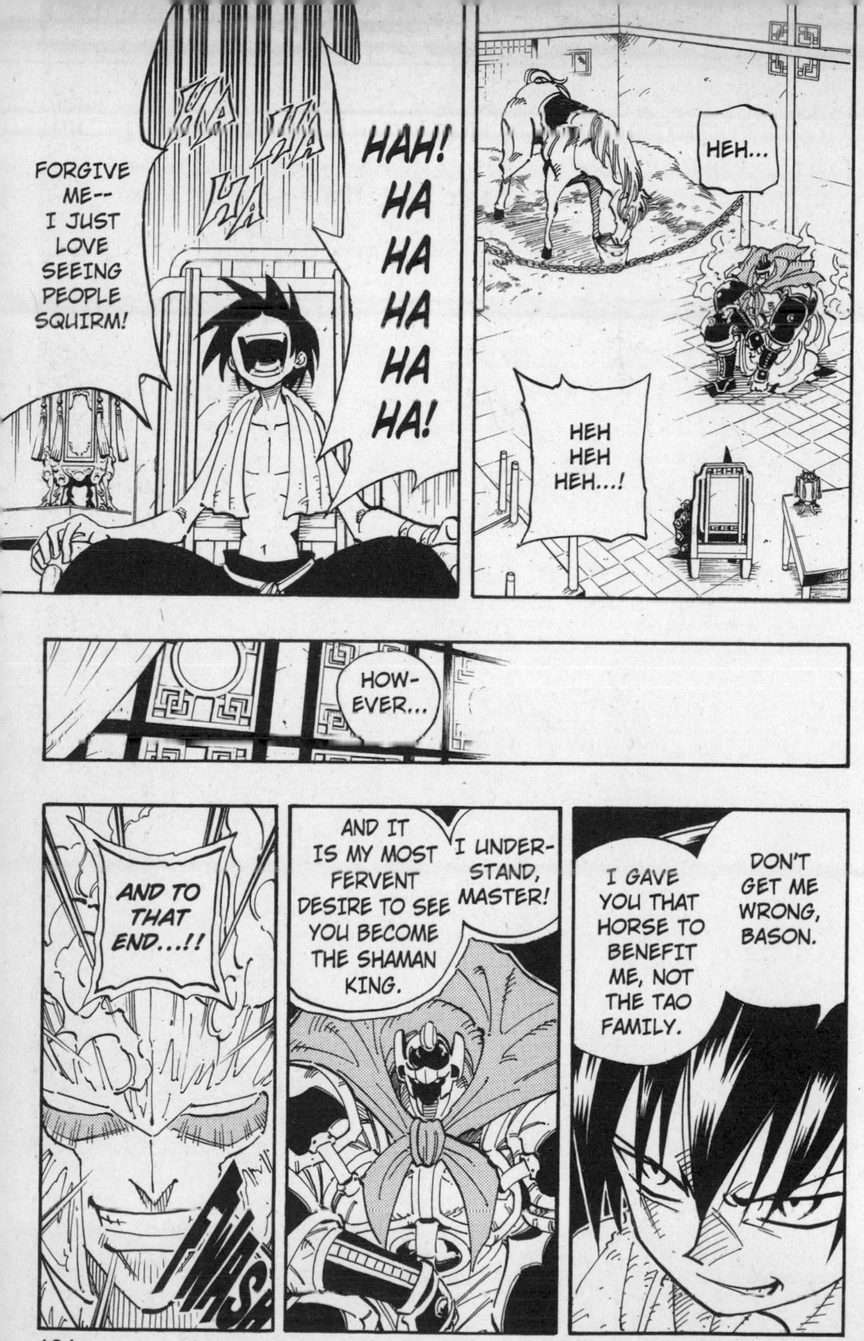
HEH...
HEH HEH HEH...!
HAH! HA HA HA HA HA!
HA HA HA
FORGIVE ME-- I JUST LOVE SEEING PEOPLE SQUIRM!
HOW-EVER...
DON'T GET ME WRONG, BASON.
I GAVE YOU THAT HORSE TO BENEFIT ME, NOT THE TAO FAMILY.
I UNDER-STAND, MASTER!
AND IT IS MY MOST FERVENT DESIRE TO SEE YOU BECOME THE SHAMAN KING.
AND TO THAT END...!!
FWASH

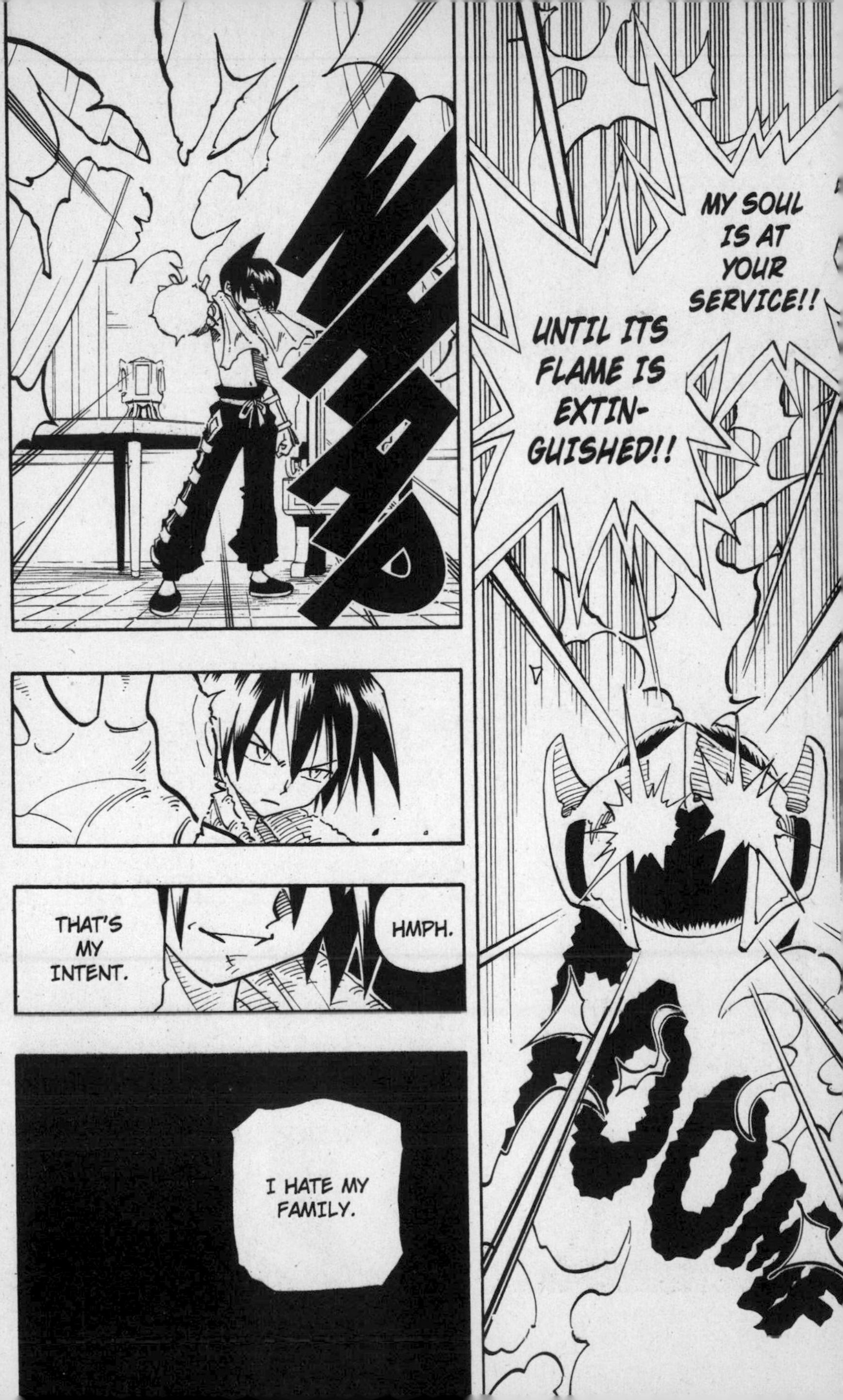
MY SOUL IS AT YOUR SERVICE!!
UNTIL ITS FLAME IS EXTIN-GUISHED!!
OOM
WHAAP
HMPH.
THAT'S MY INTENT.
I HATE MY FAMILY.

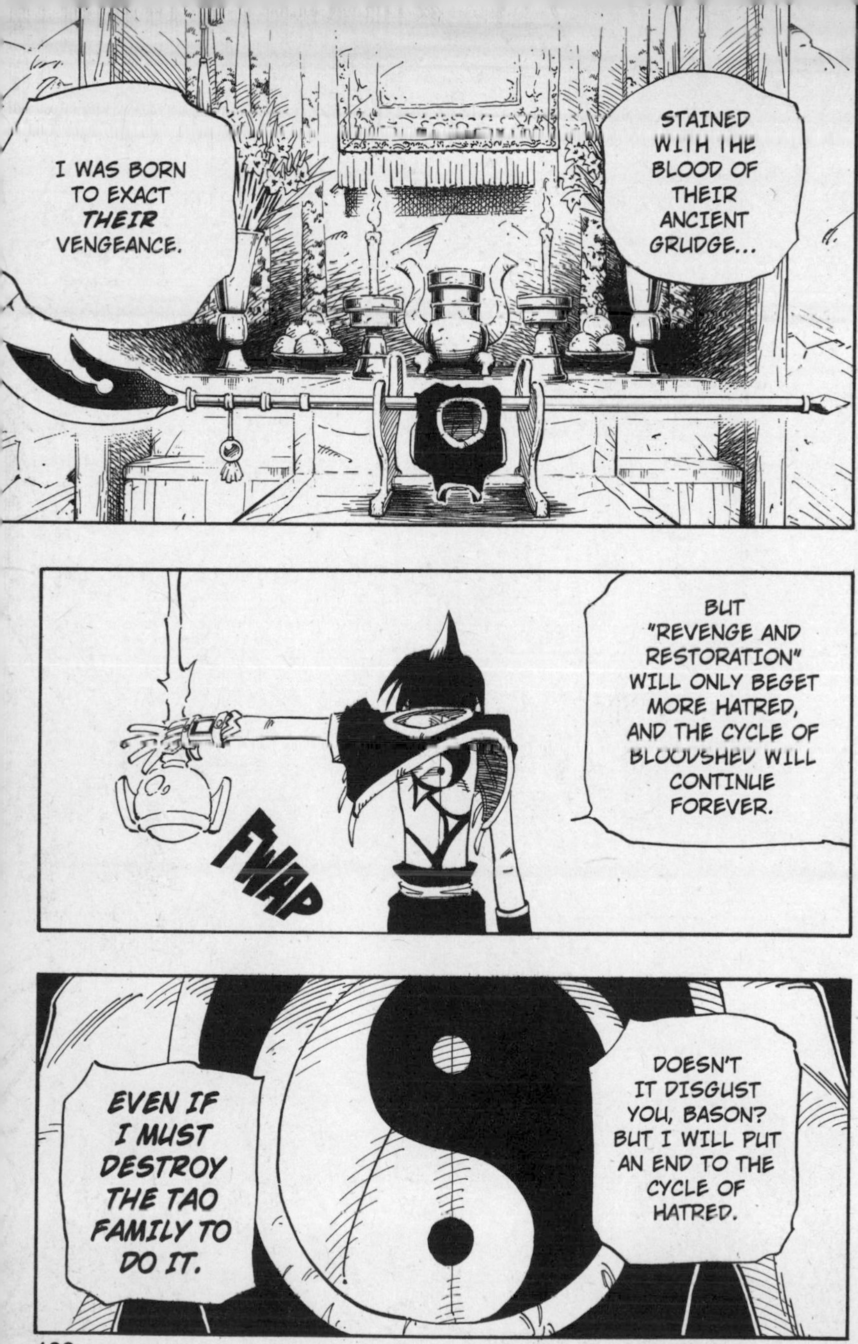
STAINED WITH THE BLOOD OF THEIR ANCIENT GRUDGE...
I WAS BORN TO EXACT *THEIR* VENGEANCE.
BUT "REVENGE AND RESTORATION" WILL ONLY BEGET MORE HATRED, AND THE CYCLE OF BLOODSHED WILL CONTINUE FOREVER.
FWAP
DOESN'T IT DISGUST YOU, BASON? BUT I WILL PUT AN END TO THE CYCLE OF HATRED.
*EVEN IF I MUST DESTROY THE TAO FAMILY TO DO IT.*

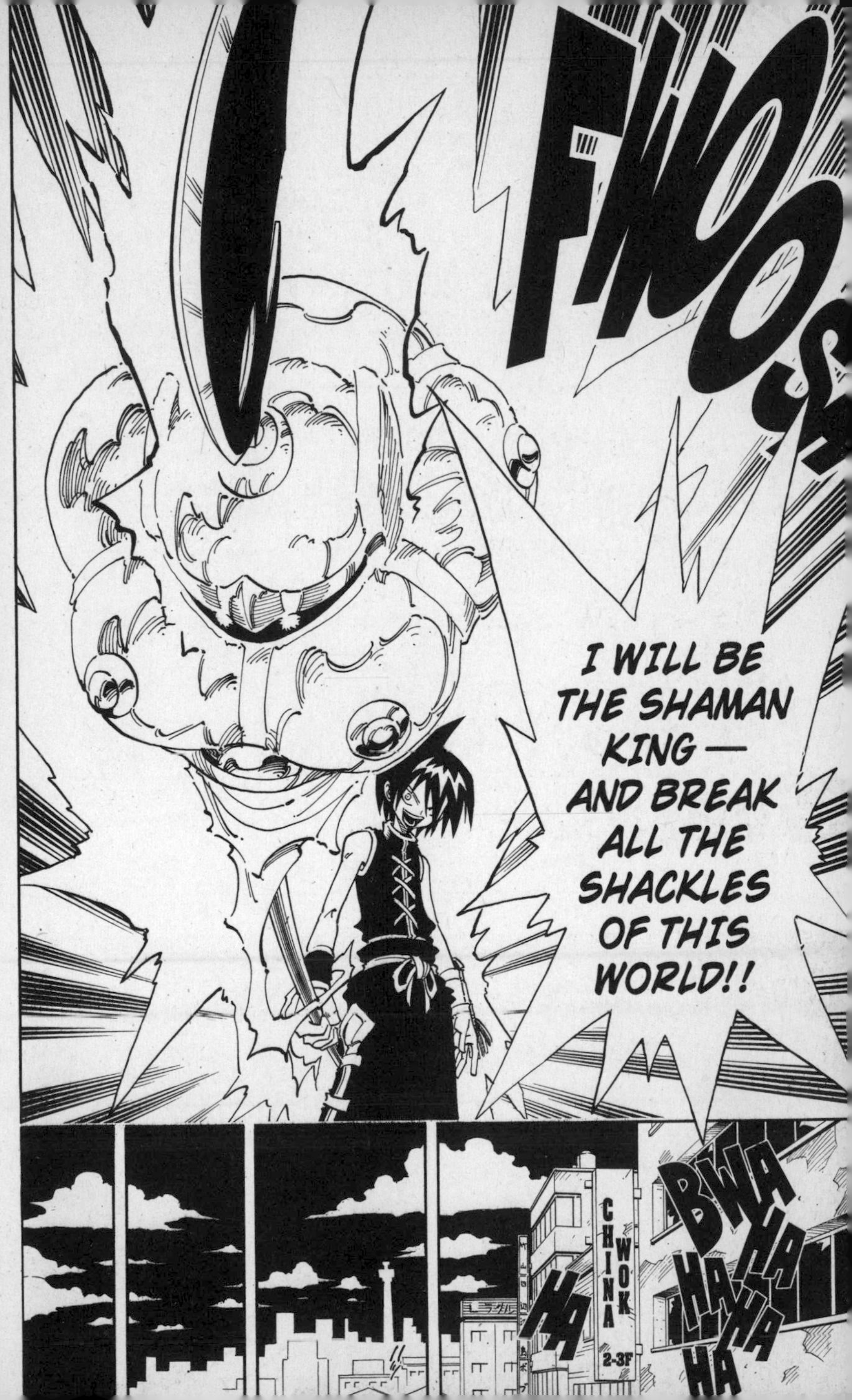
FWOOS
I WILL BE THE SHAMAN KING— AND BREAK ALL THE SHACKLES OF THIS WORLD!!
BWAHAHAHAHAHA
CHINA WOK 2-3F
HA

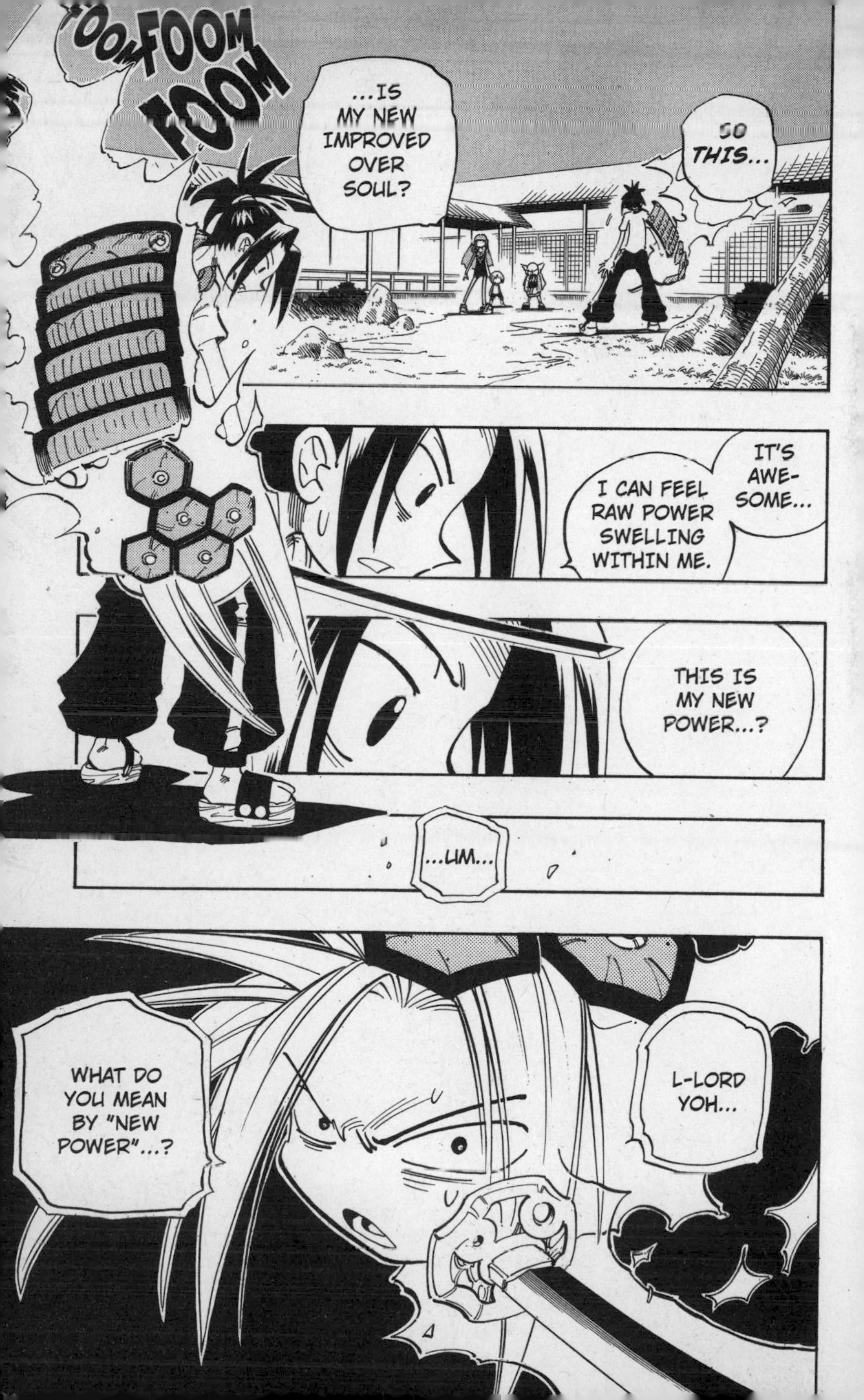
SO THIS...
...IS MY NEW IMPROVED OVER SOUL?
FOOM FOOM FOOM
IT'S AWE-SOME...
I CAN FEEL RAW POWER SWELLING WITHIN ME.
THIS IS MY NEW POWER...?
...UM...
L-LORD YOH...
WHAT DO YOU MEAN BY "NEW POWER"...?

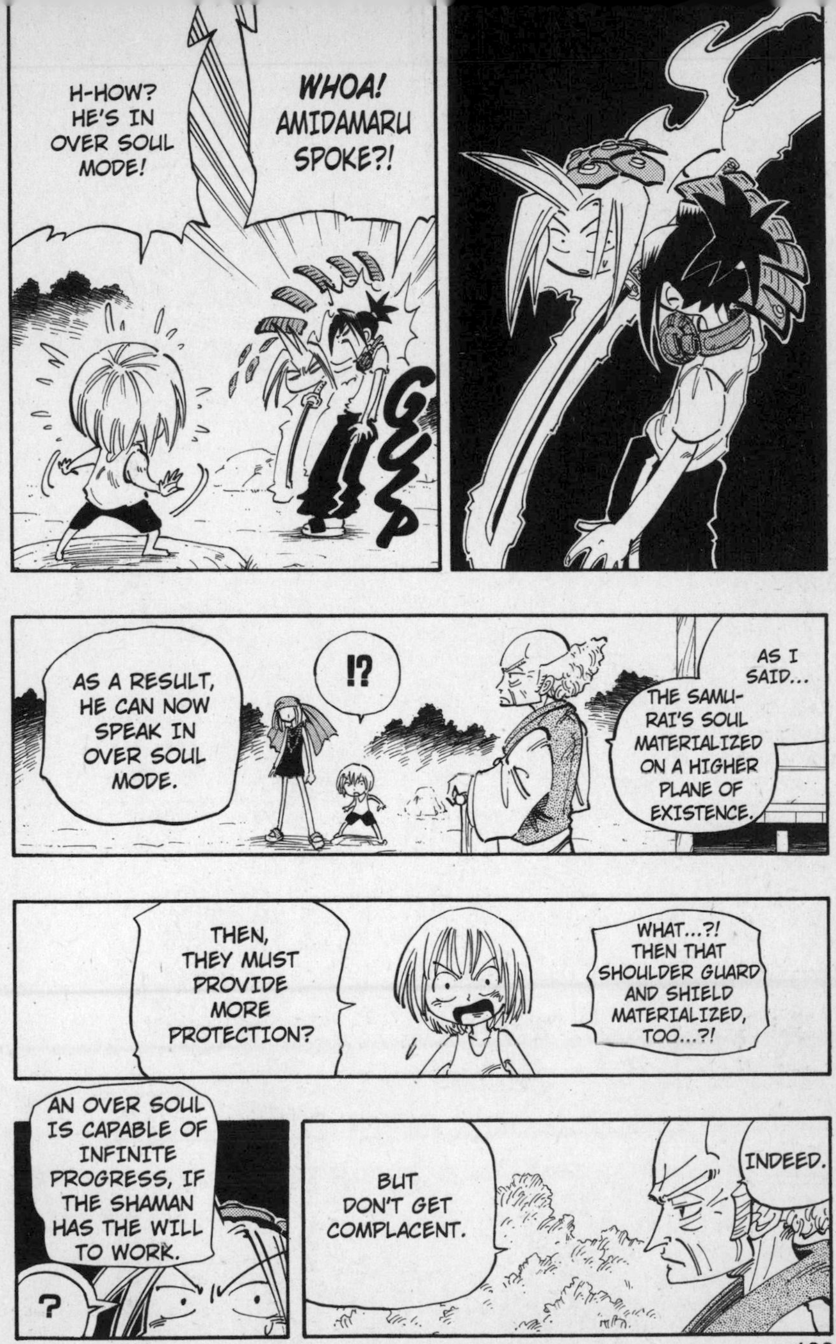
WHOA! AMIDAMARU SPOKE?!
H-HOW? HE'S IN OVER SOUL MODE!
GULP
AS I SAID...
THE SAMU-RAI'S SOUL MATERIALIZED ON A HIGHER PLANE OF EXISTENCE.
!?
AS A RESULT, HE CAN NOW SPEAK IN OVER SOUL MODE.
WHAT...?! THEN THAT SHOULDER GUARD AND SHIELD MATERIALIZED, TOO...?!
THEN, THEY MUST PROVIDE MORE PROTECTION?
INDEED.
BUT DON'T GET COMPLACENT.
AN OVER SOUL IS CAPABLE OF INFINITE PROGRESS, IF THE SHAMAN HAS THE WILL TO WORK.
?

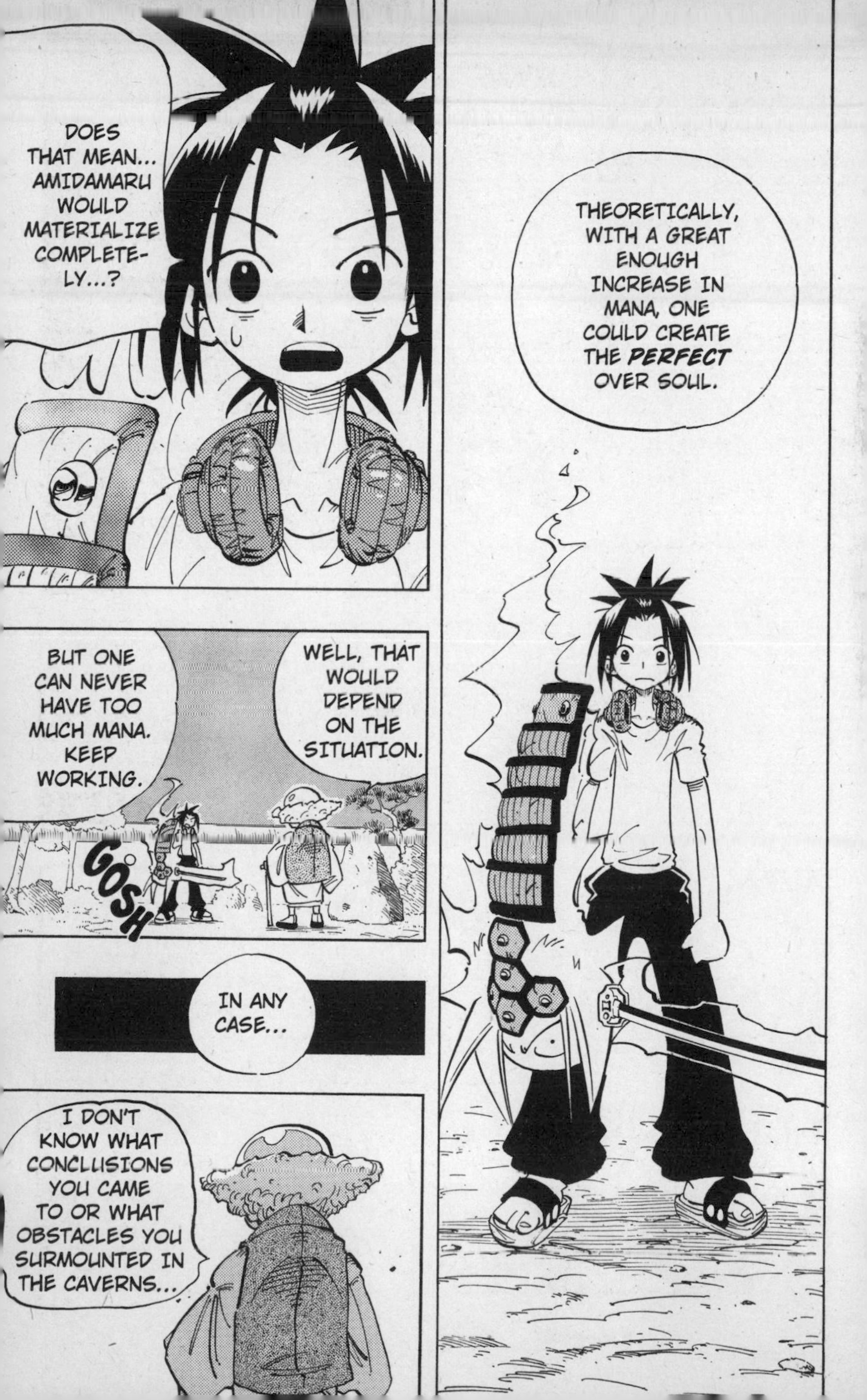
THEORETICALLY, WITH A GREAT ENOUGH INCREASE IN MANA, ONE COULD CREATE THE *PERFECT* OVER SOUL.
DOES THAT MEAN... AMIDAMARU WOULD MATERIALIZE COMPLETE-LY...?
WELL, THAT WOULD DEPEND ON THE SITUATION.
BUT ONE CAN NEVER HAVE TOO MUCH MANA. KEEP WORKING.
GOSH
IN ANY CASE...
I DON'T KNOW WHAT CONCLUSIONS YOU CAME TO OR WHAT OBSTACLES YOU SURMOUNTED IN THE CAVERNS...

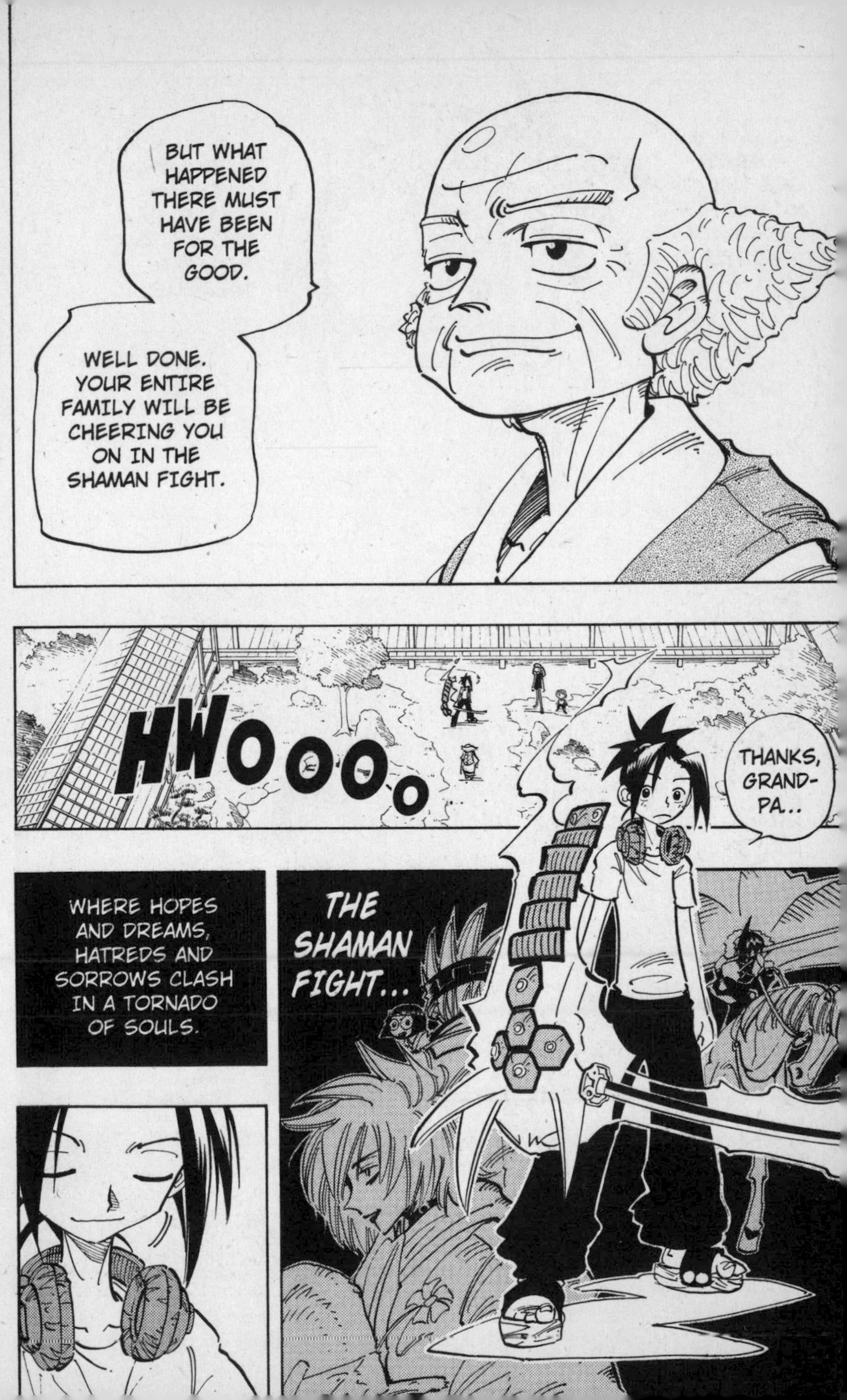
BUT WHAT HAPPENED THERE MUST HAVE BEEN FOR THE GOOD.
WELL DONE. YOUR ENTIRE FAMILY WILL BE CHEERING YOU ON IN THE SHAMAN FIGHT.
THANKS, GRAND-PA...
HWOOOO
THE SHAMAN FIGHT...
WHERE HOPES AND DREAMS, HATREDS AND SORROWS CLASH IN A TORNADO OF SOULS.

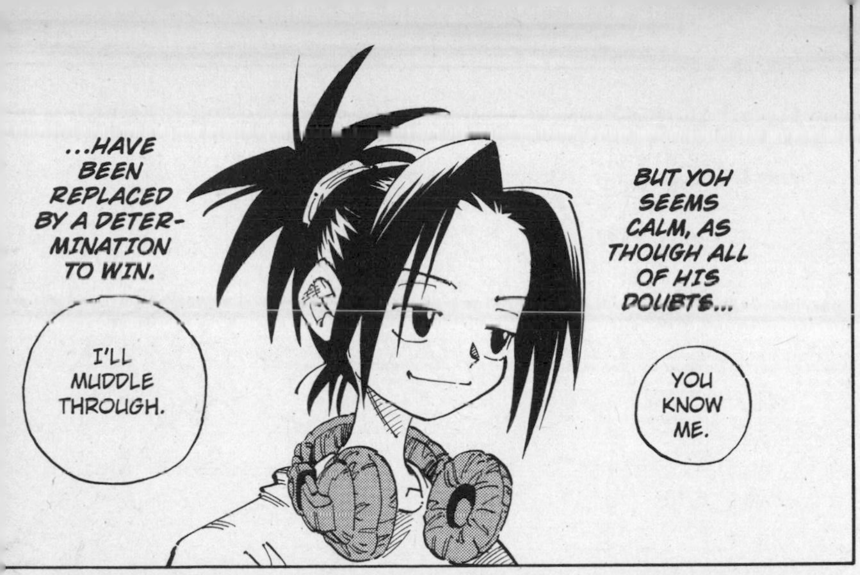
BUT YOH SEEMS CALM, AS THOUGH ALL OF HIS DOUBTS...
...HAVE BEEN REPLACED BY A DETERMINATION TO WIN.
YOU KNOW ME.
I'LL MUDDLE THROUGH.

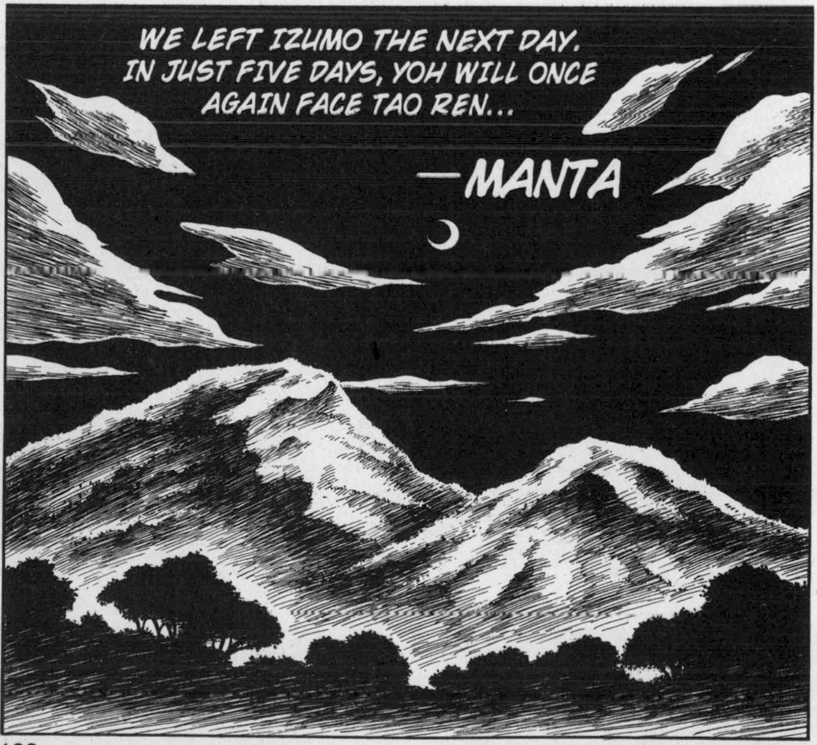
WE LEFT IZUMO THE NEXT DAY. IN JUST FIVE DAYS, YOH WILL ONCE AGAIN FACE TAO REN...
—MANTA

WHEN EVILDOERS APPEAR, LEAVE IT TO TAMAO!

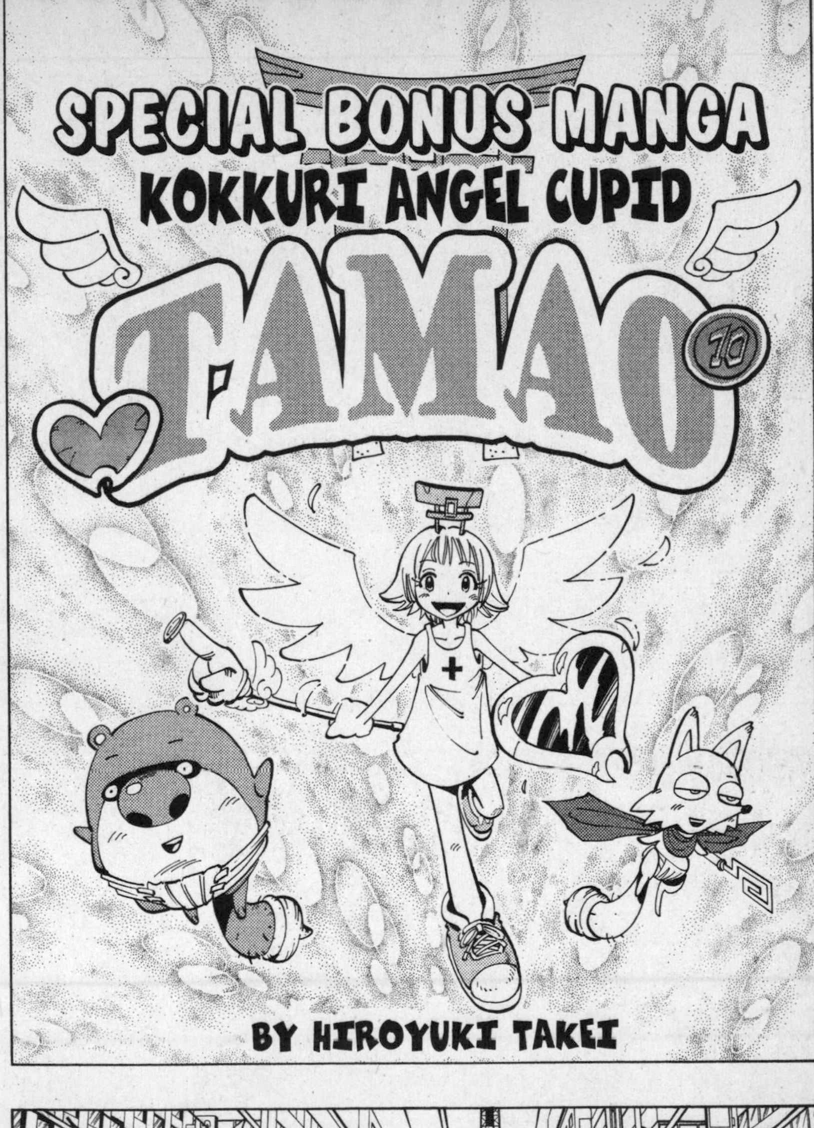
SPECIAL BONUS MANGA
KOKKURI ANGEL CUPID
TAMAO
10
BY HIROYUKI TAKEI

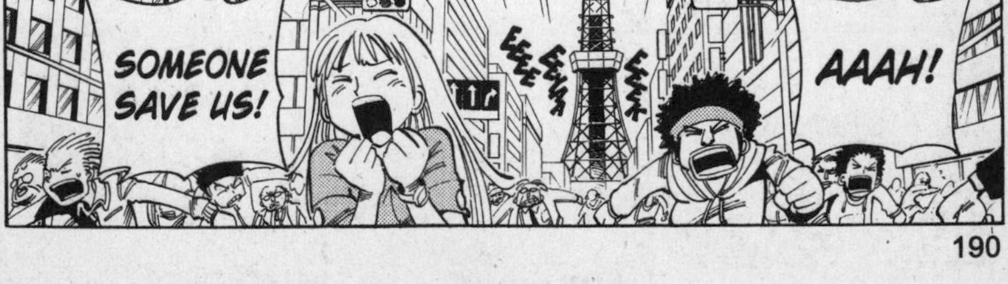
AAAH!
SOMEONE SAVE US!

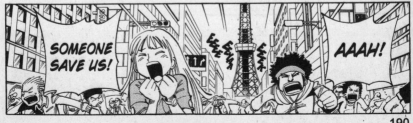

EVILDOERS WILL BE SWIFTLY PUNISHED!! WHAT WILL HAPPEN TO THE EVIL RYU...?! STAY TUNED!!

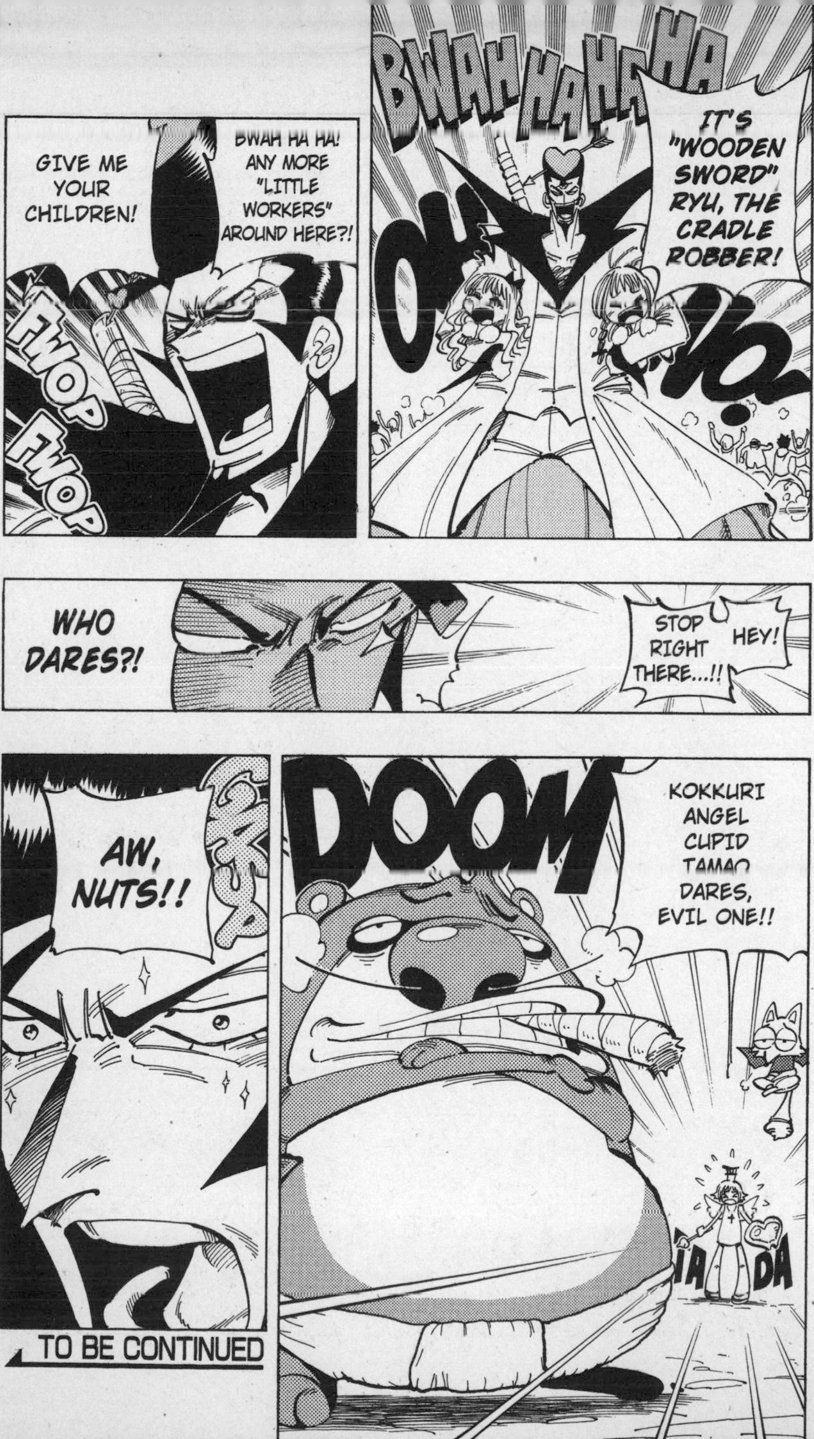
BWAH HA HA HA
IT'S "WOODEN SWORD" RYU, THE CRADLE ROBBER!
OH
YO!
BWAH HA HA! ANY MORE "LITTLE WORKERS" AROUND HERE?!
GIVE ME YOUR CHILDREN!
FWOP
FWOP
HEY!
STOP RIGHT THERE...!!
WHO DARES?!
DOOM
KOKKURI ANGEL CUPID TAMAO DARES, EVIL ONE!!
DA
AW, NUTS!!
TO BE CONTINUED

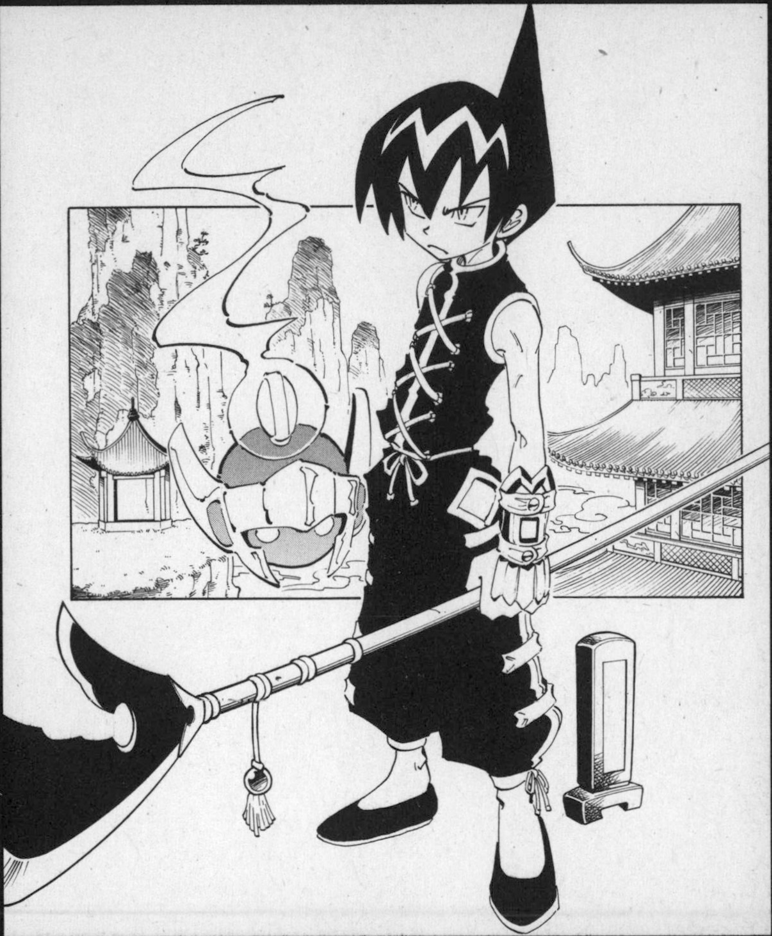

# IN THE NEXT VOLUME...

REMATCH WITH REN! This is the moment Yoh has trained for: his second fight against his fiercest rival. And this time he can't afford to lose...because he won't just be disqualified, he'll die! As Ren's golden Over Soul clashes against the samurai steel of Amidamaru, Ren's family of shamans waits for the outcome. And whoever wins will have to face the strongest and most ruthless shaman in China...Ren's dad!

***AVAILABLE SEPTEMBER 2005!***

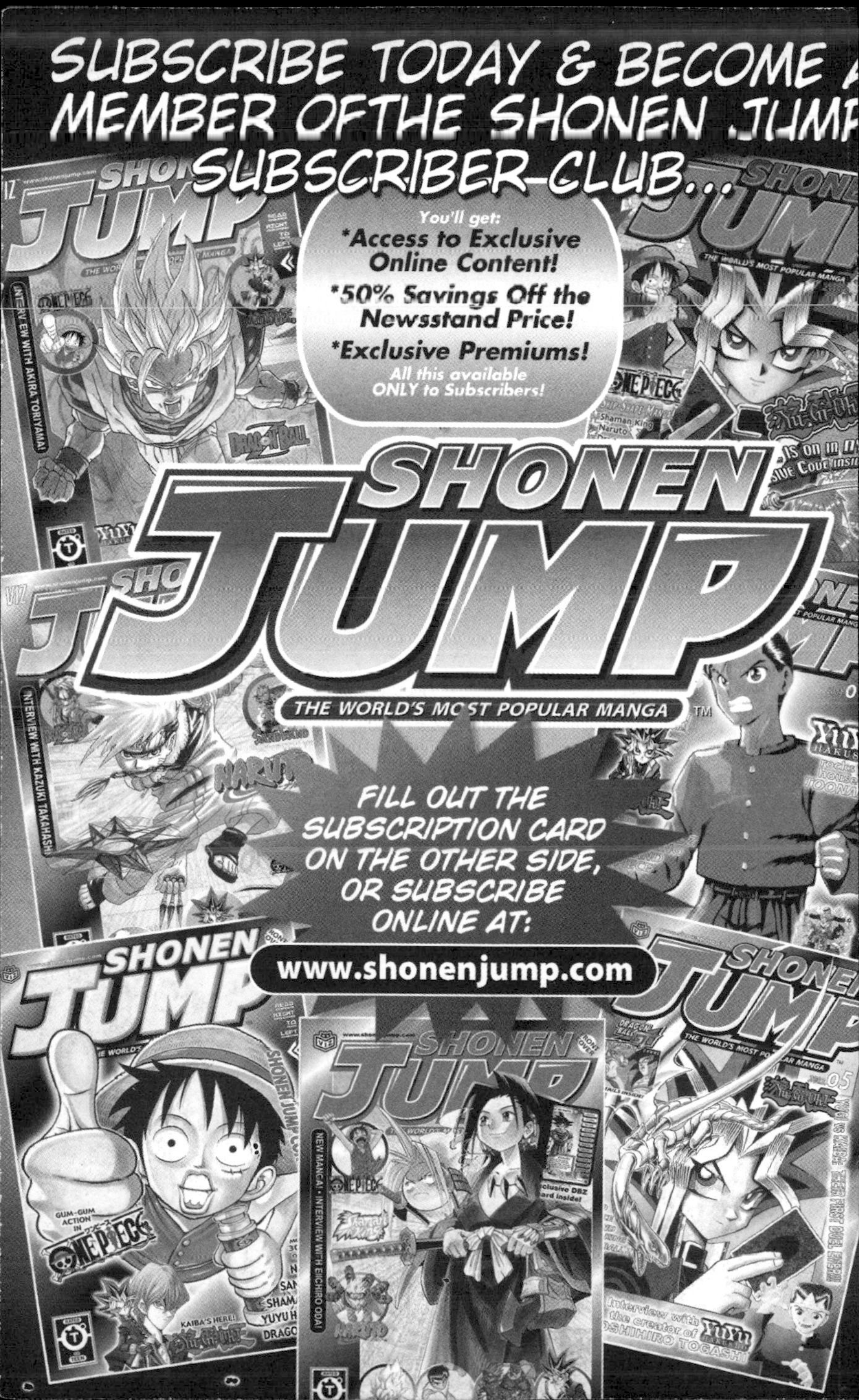
SUBSCRIBE TODAY & BECOME A MEMBER OF THE SHONEN JUMP SUBSCRIBER CLUB...
You'll get:
*Access to Exclusive Online Content!
*50% Savings Off the Newsstand Price!
*Exclusive Premiums!
All this available ONLY to Subscribers!
SHONEN JUMP
THE WORLD'S MOST POPULAR MANGA
TM
FILL OUT THE SUBSCRIPTION CARD ON THE OTHER SIDE, OR SUBSCRIBE ONLINE AT:
www.shonenjump.com

# Save 50% off the newsstand price!

# SHONEN JUMP

### THE WORLD'S MOST POPULAR MANGA

**SUBSCRIBE TODAY and SAVE 50% OFF the cover price PLUS enjoy all the benefits of the SHONEN JUMP SUBSCRIBER CLUB, exclusive online content & special premiums ONLY AVAILABLE to SUBSCRIBERS!**

☑ **YES!** Please enter my 1 year subscription (12 issues) to *SHONEN JUMP* at the INCREDIBLY LOW SUBSCRIPTION RATE of $29.95 and sign me up for the SHONEN JUMP Subscriber Club!

Only
**$29⁹⁵!**

NAME

ADDRESS

CITY                          STATE        ZIP

E-MAIL ADDRESS

☐ **MY CHECK IS ENCLOSED**     ☐ **BILL ME LATER**

**CREDIT CARD:**     ☐ **VISA**     ☐ **MASTERCARD**

ACCOUNT #                                          EXP. DATE

SIGNATURE

**CLIP AND MAIL TO** ➤ SHONEN JUMP
Subscriptions Service Dept.
P.O. Box 515
Mount Morris, IL 61054-0515

Make checks payable to: **SHONEN JUMP.**
Canada add US $12. No foreign orders. Allow 6-8 weeks for delivery.

**P5SJGN**   YU-GI-OH! © 1996 by KAZUKI TAKAHASHI / SHUEISHA Inc.

SHONEN JUMP
THE WORLD'S MOST POPULAR MANGA

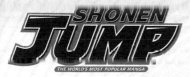

# COMPLETE OUR SURVEY AND LET US KNOW WHAT YOU THINK!

☐ Please do NOT send me information about VIZ and SHONEN JUMP products, news and events, special offers, or other information.

☐ Please do NOT send me information from VIZ's trusted business partners.

**Name:** ______________________________

**Address:** ______________________________

**City:** ____________ **State:** ________ **Zip:** ____________

**E-mail:** ______________________________

☐ **Male** ☐ **Female** **Date of Birth** (mm/dd/yyyy): ____/____/____ ( **Under 13? Parental consent required** )

**1 Do you purchase SHONEN JUMP Magazine?**

☐ Yes ☐ No **(if no, skip the next two questions)**

If **YES**, do you subscribe?

☐ Yes ☐ No

If **NO**, how often do you purchase SHONEN JUMP Magazine?

☐ 1-3 issues a year

☐ 4-6 issues a year

☐ more than 7 issues a year

**2 Which SHONEN JUMP Graphic Novel did you purchase?** **(please check one)**

| | | |
|---|---|---|
| ☐ Beet the Vandel Buster | ☐ Bleach | ☐ Dragon Ball |
| ☐ Dragon Ball Z | ☐ Dr. Slump | ☐ Eyeshield 21 |
| ☐ Hikaru no Go | ☐ Hunter x Hunter | ☐ I"s |
| ☐ Knights of the Zodiac | ☐ Legendz | ☐ Naruto |
| ☐ One Piece | ☐ Rurouni Kenshin | ☐ Shaman King |
| ☐ The Prince of Tennis | ☐ Ultimate Muscle | ☐ Whistle! |
| ☐ Yu-Gi-Oh! | ☐ Yu-Gi-Oh!: Duelist | ☐ YuYu Hakusho |
| ☐ Other ______________ | | |

Will you purchase subsequent volumes?

☐ Yes ☐ No

**3 How did you learn about this title?** **(check all that apply)**

| | | |
|---|---|---|
| ☐ Favorite title | ☐ Advertisement | ☐ Article |
| ☐ Gift | ☐ Read excerpt in SHONEN JUMP Magazine | |
| ☐ Recommendation | ☐ Special offer | ☐ Through TV animation |
| ☐ Website | ☐ Other ______________ | |

**4 Of the titles that are serialized in SHONEN JUMP Magazine, have you purchased the Graphic Novels?**

☐ Yes ☐ No

If **YES**, which ones have you purchased? (check all that apply)

☐ Dragon Ball Z ☐ Hikaru no Go ☐ Naruto ☐ One Piece
☐ Shaman King ☐ Yu-Gi-Oh! ☐ YuYu Hakusho

If **YES**, what were your reasons for purchasing? (please pick up to 3)

☐ A favorite title ☐ A favorite creator/artist ☐ I want to read it in one go
☐ I want to read it over and over again ☐ There are extras that aren't in the magazine
☐ The quality of printing is better than the magazine ☐ Recommendation
☐ Special offer ☐ Other

If **NO**, why did/would you not purchase it?

☐ I'm happy just reading it in the magazine ☐ It's not worth buying the graphic novel
☐ All the manga pages are in black and white unlike the magazine
☐ There are other graphic novels that I prefer ☐ There are too many to collect for each title
☐ It's too small ☐ Other ______________________

**5 Of the titles NOT serialized in the Magazine, which ones have you purchased?**
**(check all that apply)**

☐ Beet the Vandel Buster ☐ Bleach ☐ Dragon Ball ☐ Dr. Slump
☐ Eyeshield 21 ☐ Hunter x Hunter ☐ I"s ☐ Knights of the Zodiac
☐ Legendz ☐ The Prince of Tennis ☐ Rurouni Kenshin ☐ Whistle!
☐ Yu-Gi-Oh!: Duelist ☐ None ☐ Other ______________

If you did purchase any of the above, what were your reasons for purchase?

☐ A favorite title ☐ A favorite creator/artist
☐ Read a preview in SHONEN JUMP Magazine and wanted to read the rest of the story
☐ Recommendation ☐ Other

Will you purchase subsequent volumes?

☐ Yes ☐ No

**6 What race/ethnicity do you consider yourself?** (please check one)

☐ Asian/Pacific Islander ☐ Black/African American ☐ Hispanic/Latino
☐ Native American/Alaskan Native ☐ White/Caucasian ☐ Other

**THANK YOU! Please send the completed form to:** VIZ Survey
42 Catharine St.
Poughkeepsie, NY 12601

**All information provided will be used for internal purposes only. We promise not to sell or otherwise divulge your information.**